Romantic Desire

in (Post)modern

Art and Philosophy

THE SUNY SERIES IN
POSTMODERN CULTURE

Joseph Natoli, *Editor*

Romantic Desire

in (Post)modern

Art and Philosophy

Jos de Mul

STATE UNIVERSITY OF NEW YORK PRESS

Originally published as Het romantische verlangen in (post)moderne kunst en filosofie
©1990 Erasmus University Rotterdam
Revised third Dutch edition, © 1995 Kok Agora Publishers.

Published by
State University of New York Press, Albany

For information, address State University of New York Press,
State University Plaza, Albany, NY 12246

Production by Laurie Searl
Marketing by Anne M. Valentine

Library of Congress Cataloging-in-Publication Data
de Mul, Jos, 1956–
    [Romantische verlangen in (post)moderne kunst en filosofie.
English]
    Romantic desire in (post)modern art and philosophy / Jos de Mul
    p. cm.
    Includes bibliographical references and index.
    ISBN 0-7914-4217-9 (hc. : alk. paper)
    ISBN 0-7914-4218-7 (pbk. : alk. paper)
    1. Aesthetics, Modern.   2. Romanticism.   3. Postmodernism.   I. Title.
    BH188.D8 M8513   1999
    111'.85—ddc21
                                                                    98-41220
                                                                    CIP

10 9 8 7 6 5 4 3 2 1

Die Romantik ist noch nicht zu Ende gebracht.
Romanticism is not yet brought to an end.
—Martin Heidegger

Nur um der Hoffnungslosen Willen ist uns die Hoffnung gegeben.
Only for the sake of the hopeless hope is given to us.
—Walter Benjamin

Es giebt vielleicht auch für das Lachen noch eine Zukunft!
Even laughter may yet have a future!
—Friedrich Nietzsche

Contents

Illustrations

Reproduction of figures 1, 2, and 3 by kind permission of Sigurdur Gudmundsson. Reproduction of figures 4 and 6 by kind permission of the Louvre, Paris. Reproduction of figure 5 by kind permission of the Pinacoteca di Brera, Milan. Reproduction of figures 7–11 and 14 by kind permission of Beeldrecht Amsterdam.

Abbreviations

Ä	*Ästhetik*, Hegel, 1955
B	*Birth of Tragedy*, Nietzsche, 1993
BDT	"Building Dwelling Thinking," Heidegger, 1978
BGE	*Beyond Good and Evil*, Nietzsche, 1990
BPh	*Beiträge zur Philosophie*, Heidegger, 1989
BT	*Being and Time*, Heidegger, 1962
BW	*Basic Writings*, Heidegger, 1978
CR	*Critique of Pure Reason*, Kant, 1978
CJ	*Critique of Judgement*, Kant, 1987
D	*Daybreak*, Nietzsche, 1982
DT	*Discourse on Thinking*, Heidegger, 1966
É	*Écrits*, Lacan, 1966
EH	*Ecce Homo*, Nietzsche, 1992
EM	*Einführung in die Metaphysik*, Heidegger, 1953
ER	*Essence of Reasons*, Heidegger, 1969
G	*Gelassenheit*, Heidegger, 1985
GA	*Gesamtausgabe*, Heidegger, 1976, 1977
GM	*Genealogy of Morals*, Nietzsche, 1956
GS	*The Gay Science*, Nietzsche, 1974
H	"Uses and Disadvantages of History for Life," Nietzsche, 1983
HEP	"Hölderlin and the Essence of Poetry," Heidegger, 1949

HH	*Human, All Too Human*, Nietzsche, 1986
HW	*Holzwege*, Heidegger, 1977
ID	*Identity and Difference*, Heidegger, 1960
IM	*Introduction to Metaphysics*, Heidegger, 1958
KM	*Kant and the Problem of Metaphysics*, Heidegger, 1962
KSA	*Sämtliche Werke. Kritische Studienausgabe*, Nietzsche, 1980
KU	*Kritik der Urteilskraft*, Kant 1968
KrV	*Kritik der reinen Vernunft*, Kant 1968
L	"Language," Heidegger, 1971
Logic	*Logik*, Kant, 1968
MA	*Gesammelte Werke. Musarionausgab*, Nietzsche, 1920–29
N	*Nietzsche*, Heidegger, 1991b
O	"The Origin of the Work of Art," Heidegger, 1978
OWL	*On the Way to Language*, Heidegger, 1971
P	"Preface," Heidegger, 1974
PLT	*Poetry, Language, Thought*, Heidegger, 1975
PR	*The Principle of Reason*, Heidegger, 1991
QT	"The Question Concerning Technology," Heidegger, 1978
R	*Das Rektorat 1933/34*, Heidegger, 1983
Religion	*Die Religion innerhalb der Grenzen der bloßen Vernunft*, Kant, 1968
TEP	*Toward Eternal Peace*, Kant, 1968
TI	*Twilight of the Idols*, Nietzsche, 1976
S	*Silence*, Cage, 1973
SE	*Standard Edition*, Freud, 1953–74
VA	*Vorträge und Aufsätze*, Heidegger, 1967
VS	*Vier Seminare*, Heidegger, 1977
W	*Werke. Sämtliche Werke*, Schelling, 1907

WCT	"What Calls for Thinking?" Heidegger, 1978
WDB	*Werke in Drie Bänden*, Nietzsche, 1976
WG	*Vom Wesen des Grundes*, Heidegger, 1976
WM	*Wegmarken*, Heidegger, 1976
ZW	"Die Zeit des Weltbildes," Heidegger, 1977
Z	*Thus Spoke Zarathustra*, Nietzsche, 1969

Preface

This book stems from a series of lectures I delivered over the past decade at conferences in the Netherlands, Germany, the United Kingdom, Canada, and the United States. The common thread running through the papers in this volume is that they all deal with the relationship between (post)modern—that is, the interwoven field of modern *and* postmodern—art and philosophy. Moreover, these papers emerged from reflections on one or more concrete works of visual art, literature, and music and share as their common theme a fascination for what I have called Romantic desire.

Human beings are characterized by an insatiable desire to understand the meaning of their existence and to find some form of happiness. Since the loss of faith in religion in modern culture, this desire has turned in new directions. From the era of the Romantics on, we find an extensive and diverse tradition that attributes to art the power of realizing our desire for meaning and happiness. According to the Romantic artists and philosophers, only an aesthetization of life will offer us a prospect of happiness. However, this Romantic desire is accompanied by a tragic consciousness of the final unachievability of this desire. In this respect the Romantic experience anticipates postmodern doubt and irony with regard to the 'controllability of happiness.'

Although this book contains extensive discussions of the works of nineteenth- and twentieth-century philosophers belonging to various continental traditions, and for that reason can be read as an historical introduction to continental aesthetics, its aim is not primarily historical. My main aim has been to contribute to the 'ontology of the present.' The argument does not dwell on the Romantic tradition from an antiquarian perspective, but is driven by a desire to understand the complex nature of our present culture. Its presupposition is that the study of the traditions on which culture rests will offer insights into our present and future condition.

This book was originally published in Dutch. For the convenience of the English-speaking audience, translations have been provided for foreign-language quotations. Whenever English translations were available, the quotations and references refer to these. In all other cases the translations are the author's. Some references to Dutch publications for which no English translations exist have been omitted, since they would not be of much use to most English readers. Only in cases where quotations were taken from the works referred to, have I included them in the bibliography. For convenience and brevity 'he' has been used throughout the book. This, of course, should be read as 'he or she'.

Though my reflections on the subjects discussed in this book have developed further since its first publication, I have decided not to alter the original publication drastically. Not only because I still adhere to most of the ideas developed in this book, but also because the result would have been another book. However, in order to link the book to more recent publications, I have added an afterword—"Virtual Romantics"—in which some further developments of the ideas presented in this book are sketched especially with regard to the cultural implications of information and communication technology. Those who are interested in a more detailed discussion of the anthropological and methodological presuppositions of the present book might read my book *The Tragedy of Finitude* (Yale University Press, 2000).

I would like to thank my colleagues who discussed the contents of this book with me during the various stages of its genesis. Apart from my colleagues from the University of Nijmegen and the Erasmus University Rotterdam, I would especially like to thank Tom Rockmore for his help in finding the right publisher for this edition. I further want to thank Alan Murphy-Reeve, for his substantive contribution to the translation, and Ronald van Raak, Maarten Reith, and Laurie Searl for their assistance during the different stages of the preparation of this book. My muse, Gerry, introduced me to the living and lasting experience of Romantic desire. For that reason this book is dedicated to her.

Acknowledgments

The original Dutch version of this book appeared in 1990 in the series Studies in Philosophy of the Erasmus University Rotterdam. The second and revised third edition were published by Donker Publishers and Kok Agora Publishers respectively in 1991 and 1995. This English edition is based on the revised third Dutch edition of 1995. In the present edition some minor revisions were made in the body of the text, an afterword was added, and the bibliography has been supplemented by a number of recent titles on the subjects discussed.

Earlier versions of some parts of this book have been previously published in English. A substantial part of "Frozen Metaphors" appeared under the title "Image without Origin: On Nietzsche's Transcendental Metaphor," in P. J. McCormick (ed.), *The Reasons of Art/L'Art a ses raisons* (Ottawa: University of Ottawa Press, 1985), 273–86.

Parts of *"The Art of Forgetting"* were published as *"The Art of Forgetfulness: Schopenhauer and Recent Repetitive Music,"* in R. Woodfield (ed.), *XIth International Congress in Aesthetics: Sixty-Four Selected Papers* (Nottingham, 1990), 143–46.

"Disavowal and Representation" appeared as "Disavowal and Representation in Magritte's 'La trahison des images,'" in *Filozofski Vestnik* 17.2 (1996): 107–26.

Some of the ideas presented in the afterword were taken from more extensive discussions presented in "Networked Identities," published in Michael B. Roetto (ed.), *Proceedings of the Seventh International Symposium on Electronic Art* (Rotterdam: ISEA, 1997), 11–16, and "The Digitalization of the Worldview: The End of Photography and the Return of the Aura," published in Annette W. Balkema and Henk Slager (eds.), *The Photographic Paradigm* (Amsterdam/Atlanta: Rodopi, 1997), 44–56.

Introduction

> The epithet 'romantic' and the antithetical terms 'classic' and 'romantic' are approximate labels which have long been in use. The philosopher solemnly refuses to allow them, exorcising them with unerring logic, but they creep quietly in again and are always obtruding themselves, elusive, tiresome, indispensable; the grammarian attempts to give them their proper status, their rank and fixed definition, but in spite of all his laborious efforts he discovers that he has been treating shadows as though they were solid substance.
>
> Mario Praz

The six chapters in this book constitute part of the ongoing dialogue between philosophy and art. Conceptualizations by philosophers and philosophically oriented scientists such as Plato, Kant, Schopenhauer, Nietzsche, Weber, Freud, Heidegger, Piaget, Adorno, Benjamin, Habermas, Lacan, Mannoni, Barthes, and Vattimo are discussed in their relations with sculptures, photographs, and paintings by Magritte, Gudmundsson, and Stella, with musical compositions by Schönberg, Cage, and Reich, and with poetry by Coleridge, George, Rilke, and Achterberg. I have deliberately chosen the concept of *dialogue* because my concern is not so much with an interpretation of artistic works on the basis of a particular theory, although it must not be forgotten that a conversation can never occur without some form of explanation, but rather with the *meaning* that arises from the reciprocal interpenetration of image and concept.

Meaning is established only when the participants in a dialogue dismiss their prejudices and open themselves to what the others have to say. Philosophical and scientific interpretations that impose their conceptual frameworks as indisputable truths upon a work of art do not often discover anything new; they more frequently only multiply their own bias. It is true that the philosopher and the scientist can only enter into a conversation with art from within their already established conceptual boundaries, but it is only when they are prepared to permit such boundaries to be penetrated by that which art presents to them that, to employ a hermeneutic term, they enter into the effective history of the artwork in question (cf. Gadamer, 1975, 267 ff.). Although every interpretation presupposes the contribution of the interpreter, the meaning that emerges from concealment during a fruitful conversation rises above prejudice.

In the Western tradition many names have been given to the mysterious origins of meaning in the creation and experiencing of artistic works. However, whether this creation is conceived as the divine inspiration of the muses (as occurred in Greek mythology), as the voice of the unconscious (as with the reflections of the Romantics, the surrealists, and the psychoanalysts), as a common fortune (*Geschick*) of Being (Heidegger), or as the uncontrollable exteriority of the text (Derrida), each time the formulation specifies that the meanings we assign to the world are not exclusively the product of our autonomous spirit, that they are— at least partially—the product of fortune and fate.

The six chapters in this book are fragments that permit of various combinations but cannot be subjected to a hierarchy wherein a unidimensional line is determined. They could be compared to a collection of jigsaw puzzles where the pieces may be slotted together in a variety of ways, persistently suggesting that they constitute parts of a coherent whole, but from which, regardless of our conscientious attempts and the pleasure that we derive from them, no completed product emerges and apparently superfluous pieces remain on the table. At some moment we could begin to doubt whether or not these pieces ever constituted a coherent picture, and, disappointed in our desire for continuity and coherence, we could abandon our endeavour and seek another game that could provide more satisfaction. Equally, however, we could, during the exertions of seeking coherence in the puzzle, arrive at the insight that it is precisely the open character of the exercise that constitutes the pleasure of puzzling. The sense of our unquenchable desire for encompassing meaning resides not in the completion of a task but rather in the processes of achieving understanding.

Perhaps this imagery of the fragmentary and therefore unresolvable puzzle is not only applicable to this book but also offers some insight into how we at present appreciate reality. Is it not so that our contemporary experience is determined by innumerable perspectives that, at best, when a number of them temporarily combine to produce a coherent image, only offer the *illusion* of a totality? If this suspicion is correct—and I shall argue herein that it is—then not only the contents of this book may be considered as an attempt to articulate a number of aspects of contemporary experience, but also its fragmentary form expresses our current *worldview*.

Although the chapters of this book connect with each other in several ways, regularly presuming and sometimes overlapping each other, the sequence in which they are presented is not compulsory. They could, in fact, be read in an arbitrary sequence[1]. According to the trajectory that is pursued, and the accents that are thereby imposed, a variety of different yet equally incomplete totalities can emerge. In this introduction I want to explicate just one of the possible trajectories—that of Romantic desire. In contrast to the following chapters, wherein the starting point for the dialogue is each time determined by one concrete work of art, this introduction has a more general and abstract character: matters that are, in subsequent chapters, extensively discussed, are simply mentioned without much further deliberation in this introduction. Readers who prefer their literature to be more concrete in tone may skip the following eight sections, and, should they so wish, return here later for a more abstract contextualization. In such a case, the overview provided in section 0.9, below, will provide a signpost for subsequent chapters.

0.1   THE KANTIAN ORIGINS OF MODERN AESTHETICS

The dialogue between philosophy and art has a long history; in the Western cultural tradition, the commencement of the conversation is to be found together with the birth of philosophy. Fascinating speculations concerning art are found in the works of the pre-Socratics, and Plato and Aristotle, as well as their successors, also exhibited regular concern with the subject. However, those who examine the subject in any depth quickly note that the conversation does not always show the characteristics of a real dialogue. Philosophers have often cherished the pretension that they uttered the last word concerning art: with Plato, and a significant part of the great tradition that follows in his footsteps, the pretension is combined with a sharp condemnation of art wherein it is portrayed as both intellectually and morally inferior to philosophy. Not infrequently, the theoretical condemnation goes hand in hand with a practical censorship (see sect. 1.1).

Since the end of the eighteenth century, however, a remarkable change is noticeable with regard to both art's relationship to philosophy and philosophy's assessment of art. The view that Kant initiated a fundamental change in Western philosophy is confirmed in this context: Kant is not only the first philosopher to give a definite place to aesthetic reflection within the "system of philosophy,"[2] but, in addition, he cleared the way for a more positive assessment of both aesthetic experience and art. The transcendental critique (i.e., analysis, justification, and delimitation) of aesthetic judgmental competence is, for Kant, not only a complement to theoretical and practical reason, but also in a certain sense, the very keystone (i.e., the stone that, resting upon all the other stones, holds the arch in place) of transcendental philosophy. In the *Critique of Pure Reason* (1781) and the *Critique of Practical Reason* (1787) Kant sharply contrasted the causally determined world of nature and the moral world of freedom. Subsequently, in the *Critique of Judgment* (1790), he posed the question as to whether or not this gulf between nature and freedom can be bridged, that is, whether or not the goals proposed within human freedom can be found in the deterministic world of phenomena. Kant attributed the ability to reconcile the dimensions of nature and freedom to aesthetic judgment: according to Kant, aesthetic judgment does not so much provide factual knowledge of reality, but rather provides the human subject with a point of view wherefrom nature and freedom can be brought into harmony with each other. For this reason, Kant interprets the work of art as a symbol of the moral (CJ, 254/KU, B254). The supersensible Ideas of reason may well not be susceptible of representation by means of any particular sensory phenomenon, but, indirectly, by means of an *analogy*, they *can* be represented. Aesthetic judgment regulates the relationship between the human subject and reality by permitting us to experience nature as appropriately teleological (CJ, Bxxviii/KU, Bxxviii). The *Critique of Judgment* offers on this issue an answer to the third of Kant's three fundamental questions: "What can I know? What ought I to do? What may I hope?" (CR, 635/KrV, A805). The (human) individual may hope that his finite freedom can be realized in this world.[3] In the feeling of pleasure, which is connected with aesthetic judgment, the individual finds this hope confirmed. The beauty that we experience in the world is, in Stendhal's words, "a promise of the beatitude" (*une promesse de bonheur*) that we can achieve in our own lives.

Although Kant, with this conceptualization of the aesthetic judgment, breaks fundamentally with the pejorative attitude that characterized the preceding tradition, his thinking about art was in important ways determined by that tradition, something that gives his work an irresolvable tension (Biemel, 1959). These tensions are consequent to the fact that Kant maintains the subject-object dichotomy that, from the Greek thinkers onward, decisively characterized Western thinking. Kant, connecting into this tradition, especially with respect to Descartes, the "father" of modern thought, conceives of knowledge primarily as *objectivization*. On the basis of his "Copernican revolution," the insight that human experience does not conform to the object, but rather that the object conforms to the nature of the human reason (CR, 22/KrV, Bxvii), Kant presumes that valid knowledge consists of, or is at least based upon, a theoretical objectivization wherein the objects of experience are constituted. Given that the aesthetic judgment, according to Kant, is exclusively a *secondary* subjective appreciation of the natural object that has been constituted in theoretical reason, the aesthetic experience does not provide knowledge in the sense just elaborated: the aesthetic judgment is therefore not conceived as a commentary concerning the characteristics of an object but as an expression of our *subjective experience* of this natural object. For this reason Kant's theory of aesthetics is more reasonably described as a theory of natural beauty than a theory of art (CJ, 165/KU, B166; cf. Gadamer, 1975, 46). Just as in many classical theories concerning beauty—Plotinus' philosophy, for example—Kant's conceptualization of natural beauty forms the context wherein the beauty of art is interpreted: "Therefore, even though the purposiveness in a product of fine art is intentional, it must still not seem intentional; i.e., fine art must have the *look* of nature even though we are conscious of it as art. And a product of art appears to be like nature if, though we find it to agree quite *punctiliously* with the rules that have to be followed for the product to become what it is intended to be, it does not do so *painstakingly*" (CJ, 174/KU, B179). The primary orientation toward theoretical reason means that Kant, despite the significant steps he took in terms of the emancipation of aesthetic experience, ultimately provided no facility for art to provide us with knowledge of the world.

At this point it is important to add that the aesthetic judgment, interpreted as subjective experience, was at no time conceived by Kant as being of an arbitrary nature. In contrast to the purely pleasant, which differs from person to person, aesthetic judgment is, according to Kant, of no less universal validity than theoretical and practical judgment (CJ, 85 ff./KU, B62 ff.): according to him, the basis of aesthetic pleasure in an object is formed by the harmony of faculties of cognition among themselves and by the harmony of man with nature, something that must be assumed as equal among "all human beings" (CJ, 64/KU, B64). In other words, Kant assumes a timeless transcendental subject that all reasonable subjects have in common. For this reason, the aesthetic domain is based upon a common sense (*sensus communis* or *Gemeinsinn*) (CJ, 87/KU, B76). It is, however, self-evident that the subjective character is not removed by this extension of the notion of subjectivity to intersubjectivity.

Nonetheless, with the emphasis on the subjective character of Kant's aesthetics the last word has not been spoken. Although his thought operates within the subject-object dichotomy, a number of other aspects of his aesthetics show that he had the tendency to go beyond it such that there also appears room for art to provide us with a specific experience of reality outside ourselves. Though Kant primarily determined beauty on the basis of the subject's aesthetic taste, emphatically stating that beauty is not an intrinsic attribute of an object, he otherwise defined aesthetic taste as judgmental competence relating to objects by virtue of *disinterested* pleasure or displeasure. By this formulation was meant that "the liking that determines a judgment of taste is devoid of all interest" (CJ, 45/KU, B4). In other words: the aesthetic experience postulated has no theoretical or practical interest in the object of contemplation. However, as Heidegger has noticed, this does not imply that with the elimination of these interests our relation with the object is severed such that the aesthetic experience becomes a purely subjective feeling. On the contrary, according to Heidegger, precisely because there are no theoretical or practical interests involved, the object of aesthetic experience appears as a *pure* object (N, 1:130). The aesthetic experience hereby becomes a preeminently original experience of the world, an experience that surpasses subjectivism without thereby collapsing into its opposite, namely, objectivism. Kant also comes close to a recognition of the cognitive claims of art in his concept of the aesthetic Idea. An aesthetic Idea is a representation that prompts much thought without the corresponding compliance of a *determinate* concept, that is, without discursive language being able to express this Idea completely (CJ, 182/KU, B192 ff.). The presentation aesthetically "expands the concept itself in an unlimited way" (CJ, 183/KU, B194).

0.2   THE UNFULFILLABLE ROMANTIC DESIRE

Though Kant, trapped in the subject-object dichotomy and his subjective determination of the aesthetic judgment, did not completely elaborate his reevaluation of aesthetics, a large group of philosophers and artists subsequently pushed on through the breach in the unidimensional intellectualism of rationalism that he had constructed in the *Critique of Judgment*. In combination with a progressively more radical undermining of the subject-object dichotomy, the works of Schiller, the Schlegel brothers, Novalis, Schelling, Schopenhauer, Nietzsche, and Dilthey express an aestheticization of the worldview.[4]

It is characteristic of the Romantic attitude that reality in its entirety is understood from within an aesthetic perspective.[5] In accordance with Kant, aesthetics is conceived as the dimension wherein theoretical and practical reason can be brought into harmony with each other; aesthetics hereby becomes "Fundamentalphilosophie" (Marquard, 1962, 232). Disappointed by the violent bankruptcy of the French Revolution, Schiller, in his influential series of letters, *On the Aesthetic Education of Man* (1795), pleaded for a more fundamental, aesthetic revolution.[6] According to Schiller, when theoretical *or* practical reason dominates, then one side of human nature is oppressed in favor of the other and a fundamental alienation ensues. Only when the individual abandons himself to his aesthetic *Spieltrieb* can nature and freedom, and thus also theoretical and practical reason, be reconciled, and only then can the individual become a *human individual* in the full meaning of the term (Schiller, 1981, 58).

While Schiller remained, in many respects, true to Kant's notion of the finiteness of human reason, the thinking of subsequent Romantics is frequently characterized by a passionate desire (*Sehnsucht*) for the infinite and the absolute. The Romantic aspiration was directed at reconciling the infinite with the *here and now*. In 1800, Novalis provided the following formulation of the Romantic project:

> *The world must be Romanticized.* In this way, one will re-find the original meaning. Romantic thought is nothing less than a qualitative improvement (*Potentierung*): the humble Self becomes, in this operation, identified with a better Self. By giving a higher meaning to the ordinary, a mysterious stature to the everyday, the value of the unknown to the known, and the appearance of the infinite to the finite, I romanticize them. And, by inverting the process with regard to the higher, the unknown, the mysterious, and the infinite . . . they receive an ordinariness of expression. (quoted in Rothmann, 1981, 113)

The tendency of the Romantics to postulate, in opposition to Kant's strict separation of subject and object, an almost mystical identity of subject and object, spirit and nature, is noticeable in the foregoing quotation from Novalis. This tendency is especially noticeable in their conceptualization of nature: while Kant, in the context of his critique of theoretical reason, conceived of nature as a lifeless totality, that is, as an atomic collection of phenomena that derive their unity from the rules that reason designates (*Logic*, A1), the Romantics conceived of nature as an organic, living totality. The spirit does not so much stand in opposition to nature, but rather is a phase in its development wherein it becomes self-conscious.[7]

In Schelling's philosophy of Identity, spirit and nature are conceived in their original identity.[8] Art is herein attributed the sacred task of embodying this absolute identity (or indifferentiation of the antithesis of spirit and nature): the work of art is the finite representation of the infinite (W 3:620). In Schelling's *System of Transcendental Idealism* (1800), art is thereby promoted to "the only true and eternal organon which always and unremittingly documents anew what philosophy cannot represent: the unconscious in action and production and its original identity with consciousness. For the philosopher, therefore, art is the pinnacle because it, in a manner of speaking, opens what is most holy, what is burning in an eternal and original union, what in nature and history is separated and which, in life and action, equally in thought, must eternally seek to escape from each other" (W 3:627–28).[9] Ultimately, Schelling conceives of the totality of reality as a work of art. Thus, we read in the *System* that "the objective world is only the original, still unconscious poetry of the spirit" (W 3:349). "What we call nature is a poem which is written in a secret, miraculous text" (W 3:628).

Without doubt, after Schelling we find the most pregnant expression of this aestheticization of worldview in the philosophy of Nietzsche. Initially, still strongly under the influence of Schopenhauer's philosophy, Nietzsche ascribes to art not only the capacity, as a *healing magician*, to absorb the artist into the *primal unity* (B, 24), but also conceives the totality of reality as a work of art that creates itself. Most especially, in the effective history of Nietzsche's philosophy, the aestheticization of worldview has continued in twentieth century philosophy. Megill argues in *The Prophets of Extremity: Nietzsche, Heidegger, Foucault, Derrida*, that the latter three can also be considered as the heirs of the Romantic project. He notes immediately, however, that the aesthetic philosophy of these thinkers can no longer be borne by the belief in the reconciling, unity-creating function of art, but rather that it is characterized by the conviction that modern culture finds itself in an unconquerable crisis. In this sense, according to Megill, there is an immense chasm between the thinking of nineteenth-century Romantics, such as Schelling, and their twentieth-century heirs (Megill, 1985, 18–19).

Against Megill's arguments, however, I want to propose that the crisis of consciousness is already inherent to the Romantic project. The Romantic enthusiasm for art's function of reconciliation is merely one side of Romantic desire. The Romantic *Sehnsucht* in relation to the absolute is actually emphatically associated with the consciousness that such desire is, fundamentally, not susceptible of realization. According to Schiller, for example, although his proposed aesthetic harmony between theoretical and practical reason is embodied, in an unreflected manner, by the *naive* Greek artist, such a unity is no longer possible for the modern individual. The modern artist, described by Schiller as *sentimental*, can, at best, only hope to *approach* such a unity, much as a seriously ill person hopes to become well again. Speaking about the Greeks in *On Naive and Sentimental Poetry* (1795–96), Schiller states: "They are what we once were and what we must once again become. For centuries we have seen in them what we are not, what we are continuously forced to strive to be; what we can never achieve, yet what we hope to approach in an endless progress" (Schiller, 1962, 414). Connecting to this, Schlegel, in a programmatic fragment dating from 1798, postulates that the Romantic project is a *literally* unending project. Contrary to Enlightenment thinking, wherein the infinite was conceived as a *potential* inherent to the finite world, something that could be realized in the future, the infinite for the Romantics is an *actual* infinite that decisively determines our thought and action without our actually being able to achieve it (cf. Knittermeyer, 1929, 15–35). Although the German Romantics felt themselves closely allied to the Idealist metaphysicians in their striving toward the absolute, the Romantic project distinguishes itself in a fundamental manner from the absolute Idealism of Hegel by virtue of an awareness of the fundamental unachievability of this ambition. It is true that Schlegel speaks of an infinite historical progress, but, in a paradoxical manner, this progress is simultaneously understood as being cyclical, something that, for him, makes modern European history a process without possibility of completion.

0.3   ROMANTIC IRONY

It is clear this insight can lead to a nostalgic sentimentality, especially when one, as in the case of Schiller, proceeds from the assumption that this harmony, in a far-off time, once constituted reality. When, as was later the case with Nietzsche, it is understood that this original harmony is actually a historical fiction, then the Romantic desire can shatter into a lethargic passivity and a *Weltschmerz* bordering on madness (c.f. 1.6). Nonetheless, this reaction is not the most representative of the Romantic attitude to life. What is most characteristic of the Romantic reaction to insight into the unachievability of Romantic desire is its fundamental *irony*. In the context of Romantic art, Schlegel speaks of an "eternal oscillation of enthusiasm and irony" (Schlegel, 1882, 2:361). Irony is, in the first place, a method of exorcizing the threat of lethargic passivity: by treating with irony the unachievable desire that is characteristic of human involvement with the world, the Romantic can cherish that desire without falling prey to the despair that is attached to it. But irony is in this context more than merely a *method* of combating lethargy; it is simultaneously an expression of the insight that the grandeur of Romantic desire resides precisely in the fact that it is fundamentally unachievable. Thus, for this reason, irony constitutes the *goal* of Romantic desire: it embodies the fundamental openness, the transcendent character of this desire. It is for this reason that "for Schlegel, there is a fundamental necessity of Romantic irony, whereby the artist self-critically disturbs the illusion created by his work in order to ensure that the progressive, creative process does not become definitive, rigid" (Rothmann, 1981, 114). In other words, irony hinders our falling into the illusion of a last, absolute interpretation of the world.

What hereby becomes clear is that Romantic irony is not merely a stylistic method, but rather that it forms an *ontology*, that is, a view of the most elementary characteristics of reality (Furst, 1984, 225 ff.). The irony-evoking realization of the unachievability of the aspiration for absolute truths and values is based upon the comprehension of the fundamental changeability of reality (see 1.5). The Romantic's irony "is the instrument for registering the obdurate paradoxicality of a universe in eternal flux. . . . The divergence between traditional and romantic irony is thus as much a matter of ontology and epistemology rather as of literary technique" (Furst, 1984, 229).[10] Ontologically comprehended irony is, as Jankélévitch expressed it, "an expression of the transcendental subjectivism" (*une ivresse de la subjectivité transcendentale*) that considers man to be the basis of absolute truth (Jankélévitch, 1964, 17). But, at the same time, irony embodies the capacity that people have to reflect upon their impotence, to distance themselves from it and thus, to a certain extend, to rise above it. Romantic irony makes it possible to live with the knowledge that everything is changeable, and this transcendent character is what differentiates Romantic irony from sarcasm, making it a weapon against the nihilism that announces its presence when transcendental subjectivism is undermined.

The realization of the fundamental unachievability of Romantic desire is also expressed in a number of other specific (stylistic) characteristics of Romanticism. Given that the absolute work of art cannot, in principle, be achieved, the Romantic artists set the open form of the *fragment* in contrast to the self-enclosed unity of the classical work of art (see chapter 6, especially the remarks concerning Schumann's *intermezzi* in the chapter's introduction). On the theoretical level, the preference for the fragmentary is expressed in Schelling's thesis that beauty is the representation of the infinite in the finite (W 3:620; cf. Beierwaltes, 1982, 9). As Schelling remarked in *Über das Verhältnis der bildende Künste zu der Natur* (1807), without boundaries it is impossible for the infinite to appear (W 7:310).

In combination with the foregoing, it is not the beautiful but the *sublime* that is central to Romantic works of art: at this point the Romantics ally themselves with the terminology which Kant developed in the *Critique of Judgment*. While the beautiful is based upon the bounded form of an object, the sublime, according to Kant, relates to formless, unbounded objects. Whereas the beautiful pleases us because it appears to be appropriate, that which is sublime brings a "negative pleasure" into play, because of its chaotic, disordered, and wild character (CJ, 98 ff./KU, B76 ff.). While beauty rests upon the harmony between our imagination and our reason, the sublime is an expression of the conflict between our imagination and the absolute. Through the expression of the sublime, the Romantic artist attempts to evoke an experience that transcends human imagination. According to Schelling, the beautiful and the sublime meet each other in the work of art (Schelling, W 3:621). Thus, accordingly, the "infinite harmony" (W 3:617) toward which the artist strives is not a harmony without tension, but rather a conflicting harmony in the sense found in Heraclitus (see Heraclitus, in Kirk and Raven, 1980, 195 ff.; cf. Beierwaltes, 1982, 14; in this connection see also 1.6).[11]

The Romantic appreciation of the fundamental *finiteness* of aspiring to the infinite also reaches a pregnant expressiveness in the insight that the aspired identity of spirit and nature, to the extent that this really is approached in the aesthetic experience, can never be fully under the control of the conscious subject, but rather falls to that subject, at least in part, as a gift of fate. Hereby, German Romanticism, unlike Kant's transcendental philosophy and Hegel's absolute Idealism, breaks in a radical manner with the Cartesian philosophy of consciousness. Nonetheless, in a certain way this insight is already present in Kant's concept of the genius, a concept that eventually becomes central to Romantic aesthetics. In the *Critique of Judgment,* the genius refers to the "innate mental predisposition (*ingenium*) *through which* nature gives the rule to art" (CJ, 174/KU, B180): really great art originates not by virtue of consciously following aesthetic rules, but rather in imitation of the genius yet *unconscious* powers of imagination.[12] Schelling radicalizes Kant's concept with his thesis that the identity of spirit and nature is only embodied in the work of art itself and can never be achieved in conscious reflection. He links up here with the Kantian conception of the "aesthetic Idea," mentioned above, which "prompts much thought, but to which no determinated thought whatsoever, i.e. no determinate *concept,* can be adequate, so that no language can express it completely and allow us to grasp it" (CJ, 182/KU, B192 ff.). According to Schelling, this unbounded quality that is embodied in the finite work implies that the meaning of the work of art contains an infinite number of possible interpretations that cannot be comprehended by finite reason, but can only surface in the fundamentally open history of the aesthetic experience of that work (W 3:620).

Schopenhauer and Nietzsche emphasize even more categorically the unconscious character of the aesthetic reconciliation. For Schopenhauer, music, the highest expression of the cognitive capacity for art, is an "*unconscious* exercise in metaphysics" (Schopenhauer, 1969, 264; cf. 3.1). And in Nietzsche's *The Birth of Tragedy out of the Spirit of Music* we read that the aesthetic experience of the "primal unity" can only occur when the artist abandons himself to the Dionysian ecstasy wherein subjective consciousness is sacrificed (B, 29; cf. 1.5-6). Only afterwards, in reflection, is it possible to see into what gave us the aesthetic experience, but such reflection necessarily implies a distance with respect to the immediacy of the experience.

Marquard, in an ingenious study of Schelling and Freud, has argued that the process of aestheticization in nineteenth-century German philosophy must be seen not so much as an indication of spiritual overconfidence (cf. the critique that Hegel, in his *Aesthetics,* directed at Romantic irony—Ä 1:101), but rather as a reaction to the experience of the *impotence* of theoretical and practical reason (cf. note 6). That which achieves expression in Schelling (and the other Romantics) is the hope that when theoretical and practical reason are no longer able to control (external and internal) nature, art will be able to allay nature's threat. This, too, can clearly be inferred from the Romantic concept of genius: on the one hand, genius is itself deceptive nature (which is why, for the Romantics, genius and madness are so close to each other), while, on the other hand, it is capable of transforming the deceptiveness of nature into a nonrisk presence (Marquard, 1982, 96, 106).

According to Marquard, the agreement between Schelling's philosophy and Freud's psychoanalytic therapy lies in the fact that both are intended to allay the dominance of (internal) nature precisely by appealing to that deceptive nature itself. Psychoanalytic therapy, too, claims to heal by permitting the unconscious *itself* to speak (see 4.1). In this sense, both Schelling and Freud develop a theory of sublimation: "Aesthetics and therapy—when, in the nineteenth century, they became respectable, both had, therefore, at least one common function: they may both be defined as attempts, under the influence of the impotence and the resignation of historical-world bourgeois reason, that is, under the influence of the dominance of nature, to preserve the presence of humanity" (Marquard, 1982, 106).

According to Marquard, the high point of Romantic aesthetics was merely a temporary circumstance. He asserts that this high point was succeeded by therapy when it became clear that the aestheticization of reality was doomed to failure. Hölderlin is the paradigmatic and tragic symbol of this development: the admiring reception of the divine genius of the artist gave way to a therapeutic concern for the pathology of his madness. This alternation of high point culminates, according to Marquard, in Freud's pretention to have provided, with psychoanalysis, a general theory of humanity and culture that can succeed philosophy (c.q. aesthetics). Marquard's analysis appears to support Hegel's thesis "that art, according to its highest definition, . . . is something from the past," a phenomenon that should not be followed, but rather in thoughtful appreciation should be scientifically understood. This could lead us to the temptation to consider the Romantic project as a finished chapter from the history of the spirit (cf. Hegel, Ä 1:22; also see 0.8 below).

In my view Marquard reaches this conclusion too rapidly. He assumes, following Hegel, that art reaches its climax in the reconciliation of spirit and nature, that is, in its *healing effect*. Against this could be argued that the climax of *modern* art lies more in the representation of the impossibility of the absolute Identity and of the gaping abyss that eternally separates us from that identity. In much no-longer-fine art, such as the music of Schönberg, the plays of Beckett, and the paintings of Bacon, it appears that nonidentity has been elevated to the highest principle. It appears that Marquard ignores the fact that Romantic art and aesthetics can no longer be understood by reference to some absolute-idealistic measure, but, on the contrary, through their characteristic tension between enthusiasm and irony, anticipate an experience of reality that in the no-longer-fine arts probably finds its most pregnant expression.[13]

The thesis that I defend in this book is that the tension that is inherent to the Romantic project is characteristic for an important part of nineteenth- and twentieth-century Western art and philosophy. I shall argue that an analysis of contemporary culture from the perspective of the Romantic project throws clarifying light on the current *condition humaine*.

0.4   THE (POST)MODERNISM DEBATE

I want to illustrate the topicality of the romantic project by locating it in the context of the (post)modernism debate, which, in the last decades, has engaged rather a lot of intellectual interest. I appreciate that a certain amount of confusion lurks within this attempt: the concept *postmodernism* is currently employed with such diverse meanings that it gradually appears to be applicable in every situation (see Eco, 1983, 65; and Welsch, 1987, 1, 9). In this respect, the concept cannot really be differentiated from the equally extensively employed concept *modernism* that forms its basis. The term postmodernism, used for the first time, as far as I know, in a 1917 document (provisionally without imitators) from the little-known German Nietzschean Pannwitz, reemerged during the 1930s in American literary theory. Following World War II the term rapidly gained adherents in other disciplines; the historian, Toynbee, for example, employed it in a book (1947) in order to indicate a particular historical period.[14] The term appeared again in the 1960s in reflections concerning architecture and painting; in the 1970s it became a part of the conceptual terminology of the social sciences. When Lyotard's *The Postmodern Condition* was published in 1979 it appeared that postmodernism had returned to its philosophical roots, with the annotation that what was originally a marginal phenomenon had now become a central theme in philosophical discussion. Now, there are only a few subjects with which the term has *not* been brought into association: the application reaches from postmodern theology and body-culture to postmodern travel-guides and furniture shows. Apart from the spatial spread of the term over the aforementioned domains, it appears that postmodernism is also being applied to a constantly expanding period in history. Where the term was originally and primarily employed to indicate a future or current development (Pannwitz, for example, found that the postmodern individual modeled on Nietzsche's *Übermensch* was a development in the future), the historian Toynbee employed it for a previous historical period, namely, since circa 1875. Other authors go even further back, pointing to a relationship between postmodernism and the Baroque. Eco, who examined postmodernism in relation to mannerism, joked in 1983 that it would not be long before it was used in connection with Homer (Eco, 1983, 66). Lyotard, one of the trendsetting theorists of postmodernism, had several years previously already mentioned his affinity with Aristotle. The multiple referential utility of the concept postmodernism is extended by the fact that, in terms of content, so many mutually contradictory phenomena are indicated (Welsch, 1987, 10). Where the term is used by some to indicate a connection with the era of postindustrial information and communcation technology, for others it stands for the "green" world, ecology, and everything that is associated with alternative lifestyles. While for one group of theorists postmodernism represents a new integration—in the form of a new mythology or a "New Age" ideology—of the fragmented communities that are a product of modernism, yet another group considers it a descriptive affirmation of precisely that fragmentation and pluralism. Aspiring to a good understanding of the term postmodernism is also seriously frustrated by the fact that, in a number of journals that present themselves as postmodern, incomprehensibility appears to have been promoted to the ultimate in style.

For some philosophers, the vague and fashionable character of the term postmodernism is a reason to rigorously avoid its use: the point at issue, however, the crisis wherein modern thought finds itself, cannot be so easily avoided. For this reason, I intend to continue employing the term. In order that possible confusion will be kept within acceptable boundaries, I shall stipulate what it is that I, here and in the following chapters, understand to be involved with the terms *modernism* and *postmodernism*. What I offer is an operationalization of the concepts without the pretension that I thereby provide a terminology that satisfies the complex, pluralistic reality, in its totality. If there is anything that is really characteristic for our present, postmodern condition, then it is the appreciation of the precariousness of such "totalitarian" pretensions. The stipulation that now follows is the result of a necessary fragmentary (re)construction of the cultural and philosophical history of the centuries preceding our own. I will hereby maintain the concepts modern and postmodern in different ways: as *historical* concepts in order to distinguish between different historical eras, as *thematic* concepts in order to indicate the characteristics of the philosophical, social, and artistic movements that are presented as modern, respectively postmodern, and, finally, as concepts that indicate different *worldviews*. That which follows is necessarily summary, but in subsequent chapters the various themes will be dealt with more extensively.

0.5 THE FOUNDATIONS OF MODERNISM

Referring to historical periods, I maintain the term *modernism* in the first place as a synonym for what the Germans refer to with the term *Neuzeit,* that is, the period that begins in the seventeenth century and for which the work of Descartes and Bacon provides the starting point (cf. Welsch, 1987, 65 ff.).[15] Given that the culturally thematic characteristics that I will be specifying are still of decisive significance in contemporary thought, it could be argued that this period has not yet ended. Among the thematically determined characteristics of modernism, the aspiration toward a universal science (a *scientia* or *mathesis universalis*) deserves primary mention. For this universal science, the experimental physical sciences increasingly form the dominant model; this universally unifying scientific endeavor is considered as providing a conceptualization of reality in its totality. In this fashion, it lays claim to infinity. From the basis of this unifying conceptualization, which provides the foundations of the *scientia universalis,* not only nature but also politics (Hobbes) and ethics (Spinoza) are approached. Universal science not only offers the possibility of providing better *explanations* with respect to the totality of reality, but also it provides increasingly more efficient methods of *predicting* and *controlling:* the Industrial Revolution and modern technology are, thus, inherently connected with the development of the instrumental rationality of the *scientia universalis* (cf. 2.5 and 4.5).

Also characteristic for modernism is what we can call *a pathos of the radical new beginning:* modernism presents itself primarily as a break with the past *and* a new beginning. This is already apparent in the title, *Novum organon,* that Bacon chose for one of his most important works, and in Descartes' methodological doubt that aimed at finding a starting point to build the *mathesis universalis,* and remains a determinant of modernistic self-reflection until late in the twentieth century. Still Husserl, perhaps the last great representative of modernism in philosophy, understood the phenomenology he developed as a *Neustiftung der Philosophie.* The pathos of a new beginning is closely connected with a dynamic, optimistic belief in progress: most especially, in the Enlightenment, the criticism of the authority of tradition (of revealed religion, the dominance of Aristotelian science, and the feudal organization of society) is related to the belief that the path of universal reason will lead mankind into a paradise on earth. The French Revolution, and the European movement toward democracy that flowed from it, is in this sense intrinsically joined to modernism.

The pathos of the radical new beginning and the belief in progress results in an exaltation of change: "The modern age is the first to exalt change and convert it into a foundation. Difference, seperation, otherness, plurality, novelty, evolution, revolution, history—all these words can be condensed in one: future. Not past nor eternity, not time which is but time which is not yet and which always will be to come: this is our archetype" (Paz, 1974, 17).

At first sight, it appears to be a paradoxical characteristic of the modernization of European culture that, in contrast to the aspiration for unity, this modernization has occurred in combination with a powerful process of social, cultural, and theoretical differentiation. Although the dominance of instrumental rationality is not really hereby effected, modern culture shows an increasing differentiation of the various systems of social and cultural action (Habermas), for example, science, morality, law, and religion, as well as increasing differentiation within these systems. The emancipation or autonomous development of art, marked by the Art for Art's Sake (*L'art pour l'art*) movement at the end of the nineteenth century, and the development of pluralistic modern art, form an expression of this process of external and internal differentiation. At the theoretical level, this differentiation or disintegration (*Entzweiung*) of culture finds expression in Kant's achieved separation of the contents of philosophy, science, morality, and art. It is characteristic for the modernists' project that in their fundamental aspiration toward unity they attempt to force, in one way or another, a *pattern* of unity upon that differentiation that is inherent to the modernization process. The absolute Idealism of Hegel, wherein *reality in its totality* is understood in terms of an all-embracing teleology of the Spirit, can be seen, according to Habermas, as an attempt to repair the crumbled unity of the modern project (cf. Habermas, 1985, 26). According to Lyotard, such attempts are only possible when one reaches back to some sort of metanarrative (*grand récit*): he maintains that, in addition to the Hegelian teleology, the idea of human emancipation (such as was propagated during the Enlightenment and in Marxism) and the hermeneutic assumption of an all-embracing meaning are examples of such metanarrative (Lyotard, 1984, 31 ff.). Even a contemporary defender of the modernist project such as Habermas appears, in his theory of communicative rationality, and regardless of his significant criticism of Hegel's "reasonable" totalitarianism, to be ultimately concerned with the reintegration of the differentiated systems of social and cultural action.

The basis of the modern worldview, as sketched above, is the metaphysical assumption that the human subject forms the foundation of reality *in its totality.* Not only is everything that exists reduced, in modern thought, to an object for the representative subject, but also human subjectivity is itself understood as the ultimate foundation, the archimedian point, upon which the *scientia universalis* rests.[16] The great metanarratives of modernism aim in one way or another at this (at least potentially) autonomous subject.[17] Undoubtedly, this *theoretical humanism* of modernism is closely connected with what Nietzsche announced as "the death of God" (see 1.7). The *demythologizing* of the world, occasioned by instrumental rationality, and the nestling of transcendental subjectivism in the vacuum that therefore appeared, form two sides of the same coin (see in this respect the discussion of Foucault's archaeology of modern subjectivism in 6.3).

0.6   THE POSTMODERN *VERWINDUNG* OF MODERNISM

It is tempting, against the background of what I have just sketched, to characterize postmodernism as merely an antimodernist phenomenon, a *Gegenaufklärung.* Although such an interpretation, as we will shortly see, misses an essential characteristic of postmodernism, it is nonetheless serviceable as a first determination of the prefix (cf. the definition of postmodern art in 2.6). In contrast to the modernist aspiration for unity, totality, and universalism, postmodernism stands for differentiation, pluralism, and particularism. In contrast to the modernist optimism relating to progress, postmodernism places a fundamental scepticism, and, in contrast to the pathos of a radical new beginning it places the inevitability of tradition. Other than modernism, postmodernism no longer believes in the possibility of a last foundation in some one or other metanarrative, and, in contrast to modernism's claim to infinity, postmodernism stipulates the radical finiteness of the human existence. Finally, and in relation with the foregoing, postmodernism contrasts the modern subjectivism, which has decisively determined philosophy since Descartes, with the "death" of the subject.

Although the history of the term postmodernism does not lead us further back than the beginning of the twentieth century, one can postulate that, in some ways, the foregoing critique of modernism has existed since its inception. We could, for example, point to Vico, whose 1725 publication, *Scienza nuova,* was a critical reflection against Descartes' one-sided orientation to mathematics and physics, and who replaced the image of unilinear progress with that of cyclical development, or to Rousseau's early critique of the process of social rationalization. The critique located in the orientation of practical philosophy, which, beginning with Marx, has determined, in a significant manner, much of modern thinking, can also be understood as a critique of the primacy of instrumentalist rationality. We could agree with Lyotard that this is not a coincidental phenomenon, but rather that postmodernism was implicit in modernism from its inception. The differentiation that is characteristic of modernization formed in this manner the source for postmodern doubt concerning the modernistic starting point, especially the pretensions to totality and unity. In this sense one could regard postmodernism as a critical reflection upon the starting points of modern existence that was made possible by modernism itself: postmodernism forms, in a manner of speaking, the guilty conscience of modernism, following, like a shadow, the modern aspiration toward an all-embracing meaning.

In the event that the postmodern doubt relating to the starting-points of modernism is something that comes from the process of modernization itself, then such doubt is in no way a free choice of twentieth-century man such that one may take it or leave it according to personal inclination. It appears that, as a consequence of modernization, postmodern doubt has overtaken *us*. The doubt residing in the foundations of modernism has emphatically announced itself through various social and cultural developments: the succession of increasingly destructive wars that the twentieth century has witnessed, the genocide practiced under diverse ideological flags, and the ecological catastrophe that perhaps threatens us in the very heart of our material existence, makes it almost impossible not to cherish doubts concerning the modern optimism relating to progress (De Mul and Korthals, 1997).

Nowadays, there are very few people who can share Kant's modernist belief that, in the foreseeable future, a situation of permanent peace, based upon some secret plan of nature, will *necessarily* be realized (TEP, 205). But, while today's followers of contemporary modernism at least hold onto the *possibility* of achieving the modern project (see, for example, Habermas, 1996), philosophers such as the later Heidegger and Foucault plainly state that modernism's project inevitably leads to the aforementioned problems. According to Foucault, fascism and Stalinism are the products of the type of rationality that is characteristic of modern society (Foucault, 1982, 209). The postmodern philosophers postulate that every form of totalitarian thought and action inevitably leads to one or another form of terror (see Welsch, 1987, 62).

Although modernism has, from its inception, been involved with an inherently fundamental critique of its own starting points—Foucault finds that this digging in the ground whereon we stand is one of the central characteristics of modern thinking (see the interview with Carusso, 1974, 14)—there is nonetheless an important difference between the early countermovements and contemporary postmodernism, a difference that makes it extremely difficult for us to consider the latter as merely *anti*-modernism. The early critiques shared in many respects a number of the fundamental starting points of the modernist project. Marxism is a case in point; despite its fundamental criticisms it merely replaces, ultimately, one vision of a totality (i.e., the Hegelian) with another, which it then presents as a radical new beginning. Contemporary postmodernism appears to distinguish itself from these modern countermovements by virtue of its affirmation of the radical finiteness of human existence and the associated difference, pluralism, and particularism that have become increasingly characteristic of modern society and culture. Difference, pluralism, and particularism no longer form merely the occasion for a nostalgic, old-fashioned desire for unity, but are, rather, applauded as an alternative for the inevitable terror that flows from theoretical totalitarianism. Lyotard argues, in an interview, that the issue is "acknowledging the autonomy and specificity of multiple and uninterpretable language games which are entangled with each other, not reducing them to a common denominator; in one sentence: play, and let us play in peace" (quoted in Welsch, 1987, 33).

Current postmodernism, however, also distinguishes itself from the modern countermovements such as Marxism because it no longer believes in the feasibility of a final foundation (*Letztbegründung*) that would make a new beginning possible. It is primarily on this point that the interpretation of postmodernism as an antimodernism fails: a belief in the possibility of a radical overcoming (*Überwindung*) of tradition is an assumption of modernism that postmodernism most resolutely doubts. According to Vattimo, who allies himself with Nietzsche and Heidegger on this point, postmodernism should be considered as a *Verwindung* of modernism, a *solution* that exists in the radicalization of the inherent disintegrating tendencies of modern metaphysics.[18] Hereby we should, perhaps, be able to distance ourselves from modernism without falling prey to the illusion of the possibility of a radical *new* beginning (Vattimo, 1988, 164 ff.). Derrida's deconstruction of metaphysics, too, by showing the multiplicative complexity of meaning and indeterminacy of texts, can be understood as a form of *Verwindung* in the sense just explicated. This also appears to me to be the tenor of Eco's interpretation of cultural postmodernism, which he defines as the *mannerism* of modernism. Eco conceives of the postmodern as the answer to the fact that modernism cannot go any further: "The postmodern reply to the modern consists of recognition that the past, since it cannot really be destroyed, because its destruction leads to silence, must be revisited: but with irony, not innocently" (Eco, 1983, 67). Varying the words of Derrida, we could say that no postmodern experience exists that, in one way or another, does not *a priori* assume modern experience (cf. Derrida, 1981, 280–81): the conditions of the possibility of postmodernism lie in its parasitical relation to modernism. Derrida is therefore aware that even in the most radical deconstruction an hermeneutic desire for meaning is assumed.

On the other hand, by virtue of the foregoing argument, postmodernism is immediately exposed to the criticism that it inevitably leads to one or another sort of nihilism or fatalism. The postmodern *Verwindung* of modern subjectivism—that is at work in the work of Heidegger and partly following in his footsteps, in that of Vattimo and (post)structuralist thinkers such as Lacan, Foucault, Derrida, and Baudrillard—appears to frustrate in advance every (modern) hope for change occasioned by human intervention. The unmasking of the phantasies of omnipotence surrounding the autonomous subject leads—in the latter thinkers, though in different ways—to the acknowledgment, or even to the affirmation, of the supremacy of autonomous signification systems, technologies, or mass media. If the search for an ultimate foundation, the "transcendental signified" (*signifié transcendental*) (Derrida), is abandoned, then every act of speech threatens to degenerate into a swirling madness of "freely circulating signifiers" (Lacan) lacking every referential power (see 5.5).[19] Through the devaluation of every value and truth that had until now existed, which is the consequence of this situation—something that, following Nietzsche, we could refer to as a passive nihilism—the sensible world can no longer be understood as real, nor the real world as sensible (Bröcker, 1963, 14; see below, 1.7). Following Nietzsche, one could therefore ask oneself whether or not postmodernism is actually a phenomenon of decadence, Europe's swan song, a symptom of a culture that, having lost all belief in its own future, has become powerless. Postmodernism appears to result in an irony that leaves no space available for enthusiasm; indeterminacy rules, ok. Because clear criteria are missing from the postmodern devaluation of the past, it becomes no more than a colorful collection of events and styles that may be used without obligation.[20] That which is presented as pluralistic differentiation declines into a complete lack of differentiation or into total indifference.

In the terrain of art this nihilism is expressed in a radical blurring of modernism's characteristic distinction between high and low art. "As long as they carry the name of a great designer," mocks Finkielkraut in his attack on postmodernist culture,

> a pair of boots is worth a play by Shakespeare. And in keeping with this, a comic strip that combines an exciting love story with beautiful pictures is worth a novel by Nabokov; these little Lolitas are the same as *Lolita*, a clever piece of advertising is worth a poem by Apollinaire or Francis Ponge, the rhythm of a rock song, a melody by Duke Ellington; a beautiful soccer match, a ballet by Pina Bausch; a great couturier, Manet, Picasso, or Michelangelo; contemporary opera—"about life, a music video, a jingle, a spot"—is basically the same as Verdi or Wagner. The soccer player and the choreographer, the painter and couturier, the writer and the ideas man, the musician and the rock star are all in the same way *creative artists*. We must stop clinging to academic prejudices that reserve the title *artist* only for certain people and demote all others to a subcultural category instead. (Finkielkraut, 1995, 113–14)

The "higher" arts even take the "lower" as example: Warhol's cans of Campbell tomato soup were inspired by the advertisements of the soup industry, the sculptures of Jeff Koons seem to seek their example in the most authentic kitsch, and the repetitive music of Phillip Glass is these days only with difficulty distinguishable from the mindless repetitions found in the hit parades. Originality, too, closely connected with the modern pathos of the new, is no longer the differentiating criterion in art. After the postmodern breakthrough of the primacy of the abstract, traditions are quoted without the least reservation (cf. 2.6–7). And why not? Why try something new if everything has already been done?

0.7 THE TOPICALITY OF ROMANTIC DESIRE

Against the background of this exposition of the relation between modernism and postmodernism I want to explain why, in my opinion, we can speak of the topicality of Romantic desire.[21] When we try to situate the Romantic project in relation to these two movements it is immediately clear that it cannot be identified completely with either position. Depending upon which characteristics we place in the foreground, the Romantic project appears as either a modernistic *Gegenaufklärung* or as a postmodernism *avant la lettre*. I shall elaborate on this point by reference to the definition given earlier whereby the Romantic position is postulated as an infinite movement between enthusiasm and irony.

That which the Romantic project primarily connects with modernism is *enthusiasm*: the Romantic desire to aestheticize reality is characterized by the same utopian hope as many other modern projects. The view that it could be possible to aesthetically transform the *totality* of reality gives the Romantic project not only a *modern* totalitarian character—with Schiller, for example, the aesthetic State is *the* ideal for the *whole* of humanity (Welsch, 1987, 76)—but, in addition, it makes clear that the project is borne by the modernist pathos of a radical new beginning. Seen from this perspective, Romanticism is no less a dogmatic representative of the *Gegenaufklärung* than Marxism (Finkielkraut, 1995, 21 ff.). The Romantic project also remains modernistic in its appeal to individual responsibility: while it is true that Romanticism is in tension with the subject-centrism of the Enlightenment, and, as in the case of Schelling's philosophy of the unconscious, it takes fundamental steps in the direction of a postmodernist decentring of subjectivity, it does not distance itself in any way from the conception that it is possible for man to aesthetically transform reality from within his subjectivity. Even Nietzsche, who, because of his radical critique with respect to subject-centrism has been elevated by many postmodernists to the position of star witness in the case of the "death of the subject," does not really distance himself from the idea that "man is a subject, especially an artistically creative subject" (KSA, 1:883–84; see below, 1.3). In the Romantic vision, art is conceived as an experiential domain wherein forms of subjectivity can be developed other than those which have been imposed upon us in centuries past.

The fact that Romantics have cherished the ideas of totality and unity in another way has led a number of authors into the temptation to dismiss the Romantic project as a purely nostalgic repetition of modernism's aspiration for a meaningful unity (see, for example, Welsch, 1987, 36, 76). Such an interpretation, however, unjustifiably misses the ironic side of the Romantic project, which, as I have attempted to make clear in my foregoing remarks, is no less constitutive for Romantic experience. It is true that the characteristic irony of the Romantic project does not do any damage to the modernist hope for unity and totality, but it does mean a simultaneous acknowledgment of the unachievability of this aspiration.[22] This irony ensures that Romantic enthusiasm is essentially distinguished from the dogmatic enthusiasm that is characteristic of modernism.

The fundamental role that irony plays in Romantic experience precedes the postmodern pathos of irony. But, where radical postmodern irony, as we have seen above, threatens to result in a passive-nihilistic or even fatalistic attitude, the Romantic project is borne by the idea that the transcendental movement in the direction of unity and totality is not only constitutive for human existence, but also that it expresses the humanity of man. And this precisely in a world wherein meaning has lost its self-evident certainty. Human existence is, in fact, impossible without the aspirational striving toward sense, even though this aspiration in its totality is unachievable. A complete affirmation of pluralism and particularism, of the radical finiteness of all objects, is, in the final analysis, an impossible mode of Being for man. Only an *Übermensch* would, perhaps, be able to bear such a position (cf. 1.6 and 1.9). We can, perhaps, best conceive of the aspirational striving toward sense in existence by analogy with Kant's regulative ideas: the aspired unity is not a (future) given, but rather a necessary though insoluble task for man. In other words, we are confronted here not with an immanent but with a transcendent usage of terms such as unity, infinity, and sense (Kant, Prol. 328; cf. CR, 318/KrV, A326 ff.).

The relationship between the Romantic project and an important part of postmodern philosophy is also expressed in the significance of the role that they both ascribe to art.[23] We already find the postmodern presumption that the artist is an equal conversational partner to the philosopher in Schelling's 1803 publication *Lectures on the Method of Academic Studies* and in his posthumously published work *Philosophy of Art.* In these texts, Schelling corrects the conception of the relationships between art and philosophy that he had earlier published in *System of Transcendental Idealism* (1800): he no longer speaks of the superiority of art (an expression of the modernist desire for the one, exclusive perspective of totality that had characterized his *System*—cf. 0.2, above). "Art," remarks Schelling, "although it is an absolute, perfect unitary identification of the real and the ideal, holds itself in its relation to philosophy as something real to something ideal. In philosophy, the last contradiction resolves itself in pure identity, but, nonetheless, in this identity philosophy remains merely ideal. Both meet each other on the final pinnacle, and, in relation to each other, precisely because of their common attribute of absoluteness, they are each others model and counterpart (*Vorbild und Gegenbild*)" (W, 5:348). Philosophy and art stand together here "on the same pinnacle" (W, 5:369), regarded as partners that possess, in the Absolute, an identical content, but that differ from each other in form, the one in the form of truth and the other in the form of beauty (W, 5:370). Heidegger, in the afterword of *What Is Metaphysics?*, appears to agree with Schelling's remark that art and philosophy are on equal heights when he remarks that "poets and thinkers live close to each other on separated mountains" (GA, 7:122).

The accessibility of this dialogue has resulted in philosophy undergoing an important transformation in postmodern experience: it marks the end of what we, with Rorty, may call philosophy in its epistemological form. In modern times, when philosophy has lost so much terrain to science, it has, with increasing determination, presented itself as the critical authority providing analysis and epistemological verification of scientific propositions, hereby attempting to maintain the supremacy over science that, formerly, as queen of the sciences, it had possessed. Here, too, Kant's transcendental philosophy marks a break in the history of philosophy: in contrast to the philosophers before him, Kant no longer speaks of things as such, but rather of our knowledge of things (CR, 59/KrV, A12), thereby making philosophy primarily a theory of knowledge (epistemology). This is also applicable to modern aesthetics, which has in modern times developed itself as the epistemology and methodology of the experiencing of beauty. Aesthetics, as Kant had designed it, became an investigation into the conditions of the possibility of the aesthetic experience of works of art (Vattimo, 1985, 288). Given that this contains a pretension to speaking the last word about art and the aesthetic experience, such an *epistemological* aesthetics is still located in the Platonic tradition. Postmodern philosophy no longer utters the last word concerning science or art, but rather is one contributor to a pluralistic *conversation of mankind* wherein the conversational partners are equivalent but self-evidently not equal (Rorty, 1979, 389 ff.).[24]

On the basis of the foregoing we could describe the Romantic experience as one that occurs in the field of tension between modernity and postmodernity. If most of us are, as Hassan has rightly remarked, "a little Modern, and Postmodern at once" (Hassan, 1987, 88), then, in fact, the topicality of the Romantic experience is hereby already established. However, the Romantic oscillation between the poles of modernity and postmodernity may not hereby be considered as a *reconciliation* of those poles or as a victory over their contradiction. In principle, the Romantic experience is an ambivalent experience, an expression of the ambivalence that is inherent to the (post)modern individual. The Romantic experience oscillates between modern enthusiasm and postmodern irony, between the modern aspiration for totality and postmodern pluralism, between the modern desire for infinity and the radical postmodern appreciation of human finiteness.

With this determination of the Romantic experience, the contours become apparent of what we can refer to as a Romantic anthropology of discord. Such an anthropology departs from the real existing discord that appears in the world and in our existence, and, therefore, in our reflections about and our interpretation of both world and existence (cf. Van Nierop, 1989, 11). Philosophical reflection can illuminate this discord, but it cannot triumph over it, reconcile it, or liberate us from it.

0.8   THE ROMANTIC IMAGE OF MAN

I want to further specify the contours of this Romantic anthropology of discord by comparing it with the anthropological design that the Dutch philosopher Oudemans offers in his book *Divided Man*. Such a comparison is useful because it illuminates a number of agreements as well as a number of important points of difference. Oudemans summarizes his postmodern philosophy of finitenes, which in large part rests upon Heidegger's philosophy, as follows: "Human discord resides in the fact that we permanently turn away from the unity to which we were called and that we cannot move in the direction of that unity, while it is just as difficult for us to accept its lack: we are called to be ourselves, but we cannot be ourselves. But, while we cannot be ourselves, and occasionally recognize this fact, we actually have no other choice than to assume and desire our complete unity" (Oudemans, 1980, 247). For this reason, according to Oudemans, man lives in "inevitable inauthenticity": "We hope to show that man is incapable of forging himself into unity through a gradual reduction of inauthenticity via intervention and insight, and that he equally cannot achieve his unification through resigned acceptance of his inauthenticity" (Oudemans, 1980, 52).

While, on the basis of this determination of "human life in general" (Oudemans, 1980, 9), one could expect a Schopenhauerian pessimism, Oudemans in no way ends his book on such a depressed note. It is perhaps true that being a human individual is necessarily and without surcease a question of being unreal and divided, but we are, according to him, so finite and unreal that we simply cover this truth with illusions and blind hope. According to Oudemans, we cannot, because of our fundamental finiteness, really permit the tragedy that determines human life to actually penetrate our awareness. "The delusion," as Peperzak summarizes Oudemans' position, "which beats us down in our existence is not only a destiny but also the greatest comfort" (Peperzak, 1981, 260). On the basis of this conception of the inevitable inauthenticity of the human existence, Oudemans criticizes Heidegger, who, unjustly according to him, considers that we can accept our finiteness, heroically or not, and thereby achieve some form of authenticity (cf. below, 4.3).[25] We are constantly "divided between amazement at the beauty of the world and bewilderment at what is diabolical about it" (Oudemans, 1980, 259).

Oudemans' anthropology of discord meshes in many respects with the portrayal of mankind that lies in the foundations of the Romantic project. Nonetheless, there is a fundamental difference with respect to the evaluation of hope and the desire for unity. It is clear from the foregoing quotations that Oudemans resolutely dismisses every aspiration toward infinity as an illusion. Peperzak has justifiably remarked that this is connected with the remarkable fact that Oudemans equates this aspiration with a *claim* to completion, and, on this basis, must conclude that such an aspiration is necessarily of an illusory character (Peperzak, 1981, 262). This results from the remarkable fact that Oudemans, in contrast to his postmodern starting points, continues to maintain typically modern criteria such as *complete* autonomy, freedom, and responsibility in his judgment of human existence. This leads, according to Peperzak, to an unjustifiably dichotomous approach: "Everything which a person does not do from a basis of infinite authority, is alienation; world and community resound henceforth with unachievable demands and endless dissatisfaction" (Peperzak, 1981, 265).

It is equally on these grounds that Oudemans rejects the Romantic attitude to life. "The misconception of human discord in the Romantic attitude receives an unusual form hereby: the Romantic recognizes human discord and also sees that humans cannot bear such discord—nonetheless, he lives alongside and through that discord because he thinks he can achieve a victory with an aesthetic attitude to life which exults in its own despair" (Oudemans, 1980, 246). Oudemans, with Wittgenstein, rejects this attitude because, according to him, the harshness and the conflict in life cannot be made pleasant, but rather continue to torment us, whatever our desires may be.

Apart from the fact that Oudemans maintains a rather one-sided conceptualization of the Romantic, whereby he completely ignores the role played by irony, he also gives too little consideration to the transcendent character that the aesthetic experience shares with a number of other experiential domains such as love and religious hope. Their grandeur does not reside in the completion of these desires (such completion is indeed denied to us because of our radical finiteness), but rather in the fact that they can permit us, in a certain sense, to go beyond such finiteness. "Action is not a sum of the factually finite and the illusory infinite, but a *limited* realization of something positive on the basis of our desire for the infinite (which, if it is good, does not imagine that the desired can be demanded)" (Peperzak, 1981, 264). Those, such as Oudemans, who are tempted to reject every hope and desire as an illusion misunderstand that Romantic desire literally promotes living.[26] The aesthetic experience is, for this reason, not merely a blinding that forces us to live alongside and through our finiteness in inauthenticity. We can immediately agree with Oudemans that we live large parts of our lives in inauthenticity and that an aestheticistic attitude can play an important role in that living, but this is merely viewing one side of the aesthetic Janus-mask. Aesthetic experience can put us in such a contemplative relationship to the finiteness of our lives that we actually, even if only for a mere moment, transcend it. This is not only that of which the greatness of Greek tragedies consists, but, in fact, it is applicable to all sublime works of art, even—or, especially—when they belong to the contemporary no-longer-fine arts.

The transcendence does not completely lie within the capacity of desiring man—the issue is more one of being open to it—but it can certainly not take place *without* man. The aspiration for transcendence always remains, in this sense, an adventure, the ending of which is not determined by us alone. Life, also aesthetic life, always implies a risk, a dance above the abyss of the inauthentic. But it is precisely herein that the grandeur of the fundamental openness of Romantic desire hides. In Nietzsche's words (GS, 47):

Smooth ice	Glattes eis
is paradise	Ein Paradeis
for those who dance with expertise	Für den, der gut zu tanzen weiss

When, in the following chapters, I speak of art and works of art, it will be done in the light of the Romantic discord I have just explicated. Before giving a survey of the rest of this book, I will first enumerate a number of this discord's characteristics .

In the context of the anthropology of discord, art appears as a phenomenon that cannot be unambiguously associated with modernism or postmodernism. As an autonomous *cultural domain,* art has developed itself, in the past century, as an undisputable aspect of the modern project. Habermas comments, correctly, that: "The idea of modernity is intimately bound up with the development of European art" (Habermas, 1996, 44). This idea of modernity is, for example, expressed in the autonomization of art, in the belief in artistic progress and social emancipation through art, in the emphasis on criteria such as originality and authenticity, and, especially, in the real significance that modern art attributes to renewal. The strong differentiation between different forms of art as a consequence of a "pathos of purity" that is inherent to modern art is, as was remarked above, characteristic for modernism, too (Bürger, 1987, 10; see chapter 2). On the other hand, the extreme pluralism of modern art, expressed in the great number of -*isms* that currently exist, is a real characteristic of postmodern experience of life. Moreover, art has not only been an emancipatory power from its inception, but also it has been a "form of disappearance of reality" in the sense that as autonomous art it easily results in a reservation wherein the subject, disciplined by instrumental reason, can cherish an imaginary freedom. "Art," as Sanders expressed this ambivalence in his analysis of postmodernism, "is a part of the modernist project and, simultaneously, contradicts this project" (Sanders, 1987, 76).

In both its modern and postmodern forms, art is a domain of experience that oscillates between reconciliation and criticism. On the one hand, since the Romantic period art has been an expression of the modern aspiration for a meaningful totality and, on the other hand, it has appeared as an *antidote to utopianism* that constantly reminds us of the tragedy of human existence. This latter is especially relevant for the no-longer-fine arts. On the other hand, the Romantic enthusiasm for reconciliation has not been abandoned by an important part of modern art: the historical avant-garde movements at the beginning of the present century, such as dadaism and surrealism—in contrast to their ironic content, which indisputably foreshadowed later postmodern art—remained loyal to the Romantic imperative to aesthetically transform life. Reconciliation and criticism reflexively interpenetrate: after all, the illusory aesthetic reconciliation also means a complaint against everyday fallen-ness, and the critical presentation of it simultaneously reconciles us to it through its aestheticization.

The aestheticization of existence, too, sometimes identified with the postmodern experience of existence, has, for this reason, two aspects. In contemporary postmodern society, the aestheticization of existence, in a certain sense, has been realized. But, according to Vuyk in the essay previously cited, this postmodern "aestheticization of worldview" does not automatically mean that the world has been made more beautiful (Vuyk, 1988, 181). The stylization of life, which meets the many requirements cherished by the postmodern individual, easily turns out to be a relaxation into one or another *lifestyle*. And this stands in diametrical opposition to the stake of the Romantic project: "Living with taste is not an unproblematic swanning along the boulevards of the welfare State. Looking, acting, judging from an aesthetic perspective poses conditions, and, if they are not met, then the world is merely a game of mirrors: ultimately, everything hurts the eyes, and, finally, one sees nothing other than one's own delusion" (Vuyk, 1988, 181).

The blinding character of the postmodern game of mirrors resides partly in the fact that it makes the ironic character of Romantic irony invisible. Eco understood this well when he remarked: "Irony, metalinguistic play, enunciation squared. Thus, with the modern, anyone who does not understand the game can only reject it, but with the postmodern, it is possible not to understand the game and yet take it seriously. Which is, after all, the quality (the risk) of irony. There are always those who understand the ironic argument as something serious" (Eco, 1983, 68).

0.9 SURVEY OF THE BOOK'S CONTENTS

The following six dialogues between art and philosophy take place in the field of tension generated between Romantic enthusiasm, Romantic irony, and the polarized concepts that thereby arise. The themes that are discussed may be read as a more detailed explication of a number of issues that, in their mutual relationships, have been introduced in the foregoing pages. The separate chapters carry, as is usual in the hermeneutic circle of understanding, the comprehension of the *totality* of the relationships, while their meaning can only be grasped against the background of that totality. At the same time, however, the separate parts have a diffuse effect; the totality constantly shifts in the process of understanding. Every unveiling of meaning also means a concealing of other, often no less significant, aspects of the interpreted issue. For this reason, it is not my intention to tempt the reader of this book into accepting, with me, only one perspective of Romantic desire, but rather to lead him—carefully noting Nietzsche's remark that the understanding of an issue increases to the extent that we use more eyes, *different* eyes, in examining that issue (GM, 255)—along a diversity of perspectives.

In the first chapter, *"Frozen Metaphors"* enthusiasm and irony, which are characteristic of the Romantic project, are discussed in relation to several works by the sculptor Sigurder Gudmundsson, a poem by the Dutch poet and film director Peter Delpeut, and a number of texts by Friedrich Nietzsche. Although the work of each of these persons is characterized by the Romantic aspiration toward unity, they also show the principle of the unachievability of this Romantic aspiration. The view from which this thematic is approached is formed by the metaphoric character of the works of Gudmundsson, Delpeut, and

Nietzsche. The metaphorical character of their work is not merely stylistic; it forms the expression of an aesthetic ontology standing in vital contrast to the metaphysics that have decisively determined Western thinking since Plato. The aesthetic imperative that flows from this ontology is, however, presented with the necessary irony.

In chapter 2, *"The Path of Autonomy,"* in a constructed conversation between the works of the American painter Frank Stella and the genetic epistemology of the Swiss scholar Jean Piaget, a more detailed examination of the rationalization of modern art is to be found. The *medium* for this conversation is the study by the art historian Suzi Gablik concerning the process of rationalization and progress in art. In this conversation it becomes clear that the development of modern art, which has made an important contribution to the origins of modern subjectivity, reached a dead-end in the early work of Stella, in consequence of which, in his work of the 1970s and 1980s he has entered new, postmodern pathways in order to escape from the silting up of modernism. In a comparison with Dadaism and Surrealism, two important representatives of the historical avant-garde, I subsequently examine more closely the position that the later Stella occupies between modernism and postmodernism. At this stage, the interpretations of modern and avant-garde art provided by Adorno, Benjamin, and Habermas, representatives of the Frankfurt School, enter the discussion: art appears also in their interpretations as a domain of experience that can mean, as well as a *promesse de bonheur*, a promise of significant unity, a radical expression of nonidentity, as is especially the case in the no-longer-fine arts.

In the conversation between Schopenhauer's aesthetic of music and Steve Reich's repetitive music that takes place in the third chapter, *"The Art of Forgetting"* it becomes clear that Schopenhauer's variant on the Romantic project can throw a clarifying light on a striking form of contemporary music that is deemed to be postmodern. Moreover, the nonteleological experience of Reich's music gives us the opportunity to listen to Schopenhauer's Romantic aesthetic of music with different—postmodern?—ears. Just as in the previous chapter the role that aesthetic experience, in this case, the experience of music, has played in the origin of the modern subject is discussed, whereby a first attempt is made to think beyond modern subjectivism. The other side of the aestheticization of subjectivism, the danger of aestheticism, also arises at this point in the discussion. In addition to Nietzsche, Freud, like the former a student of Schopenhauer, begins to speak in this chapter; he has an important role to play in later chapters. The concluding reflections, which, on the basis of the works of Deleuze and Lyotard, concern the libidinal interpretation of repetitive music, give a foretaste of the final three chapters in the book, wherein a number of representatives of (post)structuralist French philosophy join the conversations.

In chapter 4, *"The First and the Last Word,"* mediated by one of the Dutch poet Achterberg's poems, Heidegger's hermeneutics enter into dialogue with the psychoanalyses of Freud and Lacan. Hereby, along with some important points of agreement, several fundamental differences are shown. The central question here is whether art is merely the *object* of scientific or philosophical knowledge, or precisely the *region* of something else, that is, aesthetic knowledge. Connecting into what was said above about the relief from aesthetics in nineteenth-century German philosophy by virtue of therapy, it will be argued that psychoanalysis, regardless of its substantial relationship to artistic imagination, ultimately cherishes the pretension to speak the last, liberating word about art. In contrast, in Heidegger's hermeneutics the word of the poet is conceived as the region where the truth of *Being* is found. In this chapter the destruction of the metaphysical tradition that Heidegger, in succession to Nietzsche, took upon himself, is also extensively discussed. Heidegger especially points, in this destruction, to the far-reaching consequences of modern, theoretical subjectivism. The question, however, is whether the hope that Heidegger located in the poet and the thinker can be brought into agreement with his interpretation of modern culture, an interpretation wherein instrumental (*calculative*) thought has subordinated all other forms of rationality to itself. In combination with this point, one can pose the question as to whether or not Heidegger's thinking remained *too* dominated by the totalizing thought that he so thoroughly investigated. Posed in terms of the Romantic project, it seems that irony is clearly a missing ingredient in Heidegger's work.

In the case of the surrealistic painter Magritte, who was inspired by Heidegger, irony is certainly no missing ingredient. In the fifth chapter, *"Disavowal and Representation,"* an attempt is made, on the basis of a confrontation between Magritte's famous painting *La trahison des images* and the theory of the disavowal (*Verleugnung*), developed by Freud and Mannoni, to ascertain and elaborate insights into the nature of discord in the aesthetic experience. In this chapter the central theme, which has already been superficially addressed in previous chapters, is the distinction between the *aesthetic* and *aestheticistic experience*. Magritte's recalcitrant painting of a pipe that turns out *not* to be a pipe gives us, moreover, a better understanding of the parasitical character of the postmodern (more especially the poststructuralist) denial of representation. Magritte's work demonstrates hereby the shocking power of art to break with aesthetic blinding, even if only for a moment, thereby providing us with an original experience of the world.

The work of Barthes, which enters the discussion in the fifth chapter, has a leading role in the sixth, concluding chapter, *"The Oldest Nobility in the World."* In an interpretation of the place that the *fragment*—one of the characteristics of Romantic style and ontology—takes in the (post)structuralist work of Barthes and the compositions of John Cage, it becomes clear that the agreements collapse because of their different attitudes with respect to chance. Where for Cage chance is a *technique* to permit the sound to speak for itself, thereby liberating itself from dominance by the musical subject, Barthes announced his earlier works to be a war against chance. Although Barthes' later works appear to mesh more closely with Cage's *aesthetic ontology*, he remains in crucial points connected with modern metaphysics. This ensures that the new notion of subjectivity, as it is expressed in Cage's musical experience, is primarily understood by Barthes to be a *loss* for modern subjectivity. Connecting to the analyses of Nietzsche's and Heidegger's version of the Romantic project that was worked out in the preceding chapters, this concluding chapter ends with an attempt to delineate the contours of aesthetic subjectivity as it is given voice in Cage's aleatory music.

I

Frozen Metaphors

Critical reason depopulated heaven and hell, but the spirits returned to earth, to air, to fire, and to water—they returned to the bodies of men and women. This return is called Romanticism.

Octavio Paz

I asked for ice, but this is ridiculous.

Titanic, 1913, anonymous

Questions relating to the (most) fundamental characteristics of beings hold a prominent place in the tradition of Western philosophy. This is one of the major distinguishing characteristics of philosophy in relation to science: it does not question the variety of beings, but rather what gives beings their Being. Since the thirteenth century this metaphysical or ontological questioning has been referred to as *transcendental*. In the Scholastic tradition, the transcendental characteristics, or *transcendentalia* (such as Being, Object, Truth, Good, Beauty), are conceived as independent characteristics that enable beings to *be*. Since Kant's Copernican Revolution the general concepts that, in Scholasticism, were referred to as transcendental, have become more commonly designated as *a priori* concepts of the human subject.[1] Given that transcendental concepts maintain a relation to beings, even if only to the extent that such beings are objects for the human subject, the term *transcendental* continues to preserve an ontological stature.[2]

Although the Kantian shift to transcendental subjectivism signifies an important discontinuity in the development of transcendental philosophy, Kant nonetheless does, with respect to another fundamental characteristic, remain loyal to this tradition. He continues to consider that the transcendentalia are universal and timeless characteristics of reality. Kantian transcendentalism, too, remains concerned with the unchanging within everything that changes, and, in this respect, it is, like Scholasticism, an heir of Plato.

In this chapter, on the basis of a poem by the Dutch poet Peter Delpeut, two works by the Icelandic sculptor Sigurdur Gudmundsson, and some texts from the German philosopher Nietzsche, an aesthetic experience of reality is examined that, in contrast to the transcendental tradition, sees in the changeable *as such* that which is the only constant. This paradoxical experience brings into sharp relief, on the basis of the words and images provided by the aforementioned persons, a fascination for metaphors, and this will be discussed. Without exception, the conceptualizations that are brought into discussion with each other in this context are not only exceptionally metaphorical, but, at the same time, they form a (more or less explicit) *reflection* on the metaphorical character of language and reality. The process of the metaphorical transfer is hereby understood as a metaphor for a reality that is constantly transforming itself. The metaphorical conceptualization that emerges in the following dialogue implies a sharp critique of the traditional view of the metaphor, rooted in Platonic metaphysics, that sees the metaphor, in relation to the abstract, philosophical concept, as an inferior instrument of knowledge. This critique goes hand in hand with a fundamental reevaluation of art's cognitive capacity that receives, for this reason, a prominent place in reflections concerning man and his place in the world.

A theme that runs as a red line through this chapter is the relationship of the views here discussed and the Romantic project. These views are located between the poles of enthusiasm for the aesthetic affirmation of the constantly-transforming reality and the ironic appreciation of the tragic, human-strength-exceeding character of this affirmation.

1.1 A METAPHOR OF WINTER:
THE WINTER OF METAPHOR

Several years ago, Peter Delpeut sent me one of his poems entitled: "The Man Who Came from the Cold."[3] The following lines appear in the poem:

those who come from the cold are themselves winter,—he said.

They love their sledges and their dogs.
It is not through a landscape they travel,

but seasons of storm and ice:
it freezes their thought.

zij die van de kou komen zijn zelf winter,—zij hij

Zij houden van hun slee en van de honden.
Het is niet het landschap dat zij reizen,

Maar een seizoen van storm en ijs:
Zij bevriezen hun denken.

It was the metaphorical language of the last line that struck me in this excerpt: *it freezes their thought*. A metaphor is a speech act whereby a particular thing is replaced by another. Ordinarily, it is presumed that this replacement is facilitated by the fact that the two things that are brought into a nexus are in one way or another related to each other; the second referent is then referred to as *an image* of the first. In the excerpted poem a comment is given concerning the thinking of people who come from the cold. Such thinking is illustrated by blending it with the imagery of extreme cold: *it freezes their thought*. This blending of both elements is expressively illustrated by the pictorial language in the poem:

He told stories of sleet and snow,
blending them into a legend for radio and TV:

those who come from the cold are themselves winter,—he said.

Hij vertelde verhalen van hagel en sneeuw,
versmolt ze voor radio en t.v. tot een legende:

zij die van de kou komen zijn zelf winter,—zei hij.

The metaphor is traditionally presented as a specific form of figurative speech that is based upon a particular analogy between two elements that, in the metaphor, are combined. In his *Poetics* (1457b) Aristotle maintained that a substitution occurs on the basis of this analogy: a thing receives the name of another thing. Quintilianus conceived of the metaphor as a condensed comparison. In his *Institutio Oratoria* he defined the metaphor as: "Metaphora brevior est similitudo" (VIII.6.4). However, the condensed comparison may justifiably be regarded as a special case of the substitution thesis: both are based upon analogy (cf. Whately, 1864, 280). When a camel is portrayed as the ship of the desert, then the metaphorical expression involved depends upon an analogy of movement—both referents demonstrate a rolling motion. An analogy always presumes a differentiation between two separate areas, while a metaphor expresses a transition of meaning from one area to the other on the basis of an analogy between the two areas. The Greek *metaphorein*—literary meaning 'transfer'—is a particularly apt description for this phenomenon.

In the excerpted poem a transition is made between what is sensorially perceptible—freezing in winter—and what is not sensorially perceptible—the thinking of people who come from the cold. These people freeze their thinking. According to Heidegger, the transition from the sensible to the nonsensible is characteristic for the metaphorical. In *The Principle of Reason* he maintains that every use of metaphorical language is based upon the distinction between them: "The idea of 'transposing' and of metaphor is based upon the distinguishing, if not complete separation, of the sensible and the nonsensible as two realms that exist on their own" (PR, 48).

Heidegger's remark concerning the distinction between sensible image and nonsensible concept makes it clear that the study of metaphors is of significance for at least two philosophical disciplines. In the first place, the metaphor brings us onto the terrain of aesthetics. This discipline, which concerns itself with providing discursive commentaries about non-discursive (visual, tactile, auditory) images, cannot avoid the issues of the relationship between image and concept and of the conditions of the possibility of the transition from one area to the other. Accordingly, the study of metaphors belongs to the fundamental research concerns of aesthetics: without an explication of the relationship between image and concept, every aesthetic analysis ultimately remains unclear.

In the second place, Heidegger focuses our attention on the relationship between the metaphorical and the metaphysical. The quotation above continues: "The setting up of this partition between the sensible and the nonsensible, between the physical and the nonphysical is a basic trait of what is called metaphysics and which normatively determines Western thinking. . . . The metaphorical exists only within metaphysics" (PR, 48). According to Heidegger, every metaphorical figure of speech is founded in a particular metaphysical conceptualization of the relationship between image and concept. However, in almost the entire Western tradition metaphor is simultaneously, on the grounds of this conceptualization, excluded from the domain of metaphysics. In order that this latter point be clarified I must briefly refer to one of the origins of the tradition to which Heidegger's remark refers, that is, Plato's theory of Ideas. In Plato's metaphysics a sharp distinction is made between, on the one hand, the perfect, unchangeable and suprasensible world of the Idea, and, on the other hand, the imperfect, changeable and sensible world of concrete things. For Plato, the world of the Idea possesses an ontological priority, something that makes clear that for him "not the visible but the invisible thing is the primary reality," that is, the *essence* of the visible thing (De Vogel, 1967, 107). Real knowledge (*episteme*) is only achievable through pure, philosophical thinking and relates exclusively to the unchangeable, real Being. Plato assumes hereby that the characteristics and value of a form of knowledge are completely determined by the nature of the known objects. Sensory perception offers only an image of the changeable world of Becoming and accordingly leads to only transitory meaning (*doxa*). Only the philosophical concept offers an immediate representation of an Idea. The thinker should for this reason apply himself to the dialectic and detach himself as far as is possible from his sensory organs (cf. Matthews, 1972, 15).

Already on basis of this summary sketch of Plato's metaphysics and epistemology, it is not difficult to comprehend his rejection of rhetoric. If the world of the unchangeable Idea can only be comprehended by pure, dialectical thinking, then metaphorical speech damages the correct conceptualization. The metaphor shifts attention away from the origin (the concept) to the derivative (the image), leading the thinker away from his citadel of concepts and deluding him with illusions in an apparent world of images. In the *Gorgias*, a dialogue concerned with rhetoric, Plato maintains that rhetoric can only lead to *doxa* and, for this reason, he condemns it quite sharply. In *The Republic* the comment is that a poet using figures of speech fashions "phantoms far removed from the truth" (X: 605c). Although more nuance is introduced in the treatment of rhetoric in the *Phaidros*, even there it is only accorded, at best, a didactic function. Metaphorical speech forms merely an illustration of a more fundamental conceptual demonstration.

Even without completely agreeing with Whitehead's idea that the totality of Western philosophy consists of writing footnotes to Plato, it can be maintained, without exaggeration, that Plato's condemnation of rhetoric is characteristic for the pejorative attitude toward it that is found in the Western philosophical tradition.[4] There is a complete tradition that considers rhetoric as a manner of speaking that moves away from the truth, that is, from a direct representation of reality through the medium of pure concept. Especially after the victory of Cartesian philosophical self-knowledge, the ideal of pure (*clare et distincte*) thought, the condemnation of rhetoric is indubitably apparent. According to Kant, the *ars oratoria* is even a danger for freedom: rhetoric hampers thinking and subjects the hearer to an unreasonable authority (CJ, 197 ff./KU, B216 ff.). In his *Encyclopedia of Philosophical Sciences* (sections 446–64), Hegel maintains that the dialectical development toward the Truth moves from image to pure concept. Even a more sceptical thinker such as the later Wittgenstein, who no longer believed in the possibility that language could represent reality like a mirror, maintained that philosophical illusions are the result of metaphorical appearance. In the mainstream of Western philosophy, metaphorical expressions are, in the best case, permitted as a didactic decoration that, however, because of their dubious character, should be avoided as far as possible. With a nod to the famous seventh thesis of Wittgenstein's *Tractatus*, Black, in an article concerning the relationship between philosophy and metaphor, summarizes the pejorative attitude of philosophers as follows: "Addiction to metaphor is held to be illicit, on the principle that whereof one can speak only metaphorically, thereof one ought not to speak at all" (Black, 1978, 451). It is indeed legitimate to maintain that the metaphorical, in a complete tradition, is excluded from philosophical argument. In the metaphysical tradition the metaphor appears to be in hibernation.

Given that the metaphor is a characteristic method of expressiveness in art, it is not surprising that it is also effected by the condemnation of rhetoric in Plato's metaphysics. Plato conceived of the different forms of art as parts of the broader class of *technē* or (handi)craft. Moreover, Plato understood art as belonging to the subclass of productive crafts: the artist, however, does not produce real things such as, for example, the furniture-maker, but rather merely images (*idoola*) of things. Images may completely imitate the original, or they may merely give the appearance of doing so: in the first case, one speaks of an *eikoon*, and in the second, of a *fantasma*. For Plato, in a certain sense, works of art are always *fantasmata* because a perfect reproduction or *eikon* is no longer an image but rather a duplicate of the real thing. A perfect imitation of a chair, for example, is itself a chair. Given that, for Plato, all transitory things in the world of Becoming are already reflections of the eternal, unchangeable Ideas, works of art are merely reflections of the second degree. Plato's banishment of artists from the ideal Republic is, therefore, an unavoidable consequence of his metaphysics (*The Republic*, X: 607b). Just as in the case of rhetoric, this condemnation of art is characteristic for almost the entire metaphysical tradition: only when traditional metaphysics loses its quality of self-evident truth—and, beginning with the period of Kant's critique of reason, this increasingly occurs—does the philosophical condemnation of art *also* lose its self-evident character.

Now, after this exposition, we return to the poem. What is fascinating for me in this fragment is that the metaphor appears to be reflexive in terms of the linguistic expressiveness itself: the poem treats the metaphorical processes of creating poetry. This process appears to me to be suggested in the image of the freezing of thinking. That the poem possesses a self-reflexive character is not in itself surprising: since its emancipation at the end of the nineteenth century, modern art has increasingly been characterized by a reflexive relationship to itself. Just as much of modern philosophy, modern art explores primarily its own medium.[5] However, what is fascinating in this fragment is the specific content of this reflexive, metaphorical image. Initially, I could not come to grips with the analogy upon which it was based. The people love their sledges and their dogs, simultaneously, and, for one reason or another, they freeze their thinking. However, another line from the poem gives an indication of which analogy provides the basis for the metaphor: *those who come from the cold are themselves winter*. The areas of the sensible and the nonsensible are not sharply distinguished from each other, and, in fact, they cannot, ultimately, be differentiated: they merge, blending in the poetic metaphor. The image of the freezing of thinking forms an evocation of a romantic longing toward the overcoming of the distinction between the spheres of the sensible and the nonsensible.

1.2 GUDMUNDSSON'S *GREAT POEM*

In 1982, the year Peter Delpeut sent me his poem, a rather enigmatic sculpture by Sigurdur Gudmundsson, entitled *The Great Poem*, was on show in the exhibition '60–'80 that was held in the Stedelijk Museum, Amsterdam. It was not only the title that made me think about the poem that had only recently been sent to me.

Gudmundsson, born in Iceland but living and working as a sculptor in Amsterdam since the 1960s, made his debut in 1969 as a member of the Icelandic AUM group, a circle of sculptors, composers, poets, and writers related to the Fluxus movement. His early work possesses a strong poetic character and, among other features, presents various visual metaphors: objects and actions that are combined on the basis of the fact that their names rhyme with each other. For example, *Moss-Gross* (1973) consists of two squares, the first of which is formed by a quantity of moss and the second of which comprises 144 matches. *Hestur-Lestur,* from the same year, portrays a man, reading, and a horse ("reading" and "horse" rhyme with each other in Icelandic). In this period, too, Gudmundsson organized so-called *Full-House* performances. A photograph produced in 1971 shows a group of five men standing in front of the Balderich Gallery: according to the caption, two of the group had read Heine, and three of them had seen the Shetland Islands from the air.

After his definitive settling in The Netherlands, where he came in contact with a number of Dutch conceptual artists, Gudmundsson produced several photographic works that he called *situations.* These are tableaux vivants wherein, besides a diversity of landscapes and objects, Gudmundsson himself constantly appears as the central figure. These works, too, are strongly metaphorical in character. *Dialogue,* from 1979, shows a motionless Gudmundsson in an ambivalent position: a number of balloons, attached to his hair, attempt to pull him upward, while a block of stone in his arms attempts the opposite. *Mathematics,* also from 1979, shows Gudmundsson, wrapped in wool, sitting next to a pyramid of sand. Since the beginning of the 1980s, Gudmundsson has been making large sculptures from diverse materials such as concrete, glass, paper, and plaster; he also uses natural materials such as seaweed. Once again, metaphors play a significant role in these works. *Kantadorum* (1981) consists of a high pedestal topped with an arrow pointing upward, and *Stella Maris,* from the same year, shows a giant paper boat placed high above the pedestal (this piece can be seen in the Academic Medical Centre, Amsterdam). In a publication from the Public Art Collection concerning Gudmundsson, the art historian Marlies Levels justifiably maintains that "everything which is visible and tangible in Gudmundsson's work has a metaphorical and poetic meaning. Motifs such as the scenic (earth, air, mountain, balloon, paving stone) and geometric or abstract forms (arrow, pyramid, line, colour) together comprise the alphabet of a language of signs. . . . Such a symbolic language can only be 'interpreted' via a figure of speech" (Levels, 1982, 6).

The Great Poem, which was on show in the Stedelijk Museum, belongs to the sculptures from the beginning of the 1980s. We see a trinity of cement pyramids standing on a wooden base (figure 1), with the head and neck of a swan achingly reaching out from each pyramid. It is as if the swans long to fly away, but are uncompromisingly doomed to failure because they are imprisoned in the cement. It is tempting to consider this sculpture, too, as a striking metaphor of the culture-nature relationship. *The Great Poem* embodies a theme that plays a large role in Gudmundsson's work: nature and culture are presented as an antago-

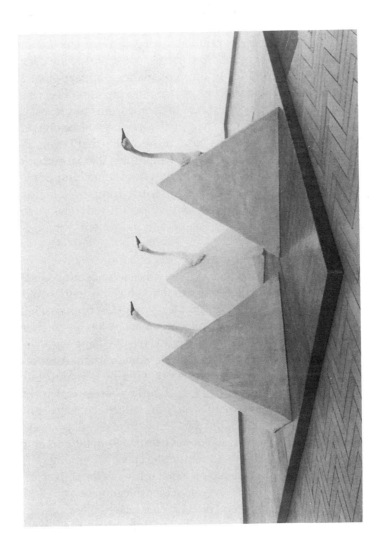

FIGURE 1

The Great Poem, Sigurdur Gudmundsson, 1981, concrete, stuffed swans and steel, 350 × 350 × 150 cm. Stedelijk Museum, Amsterdam.

nistic polarity. In the publication already cited, Marlies Levels interprets the work in this light, adding: "If creating art is compared with the longing to free oneself from earthly constraints, then this work could be comprehended as a metaphor for art itself" (Levels, 1982, 14). Levels points to the reflexive character of *The Great Poem*: it is a metaphor of the artistic, metaphoric desire. She maintains that the attempt by the swans (read: nature) to escape from the pyramids (read: culture) is a metaphor for the artistic longing to free oneself from earthly constraints. However, this interpretation is not completely unproblematic: it appears that a transposition of terms has occurred in Levels' interpretation because, while the swans in *The Great Poem* attempt to escape from culture, art is precisely characterized, according to her, by the longing to free oneself from earthly constraints, from nature. Now, it is possible that Levels, in her interpretation, only has a formal analogy in mind—that is, both art and the swans are attempting to free themselves from something. Some metaphors, do, after all, rest entirely upon such formal analogies. Nonetheless, I wonder if Levels has not, in this case, missed a chance to achieve a deeper interpretation, with respect to its contents, of Gudmundsson's sculptures.

It is Levels herself who set me on the trail of a more extensive interpretation of *The Great Poem*. In her master's thesis concerning Gudmundsson's work, she investigated the extent to which his work could be placed in a Romantic tradition. The brief foregoing description of his work already suggests an affirmative answer: the inclusion of material elements in reality as symbols in a universal, divine "language" is, namely, typical of nineteenth-century aesthetic Romanticism. After an extensive comparison of Gudmundsson's work with the Romantic tradition, Levels concludes that his work, too, "at the level of content, form (composition), and method of presentation, can, indeed, be called Romantic" (Levels, 1981, 128). In the first part of her investigation Levels also remarks that nature has a central place in German Romantic art and aesthetics. As characteristics of the Romantic she specifies, among others, the view that nature is considered as a metaphor for the universal, and that the Romantic artist is in search of an identification of spirit and nature (cf. 0.2). Following Sørensen (1963), Levels places these characteristics in a tradition of mystic naturalism: the Romantic artist is connected to this tradition to the extent that, through the medium of metaphorical imagery, he too hopes to evoke a blending of spirit and nature, subject and object.

Given these characteristics of the Romantic tradition, Levels' interpretation of *The Great Poem* is rather surprising. After all, she maintains that art characterizes itself through the longing to liberate itself from earthly constraints, from nature. It would appear more reasonable to present the metaphor of *The Great Poem* as follows: just as the swans attempt to escape from culture, represented in the geometric pyramids, so also does Romantic art, to which Gudmundsson's work is closely related, attempt, in its striving for a fusion with nature, to escape from the constraining pressures of an alienating culture. In the Romantic work of art, nature attempts to free itself from the dominion by culture.

This Romantic conceptualization of art's task can be clarified by a brief reference to Kant's *Critique of Judgment*, a text that, although difficult to locate in the authentic Romantic tradition, nonetheless, in important respects, paved the way for Romanticism (see 0.2 above). Kant concluded, on the basis of the first two critiques, that an "immense gulf" (*unübersehbare Kluft;* CJ, 14—literally: an "unsurveyable gulf") exists between the terrains of nature and freedom (whereon culture is founded). According to Kant, man occupies a remarkable middle position because, as a physical being, he constitutes a part of nature and is subjected to its laws, he is simultaneously also, as a thinking being, a constituent part of the freedom of Reason. For this reason, for Kant, man is a citizen of two worlds. In the *Critique of Judgment* Kant undertakes an attempt to bridge the gulf between these two worlds, accrediting art, in the attempt, with an important role. This view, regardless of the caution and hesitancy with which it is formulated, locates Kant at the dawn of Romantic aesthetics.

A pregnant expression of this Romantic attitude with respect to art is found in section 46 of the *Critique of Judgment* wherein Kant addresses artistic genius. Genius, a central concept in Romantic aesthetics, is defined by Kant as "the innate disposition of the mind with which nature provides its rules" (CJ, 179/KU, B179). In this definition, the Romantic distrust of the grandiose pretensions of a culture based upon human Reason is specified: when Reason is no longer considered to be able to close the gap between nature and freedom (an Enlightenment ideal that achieved its magnificent apotheosis in Hegel's Odyssey of the Spirit), then this reconciliatory capacity is ascribed to nature itself. Art, as nature's "mouthpiece" in humans, thereby receives the task of realizing the reconciliation of nature and freedom (cf. Marquard, 1982, 96).

On the basis of the foregoing it can now be argued that Gudmundsson's place in the Romantic tradition, made plausible by the art historian Levels in her analysis, is intimately connected with the recognition, embodied in his work, of the reconciliatory claims of nature at the expense of the totalitarian pretensions of Reason. The metaphor of

The Great Poem points, for this reason, not to the longing of art to escape from nature, but rather to art's attempt to realize a reconciliation by submitting to nature. *The Great Poem*, however, can also be read as a symbol of the precarious character of art's escape attempt: although the swans in the work reach for their freedom, they remain imprisoned in the stone pyramids. Art reaches toward the natural, but remains imprisoned within the constraints of the culture of Reason. In this sense, *The Great Poem* is, indeed, a metaphor for Romantic art: it binds, in an ironic fashion, enthusiastic desire for an absolute reconciliation of nature and freedom with the insight of the unachievable character of this desire.

1.3   NIETZSCHE AND METAPHOR

Regardless of how multifaceted the contents of Nietzsche's texts are, they share a common extreme metaphoricism: one is confronted with little argumentation but much suggestion, seduction, and enchantment.[6] Accordingly, the dividing line between a philosophical explication and a poetic eruption of images is not always easy to establish: for Nietzsche, philosophy is a "reasoning in images" (*Bilderrede*), an "artwork made of language" (*sprachliches Kunstwerk*) (D, 74). He was convinced of the impossibility of making a distinction between analysis and imagination: the philosopher "knows if he poeticizes, and poeticizes if he knows" (KSA, 7:439). Time and again Nietzsche emphasises that his metaphorical style is in no way decorative, but rather that it is inextricably connected to the contents of his philosophy. He maintains the metaphor as a strategic weapon against a philosophical, moral, and religious tradition that, in a radical manner, has suppressed its metaphorical origins and thereby excluded them from its domain.

Just as is the case with Gudmundsson, a century later, it is easy to refer to Nietzsche's relation to the metaphor as being Romantic. This Romantic root is especially and explicitly expressed in early works such as *The Birth of Tragedy out of the Spirit of Music* (1872). Nietzsche refers to art with the imagery of the "healing enchantress" that enables man to be absorbed by the primal unity of nature (B, 23, 35, 40). Although, in the "Versuch einer Selbskritik" that he added to *The Birth* in 1886, Nietzsche distances himself from the *Artisten-Metaphysik* of his early ideas, this self-criticism does not so much constitute a change of viewpoint as a radicalization of his position. He criticizes, namely, his attempt in *The Birth* to discursively explicate his insights: "It should have been singing, this 'new soul,' not speaking! What a shame that I dared not say what I had to say then as a poet: I might have been able to do it" (B, 6). According to Nietzsche, the radical critique of his book made by his philologist colleagues made it clear what the motive was behind his *Artisten-Metaphysik:* in *The Birth*, science was presented, for the first time, as problematic (B, 4). The audacious step taken in that work was *"to see science under the lens of the artist, but art under the lens of life"* (B, 5).

If we want to understand the rehabilitation of art at the expense of discursive science and Nietzsche's extremely metaphoric expression of this program in their connection, then the lectures concerning classical rhetoric that he gave in Basel at the time of the publication of *The Birth*, along with the linguistic views he developed at that time, form a good starting point (cf. De Man, 1974). In these lectures Nietzsche gave a lot of attention to classical rhetoric and, in contrast to the Platonic tradition, he placed it in a remarkably positive light. He conceived of the rhetoric of the Greeks as "the breath of life for this artistic people" (MA, 5:3). In that time, according to Nietzsche, rhetoric did not possess the pejorative connotation which it gained from the time of Socrates; on the contrary, it was highly regarded by the Greeks. Rhetoric is related to the probable (*pithanon*): rhetoricians, he maintained, "have the meaning about things and therefore the effects of those things upon people in their control, and they know that, too!" (MA, 5:4). The rhetorical figure upon which Nietzsche concentrated in his Basel lectures was the metaphor: he conceives of this figure as a collective name for all rhetorical figures that establish a transference of meaning. He conceives of this *transference* (*Übertragung*) as having two meanings: it refers to both the result of the transfer and to its process. That Nietzsche gives such a central place to the metaphor in his lectures is an equal expression of his view that the totality of language is ultimately based upon metaphors: he quotes the Romantic Jean Paul: "Every language is a dictionary of faded metaphors" (*Jede Sprache ist ein Wörterbuch erblasseter Metaphern*) (MA, 5:315).[7]

This idea was further elaborated by Nietzsche in his essay "Über Wahrheit und Lüge im aussermoralischen Sinn" (1873), written at the time of the Basel lectures but only published posthumously. The essay, which, although only sixteen pages in length, is of cardinal significance for an understanding of Nietzsche's metaphorical crusade, has as its central question the extent to which language offers us an adequate expression of things. According to Nietzsche language does not provide such an adequate expression because what we call the truth rests upon a double metaphor: "A nervous impulse transferred by an image. First metaphor. The image once again transferred by a sound. Second metaphor. . . . We believe that we know something of the things when we speak of trees, colours, snow, and flowers, yet we possess nonetheless nothing other than metaphors of these things, metaphors which, in their totality, do not refer to the original *Being* of those things" (KSA, 1:879).

There is, thus, no logic here with relation to the origin of language: the totality of the material with which humans work and build does not originate from the essences of things. There is, however, yet a third transfer that concerns the transformation from word to concept. According to Nietzsche, this is where contact with things is lost: a word becomes a concept at that moment when it no longer functions as the expression of a unique, individualized primeval experience to which it owes its original existence, but rather when it is used to refer to a multitude of more or less similar but never identical experiences. Use of the word *leaf* prompts the image of a primal leaf in us, although there is only the multitude of different leaves in our world. "Every concept," concludes Nietzsche, "originates by virtue of an imposed identity upon what is not identical" (KSA, 1:880).

For this reason, for Nietzsche, our entire world of concepts is completely anthropomorphous. That which we call truth is ultimately "a moving army of metaphors, metonyms, anthropomorphicisms, in brief, the sum of human relations which, in a poetic or rhetorical manner, are elevated, transferred, and romanticized, and which appear to a people, after long usage, as canonic and binding: truths are illusions which people have forgotten to be illusions, metaphors which have become threadbare and impotent, coins which have lost their portraits and which are no longer used as coins but only as metal" (KSA, 1:880–81). Because man has forgotten the illusory character of truth, he lies when he thinks that he speaks it.[8]

The foregoing quotations make it expressively clear that Nietzsche is here maintaining a metaphor that differs radically from those employed by Aristotle and Quintilianus. For him, there is absolutely no meaning beyond the metaphorical transfer, or, more rigorously formulated: in the final analysis, the meaning of a word or concept is the result of the (metaphorical) interpretation whereby the relationships between words and things are instantiated in an aesthetic manner. Between the two domains that metaphor in a single movement unites and equally articulates the distinction between them, there "exists no causality, no correctness, no expression, but, at the most, merely an aesthetic relation" (KSA, 1:884). The concept completely derives its meaning from this metaphorical interpretation; it is a derivative phenomenon. Here, Nietzsche appears to defend a position that is the converse to that expressed in the already quoted view of Heidegger. According to Nietzsche, metaphysics is only possible on the basis of the metaphorical transference.[9]

In his argument, Nietzsche also employs the metaphor of fossilization that we earlier saw embodied in Gudmundsson's *The Great Poem:* "While each perceived metaphor is individual and unique, moreover remaining free from every possibility of being placed in a given rubric, the constructed edifice of the concepts demonstrates the rigid regularity of a Roman columbarium" (KSA, 1:882). Anyone familiar with the severity of this conceptual structure will hardly be able to believe that the concept is merely a residue of a metaphor and that "the illusion relating to the artistic transference of a nervous impulse into images is, if not the mother, then at least the grandmother of each concept" (KSA, 1:882). Only by forgetting the primitive world of metaphors, only by the hardening and stiffening of the stream of images that originally, like molten lava, flowed outward from human phantasy, only by the invincible belief that this sun, this window, this table, constitutes in itself a truth, in brief, only by forgetting that man is a subject, and an artistically creative subject, nota bene, can one live with any peace, certainty, and consequence; if one could escape for even one moment from the prison walls of this belief, then one's 'self-consciousness,' in that moment, would be shattered" (KSA, 1:883–84).

Nietzsche does not unambiguously reject conceptualization; it is also, after all, a symbol of human grandeur: "In this sense, one may certainly admire the human being as a magnificent constructive genius who succeeds in building, on shifting foundations and running water, as it were, a towering, infinitely complex cathedral of concepts" (KSA, 1:882). When, in *The Birth,* Nietzsche nonetheless comes to the defense of the artist at the expense of the *theoretical person,* this is because art, along with the myth, has become the refuge for the basic capacities of the metaphor: "The compulsion to form metaphors, the fundamental compulsion of man, which one cannot dispense with unless one also dispenses with people, this compulsion is truly not suppressed, scarcely even curbed, because, from its evaporated products, the concepts, a regular and rigid new world is built as a dungeon for man. It merely seeks another territory and other channels for its activities, and finds these in myths and, even more, in art" (KSA, 1:887).

1.4   FOSSILIZATION AND FREEZING

With both Gudmundsson and Nietzsche the domination of the rhetorical imagination of reality by conceptual rationality is presented with the image of fossilization. And, in contrast to the fossilized discursiveness of the concept, both place poetic thinking in images that do more justice to the metaphorical primal capacity of man. In the poem by Peter Delpeut, which I interpreted above as a reflection on the writing of poetry, this poetic imagination was evoked as follows:

> those who come from the cold are themselves winter,—he said.
> . . . .
> it freezes their thought.

> zij die van de kou komen zijn zelf winter,—zei hij.
> . . . .
> zij bevriezen hun denken.

The process of the poetic imagination of reality is presented in this fragment as a process of freezing: in the poetic imagination, the constantly shifting reality is frozen. Just as one gets to grips with water by freezing it, so does the poet freeze the upward streaming wealth of imagery in his language. In the poetic imagination, subject and world are blended together so that they can, subsequently, be frozen in the work of art. This "freezing" of thinking is essentially different from the fossilized working of conceptual thinking: the unity evoked in the poetic work is not definitively fixed, as in theoretical concepts, but rather it maintains *in potential* its liquidity. In our interpretation of the work, it recuperates this liquidity once again. We could, following Schelling (see 0.3), also express this point by saying that the poem is characterized by a fundamental openness, an abundance of meaning that necessarily transcends every individual interpretation.

Gudmundsson, too, maintains the metaphor of freezing in a work from 1970: *Untitled* (figure 2) consists of the documentation of an event. That which remains to us of this event is merely a number of "frozen" images in the form of six photographs and an annotation. The annotation reads: "this is about how my philosophy becomes a part of human beings and their surroundings." The first photo shows us a hand that, holding a pen, writes six sentences on a piece of paper. The writing reads: "writing the philosophy and simplifying it to six sentences." The second photo shows a number of molds of the individual letters that make up the six sentences. The molds are filled with water. The caption informs us that the water in the molds is subsequently frozen. In the third photo, we see Gudmundsson, with the frozen sentence, on his way to the gallery *Now Constructions*. This sentence, according to what we see in the fourth photograph, is displayed on the floor of the gallery. In

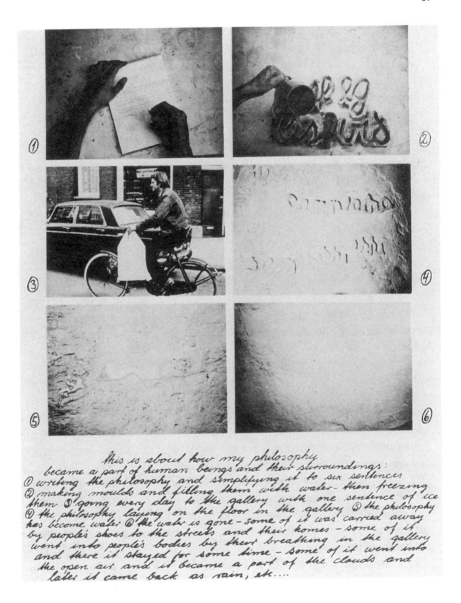

FIGURE 2

Untitled, Sigurdur Gudmundsson, 1970, project with a report in photographs and text, Poster Gallery Now Constructions, 63 × 46.5 cm. Collection of J. de Mul, Molenhoek.

the fifth photo, there is still some water to be seen, and in the sixth and final photo we see the empty floor of the gallery. The caption to the sixth photograph reads: "the water is gone—some of it was carried away by people's shoes to the streets and their homes—some of it went into people's bodies by their breathing in the gallery and there it stayed for some time—some of it went into the open air and it became a part of the clouds and later it came back as rain, etc."

Untitled, too, should be understood as a metaphor of the artistic imagination. In this sense, the metaphor comprises both the form and the content of the work. In the six sentences, Gudmundsson attempted to "conceptualize" this philosophy. The six sentences had been written in Icelandic, and, when I asked him to translate them for me he only did so after some hesitation. He later told me that he would now formulate his philosophy differently, with more nuance, than he had done in 1970. The conceptual expression of his philosophy appeared rather rigid, no longer able to adequately represent the abundance of meaning of the image. But he nonetheless remained loyal to the image that had been evoked in *Untitled*. Because of its ability to constantly summon different meanings, the image appears more able to function as a metaphor of the poetic process.

However, *Untitled* does not appear to exclusively point to the poetic imagination: the water that becomes frozen and is subsequently carried off on the shoes of people simultaneously refers to the reality outside of art. This reality is characterized, to use the words of Heraclitus, the pre-Socratic philosopher, by a constant flowing: all things are in flux (*panta rhei*). For this reason, according to Heraclitus, we can never step twice into the same river (Heraclitus, in Kirk and Raven, 1980, 186, 197). The constantly flowing reality is temporarily frozen in the work of art, but, after the image is melted, it returns to the stream of life: the houses of the people, the streets, the clouds. While the concepts of Gudmundsson's philosophy form a rigid and unchanging structure, the images appear able to represent more adequately the *panta rhei* of reality. In contrast to the conceptualization of the theoretical person, which petrifies reality like the glance of Medusa, art expresses the movement of life itself.

1.5 THE TRANSCENDENTAL METAPHOR

In the case of Nietzsche, too, the interpretation of metaphorical imagination is simultaneously an interpretation of the most elementary characteristic of reality. And, just as with Gudmundsson, this fundamental ontology is in accord with Heraclitus' *panta rhei*.[10] The insight that, because it is constantly in the process of change, Being can never be completely identified by understanding, is one that we could propose as Nietzsche's thesis of *ontic difference*.[11]

Nietzsche summarizes the absolute stream of the world's occurring as a metaphorical occurring, a continuous transfer. The fundamental need for metaphor on which he spoke in 1873 was not only attributed to man, but rather also to life itself, and, with certain reservations, even to nonliving nature. "A superior physiology shall undoubtedly understand the artistic processes in our development—not only in humans, but also in animals: a superior physiology shall teach us that the artistic begins in the organic. . . . Even the chemical transformations of anorganic nature are, perhaps, artistic processes" (KSA, 7:437). And, in a fragment from early in 1884, the formulation is: "Everything organic which 'judges,' behaves as an *artist*. . . . The creative—1) appropriating 2) selecting 3) transforming 4) the self-regulating element 5) the separating" (KSA, 11:97). In his later works, Nietzsche proffered this metaphorical interpretation as the creative *Will to Power*, which he understood as the "most intimate essence of Being" (WDB, 3:798). For him, the *process* of transfer is central in the concept *Will to Power*: "One must not ask 'who is it who interprets?', but the interpretation itself exists as a form of the Will to Power, (But not as a *Being*, but as a *process*, a *becoming*), as an affect" (KSA, 12:140). This creative process of the metaphorical interpretation of the Other, which for Nietzsche necessarily possessed an aspect of subjugation, simultaneously implies an aspiration to the overcoming of one's self (Z, 136).

Seen in this light, the human compulsion to metaphorical thinking, which cannot be denied without denying humanity itself, is nothing less than a metaphor for nature's constant metaphorical transformation of itself. Without this metaphorical transformation Being itself would not be able to exist. For Nietzsche, the metaphorical process forms the transcendental condition for the possibility that Being occurs. The ontic difference is rooted in the transcendental metaphor. The use of the term "transcendental" is, incidentally, not without tension because it breaks with two connotations that are closely connected with the traditional usage of the term: for Nietzsche, unlike those in the Kantian tradition, the conditions of the possibility of the appearance of Being do not reside in the human subject, but rather in the metaphorical transfer that is inherent to Being in itself and that exceeds human experience. If, in connection with Nietzsche, we actually dare to speak of Kantianism, then there is—to use an expression that Ricoeur employs in another context—a reference to a Kantianism without a transcendental subject. In addition, and here Nietzsche places himself in opposition to both the Kantian and the Scholastic traditions, *this* notion of the transcendental metaphor expresses the postulate that the only *constant* in every change is the abysmal dimension of change itself, something that, for this reason, can never be named in positive terms, but rather can only be brought into issue in the sense of a transfer, by being employed as a metaphor, for example.[12]

In *The Birth of Tragedy out of the Spirit of Music* (1872) Nietzsche first gave expression to his in every way Romantic conceptualization of reality as a constant artistic transformation. Still under the influence of the impression that Schopenhauer's *The World as Will and Representation* (1817) had made upon him, he specified, in metaphysical terms, this process of artistic transformation as *World Will* (although he also maintained other metaphors such as primeval foundation, core of Being, mother of Being, and primal unity. As is the case with Schopenhauer, Nietzsche regarded the Will as a process wherein man is nothing other than the instrument and medium of this Will (cf. the explication of Schopenhauer's metaphysics in 3.2 below). However, other than Schopenhauer, he considered the process as artistic comedy, "an artistic game which the will, in the eternal abundance of its pleasure, plays with itself" (B, 115).

> For this above all must be plain to us, to our humiliation *and* our enhancement, that the whole comedy of art is not at all performed for us, for our improvement or edification, any more than we are the actual creators of that art world: but we can indeed assume for our own part that we are images and artistic projections for the true creator of that world, and that our highest dignity lies in the meaning of works of art—for it is only as *an aesthetic phenomenon* that existence and the world are eternally *justified*—while of course our awareness of our meaning differs hardly at all from the awareness that warriors painted on canvas have of the battle portrayed. Thus all of our knowledge of art is utterly illusory, because we, as knowing subjects, are not identical with that being which, as sole creator and spectator of that comedy of art, prepares an eternal enjoyment for itself. (B, 32)

Art reveals "the spirit that playfully builds and destroys the world of individuals as the product of a primal pleasure: similarly, dark Heraclitus compares the force that builds worlds to a child placing stones here and there, and building sandcastles and knocking them down again" (B, 115).

Nietzsche explains this artistic game of the world's foundations, the eternal origin and decay of finite Being, as the eternal conflict between the Dionysian and the Apollonian. For Nietzsche, Apollo, the Greek god of light, clarity, beautiful stature, is the metaphor of the origin of Being in its spatial and temporal differentiation, "the glorious divine image of the *principium individuationis*" (B, 16). Dionysius, the Greek god of darkness, of formless chaos, of the mystical, ecstatic rite, forms the metaphor of the burst of this Apollonian world of the *principium individuationis* (cf. KSA, 13:224). Nietzsche clarifies these "powers of nature" by reference to their forms of appearance in humans and the art forms with which they are associated. He sees the Apollonian creative power primarily embodied in dreams: "The beautiful illusion of the dream worlds, in the creation of which every man is a consummate artist, is the precondition of all visual art, and indeed, as we shall see, of an important amount of poetry" (B, 15). Nietzsche sees the Dionysian abolition of the individual stature primarily reflected in the intoxication that is characteristic of sexual and narcotic ecstasy (B, 17). For him, (rhythmic) music is Dionysian art *par excellence*, while dance and lyric poetry also possess a Dionysian character. Works of art that, in the first instance, appear to be a product of human creativity, appear in the last instance to be the stage upon which the occurrences of the world (*Welt-Ereignis*) are played out in the form of a conflict between Dionysius and Apollo (cf. Fink, 1960, 25).

We are dealing here with an ontology of a definitive aesthetic character. Nietzsche himself referred to it as an "Artist's metaphysics" (B, 5). Art is not only elevated to the most fundamental activity of man (B, 13), it is also, and simultaneously, regarded as the gateway to solving the riddle of Being. In addition, this aesthetic ontology is evoked in a stream of images rather than being rationally argued. For Nietzsche, art is not only the theme of his philosophy, but, also and simultaneously, it is the medium and the method. Just as for Schelling, art is for Nietzsche the real organon of philosophy.

Fink, in his study of Nietzsche, justifiably remarks that *The Birth* already contains the seeds of the later work (Fink, 1960, 32). It is true that, especially in what we may refer to as his positivistic periods, Nietzsche distanced himself from a number of the traditional-metaphysical connotations that appeared in his artist's metaphysics, but the aesthetic ontology he developed in *The Birth* remained with him to the end.[13] Still in a fragment from 1885, Nietzsche maintains that the world is a self-producing work of art (KSA, 12:326). For the later Nietzsche, the world is a game of mirrors wherein "in the fulfilment of his existence in the game" (Visser, 1989, 329) man beyond man reflects himself as a child.

I.6 TRAGIC WISDOM

The Birth of Tragedy is indisputably a Romantic work, a "confession of a romantic" (*Romantiker-Bekenntniss*) to use Nietzsche's own words (KSA, 12:115). This is apparent not only from the enthusiastic aestheticization of the world, but also from the "wingbeat of desire" (*Flügelschlag der Sehnsucht*) and the "strive for the infinite" (*Streben in's Unendliche*) that clearly speak from this work (B, 115). The aestheticization of the world certainly does not mean that Nietzsche idealizes reality: following his teacher, Schopenhauer, he conceives of the Will as an irrational, aimless, and, more especially, cruel occurrence. Nietzsche praises the pre-Socratic Greeks, "whose piercing gaze has seen to the core of the terrible destructions of world history and nature's cruelty" (B, 39). In a preparatory study (1870) for *The Birth*, Nietzsche maintains that what a glance at the "deep source of Being" (GM, 237) reveals is the "nullity of existence" (*Nichtigkeit des Daseins*) (KSA, 1:570). Those who gain this wisdom run the risk that, as with Schopenhauer, they will begin to long for the Buddhist denial of the Will.[14] It is true that Nietzsche points out that ecstatic relaxation into Dionysian intoxication engenders profound desire, but, according to him, this desire is necessarily combined with a profound suffering: "For a brief moment," he says, "we really become the primal essence itself, and feel its unbounded lust for existence and delight in existence. Now we see the struggles, the torment, the destruction of phenomena as necessary, given the constant proliferation of forms of existence forcing and pushing their way into life, the exuberant fertility of the world will. We are pierced by the raging goad of those torments just as we become one with the vast primal delight in existence and sense the eternity of that delight in Dionysian ecstacy" (B, 80–81). Given that it occurs at the same time as a radical forgetfulness, this suffering is endured *during* the intoxication: "The ecstasy of the Dionysian state, abolishing the habitual barriers and boundaries of existence, actually contains, for its duration, a lethargic element into which all past personal experience is plunged. Thus, through this gulf of oblivion, the worlds of everyday and Dionysian reality become separated." This forgetfulness of intoxication is, however, only temporary: "But when one once more becomes aware of this everyday reality, it becomes repellent" (B, 39). This revulsion can lead to an aesthetic attitude that turns against the Will and that paralyses all action: "True understanding, insight into the terrible truth, outweighs every motive for action. . . . No consolation will be of any use from now on. . . . Aware of truth from a single glimpse of it, all man can now see is the horror and absurdity of existence" (B, 39–40). Whoever considers this truth, can only endorse what the wise Silenius said to King Midas, namely, that the very best thing for a person is not to be born, not to *be*, to be *nothing*, and the second best is: to die quickly (B, 22).

The only way open to avoid total paralysis is to transform the tragic truth concerning existing in everyday life, to *sublimate* it (see 0.3 above), or simply to forget it. In the essay "On the Uses and Disadvantages of History for Life," published several years after *The Birth*, Nietzsche maintained:

> Forgetting is essential to action of all kind, just as not only light but darkness too is essential for the life of everything organic. . . . Thus it is possible to live almost without memory, and to live happily moreover, as the animal demonstrates; but it is altogether impossible to *live* at all without forgetting. . . . Imagine the extremest possible example of a man who did not possess the power of forgetting at all and who was thus condemned to see everywhere a state of becoming: such a man would no longer believe in his own being, would no longer believe in himself, would see everything flowing asunder in moving points and would lose himself in this stream of becoming: like a true pupil of Heraclitus, he would in the end hardly dare to raise his finger. (H, 62)

In *The Genealogy of Morals*, too, published more than ten years later, it is maintained that life demands "active oblivion," because without forgetfulness "no happiness, no serenity, no hope, no pride, no *present*" can exist (GM, 189).[15]

The health of an individual or a culture, that is, the extent to which this individual or culture can survive, is, in the essay concerning historical comprehension, understood in terms of the *plastic power* "of making the past and the strange one body with the near and present, of healing wounds, replacing what is lost, repairing broken molds" (H, 7).[16] This plastic power reaches an expression *par excellence* in the metaphorical character of art.

According to Nietzsche, this forgetting is made possible by the metaphoric transformation of reality in Apollonian art. Now, it is characteristic for the metaphoric transformation, as we noted in section 1.3 with respect to the metaphor, that its metaphoric character is forgotten. On these grounds, Nietzsche interprets the Homeric Olympus as a *veiling* of the paralyzing Dionysian truth (B, 24). The Olympian world is a world of (aesthetic) appearance, "a transfiguring mirror," which the Hellenic Will presents to itself as a means of overcoming its deep-rooted talent for suffering (B, 23–25). By letting the gods determine human lives, the very existence of those lives is justified: "Existence under the bright sunlight of gods such as these was felt to be the highest goal of mankind. . . . We might now reverse Silenius' wisdom to say to them [the Homerian people—JdM]: 'The worst thing of all for them would be to die soon, the second worst to die at all' " (B, 23). In order to live in this world of appearances, the Greeks had to completely repress the Silenian wisdom. For this reason, Nietzsche, using a term derived from Schiller, designates Homer as the prototype of the naive artist.[17]

Nietzsche maintained that pre-Socratic culture can be understood as a constant struggle—in this connection, he pointed to Heraclitus' notion of *polemos*, the harmonious conflict (KSA, 1:494; see Heraclitus, in Kirk and Raven, 1980, 195 ff.; cf. Bönig, 1986, 93)—between the Dionysian and Apollonian passions of the Greeks, which, in Attic tragedy, entered into a brief union with each other: "These two very different tendencies walk side by side, usually in violent opposition to one another, inciting one another to ever more powerful births, perpetuating the struggle of the opposition only apparently bridged by the word 'art'; until, finally, by a metaphysical miracle of the Hellenic 'will,' the two seem to be coupled, and in this coupling they seem at last to beget the work of art that is as Dionysian as it is Apolline—Attic tragedy" (B, 14).[18] According to him, the basis of Attic tragedy was formed by the ecstatic Dionysian chorus that discharges itself time and again in the Apollonian dialogic world of imagery. Here, the Apollonian dream, other than is usually the case with Apollonian art, is no redemption in appearances: the tragic character of the tragedy resides in the fact that the collapse of the individual, and his unification with primal Being, is dramatically represented (B, 45).

According to Nietzsche, Attic tragedy forms a high point of Greek culture because Dionysian wisdom enters into an agreement with the Apollonian world of appearances. This is why, he maintains, the Greek worldview finds such profound and pessimistic expression in the tragedies of Aeschylus and Sophocles: they form the representation of Dionysian wisdom through Apollonian artistic methods so that, in this way, to live with this tragic wisdom becomes endurable. "Here, in this supreme menace to the will, there approaches a redeeming, healing enchantress—*art*. She alone can turn these thoughts of repulsion at the horror and absurdity of existence into ideas compatible with life: these are the *sublime*—the taming of horror through the art; and *comedy*—the artistic release from the repellence of the absurd" (B, 40).[19] In the earlier cited preparatory study with respect to *The Birth*, Nietzsche refers to the result of this agreement of Dionysius and Apollo as "a mid-world between beauty and truth," a world of "probability" (KSA, 1:567). While it is true that there is here a reference to a world of appearance, this does not, however, function as pure appearance, but rather is experienced "as symbol, as sign of the truth" (KSA, 1:571).[20] We could speak here of a tragic irony: in the sublime appearance, the disconcerting and the absurd in existence become capable of being experienced (cf. the opening lines of Rilke's first *"Duineser Elegie,"* which I quote in 6.8).

The famous grace of the Apollonian Heaven, which tempted Winckelmann to conceptualize Greek art as "noble simplicity and quiet grandeur" (*edle Einfalt und stille Grosse*) may not, according to Nietzsche, for this reason be understood as a careless pleasure: the Apollonic mask is, on the contrary, "the inevitable product(s) of a glance into the terrible depths of nature: light-patches, we might say, to heal the gaze seared by terrible night" (B, 46). Compared with Winckelmann's classical interpretation of Greek culture, Nietzsche's interpretation can justifiably be termed Romantic.

1.7   SOCRATIC TRUTH AND NIHILISM

Nietzsche's thesis that the association of Apollo and Dionysius was a fortunate but extremely short-lived exception in Western cultural history is equally Romantic. In the degenerate stature of Euripides' tragedies, and even more so in the later Attic comedies, the unique band between the Dionysian and the Apollonian was, according to Nietzsche, again bursted by a predominance in favor of the Apollonian pole. This is apparent not only from the suppression of Dionysian elements in the chorus in favor of the Apollonian dialogue, but also from the increasingly "everydayness" and "bourgeois mediocrity" of its content. Greek cheerfulness became "the cheerfulness of the slave, who has no serious responsibilities and nothing great to strive for" (B, 56). Cutting away the Dionysian element has become so drastic, according to Nietzsche, that the tragic feeling for life could no longer be expressed in the Apollonian world of imagery: the Dionysian, it is true, did not completely disappear from Greek culture, but it was indeed banned from art to "the underworld, as it were, in the degenerate form of a secret cult" (B, 85).

In connection with this, according to Nietzsche, the figure of Socrates appears together with that of theoretical man. In the reasonable philosophy of Socrates the Apollonian style of art undergoes a metamorphosis into logical schematization (B, 69–70). The arrival of theoretical man marks the end of the tragic myth in favour of the myth of a possible "earthly consonance, a *deus ex machina* of its own—the god of machines and crucibles, the powers of the spirits of nature acknowledged and employed in the services of the higher egoism; it beliefs in the rectification of the world through knowledge and in a life guided by science, and it can also truly confine the individual within a limited circle of soluble problems, from which he can cheerfully say to life: 'I want you. You are worth knowing'" (B, 85). In the Platonic dialogues the metamorphosis of the Apollonian into the optimistic, theoretical worldview receives its expression in the total subordination of artistic expression to the philosophical Will to Truth.[21] After Socrates, a common network of rational thought has been established across the globe, providing glimpses of the lawfulness of an entire solar system. "Once we remember this, and the astonishingly high pyramid of knowledge of the present day, we cannot help but see Socrates as the turning-point, the vortex of world history" (B, 73). As we have already remarked, Nietzsche did not consider this development to be completely negative. In case the immense powers that are invested in the Will to knowing would be employed for purely practical, that is, "egoistic aims of individuals and peoples" (an extreme secularization, thus, which, according to Nietzsche, reached its most terrible expression in the Roman *imperium*—B, 99), then the consequence would be a barbarism such as the world had never experienced, a barbarism wherein the instincts for life would be so weakened in "universal wars of destruction and constant migration of peoples" that the result could even be "a terrible ethic of genocide through pity" (B, 73–74).

On the other hand, Nietzsche considered the Socratic development as an ultimately risky saving of life. With Socrates, namely, according to Nietzsche, the natural relationship between instinct and critical consciousness had been inverted: "While in all productive people instinct is the power of creativity and affirmation, and consciousness assumes a critical and dissuasive role, in Socrates instinct becomes the critic, consciousness the creator—a monstrosity *per defectum*" (B, 66). The history of decadence begins with Socrates, the sapping sickness that is inextricably bonded to European culture. The opposition that begins to dominate Nietzsche's thinking from this moment is no longer that between Apollo and Dionysius, but rather that between the Apollonian-Dionysian creative artist-philosopher on the one hand and theoretical man, shackled to concepts, on the other.

It is also with theoretical man and his "heaven-reaching pyramid of knowing" that the fossilization, which we have discussed by reference to Gudmundsson's *The Great Poem,* begins. When Socratic philosophy bans metaphorical art, it can only produce conceptual mummies. In this connection, Nietzsche speaks of Plato's *Egypticism*—referring to the surviving suggestion that Plato had once visited Egypt (cf. among others, TI, 479). Gudmundsson, too, as we have seen, chooses the pyramid as a symbol for fossilizing culture: we could consider the three pyramids in *The Great Poem* as symbols for the Ideas of the True, the Good, and the Beautiful in Plato's philosophy. The Platonic "conceptual mummies" are based upon a forgetting in the second degree, a forgetting of the transition from the Apollonian images to the "primal fallacy of identity" that is characteristic for metaphysics (KSA, 9:543, 545). Only on the basis of this forgetting in the second degree, comes the metaphysical belief in a true, unchangeable world behind the world of appearances. This belief, which, according to Nietzsche, stands by the cradle of the characteristically Western cultural weakening of life, is no less naive than that of the Apollonian artist in his world of appearances. Socratic rationality is a naive rationality (KSA, 9:41).

In "Wie die 'wahre Welt' endlich zur Fabel wurde," written in 1888, Nietzsche sketched, in a few lines, the six phases of the historical centuries of decadence that were the consequence of postulating a real world (TI, 485–86). With respect to the first phase, Plato's philosophy, his critique was relatively mild: it is perhaps true that Plato was the first to conjure up a real world of Ideas as a contrast to the world of Becoming, but there is no question of a complete renunciation of life in his works (TI, 480–81). For the philosopher, the real world is at least available in the here and now. In the second phase, Christianity, which he describes in another place as the Platonism of the common people (BGE, 32), the decadence progresses even more. The real world is now banished to the hereafter, given as merely a promise to the pious, virtuous person. For Nietzsche, the Kantian acceptance of an unknowable *thing-in-itself* marks the third phase in the biographical history of Western culture's illness: "The true world—unattainable, indemonstrable, unpromisable; but the very thought of it—a consolation, an obligation, an imperative" (TI, 485). Platonism is still apparent here, but, in a manner of speaking, it is reaching its end, the dying sun in the background. Nietzsche found that with the fourth phase, the philosophy of Schopenhauer, the ultimate boundaries of Platonism had been reached: Schopenhauer concluded that when the real world is not really reachable, it can no longer be considered as comforting, redeeming, or capable of imposing obligations. Although the renunciation of the world reached its zenith in this phase, it also opened the possibility of an overcoming of Platonism.[22]

In the critical metaphysics of Kant and Schopenhauer's metaphysics of the Will, metaphysic's Will to Truth prepares its own defeat.

Nietzsche, for the first time placing quotation marks around the concept, argued that " 'The real world'—an idea that has no further use, and that can no longer obligate—a useless, redundant idea, *consequently* a refuted idea: let's abolish it." With this abolition, according to Nietzsche, the *nihilism* that is latent in the decadent development emerges into the foreground. The consequence of this abolition is that all goals, values and truths of the metaphysical Christian tradition are wiped out, devalued.[23] Herewith, the sensible world loses its reality, and the real world loses its sensibleness (cf. Bröcker, 1963, 14). Primarily in his "positivist" period, Nietzsche made himself the spokesperson for this truth about nihilism, a truth he pronounced under the rubric of "the death of God" (cf. De Mul, 1996a). In *The Gay Science*, he produces a madman who, ridiculed by a crowd, searches with a lantern in broad daylight looking for God: " 'Whither is God?' he cried, 'I will tell you. We have killed him*—you and I. All of us are his murderers. But how did we do this? How could we drink up the sea? Who gave us the sponge to wipe away the entire horizon? What were we doing when we unchained this earth from its sun? Whither is it moving now? Whither are we moving? Away from all suns? Are we not plunging continually? Backward, sideward, forward, in all directions? Is there still any up or down? Are we not straying as through an infinite nothing?" (GS, 181). Although Gudmundsson's irony is less horrifying than Nietzsche's, he expresses the same dread in his *D'où venons nous? Qui sommes nous? Où allons nous?* (1979—figure 3; the title refers to a painting of the same name painted by Gauguin in 1897 not long before his attempted suicide), wherein he portrays an insignificant man who, without destination, wanders through an immense landscape with an enormous arrow under his arm. While the comical character of this image perhaps tempers the disgust that the nihilistic insight into the absurdity of existence engenders, it in no way removes it completely.

The nihilism engendered by the Will to Truth brings with it the rebirth of the bottomless pessimism that had once forced the Greeks to choose between India and Rome: between a radical denial of the Will and an unconstrained barbarism (cf. B, 99–100). The prophesies of the later Nietzsche with respect to a terrifying war that would haunt Europe for the coming centuries makes us suspect that he gradually saw the latter alternative as the most probable (cf. among others EH, 127; WDB, 3:911). In *The Birth*, the Romantic desire led Nietzsche to pin his faith on a possible repetition of the Greek miracle: the "third path" of a tragic culture. Because the tragic culture was once born from music, Nietzsche believes that it can only return through this medium; he was thinking

FIGURE 3

D'où venons nous? Qui sommes nous? Où allons nous?, Sigurdur Gudmundsson, 1976, photograph and text, 71 × 91 cm. State Collection, The Netherlands.

of his idolized Wagnerian music in this context.[24] Nietzsche regarded the Wagnerian total work of art, specified by him in "Richard Wagner in Bayreuth" (1875) as "a colossal system of thought without the abstract form of a thought," of which theoretical man has "precisely the same amount of understanding as a dove possesses of music," as the rebirth of the tragic myth. Only such a myth could make it possible to rise above the decadence of the Socratic, Western culture without falling into one or another form of life-denying nihilism or insanity-creating Dionysian barbarism.[25] This hope for the healing powers of art continued to accompany Nietzsche's paths of thought. In 1888, several months before his psychological collapse, he noted: "Our religion, morality and philosophy are symptoms of decadence. . . . The contrary movement: art" (KSA, 13:354–56). "We have art so that we are not defeated by the truth" (KSA, 13:500). "Art and nothing other than art. It forms the possibility of life, it is the great tempter of life, the great stimulus of life" (KSA, 13:521).

1.8   THE AMBIVALENCE OF ROMANTIC DESIRE

Schlegel once defined the Romantic as a life-feeling that oscillates between enthusiasm and irony (cf. 0.3). In the cases of Delpeut, Gudmundsson, and Nietzsche, too, enthusiasm for the healing power of art is constantly combined with an unmistakable ironic distance. A first indication of this in Nietzsche's work is the plethora of gibes that he makes in the direction of art and artists: it does not appear to me to be justified to attribute such remarks to Nietzsche's tendency to contradict himself or to the development of his thinking. This latter explanation is not justified because positive and negative comments relating to art and artists are made in each phase of Nietzsche's thinking, while the former explanation diminishes the ambivalent character that he attributed to art itself (cf. Pütz, 1975, 24). If we look more closely at Nietzsche's critique of art, we can differentiate a number of separate motives. In *Human, All Too Human*, he maintains that artists have constantly been "the glorifiers of the religious and philosophical errors of mankind" (HH, 102). In *The Genealogy of Morals*, too, he says that artists "have ever been in the service of some ethics or philosophy or religion" (GM, 236). In this critique, there is a clear expression that art, too, can become a symptom of decadence. It was "the case of Wagner" that, above all others, led Nietzsche to this insight: with the saturation of *Parsifal* with Christian motifs, Wagner betrayed tragic art to the benefit of the aesthetic ideals of decadence. Art is no longer, as Stendhal said, *une promesse de bonheur*, but rather it functions, as with Schopenhauer, as an opiate designed to momentarily ("What am I saying? *for five or six hours!*") liberate man from Will (EH, 92; cf. EH, 109).[26]

On the basis of this insight, Nietzsche, in his later work, made a distinction between the life-affirming art of the Great Style and the life-denying art of decadence. He also specified this distinction, using Goethe's famous definition of Classical and Romantic art, as being between healthy and sick art. The artist of the Great Style disciplines the chaotic Becoming by imposing his perspectual meaning: "This style shares with the great passion the fact that it refuses to satisfy, that it does not wish to persuade; that it orders; that it wants. . . . To become master of the Chaos which one is; to suppress the Chaos, to become form: logical simplicity, unambiguous, mathematical, become law: this, here, is the great ambition" (KSA, 13:246–47). Contrary to this, decadent art is not able to aesthetically transform reality, it is merely "a remedy for a damaged reality" (WDB, 3:833). Decadent art is not characterized by unity and rigor of form, but rather by losing itself in details, by fragmentation, and by openness and disproportionality. In this regard, the "miniaturist" Wagner is the preeminent example.

However, Nietzsche's critique goes even further when he maintains that art in the present time of decadence is *necessarily* decadent (cf. Bröcker, 1963, 15). This is even applicable to the artist-philosopher Nietzsche, himself: "Just as much as Wagner, I am a child of my time, that is, a *decadent:* the difference is that I understand this, that I revolt against it" (KSA, 6:11). Pütz justifiably pointed out that the Romantic stylistic characteristics that Nietzsche criticizes are applicable, item by item, to his own style (Pütz, 1975, 35). That which Nietzsche combated as sickly-Romantic is also his own Romantic desire.

What is of primary importance in this context is that Nietzsche gradually came to recognize that a simple return to Greek culture is impossible. In the words of Bröcker: "We can no longer forget science. And myths can no longer become for us what they were *before* the appearance of science" (Bröcker, 1963, 27). Decadence cannot be abolished, we must learn to live with the most characteristic stature of decadence: the Will to Truth. This conflict is also observable in Nietzsche's work: on the one hand, as an artist, he constructs new myths, and on the other hand he is the indefatigable complainant busy unmasking every myth. He constantly speaks as both thinker *and* artist, constantly oscillating between the euphoria of artistic intoxication and the grief which tragic knowledge engenders (Pütz, 1975, 38). Gudmundsson's *The Great Poem* is saturated with a similar oscillation between enthusiasm and irony: the sculpture shows us art's desire to submerge in the stream of life, but is equally the reflective symbol of the impossibility of realizing this desire in the conceptuality of modern culture.

However, there is yet another motif in Nietzsche's critique of art that repeatedly appears, radicalizing it yet further because it not only relates to the necessary decadence of contemporary art but also to the healthy art of the Great Style. That which the artist of the Great Style attempts is, in fact, the imposition of the character of Being upon Becoming (WDB, 3:895). But, for Nietzsche, this means that the artist of the Great Style is necessarily a liar! In *Thus Spoke Zarathustra,* recalling the words of Plato, he plainly states that artists lie too much (Z, 149). The lie is unavoidable because it is not possible to live with the tragic truth: anyone abandoning himself to this truth would end in Dionysian barbarism and insanity. The lie, therefore, is a part of *every* culture: "All forms of culture begin with the fact that many things remain veiled" (KSA, 7:453). "Without untruth, neither community nor culture. The tragic conflict. Everything which is good and beautiful is based upon an illusion: truth kills" (KSA, 7:623).

In the poem by Peter Delpeut, too, this critique concerning art's reality-stature receives expression:

> What remained of fingers and toes
> barely kept him upright.
>
> .   .   .   .
>
> The man who came from the cold, died yesterday,
> heroes do not live long, too briefly for a legend
>
> of snow. If I die I melt, he had said.
> He has not melted.

> Wat restte van vingers en tenen
> hield hem nauwelijks overeind.
>
> .   .   .   .
>
> De man die van de kou kwam is gisteren gestorven,
> Helden leven niet lang, te kort voor een legende
>
> van sneeuw. Als ik sterf, smelt ik, had hij gezegd.
> Hij is niet gesmolten.

Here, too, the remarkable irony in relation to the promise of artistic desire. Metaphorical art appears not to fulfil its promise to make man "melt" into the stuff of the world: the artist, the man who came from the cold, said that he would melt if he died, but he did not melt. Ultimately, the ecstatic union of subject and reality has not occurred in art: the poem turns out to be a necrology of the Romantic desire that makes one think of Hegel's announcement of the death of art.[27] But, unlike the case with Hegel, scientific understanding does not offer us any alternative in this context: the Romantic genius-artist has not only died, his life was to short to live on as a modern myth.

But this interpretation, too, fails to exhaust the poetic word. In fact, it even appears to radically fail to do justice to the poem. After all, the poem, as the interpretation of the earlier line showed, also speaks of the blending of the man who came from the cold with the sleet and snow of winter. In this fashion, the poem undermines the trusted opposition of truth and lie, thereby appearing to open up the paradoxical dimension of the authentic lie. Also, when Nietzsche simultaneously criticizes the artist as liar and praises him because he thereby remains true to the constantly shifting character of reality, he appears to be underway toward another view of the opposition between truth and lies.

1.9   THE MUSIC-MAKING SOCRATES AS ÜBERMENSCH

When Nietzsche attempts to specify the essence of art with the assistance of the contradiction between truth and lies, then, to a certain extent, he remains a prisoner of the very tradition he is seeking to overcome. The result can therefore be nothing other than an inverted Platonism. Initially, Nietzsche understood his own philosophy in these terms. In 1870 he noted: "My philosophy is an inverted Platonism: the further it is from real Being, thus how purer, more beautiful, better it is. Living in appearance as goal" (KSA, 7:199; cf. Heidegger, N, 2:176, 469).

Nietzsche's dependence on the metaphysical tradition is also apparent from the fact that, in *The Birth*, following Schopenhauer, he maintained the Kantian distinction between real and apparent reality by making a distinction between the World Will and the (Apollonian) world of appearances.[28] In Nietzsche's later work, however, we come across numerous attempts to overcome the metaphysical tradition (and above the contradiction between metaphysics and metaphor that is implied therein) through a *Verwindung* of the opposition between truth and appearance.[29] This is clearly expressed in "Wie die 'wahre Welt' endlich zur Fabel wurde," from which I have already quoted. Having established that, with the philosophy of Schopenhauer, the real world has become a redundant idea that can be dispensed with, he continues: "The true world—we have abolished. What world has remained? The apparent one perhaps? But no! *With the true world we have also abolished the apparent one.* (Noon; the moment of the briefest shadow; end of the longest error; high point of humanity; INCIPIT ZARATHUSTRA)" (TI, 486). With this remark, Nietzsche's overturning of Platonism appears to be a *twist out* of Platonism (cf. Heidegger, N, 1:208). With the denial of the true, suprasensible world of the concept, one can no longer speak of an associated contrary sensory appearance. The concept of "appearance," in the sense of illusion, points to something that is other than it presents itself. Nietzsche in no way denies that something can present itself other than as in an earlier moment, but this "other" is also necessarily appearance: for this reason, it is not worthwhile to continue to speak in terms of appearance (cf. Visser, 1989, 175).

When Nietzsche nonetheless continues to employ the concept of "appearance" to signify the only reality of things (KSA, 11:654), then, according to Visser, this is not only to signify the inaccessibility of a "real" reality, but also to name the tempting appearances, the luster of what presents itself. What we name reality must be understood as an *infinite, inexhaustible* series of interpretations (GS, 336).[30] Against the background of this play of the world the metaphor can be considered, in a nonmetaphysical manner, as being, through this process, the coming into appearance of beings. If reality in its totality consists of metaphorical interpretations, then, at this level of pure Becoming, one can no longer speak in terms of truth and appearance. Using Heideggerian terminology we could say that in the process of interpretation different beings are each time unveiled, and that with these unveilings other beings themselves become concealed.

Nietzsche's thinking does not only undermine the reassuring opposition of appearance and truth, it also implies the *Verwindung* of a number of other oppositions that are characteristic of the metaphysical tradition. This can probably be best illustrated by reference to what we may call Nietzsche's most intimate and sublime thought: the doctrine of the Eternal Recurrence of the Same (*ewige Wiederkehr des Gleichen*).[31] Briefly summarized, this doctrine "jotted down on a piece of paper with the inscription: '6,000 feet beyond man and time'" (EH, 99; for the note itself, see KSA, 9:494)—comes down to this: everything that ever appears, will repeat itself *ad infinitum.* On the one hand this doctrine appears to have been intended by Nietzsche as a cosmological doctrine (in Nietzsche's notations we find numerous attempts to argue the doctrine in these terms—see, for example, KSA, 9:498), and, on the other hand, it is an (as we shall shortly hereafter see: aesthetic) imperative, a guideline for actions in a world that must do without previously given goals: "The question with everything you want to do: 'is it so, that I wish to do this *ad infinitum'* is the *most* weighty question" (KSA, 9:496; cf. GS, 273–74).[32]

In the first place, with this doctrine of the Eternal Recurrence the metaphysical distinction between Being and Becoming loses its absolute contradictory character: "The world exists: it is not something which becomes, not something which passes away. Or, rather: it becomes, it passes away, but it has never started to Become and never stopped passing away—it *maintains* itself in both" (KSA, 13:374). "*That everything returns* is the most extreme *approximation of the world of Becoming to the world of Being—the zenith of the contemplation* (WDB, 3:895). Against this background, the intention of the artist of the Great Style to impose Becoming as the characteristic of Being is seen in another light. Shortly after the introduction of the doctrine of the Eternal Recurrence Nietzsche maintained in his personal notes that we constantly wish to experience a good work of art again, and he continued: "In this way will one give stature to one's life, that one cherishes the same wish towards its parts! This is the chief thought!" (KSA, 9:505). When the artist of the Great Style wants to impose the stamp of Being upon Becoming, then this is no flight from the transitory world, but rather the highest conceivable affirmation of this world.

From the foregoing it follows that the contradiction between finitude and infinity loses its sharpness, too. In the experience of the Eternal Recurrence of the Same, eternity is no longer something that lies beyond life, but, instead, it is something that is present in each moment (cf. Bröcker, 1960, 17; Fink, 1960, 173). Thus finitude and infinity interpenetrate each other in every action. Understood in this sense, the doctrine of the Eternal Recurrence is a radicalization of Novalis' expression of the Romantic desire to have the finite and the infinite, the eternal and the momentary, the banal and the sublime interpenetrate each other (cf. 0.2.).

Another contradiction in the doctrine of the Eternal Recurrence of the Same that is subjected to a *Verwindung* is that between necessity and freedom: "The epitome of fatalism is nonetheless identical to *chance* and the creative" (KSA, 11:292; cf. Fink, 1960, 89; for a further discussion of Nietzsche's views of chance, see 6.8 below). When everything endlessly repeats itself, one can speak of an unheard of fatalism, after all, what we do has occurred so many times before, but it can also with equal justification be said that we are confronted with decisions in every moment of our existence, decisions that not only have an influence on the near future but also on every future repetition.

We have already mentioned above that Nietzsche referred to the doctrine of the Eternal Recurrence as the most substantial doctrine. Kundera, who begins his novel *The Unbearable Lightness of Being* with reflections on Nietzsche's doctrine of the Eternal Recurrence, says in this context: "If every second of our lives recurs an infinite numbers of times, we are nailed to eternity as Jesus Christ was nailed to the cross. It is a terrifying prospect. In the world of eternal return the weight of unbearable responsibility lies heavy on every move we make" (Kundera, 1984, 5). "In this world everything presents itself without the mitigating circumstances of their transitory nature" (Kundera, 1984, 4). But what does the alternative mean, a life without the heaviest burden, in a world that, with the death of God, has lost all meaning? "The absolute absence of a burden causes man to be lighter than air, to soar into the heights, take leave of the earth and his earthly being, and become only half real, his movements as free as they are insignificant" (Kundera, 1984, 5). Is it preferable to choose this unbearable lightness of Being above the heaviest burden? Is the heaviest burden not also the image of the most intense satisfaction of life? "The heavier the burden, the closer our lives come to the earth, the more real and truthful they become" (Kundera, 1984, 5). Nietzsche's Zarathustra, too, summons us to be true to the earth and to accept this burden (Z, 42).

In *The Birth*, Nietzsche utters the hope that our culture will give birth to a music-making Socrates, the artist-philosopher who will be able to bear this tragic thought without falling into one or another form of life renunciation (B, 70, 85). It would be a tragic person who creates new myths and thereby forgets his metaphorical activity, but one who simultaneously has the courage to lucidly see through this forgetting and, as an *active* nihilist, time and again acts to destroy his creations in the name of Becoming (cf. WDB, 3:557). The question, however, is whether man will ever have the courage to really bear the thought of the Eternal Recurrence. In *The Birth* Nietzsche had already shown himself to be concerned about this (B, 75), and in *Thus Spoke Zarathustra* we read that only an *Übermensch* would be able to remain true to the earth in the light of the tragic wisdom (Z, 41–42). But, given that this *Übermensch* is understood by Nietzsche as a metaphor (transfer) of man, the origin hereof is dependent on the reaching-beyond-self creation of a "superior person" who is not tainted by decadence. For this reason, the question is whether this transfer will ever actually appear. Does the ubiquitous nihilism not mean that we are eternally doomed to remain the "Ultimate Men"? Ultimate—postmodern?— man wallows pleasurably in nihilism and surrenders himself to lethargy: "A little poison now and then: that produces pleasant dreams. And a lot of poison at last, for a pleasant death. They still work, for work is entertainment. But they take care the entertainment does not exhaust them. . . . 'We have discovered happiness,' say the Ultimate Men and blink" (Z, 46–47).

1.10 IT'S SO COLD IN ALASKA

In the foregoing I argued that Gudmundsson's *The Great Poem* warns us against the danger of fossilization that is always lurking around the corner. That danger also threatens the interpretations, which I have presented in this chapter. I have carried the metaphors of Delpeut, Gudmundsson, and Nietzsche across to the domain of discursive concepts. Because of the open character of these works, it has been a precarious undertaking. Not only because the last word about this can never be spoken, but, primarily, because every comment concerning these images also brings a conceptual fixation. And, moreover, when one speaks of transcendental metaphors, of fossilization and the freezing of water, then this can lead to ludicrous results. Thales, as Nietzsche remarked, saw the unity of all Being, and when he wanted to communicate this unity he found himself stammering about water (KSA, 1:817)!

This does not mean that the philosopher who arrives at this insight must set aside his interpretations in the way that, according to Wittgenstein, one can throw away a ladder once one has climbed up it (Wittgenstein, 1975, 115). What can be expected is that he, as an "active nihilist," comprehends that his conceptual ladders "are no more than helpful constructions, a toy for the most audacious works of art of the liberated intellect" that, at its best, "once again smashes all those things, jumbles them up, and then ironically puts them together again" (KSA, 1:888). Nietzsche himself attempted to avoid the danger of fossilization with a radical metaphoricism that leads to an unavoidable frustration of every attempt at a comprehensive interpretation of his work. His earlier quoted remark concerning the convergence of poeticizing and thinking is not a confirmatory observation, but rather an imperative directed at the reader: an aesthetic imperative. This imperative demands thought that speaks to the imagination, challenging but simultaneously lucid as the sobering freezing wind above Sils Maria:

The Man Who Came from the Cold

It's so cold in Alaska

—Lou Reed

What remained of fingers and toes
barely kept him upright.

He told stories of sleet and snow,
blending them into a legend for radio and TV

those who come from the cold are themselves winter,—he said.

They love their sledges and their dogs.
It is not through a landscape they travel,

but seasons of storm and ice:
it freezes their thought.

The man who came from the cold, died yesterday,
heroes do not live long, too briefly for a legend

of snow. If I die I melt, he had said.
He has not melted.

De man die van de kou kwam

It's so cold in Alaska

—Lou Reed

Wat restte van vingers en tenen
hield hem nauwelijks overeind.

Hij vertelde verhalen van hagel en sneeuw,
Versmolt ze voor radio en t.v. tot een legende:

zij die van de kou komen zijn zelf winter,—zei hij.

Zij houden van hun slee en van de honden.
Het is niet het landschap dat zij reizen,

maar een seizoen van storm en ijs:
zij bevriezen hun denken.

De man die van de kou kwam is gisteren gestorven,
helden leven niet lang, te kort voor een legende

van sneeuw. Als ik sterf, smelt ik, had hij gezegd.
Hij is niet gesmolten.

2

The Path of Autonomy

One should be absolutely modern.
—Arthur Rimbaud (1873)

Ideal, Ideal, Ideal,
Knowledge Knowledge Knowledge,
Boomboom, Boomboom, Boomboom.
—Tristan Tzara (1918)

If we place Nietzsche's Romantic desire for the total aestheticization of existence alongside the development of modern painting, which commenced during his lifetime, then, just as for Nietzsche, it will be difficult for us to arrive at any other conclusion than that this desire possesses a rather *unzeitgemäß* character. It is perhaps true that modern artists are no longer "in the service of some ethics or philosophy or religion" (GM, 236), but the liberation of art has not led to the blending of art and life that Nietzsche announced. On the contrary: this liberation appears to have been made possible precisely because of the characteristically modern differentiation between art and other areas of life. That modern art has been able to throw off its bondage is primarily thanks to the fact that the "world of art" has increasingly become an *autonomous* domain alongside science, morality, politics, religion, and philosophy.

Before the birth of modern art, art itself was socioeconomically *and* artistically (in terms of both its iconographic content as its aesthetic form) dominated by the patronage of the church, civil authorities, rich

merchant families, and princely houses. In this period, the 'social relevance' of art also resided in this subordinate position. Works of art were
closely connected to social and religious relationships and ideals, and
they gave these relationships and ideals form, content, and meaning (cf.
Féher, 1987, 14–15). The emancipation of art was a process that occupied
many centuries. "It was the Renaissance," summarizes Habermas,
"which first saw the emergence of a specific domain categorized exclusively in terms of the beautiful. Then, in the course of the eigteenth century, literature, the plastic arts, and music were institutionalized as a specific domain of activity distinct from ecclesiastical and court life. Finally,
around the middle of the nineteenth century, there also arose an aesthetic
conception of art that obliged artists to produce their work in accordance
with the conscious outlook of *l'art pour l'art*. The autonomy of the aesthetic was thereby explicitly constituted as a project" (Habermas, 1996,
47).[1] It is perhaps true that the modern Western artist is dependent for
his income upon the free market and government subsidies, but at the
artistic level he enjoys, at least in principle, all possible freedoms.

Modern art makes a big issue of its autonomy and, for this reason,
is characterized by a "pathos of purity" (Bürger, 1987, 10). In modern
art, all external influences and judgmental criteria must give way to
pure aesthetic criteria; this process of purification also occurs between
the various art forms. Criteria from other aesthetic "disciplines" are excluded as much as is possible. Thus, beginning with impressionism,
modern painting has increasingly imposed a distance between itself
and the narrative and anecdotal aspects of earlier paintings, and attempts to derive its meaning exclusively from its own artistic means
such as form, color, line, and structure. The painter and theorist Mau-
rice Denis maintained in 1890, as one of the first, that a painting, rather
than being a representation of, for example, a horse, is simply a flat ex-
panse covered with a particular arrangement of colors. Moreover, the
purification also relates to the aesthetic criteria from the past that are
unique to the medium. Being absolutely modern means maintaining a
distance from the canonized aesthetic rules of tradition, and, for this reason, modern art, by definition, is directed at renewal (cf. 0.7–8). Gradually, in this process of emancipation, even all mimetic and expressive
criteria are put to one side in favour of the *formalist* purity of abstract
painting.[2] "The essence of modernism," argues Greenberg, one of its
most important advocates, "lies . . . in the use of characteristic methods
of a discipline to criticize the discipline itself, not in order to subvert it
but in order that to entranch it more firmly in its area of competence"
(Greenberg, 1993, 85).

Greenberg's definition of modernism appears to be applicable not only to art, but also to all of modern culture. According to sociologists and philosophers such as Weber and Habermas, the foregoing developmental sketch of modern art is an expression of the *structural differentiation* that is characteristic of the rationalization of modern society. According to these commentators, the emancipation of which we refer to here is not only characteristic of art but also of all systems of social action in modern society, such as the economic, the scientific, the judicial, and the religious.

In this chapter, on the basis of a confrontation between Piaget's theory of development and the abstract, modernist paintings of the American artist Frank Stella (whereby the aesthetic development theory of the art historian Suzi Gablik will function as intermediary), I want to pose the question as to how far, in the case of art's development, we can speak of a process of rationalization in the sense as used by Weber and Habermas.[3] Thereafter, on the basis of the Nietzschean-inspired dadaist and surrealist revolt against bourgeois culture, and the *L'art pour l'art* movement that was closely associated with it, I shall more closely examine the converse of this aesthetic rationalization. This does not only bring me into a dialogue with the views concerning *avant-gardism* and artistic autonomy elaborated by a number of representatives of the Frankfurt School (apart from Habermas, I shall principally refer to the works of his aesthetic "tutors," Adorno and Benjamin), but, in addition, it also enables me to explain why, in his later work, Stella develops a typical postmodern style. Finally, I shall argue that this postmodern style occupies an ambivalent position between autonomous modern art and the avant-garde movement that is directed against aesthetic autonomy.

2.1 PIAGET'S STUDIES OF INTELLECTUAL DEVELOPMENT AND RATIONALIZATION

The Swiss scientist and philosopher Jean Piaget is primarily known as a developmental psychologist, but, in his long career, he has also given attention to areas far beyond developmental psychology. Piaget was interested in all possible forms of the development of human knowledge: his interest was not only in the development of knowledge in individuals but also in historical development such as is expressed in the growth of scientific and technological knowledge. For this reason we could, with equal justification, refer to Piaget as a philosopher of science. Piaget himself preferred to refer to his work as a *genetic epistemology*, a genetic theory of knowledge (cf. De Mul, 1997d, 229–33). It is, incidentally, no coincidence that he is primarily known as a developmental psychologist: the experimental "garden" for his many-sided theories was primarily the extensive empirical research into the intellectual development of children that, together with his assistants, he carried out in the Centre International d'Epistémologie Génétique in Geneva.

The starting point for Piaget's genetic epistemology is that knowledge should not be considered a mental copy of an already existing reality, but rather as a process of constant interaction between subject and object whereby both the mental structures of the subject and the relations between the objects are constructed. For Piaget, knowledge is, thus, not primarily a theoretical affair, but rather it originates in *action*. For that reason, knowledge for Piaget is above all a kind of *praxis:* "Actually, in order to know objects, the subject must act upon them, and thereby transform them: he must displace, connect, combine, take apart, and reassemble them. Knowledge is constantly linked with actions or operations, that is, with *transformations*. Hence the limit between subject and objects is in no way determined beforehand, and, what is more important, it is not stable . . . Knowledge, then, at its origin, neither arises from objects nor from the subject, but from interactions,—at first inextricable—between the subject and those objects" (Piaget, 1983, 104).

Piaget's constructivist theory of knowledge can be understood as a radicalization of Kant's epistemology. Kant's Copernican Revolution consisted of the fact that he no longer viewed knowledge as a passive reflection of reality, but rather as a structuring of perception by means of *a priori* forms of sensibility (space and time) and the categories of understanding (cf. CR, 67–68, 133–34/KrV, A23–24, 104–5). He continued to assume, however, that these *a priori* forms and categories of the subject form a timeless structure. The radicalization of Kant's viewpoint in genetic epistemology comprises the fact that herein the transcendental subject, too, is itself viewed as the product of a process of construction (Piaget, 1972, 57–58).[4]

What is characteristic for Piaget's genetic epistemology is that he does not consider the development of human subjectivity as a process of quantitative growth, but rather as a development wherein a number of *qualitatively* different stages or structured totalities can be distinguished. He distinguishes four paramount stages that he specifies as the sensory-motor, the pre-operational, the concrete-operational, and the formal-operational. I shall attempt to characterize each of these four stages, which Piaget primarily elaborated with respect to the intellectual development of the individual, with a number of catchwords.

In the prelanguage *sensory-motor* stage (globally taken, the period 0–2 years) the child obtains a first realization of objects in the world and of his own body. The starting point here is what Piaget, with Baldwin, referred to as an adualistic experience wherein the future subject does not yet comprehend a distinction between the self and the nonself world.[5] Through the coordination of (partly congenital) action-schemas a primordial subjectivity arises together with a first structuring of a world separate from the subject. The behavior of the child can already be described as intelligent, although this intelligence is not yet conceptual, but it is completely related to *action.* For this reason we could specify this intelligence as a "logic of action" (cf. Kitchener, 1986, 18).

In the second, *pre-operational* stage (2–7 years) the semiotic function develops whereby reality can be symbolized and represented.[6] Next to the sensory impression and symbolic play, language, too, belongs to this stage. With the help of the semiotic function, the subject learns to internalize his actions. In this stage, representations of reality are still completely connected to sensory appreciations: the subject is not yet able to perform mental operations on these preconceptual representations.

In the third, *concrete-operational* stage (7–11 years) the child learns to apply these mental operations to concrete objects. The subject is also able to reverse these mental transformations in thought, and, thus, learns to conserve. Concepts originate in this stage. Piaget called this stage concrete because the conceptual operations can only be carried out upon concrete objects.

In the fourth and last stage, the *formal-operational* (from 11 years onwards), the child learns to apply conceptual operations to purely mental representations and concepts. Thus, without having concrete representations available, the child can now devise and mentally test abstract hypotheses. In this stage, in brief, scientific thinking becomes possible.

If we take an overview of all four stages, then a number of characteristics can be distinguished that we also encounter with almost the same terminology in Weber's theory. In the first place, increasing *differentiation* is apparent in Piaget's stages: in the course of development more and more aspects of the inner and outer world are distinguished from each other. However, at the same time we note *integration:* the distinguished aspects are in each stage once again integrated into a balanced whole. It is also important that thinking is increasingly *formalized* and also achieves an increasingly *universal* character. While thinking is initially strongly connected to concrete actions and perceptions, it increasingly achieves an abstract character and becomes applicable to more and more situations. Further, according to Piaget, an increasing *distancing* of subjectivity occurs: whereas the subject is initially completely "taken up" in the world, he gradually and increasingly comes to stand against both the world and himself.[7] Finally, Piaget points to the fact that, in the course of his development, the human individual increasingly comes to *control* his environment: we could summarize these characteristics with the Weberian term *rationalization*.[8]

This process of rationalization is understood by Piaget as one of unqualified progress: every subsequent stage in development is characterized by more objective knowledge of reality, which makes possible an increasingly effective adjustment to the environment. Development is a process of increasing balance (*equilibrium*) between man and nature. In this sense, Piaget's genetic epistemology ties in with the optimistic belief in progress that is characteristic of nineteenth-century developmental theories such as those of Spencer and Comte, and, more generally, of the worldview of modernism.

2.2 RATIONALIZATION AND PROGRESS IN ART

As has already been mentioned above, Piaget was not only interested in the intellectual development of the individual but also in the historical development of knowledge. The thesis that he defends is that there is a relationship between the mental development of the individual and the historical development in the corresponding domains of knowledge (Piaget, 1983, 104). In a number of publications, Piaget has attempted to substantiate this thesis with respect to logic, mathematics, and physics. In these disciplines, too, according to Piaget, there is evidence of *rationalization*, that is: increasing integration and decentering, formalizing, distancing, and control. In the development of these disciplines it has not only been a question of distinguishing more and more aspects of reality, but, in addition, the separate aspects have been integrated into increasingly extensive formal structures whereby the theoretical and practical control of nature also increases.

Thus, Einstein's relativity theory does not constitute a denial of Newtonian physics, but rather the latter is integrated into a more extensive theory. We are faced here with the *historical* transition from concrete-operational to formal-operational thinking: while Newton's physics was still closely tied to the everyday experiencing of space and time, the theory of relativity takes a more universal standpoint. Further, Einstein's theory was hypothetical, that is, formulated independently from experience and only *subsequently* empirically established. In the natural sciences, too, one can speak of an increasing distancing and decentering, something that is quite easy to note from the abandonment of the earth-centric position in astronomy. Finally, modern technologies make clear that the increase in theoretical control of reality goes hand in hand with increasing practical control.

Although in the philosophy of science during the foregoing decades, and more especially subsequent to Kuhn's theory of paradigms, question marks have legitimately been placed in respect to the view that science is a continuous process of knowledge acquisition, it does appear to be unquestionable that, in the sense expressed above, a process of rationalization has taken place in the natural sciences. The thesis that similar progress has been made in painting appears less obvious, yet this is precisely what the art historian Suzi Gablik argued in 1976 in her book *Progress in Art*. On the basis of Piaget's theory, Gablik argued that one can speak of progress with respect to the development of painting. With this art form, too, according to her, we can distinguish a number of qualitatively different stages wherein there is evidence of increasing differentiation and integration, formalization, distancing, and control of space, in brief: increasing rationalization. Using a great number of examples, only a few of which I can mention in the following pages, she distinguishes three "mega-periods" in the history of Western painting that, respectively, correlate with Piaget's preoperational, concrete-operational, and formal-operational stages. The development that Gablik investigates in her book relate to the manner in which *space* is represented in the different periods (Gablik, 1976, 42).

The period that correlates with Piaget's pre-operational stage comprises the entirety of Western painting until the Renaissance (that is, from Egyptian and Greek art until the Middle Ages). Despite the substantial differences in subject matter, expressiveness, and style, every painting in this long period, according to Gablik, was without exception characterized by spatial two-dimensionality. It is perhaps true that the artists of this period increasingly gained the ability to represent objects and persons in a highly detailed manner, but they were still not able to effectively portray the underlying spatial relationships of these objects and persons. In these paintings, the place and size of these separate objects and persons was not determined by their spatial relationships, but rather in an "egocentric" manner, by their emotional value to the painter and his public. An effective example of this point is the *Madonna with Angels* from the beginning of the ninth century. Although the various figures are expressed with refinement and portrayed in detail, their intrinsic spatial relationships are completely dominated by the ubiquitous presence of the Madonna.

According to Gablik, the second period begins with the Renaissance. During the Renaissance, thanks to the development of central perspective, the flat surface was "broken open" in favor of an illusionistic, three-dimensional working in depth. That this new experience of space was not handed to the artists on a plate but only gained through a difficult process is made clear to us by typical transition works such as Simone Martini's *Road to Calvary*, painted in circa 1340 (figure 4; cf. Gombrich, 1959). Although the city in the background is already represented with a certain perspective, and the different figures already overlap each other, the figures in the foreground nonetheless remain completely independent of the city walls. One hundred and fifty years later, as Raphaël's 1504 painting entitled *The Wedding of the Virgin* shows us, Renaissance artists have completely mastered perspectual representation (figure 5). The importance of surmounting illusionistic, three-dimensional space in Renaissance paintings cannot be seen as an isolated artistic phenomenon; it is a metaphor of the new experiencing of reality that enters the scene along with the Renaissance.

In the central perspective the human figure is no longer immediately absorbed in the world-space, but rather places himself over against the world. Following Piaget we can say that this perspective is an expression of an increasing differentiation between the human figure and the world. In his book *The Philosophy of the Landscape* Lemaire expressed this as follows: "The perspectual representation of the world as landscape is an act of liberation and emancipation by the individual, or, more sharply expressed: it is via one and the same movement that the individual places himself as an autonomous subject *and* the world appears as a environmental space" (Lemaire, 1970, 24–25; cf. De Mul, 1993b). With respect to Rogier van der Weyden's portrait of Maria Magdalene (figure 6), Lemaire adds: "That which was the achievement and inspiration of the Renaissance is here reduced to an elementary image: the awakening of the self-conscious person against the background of the world, the self-differentiation of the subject who separates himself from the world in order to be able to see it in overview and to control it" (Lemaire, 1970, 25). This attainment is primarily an intellectual achievement: the experience of reality is the result of an intellectual construction. Science and art are closely connected with each other through this surmounting of space. It is no coincidence that many of the major artists of the Renaissance, for example Leonardo da Vinci, were also active in the field of science.

The perspectual representation of space that was developed in the Renaissance and that maintained a central role in painting until the

FIGURE 4

The Road to Calvary, Simone Martini, ca. 1340, panel, 9 7/8 × 6 1/8 in. The Louvre, Paris.

FIGURE 5

The Wedding of the Virgin, Raphael, 1504, oil on canvas, 170 × 118 cm. Pinacoteca di Brera, Milan.

FIGURE 6

Maria Magdalena, Rogier van der Weyden, 1451, panel, part of triptych, 34 × 27 cm. Louvre, Paris.

twentieth century agrees with what Piaget regards as characteristic for the concrete-operational stage. It is perhaps true that it constitutes progress in comparison with preceding stages, but it remains tied to concrete objects. Just as the child in the concrete-operational stage needs objects such as marbles in order to be able to count, the Renaissance artist also requires concrete objects in order to realize his intellectual constructions. Accordingly, Renaissance art is still necessarily figurative art. Further, this new art, despite its rational character, remains closely connected to the world of emotions. Although the new painting loses the collective (pre-operational) magic of painting from the Middle Ages, it forms not only a window giving a view of the newly constructed external world, but, in addition, it is simultaneously and increasingly a mirror of the artist's soul. This latter characteristic of the new art finds an especial expression in the genius-art of the Romantics (cf. 0.3 and 1.3).

According to Gablik these two characteristics of concrete-operational thinking are surmounted for the first time in *modern, non figurative art*. Purely formal operations enter the domain of the aesthetic. It is probably not coincidental that a comparable transformation in the direction of abstraction takes place in science. It is also instructive to note how this transition was achieved in painting. Cézanne is considered by many art historians to be the father of modern art: although, in his landscapes, such as *Mountains in Provence*, he holds fast to the figurative, mimetic tradition, it appears that his attention was shifted to the arrangement of forms and color on flat surfaces. As, for example, Picasso's portrait of Ambroise Vollard demonstrates, the cubists, too, hold to the representation of visible reality, but they thereby also replace the closed, singular, and fixated perspective, which has its origin in Renaissance art, with a multiplicity of perspectives. In this way, a multidimensional space is created: "In a Cubist picture, the conclusion and the connections are given. They are its content. The spectator has to find his place *within* this content whilst the complexity of the forms and the 'discontinuity' of the space remind him that his view from that place is bound to be only partial" (Berger, 1969, 25). For this reason, cubism provides a good illustration of the decentering of the subject.

The breakthrough to pure abstraction occurs with artists such as Kandinsky, Malevich, and Mondrian. In this abstract art it is no longer a physical but a logical space that is expressed: this art thereby becomes a symbol of the modern experience of reality. Finally, the mimetic dimension of painting is abandoned in favor of a formal approach to aesthetics. With Kandinsky this approach is still strongly connected to his expressive intentions. However, with Malevich this is much less the case, and, in the strict, almost mathematical work of Mondrian this last piece of traditional art appears to have completely disappeared (figure 7).[9] In contradiction to tradition modern art appears not to be concerned with portraying reality or expressing the artist's emotional state, but rather is aimed at the formal relations between the colors, lines, and areas that comprise the hidden architecture of the painting. The emancipation of the aesthetic domain is connected here with a purification of all nonpainterly criteria. The formalization of the aesthetic image also leads to the universalization of art in the sense that the engagement with the here and now that was characteristic of figurative art is abandoned in favor of a search for universal aesthetic principles. This universalization also appears from the fact that modern art cannot so easily be divided up into regional schools: the development of abstract act can justifiably be called an international development.

According to Gablik, in contrast to the central perspective that is bound to concrete objects, modern abstract art has unlimited possibilities. Art has become research in the possible relations between a restricted number of elements in an infinite logical space. For this reason, many modern artists construct their works in series whereby, as in scientific research, experiments can be carried out with the variables. Artists can also make use of high-value technological resources from computers to lasers: the Russian Constructivist adage that the artist must become an engineer has become literally true in many cases. The artist conceptualizes the work of art and its concrete achievement is frequently given over to technical firms and factories. The spiritualization of art appears to have reached a temporary zenith in conceptual art. In this art, the work of art combines with its conceptualization, while its material realization is often left behind.

Although extensively argued and illustrated, Gablik's thesis of artistic progress is undoubtedly a hazardous undertaking. In contrast to the nineteenth century, with its characteristic belief in progress, to postulate progress today, especially artistic progress, meets with little support from contemporary philosophy. I must immediately add that Gablik, in contrast to the nineteenth-century followers of the optimistic belief in progress, adds important nuances to her thesis. In the first place, Gablik argues that her reconstruction is merely one possible interpretation of an extremely complex process (Gablik, 1976, 12). She postulates that the representation of space, to the extent that this can be referred to as aesthetically relevant, is merely one aspect of the aesthetic domain. If her thesis that progress is observable with respect to this

FIGURE 7

Composition with Red, Blue, and Yellow, Piet Mondrian, 1930, oil on canvas, 20 × 20 in. Collection of Mr. and Mrs. Anmand P. Bartos, New York.

aspect is true, then, according to her, this does not have to mean that art as a whole has made progress (Gablik, 1976, 9).[10] We could add to this that it is sensible to make a distinction between a descriptive claim, wherein it is postulated that this or that change follows a particular pattern, and an evaluative claim whereby a particular evaluation of that developmental pattern is attached to it (cf. Van Haaften and Korthals, 1997, 13–29). With this condition in mind, the claim that a descriptive development of the representation of space can be reconstructed in the history of art, a representation characterized by increasing differentiation, distancing, formalizing, and universalizing, appears to me to be defensible. And, in a certain sense, we can also speak of an increasingly greater aesthetic control of pictorial "space".[11] The evaluative question as to whether this development can be called progress in any normative sense is temporarily left open in this context.

2.3 STELLA AND THE COMPLETION OF MODERN ART

Gablik's model of aesthetic development forms a fruitful interpretative context for understanding the development of abstract art in the twentieth century. Specific, at first sight difficult to specify characteristics of this development receive meaning from the model. I want to illustrate this by reference to an early work of a representative "member" of abstract modernism, namely, the painter Frank Stella. Under the influence of his teacher Patrick Morgan during his education in the Phillips Academy, Andover (1950–54), Stella, born in the United States in 1936, rapidly became enamored of the modern abstract tradition. In 1954, the year in which he went to Princeton University to study painting and art history, he became acquainted with the style of what was then the Establishment: the abstract impressionism of, among others, Jackson Pollock and Willem de Kooning. For a long time, Stella painted in the style of these abstract impressionists, but, according to his own testimony, he did not feel completely at home with the style. When, in 1958, he moved to New York, then the mecca of modernism, he became acquainted with the contemporaneous most recent developments. Painters such as Jasper Johns, caught up in the "pathos of purity," abandoned the expressionist side of abstract expressionism and committed themselves to a more radical abstraction. Within several years Stella had become the most important representative of this movement.

Increasingly, he became a more emphatic opponent of abstract expressionism, a style that, according to him, remained too strongly under the influence of the figurative and the Romantic idea that a painting is a mirror of the artist's soul. Stella himself took up the development of abstract art that started with Mondrian. After he had established himself in New York his work quickly fell under the spotlight of art criticism. Most especially with his *Black Paintings,* comprising black tracks whereby the light background of the canvass gave a pattern of white lines, he gained broad and enthusiastic attention. He developed the possibilities of this form of abstraction yet further in a series of twenty-three geometric paintings: this working with series, which makes it possible, through minimal yet systematic changes, to investigate the effect of the black tracks, is characteristic for Stella's early work. He works emphatically with flat surfaces and avoids every form of spatial illusion; the lack of color also removes almost all expressiveness from the work.

That, in this period, he strongly resisted every temptation to figurative expression, spatial illusion, and the expression of inner feelings is also clear from his famous announcement about his work in the 1960s: "What you see is what you see." Nothing less, and certainly nothing more. One critic, not without reason, called this early work *minimalist*; it appears that Stella wanted to investigate how much one could remove from traditional painting without ceasing to be a painter.[12]

In a subsequent series Stella elaborated further on the idea of the *Black Paintings*. When painting the black tracks, portions of the canvass remained unused: if they remained unused, then they would disturb the composition. Stella decided to simply cut them off. In this way he arrived at his so-called *Shaped Canvass* paintings (see figure 8). Cutting away parts of the canvass removed Stella yet further from traditional painting wherein the square canvass emphasizes, as it were, that one is here concerned with a "window on the world." After the *Shaped Canvass* series he developed this starting point yet further in a large number of other series. What remains characteristic is the modernist exploration of the flat, nonillusionist surfaces. In 1970, at the age of thirty-four, Stella gave his first great retrospective exhibition in New York's Museum for Modern Art. Such a retrospective exhibition at such an early age is remarkable; it confirms the important place Stella occupies in modern art.[13] However, it appears perhaps even more of a confirmation of the triumph of modern, abstract art.

2.4 THE OTHER SIDE OF RATIONALIZATION: THE DADAIST AND SURREALIST REVOLT

We mentioned above that Gablik's reconstruction is merely one possible interpretation of the complex history of Western painting. Such an interpretation can easily lead to the over- or underillustration of certain aspects of that complex reality. The numerous realistic tendencies in twentieth-century art, such as *fauvism* and Picasso's classical period after World War I, for example, are difficult to fit into a reconstruction that conceives of the total development of painting as merely a preparation for abstract, nonfigurative art.[14] Apart from this inevitably descriptive perspectivism, the question arises as to whether or not Gablik is actually justified in her evaluation of the process of modernization.

I will elaborate on my doubts surrounding this issue by briefly examining dadaism and surrealism, two early-twentieth-century *avant-garde* movements that rebelled in a radical manner against the rationalization in modern art. The radical revolt of these movements is not

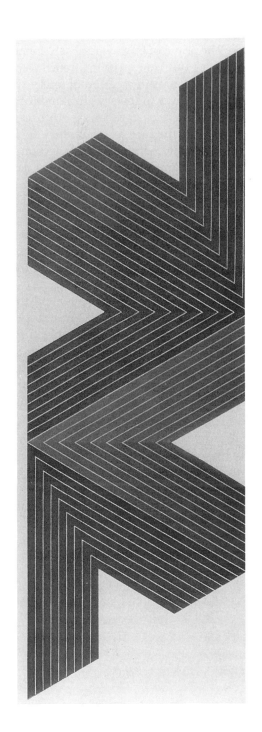

FIGURE 8

Empress of India, Frank Stella, 1965, metallic powder in polymer emulsion, 195 × 569 cm. Collection of I. Blum, Los Angeles.

really easy to comprehend if we leave the social context of their origin out of our examination. The origin of Dada was closely connected to the outbreak of World War I in 1914. This appalling trench war, which delivered more than 8 million victims in a period of four years, meant a radical break with the European bourgeois civilization's optimistic belief in progress, which had reached its brilliant apotheosis in the Belle Époque, the decades spanning the turn of the century. In 1916, in the neutrality of Switzerland, an international group of young artists including Hugo Ball, Tristan Tzara, Marcel Janco, Hans Arp, Richard Huelsenbeck, and Hans Richter, all of whom had fled from their countries to avoid being sacrificed in this senseless war, gathered in the Zurich cabaret Voltaire. The dadaist manifestations that were organized in this cabaret, and that consisted of an amazing blend of provocative jokes, exhibitions, theater, simultaneous declamations of poetry and manifestos, incomprehensible music, and slanging matches and provocations of the public, were above everything else an expression of the bankruptcy of the optimistic belief in progress and the unconditional belief in the instrumental rationality of Western civilization.[15] "The Renaissance," as Hans Arp expresses it, "taught people the arrogant glorification of Reason. The modern period, with its science and technology, drove people to delusions of grandeur. The confusion of our time springs from this over-estimation of Reason" (quoted in Richter, 1964, 55). The dadaist complaint against the type of rationality that had led to the unheard of slaughters of the First World War possessed a radicalism that bordered on what Nietzsche had described as passive nihilism (cf. 1.7 above). In the Dadaist Cannibal Manifesto from 1920 Francis Picabia[16] screamed:

You are all indicted; stand up!
Stand up as with the Marseillaise
Stand as with the Russian National Anthem
Stand as with God Save the King
Stand with the raising of the flag . . .
Shit, shit imagines the world as French fries,
and all of you who are serious, you stink worse than cow shit.
DADA stinks of nothing, it is nothing, nothing nothing.
It is just as your expectations: nothing.
as your paradises: nothing
as your idols: nothing
as your politicians: nothing
as your heroes: nothing
as your artists: nothing
as your religions: nothing

That which above all other things it had to pay for was the rationality of bourgeois civilization. The nihilistic streak of the dadaist critique did not only arise from the horrors of World War I, but, more especially, from the circumstance that the dadaists did not consider these horrors to be a more or less coincidental result of the rationalization of culture, but rather as its inevitable consequence.[17] Thus, Tzara wrote in his 1918 manifesto: "Logic is a complication. Logic is always false. It draws the superficial threads of concepts and words towards illusory conclusions and centres. Its chains kill, an enormous myriapod that asphyxiates independence" (Tzara, 1977, 11). For this reason, Dada is for the "abolition of logic, dance of those who are incapable of creation" (Tzara, 1977, 13).

Dada accuses traditional art with having entered into an especially one-sided agreement with this logic. In this line, Arp wrote in the catalogue from an exhibition in 1915: "The illusionist works of Greek and Renaissance artists have led to an overestimation of the human species, to a separation from nature and mutual recriminations." That which has thereby been lost is "the feeling for a communal reality, for a mystique, for undefined indefiniteness, for the deepest finitude."[18] Art that enters into an agreement with logic is, according to Tzara, perverse art: "If it were married to logic, art would be living in incest, engulfing, swallowing its own tail, which still belongs to its body, fornicating in itself, and temperament would become a nightmare . . . " (Tzara, 1977,11). With regard to such a lecherous art, Dada was unconditionally *anti*-art.

Although, perhaps, the nihilistic tone of the criticism suggests something else, Dada's effort was not exclusively directed at demolition. By liberating life from the dominion of rationality, Dada hoped to make possible another understanding of the world. In a communal manifesto in 1918, the dadaists postulated: "The word Dada symbolizes the most primitive relationship with encircling reality: with dadaism, a new reality demands its right of existence. Life manifests itself as a singular tangle of sounds, colours, and spiritual rhythms which in dadaist art, in a determined manner, with all possible effervescent and feverish sensations of its audacious, everyday psyche and in the totality of it brutal reality, is taken over. This is where the sharp dividing line occurs which separates dadaism from every other current in art" (in: Drijkoningen and Fontijn, 1986, 180). This quotation makes clear that Dada was not against art as such, but rather was radically against every form of autonomous art, against *L'art pour l'art*. Just as Nietzsche had done before them, the dadaists postulated art in service of life. And their accusation against modern autonomous art is that it is precisely from its forms that life ebbs away. In his 1920 "portrait" of Cézanne, which consists of a plank with a stuffed ape nailed to it, Picabia represented this criticism in a particularly apt manner (cf. Rubin, 1968, 11).

The dadaists used numerous methods to arrive at their radical transformation of life; they hoped that those methods would enable them to free themselves from logic's domination and further enable them to discover a "senseless order" (*ordre déraisonnable*). In this way, they sought their salvation in the Dionysian dimension that had been excluded by Reason, in the instinctual, the unconscious, the dream, intoxication, chance, the art of "primitives" and children.

While, in the case of Dada, these positive researches into the "other" of Reason remained somewhat in the margins of the nihilist resistance to the established order, in the surrealist movement, which originated in the lap of the Parisian citadel of Dada, these researches, under the leadership of the surrealist pope, André Breton, came to occupy a central place. In 1924 Breton's first Manifesto appeared, and the magazine *La Révolution Surréaliste* and the Bureau for Surrealist Research were founded. A large number of poets and artists, such as Antonin Artaud, André Masson, Pierre Naville, Louis Aragon, Paul Eluard, Hans Arp, Max Ernst, Yves Tanguy, Juan Miró, Salvador Dali, and René Magritte joined the movement. In the 1924 Manifesto Breton defined surrealism as follows:

> SURREALISM, n. Psychic automatism in its pure state, by which one proposes to express—verbally, by means of the written word, or in any other manner—the actual function of thought. Dictated by thought, in the absence of any control exercised by reason, exempt from aesthetic or moral concern.
> ENCYCL. *Philosophy.* Surrealism is based on the belief in the superior reality of certain forms of previously neglected associations, in the omnipotence of dreams, in the disinterested play of thought. It tends to ruin once and for all other psychic mechanisms and to substitute itself for them in solving all the principal problems of life. (Breton, 1977, 26)[19]

In this definition it is clear that the surrealists wished to aesthetically transform life. In one of the numerous political manifestos Breton stated: " 'Transform the world,' Marx said; 'change life,' Rimbaud said. These two watchwords are one for us" (Breton, 1977, 241).[20] For the surrealists, the transformation of life consisted above all other things in the abolition of the distinction, caused by the process of rationalization, between dream and reality, poetry and desire, art and life, individual and group, subject and object. In order to achieve this, the surrealists experimented with a variety of techniques such as the application of chance

operations,[21] explanations of dreams, excessive usage of drugs, black
humor, erotic escapades, spiritual seances, and artistic techniques such
as automatic writing and painting (i.e., the artistic variant on free association in psychoanalysis whereby the artist writes or paints everything
that comes into her mind), the collage (whereby the external world is literally brought into the work of art—cf. Berman, 1987, 59), and the *Ca-
davre Exquis* (whereby several painters or writers, completely independently of each other, deliver contributions to a single work of art).

Both surrealism and dadaism reach back to the ideals and aesthetics of the Romantic project (in this respect, see, among others,
Alquié, 1969, 47, and Waldberg, 1972, 25). By utilizing the techniques
specified above, the surrealists hope to repair the unity of "love, poetry
and liberty" (*l'amour, poésie, liberté*) that had been broken by rationalization. The absolute surreality the surrealists strived for was not understood by them as a transcendental world, but rather as a completely immanent reality that could be reached in the here and now: the surrealist
hope is not directed at a representation of this unity but at its immediate presentation.[22] In order to achieve this, the aesthetic, noninstrumental interaction with nature has to be liberated from the domain of autonomous art and utilized in everyday practice (Bürger, 1974, 44).
Surrealism shares the hope for a better life with modern tradition, but
in order to realize this hope both surrealism and dadaism abandon the
idea of modern autonomy (Berman, 1987, 62). The relation of surrealism
to the Romantic project reaches out to the insight of the fundamental unachievability of Romantic desire.

This tragic insight is primarily expressed in the nihilistic practice
and the merciless irony of dadaism. Picabia ended the Dadaist Cannibal Manifesto, quoted above, with the words: "Whistle at me, scream
and punch me in the mouth, and then, and then? I continue to tell you
that you are all nitwits. In a few months my friends and I will sell you
our paintings for a few francs" (Picabia, 1986, 187). The dadaists were
always aware of the fundamental finitude of their struggle. Thus, Hugo
Ball maintained: "Dada is direct like nature. Dada is for infinite sense
and definite means" (quoted in Ades, 1974, 16).

But in the case of the surrealists, too, in whose case the determined
hope of nihilism appears to win, the Romantic desire is constantly permeated by the consciousness of finitude and failure. In 1925 the surrealists declared: "We have coupled the word *surrealism* and the word *revolution* only to show the desinterested, detached, and even *totally
desperate character of this revolution*" (Breton, 1978, 317). After the brief
magic of intoxication, as the surrealists experienced like Nietzsche's

Dionysian man, everyday reality once again surrounds the poet and appears to banish the surrealist hope forever (cf. 1.6 above). We do not find this melancholic surrealist hope better expressed than in De Chirico's *Melancholy and the Mystery of the Street* (figure 9; cf. Alquié, 1969, 121). And Breton, not without irony, wrote in the first Surrealist Manifesto: "May you only take the trouble to *practice* poetry. . . . It matters not whether there is a certain disproportion between this defense and the illustration that will follow it. . . . Besides, one is never sure of really being there. . . . Be that as it may, the fact is that the way to these regions is clearly marked, and that to attain the true goal is now merely a matter of the travelers' ability to endure" (Breton, 1977, 18–19).

Many surrealist travelers, like Gudmundsson's traveler whom we met in the previous chapter (2.7, see figure 3), did not derive sufficient hope and stamina from the arrow that pointed to the surrealist regions: for a not insubstantial number of these travelers, their journey ended in humiliating suicide or the Dionysian region of madness. Nonetheless, and the grandeur of the surrealists is in this point very much in evidence, the fear of madness did not prevent them from raising "the flag of the imagination" (Breton, 1977, 6). It is perhaps true that we must agree with Peter Bürger's conclusion that the avant-garde attempt to integrate life and art did not occur (Bürger, 1974, 72), but we must not hereby ignore the heroism with which the surrealists entered into the struggle against the most monumental insanity in which instrumental reason had drowned Europe. There are times when madness is so great that the idea of humanity can only survive in yet another form of madness.

2.5 RATIONALIZATION AND MODERNISM IN FRANKFURT

Whoever agrees with the radical critique that the dadaist and surrealist avant-garde directed at modernism would perhaps be tempted to speak of the bankruptcy of the modern striving toward autonomous, abstract art. However, in such a case the question arises as to whether or not the baby is being thrown out together with the modernist bathwater. I will clarify this point by reference to a brief exposition concerning the ideas relating to modern, autonomous art of the major members of the Frankfurt School.

While the radical engagement of the dadaists and surrealists arose from their experiences of the horrors of World War I, the engagement of the Frankfurt School can not be separated from the horrors of World

FIGURE 9

Mystery and Melancholy of a Street, Giorgio de Chirico, 1914, oil on canvas, 85 × 66.7 cm. Resor Collection, New Canaan, Connecticut.

War II. This war, associated as it is with a morbid genocide, has terminally injured the remaining elements of the Enlightenment belief in progress. The indelible memories of this war have ensured that the optimism that most of the Frankfurt School continued to cherish toward the possibility of a better society has never been free of skepticism and, not infrequently, clearly pessimistic undertones.

This ambiguity especially becomes clear in the aesthetic theories of the Frankfurt School: on the one hand, in agreement with Romantic ideas and also those of German Idealism, art is accredited with the capacity to effect a reconciliation between freedom and nature, but, on the other hand, modern art is also regarded as an expression of the irreconcilable nonidentity of freedom and nature. I will elaborate somewhat on this ambivalent relationship by reference to the work of Adorno and Benjamin. Against the background of Adorno's book *Dialectic of Enlightment*, which he wrote together with Horkheimer, I will sketch the key elements of his theory of aesthetics. Subsequently, I will indicate the differences of opinion between Adorno and Benjamin with regard to their different evaluations of surrealism. Finally, I will examine Habermas' theory of aesthetics more closely; he is without doubt the most important member of the second generation from the Frankfurt School, and, in the recent modernism-postmodernism debate has shown himself to be a subtle defender of modernism and has thereby attempted to reconcile the opinions of Adorno and Benjamin.[23]

The *Dialectic of Enlightment*, published in Amsterdam in 1947, initially generated little attention. This is perhaps not so surprising when we consider that the book, which firmly attacked thinking in terms of economic and technical interests, appeared in the first years of the economic recovery following World War II. As the title already indicates, the work is concerned with the ambiguity of the Enlightenment. The Enlightenment, pregnantly defined by Kant as "man's release from his self-incurred tutelage" (Kant, 1959, 85), was described by Max Weber as a "disenchantment" (*Entzauberung*) of the world. According to Weber, the rationalization of modern society means the definitive settling of accounts with the mythical ideas of the past. In contrast to this, Adorno and Horkheimer postulate that the Enlightenment's belief in progress can also be conceived of as myth. They argue that at the basis of the Enlightenment's program of control there lies a secularized version of the religious myth that the world is administered by gods. In the Enlightenment, it is not god but man who is allocated this task. "Myth turns into enlightenment, and nature into mere objectivity" (Horkheimer and Adorno, 1973, 9).

The instrumental, goal-rational thinking that is developed hereby, facilitates a measure of control of nature of which the myth could only dream.[24] In agreement with the ideas of Piaget and Gablik, Adorno and

Horkheimer postulate that the division between subject and object creates the (material and spiritual) distance that is necessary for the control of the object by the subject. According to Adorno and Horkheimer, man pays for this increase in power with estrangement from that over which he exerts control. In distancing himself from nature, the latter is degraded to the inferior other that stands against the human subject and that one can dispose of according to personal choice. Marx, too, is placed in the Enlightenment tradition because he considered labor, understood as the transformation of nature, to be the characteristic instrument of human self-realization. This development, however, also refers to the human himself: nature in the human, too, is objectivized and made into an object of the exercise of power (Horkheimer and Adorno, 1973, 28).[25] The rationalization of modern society leads in this manner to a fundamental 'thingification': "Animism gave souls to things, and industry made things out of souls."[26]

Other than Weber, who wrote of the process of rationalization with a certain resignation, Horkheimer and Adorno radically take a position against this process and the central position accorded to man. However, other than the avant-gardists (and, for example, a Frankfurt School member such as Marcuse), they reject out of hand a total reconciliation of mankind and nature as a possible alternative because, according to them, such a reconciliation—assuming that it would be possible—would merely mean a regression (cf. Horkheimer and Adorno, 1973, 254–55). Also, they reject a glorification of nature, such as we encounter with many Romantics and the dadaists, as being a dangerous reactionary tendency. Against this, Horkheimer and Adorno emphasize the fundamental *nonidentity* of subject and object.

This view of the fundamental nonidentity of subject and object plays a central role in Adorno's theory of aesthetics. Unlike Benjamin and Marcuse, who are far closer to the enthusiasm of the Romantic tradition on this point, Adorno does not ascribe the messianic capacity for reconciliation to art. It is true that Adorno maintains the idea that works of art form the last refuge for the human desire for another existence, but with the creation of the work of art this desire is not really realized. For Adorno, art forms, in the quotation from Stendhal that he also uses, "une promesse de bonheur," a *promise* of future beatitude.[27] "Since art became autonomous," wrote Horkheimer in 1941, "it has guarded the utopia which had disappeared from religion" (Horkheimer, 1988, 421). In this sense it can be postulated that the claims that art made that it goes beyond the present world are simultaneously true and false: it is not the promise of art that is false, but rather the ideology that maintains that reality, in one way or another, already corresponds with this promise.

According to Adorno, the utopian social reconciliation is embodied by the harmonious reconciliation of form and content, function and expression, and by the subjective and objective elements in the work of art. In order to ensure that the appearance of harmony does not deceive, Adorno finds that the work of art must always contain a moment of protest by a pure and uncompromising embodiment in its innermost structure of the internal contradictions of society. At such a moment, art ceases to be purely ideological (Adorno, 1955, 27).[28] The reflection of objective reality in its complete horror elevates art to a weapon of protest in the name of the idea of humanity.

For Adorno, however, the problem with contemporary culture (and with this point he finds Marcuse on his side) is that the critical moment of art in the cultural industry is increasingly eliminated in favor of a purely affirmative culture.[29] Art is hereby elevated to a false appearance that can perhaps provide a temporary feeling of emancipation and make everyday life somewhat more bearable but that does this without attempting to achieve any real change. In order to remove itself from such an affirmative culture the only route available to art is to radically refuse to express any form of harmony. Adorno has presented this argument in its most urgent form in his studies in the philosophy of music. According to Adorno, modern music, which is absorbed in the cultural industry, threatens to completely lose its autonomy because it has been degraded into little more than something to be consumed (*muzak*). Adorno is of the opinion that the twelve-tone compositions of Schönberg, his music teacher, should be understood as a radical refusal to enter into a compromise with the unresolved dissonances of contemporary society: in this technique the realization of a false harmony is made impossible because the development of the tonal material is determined by the preceding choice for a particular order of succession for the twelve tones.[30] By retreating in this manner into the autonomous logic of music, Adorno finds that Schönberg managed to withdraw himself from affirmative culture.

Although Adorno comprehends that the autonomy of art is a product of the process of rationalization that he resists, he nonetheless defends this autonomy. Only by withdrawing into its autonomy can art protect its artistic appearance (conceived as a reflection of the truth). It is therefore not surprising that one of his last works, *Aesthetic Theory* (1970), is aimed at "saving the appearance" of autonomous works of art (Adorno, 1970, 164). On the basis of this starting point, Adorno has always expressed exceptional criticism concerning the avant-garde attempt to demolish the dividing line between art and life: he is of the opinion that the "rebellion against appearance," such as it is expressed in surrealism, for example, can only lead to a regression to "sheer objectivation" and "barbaric straightness" (*blosse Dinghaftigkeit* and *barbarische Buchstäblichkeit*) (Adorno, 1970, 157–58).

The price that must be paid for saving the appearance is not, however, particularly small. In the first place, artistic autonomy implies that the truth of the work of art is neutralized (Adorno, 1970, 339). Safely locked away in the Pantheon of culture, the truth-stature of even the most uncompromising art is damaged.[31] Moreover, uncompromising, autonomous art (the music of Schönberg is a good example here), in contrast to the art of classical tradition, is completely inaccessible for the broad public (a characteristic, incidentally, that is equally relevant to the uncompromising writings of Adorno himself). "The authentic works of art of recent times," as Horkheimer expresses it, "abandon the illusion of a real communality amongst people; they form monuments of a lonely and despairing life which finds no bridges to the Other or even to its own consciousness. . . . The work of art is the only adequate objectivization of the desolation and despair of the individual" (Horkheimer, 1988, 425). It is as equally true for the music of the great refusal as for the critical philosopher that the protection of a notion of humanity is ultimately an exceptionally impotent gesture in the middle of an ubiquitous affirmative culture. The death of art, announced by Hegel (cf. 1.8), appears more properly with the "aesthetics of silence" to take on the stature of a suicide (cf. Vattimo, 1988, 56). For this reason, in relation to uncompromising contemporary art, the pessimistic remarks concerning their own work that Horkheimer and Adorno make in the last pages of the *Dialectic of Enlightment* are applicable: "If there is anyone today to whom we can pass the responsibility for the message, we bequeath it not to the masses. And not to the individual (who is powerless), but to an imaginary witness—lest it perish with us" (Horkheimer and Adorno, 1973, 256).

As I have already remarked above, Benjamin's aesthetics, in comparison with that of Adorno, shows more agreement with the Romantic hope for a reconciliation through art. Benjamin's positive evaluation of the surrealist "rebellion against appearance" undoubtedly arises from this hope (cf. Benjamin, 1977, and Habermas, 1978, 48 ff.). The surrealist attempts to liberate the noninstrumental intercourse with nature, such as is realized in works of art, from the reservation of autonomous art and to bring it into the service of life is welcomed by Benjamin.

According to him, surrealist techniques such as automatic writing can be understood as an attempt to breach the instrumentalist use of Reason. Although, at first sight, automatism means a denial of the subjective Will, it is ultimately directed at superseding the self-denial of the subject. In his mimetic theory of language Benjamin has tried to provide a theoretical underpinning for such a noninstrumentalist use of language by interpreting it as the privileged medium of the reconciliation between humans and nature (see Jay, 1987, 8).[32]

Benjamin postulates that while surrealism has not perhaps realized the ultimate abolition of the division between art and life it has nonetheless achieved a revolutionizing of art that has enabled it to partially make a break with affirmative culture. In this connection he points to the collage and montage techniques of avant-garde artists such as Marx Ernst and John Heartfield. Collage and montage disrupts the illusionism of classical art without abandoning the mimetic character of art. Through this destruction of the *aura* that placed traditional art beyond everyday life, thereby making it an object of illusory satisfaction, a connection was made between artistic and everyday experience (Ulmer, 1983, 84 ff., and Bürger, 1974, 98 ff.). For Benjamin, that which especially makes avant-garde collage and montage into means of revolutionary expression is the shock effect that they generate. This shock disrupts the traditional aesthetic pleasure that gives the observer a feeling of liberation without actually changing the real situation, and, according to Benjamin, it prompts a real change in his practice of living.[33] The rise of the film, an art form that is strongly based upon the principle of montage, was accordingly celebrated by Benjamin by reference to the revolutionary works of Eisenstein.[34] Unlike Adorno, Benjamin refuses to make a fundamental distinction between true-to-reality "higher" art and the "lower" art that is produced by the amusement industry, and he initially ascribed revolutionary effects to mass art.

While, according to Keulartz, Adorno's rigid distinction between high and low art leads to an anti-avant-gardist position and a certain defeatism (Habermas tellingly refers to Adorno's "strategy of hibernation"—Habermas, 1978, 66), he argues that the strong relativism of this distinction in Benjamin's work threatens to result in a naive technological optimism that ignores the fact that even the most revolutionary art can unproblematically receive a place in the "monetary-bureaucratic complex" of the cultural industry (Keulartz, 1986, 32). This accusation does not appear to me to be completely acceptable; after all, in *Das Kunstwerk im Zeitalter seiner technischen Reproduzierbarkeit* Benjamin already points to the danger of a false abandonment of art's autonomy. According to Benjamin, in German and Italian fascism this false abandonment of art led to an "aestheticization of politics" instead of the "politicization of aesthetics" that he propagated (cf. also Benjamin, 1977, 303). However, introducing nuances such as this also do not remove the fact that Adorno's and Benjamin's judgment of avant-garde art are borne by a contrary vision of art's reconciliatory potential.

Although reflections about art occupy a less prominent place in the work of Habermas than that of Adorno and Benjamin, he did concern himself with the question of art's autonomy in various places in his work. It is remarkable that in this concern Habermas appears to attempt to reconcile the views of Adorno and Benjamin. In *Strukturwandel der Öffentlichkeit* (1962) he maintains a rather critical attitude in relation to autonomous art (cf. Keulartz, 1986, 13 ff.). In this book Habermas investigates the division, originating during the Enlightenment, between the private and public spheres: he maintained that the public sphere was grasped by the bourgeoisie in order to initiate a public discussion concerning the rules of economic exchange and social labor. In this public discussion it was not the relations of power of the participants that were relevant, as was the case in feudal society, but rather the relations of effect of the strongest arguments. According to Habermas, art played a key role in this process: a first form of the "communicative community," which in his later theory of communicative action he attempted to underpin, originated in the literary salons (see Habermas 1984 and 1987).

The foregoing already makes clear that Habermas assessed the Enlightenment far more positively than Horkheimer and Adorno. Apart from the "non-compulsory compulsion of the best argument," the fact that, in principle, everybody had access to the discussion was characteristic for the public nature of this literary activity. According to Habermas, this accessibility first declined with the transition from competitive to monopoly capitalism: a strict distinction between a minority of artists and the great mass of cultural consumers emerges. Art becomes autonomous for the first time in this process, separating itself from the engagement and the realism that it had possessed during the Enlightenment. Habermas views this process with reserve: "Other than is the case with Horkheimer and Adorno, Habermas views the autonomization of art with great scepticism, namely, as a process during which the communicative relationships between producer and recipient, relationships which were characterized during the Enlightenment by parity and universality, become increasingly disturbed" (Keulartz, 1986, 21).

However, in *Problems of Legitimation in Late Capitalism* (1973), under the influence of Adorno, Habermas adopts a substantially more positive attitude with respect to art's autonomy:

> Only autonomous bourgeois art has taken a position in favour of the victims of bourgeois rationalization. Bourgeois art has become the refuge for the satisfaction, even if this is only virtual, of the needs which were illegal in the material processes of life within bourgeois society. I mean here the desire to enter into a mimetic relationship with nature; the need to live in solidarity outside the group-egoism of the family; the desire for the happiness of a communicative experience which is free from the imperative of teleological rationality. . . . For these reasons, art and aesthetics (from Schiller to Marcuse), together with moral universalism, form explosive components of bourgeois ideology. (Habermas, 1973, 110)

Habermas realized, however, that avant-garde art has undermined the aura of bourgeois art and thereby also the illusion of artistic autonomy. Agreeing with Benjamin's analysis of "post-auratic" art, Habermas postulated that: "Surrealism marks the historic moment wherein modern art breaks the shell of the no-longer illusory appearance in order that it [might] exist unsublimated in life" (*ibid.*, 120). But, unlike Benjamin, he sees this as an ambivalent and thus not purely positive development. Giving up the artistic claim to autonomy, warns Habermas in agreement with Adorno's critique of mass culture, "can just as easily lead to a degeneration of art into a propagandist mass art or a commercial mass culture as into a subversive counter-culture" (*ibid.*, 120). Because, on the basis of a more positive interpretation of the Enlightenment, Habermas does not fall into Adorno's pessimistic rejection of every hope for reconciliation through art, he does not *a priori* exclude the *possibility* of a secular reconciliation of humans and nature through art (cf. Jay, 1985, 4).

In a speech with the title "Modernity: An Unfinished Project," given in 1980 on the occasion of his receiving the Adorno Prize from the city of Frankfurt, Habermas once again adopts the considerations specified above. In the speech, he once again defends the modern process of rationalization:

> The project of modernity as it was formulated by the philosophers of the Enlightenment in the eighteenth century consists in the relentless development of the objectivating sciences, of the universal foundations of morality and law, and of autonomous art, all in accord with their own immanent logic. But at the same time it also results in releasing the cognitive potentials accumulated in the process from their

esoteric high forms and attempting to apply them in the sphere of praxis, that is, to encourage the rational organization of social relations. (Habermas, 1996, 45)

Habermas acknowledges, however, that this rationalization has a price: "What the cultural sphere gains through specialized treatment and reflection does not *automatically* come into the possession of everyday practice without more ado. For with cultural rationalization, the lifeworld, once its traditional substance has been devalued, threatens rather to become *impoverished*" (Habermas, 1996, 45). For this reason Habermas, along with Benjamin, pleads for the use of aesthetic experience in giving form to the practices of life. What this aesthetic experience presents us with in this form-giving is "a decentred subjectivity which is released from the constraints of knowledge and acting" (Habermas, 1996, 48). But, other than Benjamin, Habermas can still feel no appreciation for the surrealist abolition of autonomous art. The problem is that surrealism renounces art without really shaking it off:

> All attempts to bridge the disjunction between art and life, fiction and praxis, illusion and reality, and to eliminate the distinction between artistic product and objects of utility, between premediated configuration and spontaneous impulse, the attempt to declare everything art and everyone an artist; to abolish all criteria and to equate aesthetic judgements with the expression of subjective experience: all these undertakings, well analysed as they have been, can be seen today as nonsense experiments. They only succeed, against their own intention, in illuminating even more sharply the very structures of art which they had intended to violate: the medium of semblance, the autonomous transcendence of the work, the concentrated and premediated character of artistic production, as well as the cognitive status of the judgement of taste. (Habermas, 1996, 49)

According to Habermas, in the case of the surrealist rebellion, one can speak of a *false dissolution of art*. According to him, the surrealists have achieved no integration between the different areas that have appeared in the process of rationalization, but rather have merely replaced one one-sidedness and abstraction by another. By aestheticizing all of reality (and also, for example, politics), one totalitarian pretension has merely been replaced by another.

What Habermas offers as an alternative for this false dissolution of art is an *integration* of the different spheres within the lifeworld: "In the communicative practice of everyday life, cognitive interpretations, moral expectations, expressions and evaluations must interpenetrate one another. The processes of reaching understanding which transpire in the lifeworld require the recources of an inherited culture *in its entire range*" (Habermas, 1996, 49). Only then, according to him, we will be able to "succesfully preserve something of the original intentions of the doomed surrealist rebellion, and more of Brecht's and even Benjamin's, experimental reflections on the reception of non-auratic works of art" (Habermas, 1996, 54).

A question that self-evidently demands attention is whether Habermas' proposed integration of art into everyday communicative practice offers more perspective than the "false dissolution of art" of surrealism.[35] There are different reasons for doubting this (cf. Jay, 1985, 8 ff.). In the first place, Habermas, in his speech, appears to misunderstand that the spheres of science, morality, and art in no way have been developed equally. The reason for the dadaist and surrealist revolt, as we saw in the preceding remarks, was precisely the one-sided dominance of *instrumental* rationality, a dominance that, since the beginning of this century, has rather increased than decreased. Moreover, in contrast to practical and aesthetic rationality, instrumental rationality in its totality appears not to strive for an integration with the life world, but rather to subordinate everything else to its authority. For this reason Kunneman has justifiably remarked that Habermas illegitimately considers the life world as an asylum of "non-blocked, symmetric communication," while it could be argued with Foucault, for example, that in this area, too, the instrumental working of power is unavoidable (Kunneman, 1986, 301).

These considerations make it clear that it is not really realistic to assume that the specified three spheres in the communicative lifeworld simply will or even can be integrated. In addition, in the process of rationalization the (re-)integration of the separate spheres do not relate in any balanced manner with the continuing differentiation. Modern society continues to disintegrate into fragments that can no longer be integrated. The question is whether this process, which is probably one of the primary reasons for the failure of the surrealist revolt, does not also equally foredoom Habermas' proposed communicative integration to failure. An indication for this appears to me to be that the integration of the aesthetic dimension is already problematic at the level of Habermas' *theory* of communicative action. Following Kantian aesthetics, he emphasizes the subjective character of aesthetic experience to such an extent that he *a priori* excludes the possibility of a symmetric discussion concerning these experiences and only leaves sufficient space for an asymmetric aesthetic critique (Habermas, 1984; cf. Keulartz, 1986, 11 ff.).

At a more fundamental level we can ask ourselves if Habermas ultimately, in his theory of communicative action, does not himself continue to maintain the same concept of totality which he correctly criticizes in Hegel and surrealism (see 0.5 above). From the first step, a
defence of his position would have to clarify where his proposed communicative integration precisely distinguishes itself from the integration that the avant-gardists propose. In this context, one would not be
able to avoid a serious debate concerning the postmodern critique of totalitarian thinking as such. Finally, one would also not be able to avoid
the developments that have taken place in the arts in the preceding
decades, developments to which Stella, too, has contributed.

2.6   STELLA   AS   POSTMODERNIST

In the foregoing discussion of the retrospective of Stella's work, organized in 1970, I remarked that his earlier work could be considered as a
completion of modernism. It should be self-evident that I did not mean
that the history of painting was brought to an end with that work. On
the contrary: painting since 1970, which is often referred to with the
term 'postmodern,' has blossomed enormously. I remarked in the introduction that this term cannot be easily and simply defined, a problem
that refers not only to the term in general but also to its more restricted
use with reference to a particular domain such as recent painting. The
Dutch art historian Martis has made an interesting attempt to define
postmodernism in painting. Mindful of the reactive character of the
term, he begins with a summary of what postmodern art is *not:* "Postmodernism is . . . anti-Greenberg, or anti-purist, anti-formalist, anti-
dogmatic, anti-minimalist, anti-clean, anti-cool, anti-surface" (Martis,
1986, 244). In this list we recognize the strong aversion to all those characteristics that are definitive for modern, abstract painting. The positive
attributes that Martis specifies form the opposites of the modernist characteristics: "Positively defined Postmodernism is: pluralistic, narrative,
autobiographical, spontaneous, irrational, decorative, figurative, based
on traditional methods, joyful, complex, electric" (*ibid.*, 244).

Because of the emphasis on the pluralistic character of postmodern painting, every attempt at constructing an inclusive definition appears to be condemned in advance to failure. A number of the specified
attributes remind us of premodern painting, others appear rather to
suggest a relationship with the avant-garde tradition. Should we
nonetheless attempt to bring postmodern painting under one rubric,

then it is, perhaps, the return to the past: while modernism appears above all other things to be a struggle against the past, postmodernism appears to be directed at a re-evaluation of the past. In this tenor, Eco remarks that "the moment comes when the avant-garde (the modern) can go no further, because it has produced a metalanguage that speaks about its impossible texts (conceptual art). The postmodern reply to the modern consists of recognition that the past, since it cannot be de-stroyed, because its recognition leads to silence, must be revisited: but with irony, not innocently" (Eco, 1983, 67). Perhaps we could also con-ceive of this return to the past as an attempt to reach an integration with it. While in modernism, as we remarked earlier, the enormous social and artistic differentiation did not occur with a simultaneous integration, postmodern painting appears to strive for precisely such an integration. This is expressed, for example, in postmodern impurity (referred to by Martis, above, as antipurist), in the break with the modernist pathos of purity. There is not only a blending of different, in modernism strictly distinguished, disciplines, but also life and art once against blend with each other, something that finds expression in the tendency toward the figurative, the autobiographical, the decorative. The postmodern striv-ing toward integration distinguishes itself from the integration pro-posed by the avant-gardes because it is no longer directed at an all-inclusive totality but, on the basis of its pluralistic starting point, it re-gards instead a colorful multiplicity of different integrations as possible.

I will illustrate this latter argument by reference to the develop-ment of Stella's work after 1970. At the end of 1987 Stella, then fifty-one years old, received a second retrospective in the New York Museum for Modern Art. (A critic wrote, not without irony, that this almost bordered upon sanctification.) This time, it concerned an overview of the period 1970–1987.[36] For anyone aware only of the earlier, sober works, these works are a complete surprise: we see gigantic constructions on the wall consisting of irregular forms that extrude from the flat surface and are painted in the most improbable colors that make us think of a fair or a discotheque that has been decorated with rather dubious taste. Apart from jubilant reviews there were also numerous critical commentaries. Some critics found that Stella's latest works were a betrayal of modern, abstract art. However, Rubin argued that there is no question of a real break, but rather that the later work flows with a certain logic from out of the earlier work (Rubin, 1987, 14).

As opposed to Rubin I think it is definitely justifiable to speak of a break, although this is actually more of an *ideological* than a stylistic na-ture. Despite the obvious differences it is clear that a certain stylistic continuity is perceivable. The ideological breach concerns Stella's break with the type of rationalization in art that I earlier referred to with the term 'pathos of purity'. In an interview that he gave in 1988 during the preparations for the Dutch version of the second exhibition in the Stedelijk Museum in Amsterdam, Stella argued that something has gone fundamentally wrong with abstract art: the potential that it appeared to possess in the euphoria of its youth has never, according to him, been fully realized. Minimalism has led to exhaustion, a decrease in expressiveness: retreating to the (flat) surface of a purely aesthetic language of form has brought painting into a vacuum.[37] Although, in this interview, Stella still refers to the new developments in his work as primarily arising from purely artistic motives—perhaps because he continues, in reflecting on that work, to express himself in a terminology derived from modernist aesthetics—I think that the about face in his work after 1970 equally originates from a realization of the shadow-side of the dominance of a one-sidedly developed rationality. It speaks volumes that the first series of paintings that he made in his second career bear the names of Polish cities wherein, during World War II, Jewish synagogues were destroyed. This does not detract from the fact that the new orientation in his work primarily achieves expression in the pictorial surface: in this sense, as was said above, there is still evidence of a certain continuity regardless of the ideological discontinuity. What Stella in fact does when he gives the figurative and expressive values from the past a place in his work is to realize an integration *within* the aesthetic domain. Just as with other critics of one-sided rationalization, it is not his intention to simply return to traditional values. He tries, as it were, to translate the old aesthetic values within the syntax and morphology of modern, abstract art so that he can thereby make an integration possible of the traditional and the modern manners of experience.

Stella's second retrospection once again consisted of a number of series. The largest series (*Circuits*) comprises sixty-eight works, the most of which are expressed in different formats and colors, while the smaller series always consist of at least ten pieces. The exhibition shows a number of canvasses from each series and thereby represents his development in abbreviated form. This view is further strengthened by the chronological structure of the exhibition.

The first post-1970 (from 1970 to 1973) series is the already mentioned *Polish Villages*, named after seventeenth-, eighteenth-, and nineteenth-century synagogues that were destroyed during World War II. This series consists of a total of more than 130 works, and its continuity with previous works is quite obvious. The form appears to be an extension of the "shaped-canvas" work, although the geometric shapes are more exuberant and they are more colorfully executed, characteristics that lend the paintings a certain asymmetry. It is interesting to note how Stella here begins to experiment with three-dimensional space: in *Odelsk* (figure 10), despite the maintenance of a two-dimensional space, a certain three-dimensional spatial characteristic emerges thanks to a T-formed surface that appears to be a shadow of the (yellow) form above it. Stella extends his working of this spatial dimension by making up to four different versions of each of the forty-two paintings from the *Polish Villages* series. In the second version, he emphasizes the spatial aspect by leaving areas unpainted, choosing instead to fill them with materials of varying thickness. In the third series, the modest relief-motif that has emerged is strengthened by constructing the surface of the paintings themselves from board so that real spatial contours are present. Stella painted the various series in different colors, and he made a fourth, unpainted version of some of the series whereby the spatial contouring was not influenced by the coloring. What is striking about the series as a whole is the use of such a variety of colors; this would seem to be an important break with the black-white canvasses from the period before 1970. Nonetheless, one can definitely note a certain stylistic continuity in these canvasses. In 1961–62 Stella began an extensive series of concentric squares; the series continued to the years during which he created *Polish Villages.* It is conspicuous that the colors in the series of concentric squares are already increasingly exuberant; this is seen quite clearly in the exhibition in a number of examples from the 1974 *Diderot* series.

In the years 1974–75 Stella made a series of *Brazilian Paintings.* Having become interested in the spatial aspects of the relief-motif he began to work with metal, mostly aluminum, in order to literally construct the surface of the painting. He took constructivism's adage to work as an engineer quite literally by employing different firms to fabricate the metal bases of the following hundreds of works according to his designs. The forms remain strongly geometric, but Stella now continues by painting the surfaces in a somewhat looser fashion. In the 1976–80 series *Exotic Birds* he goes a step further: what is striking about this series of twenty-eight works is that he now begins to use other forms. However, these cannot yet be called liberated: they are templates used in ship- and road-building to construct fluent lines. What does become increasingly liberated is the method of painting the metal panels; Stella comes close to the brush technique of abstract impressionism that he so fiercely resisted at the end of the 1950s.

FIGURE 10

Odelsk I, Frank Stella, 1981, mixed media on canvas, 228.6 × 335.3 cm. Private collection.

In 1977, at the invitation of the Sarabhais' Foundation, Stella stayed for some time in India, during which he designed the models for a small work, consisting of twelve pieces, which he calls *Indian Birds*. This series connects quite closely with *Exotic Birds* but is also distinguished from it by virtue of the fact that Stella stepped away from the square background and established the forms on open steel constructions. The spatial aspect was enhanced by this move. The greatest series, *Circuits* (1981–84), named after famous racing circuits in the world and consisting of sixty-eight pieces, with the works being one of two sizes, appears in some ways to be a return to square base-forms although the openness of the paintings is maintained by letting pieces from the background fall away (see figure 11). In contrast to this, the language of form becomes increasingly playful. Stella also now begins to use the redundant forms of the metal that remain after the main forms have been cut away.

In the period 1982–84 Stella also worked on three smaller series, the *Shards*, the *South African Mines,* and the *Malta* series. The *Shards* are closely connected to the series *Circuits,* and in general are rather large; in contrast, the *South African Mines* and *Malta* series show a tendency toward sculpture. The *South African Mines* consist of unpainted assemblages made up from redundant materials; there are often letters and labels observable, something that makes one think of cubist, dadaist, and surrealist collages and frottages. In the *Malta* series, moreover, the forms are painted and etched.

The series *Cones and Pillars* and *Waves,* which Stella began respectively in 1985 and 1986, form the endpoint of his development as portrayed in the second retrospective. In *Cones and Pillars* the geometric forms from his earlier works return, but this time in strongly three-dimensional form. However, he uses portrayals of these forms on flat surfaces. Because, however, he connects the surfaces to each other with different hooks, a strange experience of space emerges that Rubin refers to as "mixed space" (Rubin, 1987, 138).

According to Rubin in his catalogue, we can refer to the art from Stella's second period, in contrast to the first, minimalist period, as *maximalist*. Where, in the first period, he appeared to investigate just how much could be taken away from painting without it ceasing to be painting, Stella now appears to be interested in seeing just how much can be added to abstract painting without its ceasing to be abstract painting. In fact, in his recent paintings Stella is seeking the precarious equilibrium of an aesthetic experience that contains both the spatial expression of

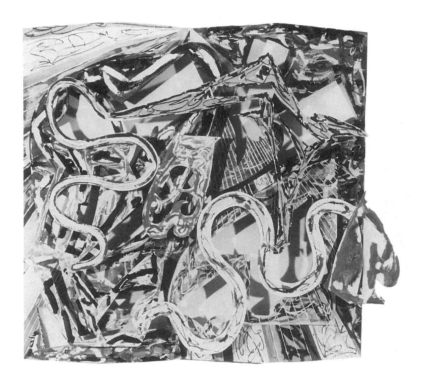

FIGURE 11

Vallelunga, Frank Stella, 1981, mixed media on aluminium, 290 × 320 × 50 cm. Collection of R. and J. Meyerhoff, Phoenix, Maryland.

the classical central perspective and the logical space that modern art works have taken over. Hereby he attempts to avoid both the illusionism of traditional art and the banality of modernism. One of the methods that Stella uses is to literally enter space with his painting without going completely into sculpture. This implies a break with the modernist dogma of purity concerning the separation of artistic disciplines. Stella himself expresses it as follows:

> Pictorial space is one which you have two-dimensional forms tricked out to give the appearance of three-dimensional ones, so that the

space you actually perceive comes down somewhere between. And somewhere in-between-them isn't a bad analogy for my work. I work away from the flat surface but I still don't want to be three-dimensional; that is: totaly literal . . . more than two dimensions, but short of three so, for me, 2.7 is probably a very good place to be. (Quoted in Rubin, 1987, 77)

In some ways, Stella appears hereby to return to the cubism that had not made the transition to complete abstraction. In contrast to older, illusionist art, Bracque and Picasso are not involved in suggesting a depth that goes away from the observer, but rather they appear to evoke a space that approaches and encloses the observer. Stella attempts to resurrect this spatial working, although in a literal sense, when he transforms his canvasses in the direction of sculpture (Rubin, 1987, 20).

In addition to a strongly expressive brush technique, a narrative moment reenters Stella's work in, for example, the lithographic series based upon El Lissitzky's illustrations of the *Had Gadya* (a moralizing story from Jewish folklore tradition) from the years 1982–84. The narrative is expressed in the later series, especially in *Waves*. With this work, it even appears that the work of art has once again received a symbolic charge. The works create the suggestion "that you see more than you see." The "2.7 dimension" of the waves symbolizes the "oceanic bond" of the old and new forms of spatial experience that Stella seeks to emulate in his later works.[38]

2.7 FROM AVANT-GARDE TO POSTMODERNISM: THE PYRRHIC VICTORY OF MODERN ART?

While Stella appears to succeed at the pictorial level in integrating the premodern into the modernist tradition—something that, while it may not thereby make it the herald of the "once-again-fine arts," does elevate it to an interesting experiment—there is little to observe, despite the cautious encouragement that the titles of the works after 1970 give, of an avant-gardist integration with life. In his new work, too, he fails to go beyond the safe boundaries of "the monetary-bureaucratic complex" of the cultural industry. The retrospective dedicated to his work forms more of a confirmation that high art, too, has definitively become an object of the cultural industry. The mega-exhibitions sponsored by industry, arttourism, and the great interest in the works of modern painters like Van Gogh and Mondrian shown by various investment funds are all indicators of the relevance of the most somber suspicions that Adorno and Marcuse cherished with respect to affirmative culture. A day out with "Stella" fits perfectly in the well-filled weekend of the wealthy culture-consumer, taking its place alongside the pretty, Italian-designed postmodern table, a meal in a Japanese restaurant, and attending Phillip Glass' latest opera.

Stella's work makes us conscious of the ambivalent position that postmodernist art occupies between modernism and the avant-garde. In a number of important respects postmodernism connects with the avant-garde rejection of modern art: the strong, sterile character of abstract modern art gives way to a renewed interest for the configuration, the *content* of the work. Hereby, just as with the dadaists and the surrealists (to whom—by taking over techniques or, more especially, via the medium of "style-quotations"—postmodern paintings not infrequently refer), life creeps back into postmodern work. But there is a crucial difference. In postmodern paintings these portrayals of life are no longer a means of transforming life, but rather an artistic goal in themselves (cf. Sanders, 1987, 76). In this respect, postmodern paintings remain remarkably true to the modernist ideal of autonomous art. Martis remarks in this respect:

> Thus, the postmodern iconograph does not use the language of imagery in order to narrate a story, but rather merely for the narration itself: images as images, iconography as iconography comparable with the colour-as-colour, the paint-as-paint from earlier avant garde movements [read: modernists—JdM[39]]. The works are just as much concerned with painting as such as with the paintings of the modernists, it is simply another form of painting. (Martis, 1986, 249)

Martis interprets this characteristic of postmodernist painting as the result of the continuance of the modernist taboo about impurity (Martis, 1986, 248).

We could, thus, refer to postmodernism in painting as the continuation of modernism by other means (Sanders, 1987, 78). Nonetheless, there is actually a definite "ideological" difference between postmodernism on the one hand and modernism and avant-gardism on the other. Where modernists and *avant-gardists* were driven by a strong engagement (the internal struggles concerned most especially the question of the correct means), such engagement is often missing with the postmodern artist. Further, the critical function of art as such was also quite frequently abandoned.[40] "The postmodern painter," remarks

Martis, "is no longer the philosopher, he is more of an alchemist and, more especially, an image-maker" (Martis, 1986, 254). Postmodern art, to vary Heidegger's provocative remark in "What Calls for Thinking" concerning science, no longer thinks (BW, 349). Instead of insight it offers a fascinating Apollonian world of images in which it is pleasant to remain. For this reason, the postmodern victory over modernism appears above everything to be a pyrrhic victory (cf. Féher, 1987). Just as in the era of modernism, art remains a reservation; the difference is that in the era of the postmodernism everyday life threatens to be totally swallowed by this reservation. The Walkman on the head of the commuter that transforms his existence into an extended advertising spot, the *design* of the watch that gives his day a disciplined progression, these provide no less the appearance of the Great Style than the Italian design furniture in his house. Is this dazzling Apollonian world of appearances not actually the result of a false dissolution of art?

This question appears to require an affirmative answer if the postmodern aestheticization of existence means, as Finkielkraut believes, that everything has become a question of "good taste," of subjective arbitrariness: "We are living in a time of *feelings,* where there is no truth or lie, no stereotype or invention, nothing beautiful or ugly, but an infinite palette of different and equal pleasures" (Finkielkraut, 1995, 117). "With this careless conglomeration of random and passing needs, the postmodern individual has forgotten that freedom means more than having the power to switch channels on the TV, and culture more than satisfying an urge" (ibid., 124). This postmodern person brings the words to mind which Nietzsche's Zarathustra speaks with regard to the ultimate, passive-nihilistic man: "They have their little pleasure for the day and their little pleasure for the night: but they respect health. . . . A little poison now and then: that produces pleasant dreams. And a lot of poison at last, for a pleasant death. . . . 'We have discovered happiness,' say the Ultimate Men and blink" (Z, 46–47). Degenerated to a narcissistic lifestyle, the postmodern individual lives in extremely satisfying inauthenticity. Certainly, if he occasionally reflects on his life then he sometimes asks himself nervously if *this* is all there is, but, fortunately, these moments are few and far between. The pleasures of the day and night quickly demand his attention again. And, moreover: "Sickness and mistrust count as sins with them: . . . whoever thinks otherwise goes voluntarily into the madhouse. 'Formerly all the world was mad,' say the most acute of them and blink" (Z, 46–47).

Abandoning the modernist striving toward the intersubjective True, Good, and Beautiful leads in the case of the postmodern individual to an ironic indifference. The sweet dream of the postmodern lifestyle threatens to destroy the moment of enthusiasm in which we decide about our existence. For this reason, Nietzsche's criticism concerning the nihilism of the last person appears still to be relevant with regard to the postmodern lifestyle. "The criticism of the crisis which is possible from Nietzsche's perspective," argues Van Tongeren in his book about Nietzsche's moral engagement,

> is directed not at relativism and subjectivism as such, but rather at the moral indifference which is connected with them. By virtue of the unmistakable multiplicity, changeability, and variable perspectives of moral evaluation, and the absence of an absolute criterion whereby they can be measured, our situation is "critical": life is experimentation, with all the attendant risks. But the opinion that it does not matter what we do, that everyone must know for themselves what they do, and that, as with taste, there is no argument possible about morality, is dangerous precisely because it misunderstands the risk, because it does not dare to experiment, and because it alienates the human individual from his own project. (Van Tongeren, 1984, 361)

Must we conclude that postmodern painting has degenerated into a nihilistic indifference? The lack of obligation, banal, and sometimes even completely empty character of much of postmodern painting—and here, in addition to Stella's later works, I am thinking, for example, of Shnabel's paintings that a couple of years ago were sold at a premium—at least *suggests* such an interpretation. But if we follow this suggestion exclusively, then we ignore the ambivalence that is characteristic of postmodern art (see 0.8 and 1.8 above). Vattimo and Kaulingfreks point out that the banal emptiness of postmodern art confronts us in a shocking manner precisely with the truth of nihilistic culture. "It is this confrontational effect which shows the power of art. By being so horribly empty and superficial it brings us on the scent of our crisis and speaks of a loss of Being. And thus, at the same time, it shows a truth, namely, the disappearance of truth. In a paradoxical manner—*via negative*—it unveils my existence, or, better expressed, my lack thereof" (Kaulingfreks, 1989, 56; cf. Vattimo, 1988, 51 ff.). Whether or not postmodern painting has this effect upon observers is, however, equally dependent upon the reflexivity of the observer: "The specified confrontation can only be operable when a feeling of dissatisfaction is present, when, in a manner of speaking, we have not yet lost it but only forgotten it. Perhaps the negative truth of postmodernism can only be recognized as such within a (modern) desire for a missing sense" (Kaulingfreks, 1988, 57).

The foregoing interpretation of postmodern painting has a rather defensive flavor. In my opinion, a more positive interpretation of postmodern painting is possible is we direct our attention to the practical dimension of this art's characteristic pluralism (see 0.6 above). In his study of postmodernism, Welsch justifiably remarks that the desire for an all-embracing sense is only sensible within a recognition of multiplicity. Every striving toward unity and totality, as we have learned time after time from modern history since the French Revolution, constantly runs the risk of becoming a massive exclusion or even elimination of that which will not or cannot bring itself to ally itself with that totality. According to Welsch, a real totality can only come about if we recognize the Other in his Otherness:

> From the idea of totality we can only extract preventive and regulatory capital. It holds up to us: be aware of the multiplicity of other real and possible discourses; do not exclude them, because precisely then will you definitively lose the totality which you are attempting to achieve. This totality, however, is actually not achievable because it consists of another quality and one can only perceive it and think of it in the structure of an open totality. Every closed totality is necessarily closed for the Other and is thereby no longer a totality. (Welsch, 1987, 62–63)

A similar conception of an open totality acknowledges the multiplicity without thereby necessarily degenerating into nihilistic indifference with respect to the differences. In this case, there is no question of an enjoyable dwelling upon one's own identity, but rather of an attempt to meet the Other in his Otherness.

Looked at from this perspective we can consider pluralistic postmodern painting as an experiment in living with the multicultural and multirational diversity of the global village that the earth has become. In such an interpretation, pluralistic postmodern painting appears as the embodiment of the striving to tack between the Scylla of an implemented terror (by one single culture or type of rationality), carried out in the disguise of integration, and the Charybdis of indifference with respect to differences. If, accordingly, we conceive of postmodernism in this manner, then the proposition that postmodernism is a continuation of modernism by other means also receives a more differentiated meaning.

The foregoing makes us at least realize that the path that autonomous art has traveled in this century is remarkably ambivalent. This realization of ambivalence will continue to accompany and guide the dialogue with (post)modern art in the following chapters.

3

The Art of Forgetting

> The piano was hammering glittering note-nails into a
> wall of air. Although in its origin this process was com-
> pletely real, the walls of the sitting-room vanished, and
> in their place arose the flowing golden walls of music,
> that mysterious room where ego and world, perception
> and feeling, inside and outside melt whirling into each
> other, quite intangibly, while the room itself consists en-
> tirely of sensation, certainty, precision, indeed of a
> whole hierarchy of the glory of ordered details.
>
> —Robert Musil

Is it possible to arrange a conversation between the philosopher Arthur
Schopenhauer and the postmodern composer Steve Reich? In a literal
sense, of course, the answer must be that this is not possible: there is not
only a temporal gap of one and a half centuries between the 1817 publication of Schopenhauer's *The World as Will and Representation* and
Reich's repetitive compositions, but, in addition, the different media in
which the two work(ed) would appear to preclude such a conversation.
Schopenhauer's medium is formed by the conceptual filter of discursive language, while Reich "speaks" by virtue of the structuring of
tones. On the other hand, our experience teaches us that acoustic images
and philosophical concepts constantly interact with each other. Not
only is our musical experience—at least in retrospective—structured by
the grid of discursive language, but, from the other side, musical tones
possess the capacity to break through this grid. In the never completely

nonviolent meeting of musical tone and philosophical concept, both sides attain new meaning: their "effective history" exists by virtue of this dialogue. What I will be arguing in this chapter is that Schopenhauer's musical aesthetics, despite the temporal distance, can clarify our experience of Reich's repetitive compositions just as those compositions make it possible for us to clarify and, in a certain sense, transcend, a number of noteworthy contradictions in Schopenhauer's aesthetics. In conclusion, I will confront the result of the following interpretation with the musical-aesthetic views of Nietzsche, Adorno, and Lyotard.

3.1 METAPHYSICS AND AESTHETICS

Before we listen to what Schopenhauer and Reich have to say to each other and to us, I want to pause to consider the close relationship between Schopenhauer's aesthetics and metaphysics. In his major work, *The World as Will and Representation*, Schopenhauer defined music as "an unconscious exercise in metaphysics in which the mind does not know it is philosophizing" (Schopenhauer, 1969, 264).[1] For Schopenhauer, music is not only an unrivaled source of beauty and comfort in the vale of tears that is life, but, more especially, a source of knowledge of the ultimate principle upon which life is based. It would appear to be a justified question to ask if this close relationship of metaphysics and aesthetics does not pose an insurmountable problem when, as (post)modern readers, we seek access to Schopenhauer's aesthetics. If we wished to point out a constant in philosophy since Nietzsche, then the fundamental break with the traditional metaphysical method of thinking, of which Schopenhauer is one of the last great exponents, is certainly one of the candidates. Does the metaphysical context wherein Schopenhauer's aesthetics appears not result in its only being interesting from the perspective of a history of ideas? In such a case the attempt to involve Schopenhauer in a contemporary aesthetic and cultural-philosophical debate would appear to be foredoomed to failure.

There is, however, a good reason not to be overhasty in reaching such a conclusion. Although the critique of the traditional-metaphysical pretension to reveal the most fundamental grounds and origins of Being is justified, the question remains whether we have thereby actually left metaphysics as such behind us. Every approach to reality occurs from within an interpretative context, an understanding of Being, without which no world at all could appear to us (see Heidegger, BT, 33, 78 ff.;

cf. De Mul, 1997d, 233–36). Even the most mundane positivism cannot avoid that; approaching reality, it permits itself to be guided by particular implied assumptions concerning what constitutes "Being." In this sense, even positivism lets itself be guided by metaphysical assumptions. Such metaphysical contexts can change during history but they can never be completely superseded or abandoned (cf. Derrida, 1981, 280–81). Dilthey, who underlined the relativity of metaphysical contexts more strongly than anyone else, remarked in this context: "Metaphysical science is an historically finite phenomenon while the metaphysical consciousness of man is infinite" (Dilthey, 1914–96, 1:386; see De Mul, 1996b, 1999). In this sense, we can only underwrite Schopenhauer's pronouncement that man is an *animal metaphysicum* (Schopenhauer, 1966, 160). If we can speak of progress in twentieth-century philosophy in comparison with traditional metaphysics, then this does not reside in the fact that we have left metaphysics behind us, but rather that we now realize that metaphysical pronouncements are actually not pronouncements about reality but should be understood as a clarification of the interpretative contexts from which Being is approached.[2]

In chapter 1, in connection with a discussion concerning Nietzsche, I pointed to the metaphorical foundations of every metaphysics. A metaphysical system originates when a particular metaphor is solidified into a transcendental foundation (what Derrida referred to as a *signifié transcendental*). The metaphor then becomes a fundamental metaphor (cf. Koestenbaum, 1960). For example, in modern anthropology, based on the works of Descartes and De Lamettrie, man is conceived as a complex machine. Such a fundamental metaphor opens up a specific reality that can subsequently be explored with empirical research. Modern Western medicine can accordingly be understood as based upon the fossilization of this metaphor. This example simultaneously shows us that, dependent upon the power of the fundamental metaphor, a systematic metaphysical fossilization of the metaphor can, theoretically, practically or aesthetically, be very successful. But the danger always exists herewith that the fundamental metaphor, to the extent that it extends to a "real world" (that is, is being naturalized), becomes worn out and impotent *as* a metaphor. According to deconstructivists, an important task of contemporary philosophy is to keep alive the metaphorical in metaphysics (cf. *White Mythology:* Derrida, 1982a, 207–71).

The role of the metaphorical in metaphysics ensures that the judgment of a metaphysical system always contains an aesthetic dimension. In his famous article concerning Schopenhauer, Thomas Mann expressed this as follows: "The joy which we experience from a metaphysical system, the satisfaction which the organisation of the world in a logically closed and harmonious world of ideas gives to us, is always of an aesthetic nature; it has the same origins as the pleasure, the great satisfaction, which the arranging, forming, and chaos-dominating function of art gives to us" (Mann, 1977, 87). It also means that in the judgment of metaphysical systems such aesthetic criteria as consistency, elegance, simplicity, and plausibility play an important part. With relatively simple means, a metaphysics of the "Great Style" opens a much-embracing perspective on reality.

These considerations mean that in my discussion of Schopenhauer's metaphysics I shall not primarily be guided by the question as to whether this metaphysics is "true" or not, in the sense of corresponding with "the most fundamental grounds of reality," but rather by the question whether or not this metaphysics makes it possible for us to clarify, in a consistent, plausible, and elegant manner, the experience that contemporary repetitive music provides us.

3.2 SCHOPENHAUER'S AESTHETICS OF MUSIC

The reason that Schopenhauer considered music as the highest form of art resides in the fact that, according to him, it shows the most fundamental grounds of reality with a definite immediacy. According to his fundamental metaphor, the principle involved here is the Will (*Wille*). This Will is the foundation and origin of everything that is given in our representations (*Vorstellungen*) of the empirical world. Will and representation (*Wille* and *Vorstellung*) are concepts that Schopenhauer constructs following the example of Kant's conceptual duo thing-as-such (*Ding an sich*) and phenomenon (*Erscheinung*). However, while for Kant the thing-as-such is fundamentally unknowable and, for that reason, functions as a conceptual asymptote in the critique of reason, Schopenhauer is of the opinion that knowledge of the Will really is possible. In this sense, Schopenhauer agrees with the program of German Idealism, especially when he more closely defines the Will in terms of transcendental subjectivity. His idealism, however, is of a very special sort: when he provides a more thorough description of the Will, he presents it as an irrational, aimless, and violent struggle (cf. Koestenbaum, 1960, 86). The world of impressions is conceived of by Schopenhauer as the objectivization of this blind Will in space, time, and causality. This objectivization occurs in stages (the mineral world, flora and fauna, the human world), and, within them, in classes and subclasses. These stages and (sub)classes constitute, as Schopenhauer expresses it in a language derived from the Platonic tradition, all levels of Being, from suprasensible Ideas to concrete individuals.

What makes Schopenhauer's metaphysics an *aesthetic* metaphysics is that he equates suprarational intuition, which provides us with insight into the Will, with aesthetic contemplation. According to him, all forms of art posses this specific cognitive capacity. In addition, art does not represent individuals, but rather the Platonic, timeless Ideas on the example of which individuals are formed. A successful portrait represents, according to Schopenhauer, not a particular person but the *Idea* of a person. Music, however, occupies a specific place among forms of art: while the other art forms represent Ideas, a domain between the Will and its empirical objectivization, music brings us into immediate contact with the Will itself: "For this reason music, in contrast to the other arts, is not a representation of the Ideas which form the objectivity of the Will, but rather a representation of the Will itself; therefore, the effect of music is also so much more powerful than that provided by the other arts: after all, these only speak from the shadow while music speaks from its essence" (Schopenhauer, 1969, 257). Music not only leads us past the empirical world of impressions such as those presented to us in the *a priori* forms of space, time, and causality, but, in addition, they also take us past the empire of Ideas through an *immediate* contact with the foundations of the world. According to Schopenhauer, the different voices of musical harmony (bass, tenor, alto, and soprano) evoke in an immediate manner the four named main stages of the Will's objectivization: the mineral kingdom, the vegetable kingdom, the animal kingdom, and the human world.

On the basis of this unique cognitive capacity Schopenhauer places music even above philosophy, which can only re-present the Will through the mediation of concepts. In contrast, music "speaks . . . not of things, but purely of the vicissitudes of life, the only reality which exists for the Will. For this reason, too, melody speaks so clearly to our hearts, because it has nothing—at least not *directly*—to say to our heads, and, as is the case with all music which paints scenes and landscapes, one misuses it if one expects this.[3] Such program music is therefore to be rejected" (Schopenhauer, 1977, 2, sect. 218). Schopenhauer goes so far as to argue that, in the final analysis, and given that we can conceive equally of the world as an embodiment of the Will or as an embodiment of music, music is even identical to the Will. Music is not so much a representation (*Abbild*) of the Will as a direct presence of the Will itself. For this reason, Schopenhauer can even remark: "Music is the melody of which the world is the text." And, not hindered by too great a false modesty, he adds: "One can only retrieve the authentic sense of this text through my explanation of music" (Schopenhauer, 1977, 2, sect. 219).

Given the distinction between music and the other forms of art it appears justified to presume that ultimately only music completely realizes aesthetic contemplation in the manner that it was explicated in the third book of *The World as Will and Representation*. In that third book Schopenhauer postulated that real aesthetic contemplation is independent of the "law of sufficient cause" (Schopenhauer, 1969, 185). This means that aesthetic contemplation leads us beyond the world of the *principium individuationis* (the multiplicity of space, time, and causality) in just as radical a manner as sleep does (cf. Schopenhauer, 1969, 197). For this reason, we can postulate that, for Schopenhauer, music is the *art of forgetting*. Music ensures that we forget—in an ontological sense—the world as it is given in space, time, and causality, and, to the extent that these *a priori* syntheses constitute typically human forms of experience, we may even postulate that music—at least temporarily—makes us forget ourselves.

3.3   CONTRADICTIONS IN SCHOPENHAUER'S AESTHETICS

Schopenhauer's aesthetics are both fascinating and puzzling. It is impracticable here to provide even a summary of all the real and putative contradictions that have been presented in commentaries concerned with this aesthetics, so I will restrict myself to only two fundamental problems. The first concerns Schopenhauer's aesthetics as a whole, while the second concerns the more specific issue of his aesthetics of music.

Not without reason, Schopenhauer's philosophy has been described as the most pessimistic in the tradition of Western philosophy. While, even when attention is paid to the issue of evil in the world, in most metaphysical systems the ultimate basis of reality is conceived as rational and good, in Schopenhauer's philosophy it is not only the case that the objectivizations of the Will (in both classes and individuals), driven by their "Will to Live" (*Wille zum Leben*), compete with each other in the empirical world in a struggle concerning life and death, but also that the Will itself is characterized by an inherent internal division. For this reason, according to Schopenhauer, happiness and joy can never be more than the temporary absence of pain and sadness. In the fourth book of *The World as Will and Representation*, asceticism, the radical negation and abandoning of the Will, is presented as the only solution for surmounting the immeasurable suffering in the world.

Against this background it is at least remarkable that Schopenhauer credited aesthetic contemplation with providing happiness and comfort: one would be more likely to expect that an immediate insight into the irrational and violent basis of our existence would precipitate a collapse into despair. For the moment, I will content myself with recording this problematic aspect of Schopenhauer's aesthetics of music; I shall return to this issue later in the chapter.

The second problem that I wish to deal with here concerns the meaning of the notion of 'time' in Schopenhauer's aesthetics of music. This notion plays a rather paradoxical role in his aesthetics. On the one hand Schopenhauer argues that music leads us beyond the empirical world as it is constituted by *a priori* syntheses of space, *time*, and causality, while on the other hand he postulates, in agreement with traditional aesthetics, that time constitutes the most important factor of music: "Music is perceived exclusively in time" (Schopenhauer, 1969, 266; cf. Schopenhauer, 1966, 453). There appears to be a contradiction here between the view that music takes us into a timeless world and the view that music can only exist by virtue of the factor of time.

A dialectical solution to the problem could consist of arguing that music presents the specified timelessness through temporary means. Music, we could argue, is always a part of the empirical world and as such is always necessarily *in* time. But this does not remove the possibility that music can evoke a feeling of timelessness in the listener. The temporal intervals are so arranged in a musical composition that they seduce the listener into forgetting the passage of time. Such a dialectical explanation of music as the "highest pastime" appears to maintain the consistency of Schopenhauer's aesthetics of music. However, apart from the question as to whether or not we would please Schopenhauer with such a dialectical movement (his radical ridiculing of the "Hegelism" (*Hegelei*) of his contemporaries makes one suspect a negative answer), the question remains as to whether or not such an interpretation is *plausible*, especially when we consider the sort of music to which he himself referred. Schopenhauer regarded the instrumental music of Mozart and Rossini as capable of bringing us into immediate contact with the Will (Schopenhauer, 1977, 2, sect. 218).[4] Memory and anticipation play a decisive role in the experience of music within the tonal tradition to which these composers belong, and this means that the experience of tonal music does not so much make the listener forget time, but, on the contrary, makes him fully conscious of its linear passage.

Inverting Schopenhauer's thesis, we could provocatively postulate that time is exclusively perceived in music.

I will illustrate this point with a brief exposition concerning the sonata (or major) form that occupied a central place in musical production in the period from *circa* 1750 to the end of the nineteenth century.[5] The sonata form consists of three parts: exposition, development, and recapitulation. In the exposition, two themes (or groups of musical themes) are introduced, one in the principal key center, called the tonic, the other in a different key (usually the dominant, the key whose scale begins on the fifth degree of the scale of the principal key). In the development, these themes are freely manipulated with brief digressions into other keys. In the recapitulation, the themes introduced earlier are repeated, only now they all occur in the tonic key. Because of this specific structure the sonata form is also referred to as teleological, something that, in the first place, means that every note in the composition has a specific place and function in the total structure. The notes receive this specific place and function thanks to their relationship to the tonal center. Moreover, the composition in its entirety heads for the final synthesis wherein the tensions are resolved. The teleological effect of the sonata form is largely dependent upon memory and anticipation. We may even say that these activities constitute the actual musical experience.

The tonal center—and here there is an important agreement with the central perspective of painting such as it was interpreted in the previous chapter—simultaneously constitutes in this way a specific place for the listening subject. The totality of the teleological structure appears as a representation of the representing subject. For this reason we cannot say here that the listening subject loses himself in the musical experience. On the contrary: the sonata form ensures that the listener becomes conscious of himself as a subject occupying a unique and individual place in time just as the central perspective situates the viewer in a unique, individual place in space.

It would appear to be an unavoidable conclusion that Schopenhauer's aesthetics of music, when placed in the context of musical practice around 1800, is, at least with respect to the notion of time, if not inconsistent then certainly not particularly plausible. However, it is self-evident that one is not saying that this applies to every musical practice. It is possible that Schopenhauer's aesthetics of music attains a greater plausibility when we bring it into relation with another sort of musical practice. The repetitive music of Steve Reich appears to me to be a suitable candidate in this connection. However, before I will discuss Reich's music, I want to briefly examine, as a transitionary movement, a small composition by Nietzsche wherein, in a playful form, a musical experience is notable that is later more thoroughly articulated by the repetitive composers.

3.4   NIETZSCHE'S *FRAGMENT AN SICH*

Without question, Nietzsche was one of Schopenhauer's best readers (cf. Schirmacher *et al.*, 1984). I have already remarked in chapter 1 that the early writings of Nietzsche can be read as being clearly influenced by Schopenhauer's "artist's metaphysics" (*Artisten-Metaphysik*), most especially by the latter's aesthetics of music. That the aesthetics of music especially generated Nietzsche's enthusiasm should not surprise us when we consider that he was a passionate lover of music and, in his youth, an enthusiastic if not particularly talented composer. In 1871, busy writing his first book, *The Birth of Tragedy out of the Spirit of Music* (which would be published a year later), and not long after he had discovered Schopenhauer's work, Nietzsche composed a short piece for the piano to which he gave the title *Das Fragment an sich* (see figure 12). This brief, fragmentary composition would perhaps not deserve our attention were it not for the fact that Nietzsche wrote *"Da capo con malinconia"* at the end of the piece. What is particularly noteworthy is that this melancholic instruction to repeat has no *fine* indicator, something that indicates that the piece is to be endlessly repeated. We could perhaps consider this musical joke as a metaphorical foreshadowing of Nietzsche's later doctrine of the Eternal Recurrence of the Same *(ewige Wiederkehr des Gleichen)*, but, in my opinion, we should primarily understand it as an ironic commentary concerning Schopenhauer's aesthetics of music and more especially concerning the problematic notion of time that was discussed above.

Just as in the major form, repetition plays an important role in *Das Fragment an sich*, but in the latter instance it is, as it were, *perverted*. Although the *Fragment an sich* is written in the idiom of the tonal system, the notions of the structured totality, the tonal center, and the final synthesis completely lose their meaning through the endless repetition of the fragment (a literally eternal recurrence of the same). Every repetition of the fragment becomes literally a fragment *an sich*. Here, the repetition does not serve a memory or an anticipation of the musical structure, but rather undermines that structure in such a radical manner that the musical experience becomes what Nietzsche in his later writings referred to as an active forgetting (cf. 1.6, above).[6]

This forgetting also has consequences for the listening subject. Not only does music lose its privileged tonal center, but, in addition, the listening subject no longer forms the archimedial point from

130

FIGURE 12

Das Fragment an sich, Friedrich Nietzsche, 1871, composition for piano, in: C. P. Janz. (1976). *Friedrich Nietzsche. Der musikalische Nachlaß*, 85. Basel: Baerenreiter.

whence the entire structure of the composition can be surveyed by virtue of memory and anticipation. In this respect, we could also refer to the *Fragment an sich* as a metaphorical foreshadowing of the crisis of the modern subject.

3.5 REPETITION AND FORGETTING: THE MUSIC OF STEVE REICH

One could offer as rebuttal that I attach disproportional importance to a musical joke were it not that later composers have developed this "joke" in a systematic manner. We may think of Eric Satie in this connection, especially his *Vexations*, which must be repeated 840 times (the first complete performance of this work, under the direction of John Cage, took place in New York in 1963). Most especially, however, a number of implications of Nietzsche's musical joke were expressed in the repetitive music, developed in the United States in the late 1960s, of the composers La Monte Young, Terry Riley, Philip Glass, and Steve Reich. I restrict myself here to Steve Reich, particularly the repetitive works he wrote in the period 1967 (*Piano Phase*) to 1980 (*Music for a Large Ensemble*).

When we listen to Reich's music from this period, a number of specific techniques spring to our attention, techniques such as "phase shifting" (an effect that arises when one of two identical parts are gradually accelerated or slowed), or a surprising return to tonality that, as we noted in the previous chapter, at least since Schönberg has had a bad reputation among many composers. The most notable feature of Reich's music from this period, however, is without doubt the dominant presence of repetition. The compositions have no teleological structure, but rather they consist of elements that apparently are endlessly repeated. The compositions are not characterized by a linear structure directed at an ultimate synthesis (A, B, C, A), but rather by a cyclical structure that knows no real beginning or ending (A, A, A, A). While the compositions of Nietzsche and Satie are still characterized by a traditional structure that is repeated as a totality, in Reich's compositions repetition plays a decisive role at both the micro and the macro levels (cf. figure 13).

One can no longer speak here of "works" in the traditional sense, but rather of processes that, once they are begun, appear to unfold themselves without any interference by the composer or performer. In the musical experience specific psycho-acoustic effects appear, the so-called "resulting patterns."[7] These are the consequences of the fact that the repetitive compositions do not permit a teleological experience. Given that here repetition merely serves forgetting, the possibility of

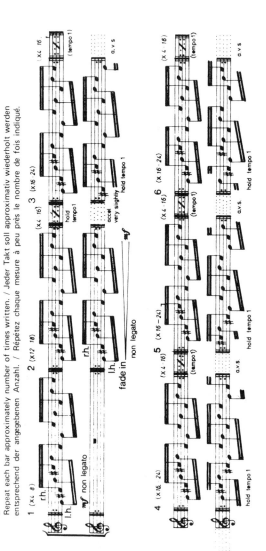

132

FIGURE 13

Piano Phase, Steve Reich, 1966, composition for two pianos or two marimbas.

remembering or anticipating does not exist, a characteristic that has led to repetitive music also being referred to as meditative music. The listener is led into a particular trance, a feeling of timelessness that is strengthened by the fact that, because of the lack of a structuring center, the subject appears to lose himself in the music.

When we approach Schopenhauer's aesthetics of music from the practice of repetitive music, then the earlier noted inconsistency with respect to the notion of time appears to resolve itself. Self-evidently, repetitive music too occurs in empirical time, but, unlike music based on the sonata form, repetitive music is not directed at remembrance or anticipation in time. The result is an experience of timelessness, a (temporary) deliverance from the *principium individuationis*. In my opinion it is not coincidental that both Schopenhauer and the repetitive composers appeal to Eastern philosophy in order to verbally articulate this specific experience of timelessness. For them, Western discursive language appears to be unable to articulate this experience.

Nonetheless, we do not necessarily need to resort to Eastern philosophy to describe the experience of timelessness; another famous reader of Schopenhauer can help us to find our way in this connection. I refer here to Sigmund Freud, thinking most especially of his theory of the unconscious (a concept that, in a number of respects, reminds us of Schopenhauer's concept of Will[8]). In connection with the unconscious, Freud argues in *Beyond the Pleasure Principle* (1920) that: "As a result of certain psychoanalytic discoveries, we are today in an position to embark on a discussion of the Kantian theorem that time and space are 'necessary forms of thought.' We have learnt that unconscious mental processes are in themselves 'timeless'" (SE, 18:28).[9] Freud also referred to the unconscious as the 'oceanic experience' whereby it is not longer possible to distinguish between subject and object.[10] These characteristics of the unconscious appear to be preeminently suitable for describing the experience of repetitive music.

3.6 DEATH THROUGH REPETITION

The first problem that I noted with Schopenhauer's aesthetics of music—the fact that he ascribes joy and comfort to the immediate musical experience of the irrational basis of the world—is not, however, hereby resolved. It is certainly not the case when we consider the great popularity that repetitive music, especially its popularized forms such as disco and, more recently, in hiphop, house and dance, enjoy. If this music brings us into immediate contact with the terrible reality of the

Will, how then can it provide such an enormous amount of pleasure? In section 1.6, we saw that Nietzsche, too, was mesmerized by this issue in his elaboration of Schopenhauer's aesthetics of music. In *The Birth* he postulated that the individual, in the experience of Dionysian musical intoxication, was transfixed by the "furious angel" of the World Will's suffering and simultaneously that he was swamped by the "immeasurability" and "eternity of pleasure" (B, 80–81). Nietzsche sought the explanation for this fact in the "lethargic forgetfulness" of Dionysian ecstasy.

Perhaps we can elucidate this paradoxical combination of pleasure and displeasure by looking more closely at Freud's analysis of the phenomenon of repetition compulsion.[11] In *Beyond the Pleasure Principle* (1920) Freud notices that, in the case of traumatic neurosis (a frequent syndrome among soldiers during and after World War I), the patients constantly reexperience their original neurosis-inducing trauma in their dreams. Seeking to explain this phenomenon, Freud postulates the existence a repetition compulsion (*Wiederholungszwang* or *Wiederholungstrieb*) that was not in the service of Eros (a concept that shows a strong similarity with Schopenhauer's Will to Life (*Wille zum Leben*), but rather of Thanatos or the death instinct (*Todestrieb*). While the sexual instinct is directed at maintaining life, the death instinct seeks the elimination of the tension that is characteristic of life. It is not surprising that Freud, too, seeks refuge here in a metaphor from Eastern thought and referred to the death instinct as the *Nirvana principle*.

Could we not also, in an analogous manner, interpret the pleasure that is derived from the experience of repetitive music in terms of this compulsion to repeat? This would mean that in the case of repetitive music, too, repetition is in the service of death instincts rather than life instincts (cf. Mertens, 1980, 156). Although the musical experience of repetitive music brings a loss of the listener's individuality and subjectivity with it, this loss is "rewarded" with a lessening of life tensions such as is also realized in many meditative techniques.

If we interpret the experience of repetitive music in this manner, then the second inconsistency in Schopenhauer's aesthetics of music also seems to vanish. The cruel reality of the Will is only anxiety-inducing when we consider it from the perspective of the subject. When the subject frees himself from his Will, then the Will itself is liberated from its dominance. This implies, incidentally, that we should relativize the distinction that Schopenhauer makes between aesthetic contemplation and the asceticism of the sacral, at least with respect to the experience of repetitive music. The experience of repetitive music, too, seen from

Schopenhauer's perspective, can be conceived as an exercise in *detaching* or *disengaging*.

3.7 BEYOND THE REALITY PRINCIPLE?

Although the interpretation I have just given of repetitive music from the perspective of Schopenhauer's aesthetics of music makes it possible for us to clarify the experience that we obtain from the music, this explanation still cannot completely satisfy. The reason for this is that hereby the experience of repetitive music is only explained in a negative fashion, something that is due to the loss of subjectivity. This is undoubtedly a consequence of the fact that the explanation is expressed in terms of psychoanalytic concepts: within this interpretative context the unconscious experience evoked by the repetition can only be presented as an hallucinatory satisfaction of desire that is combined with a *flight* from reality. Following this explanation, the experience of repetitive music could open itself to the accusation of being an expression of a perverse aestheticism.[12] After Freud had announced the timelessness of unconscious processes, he continues: "The *Ucs.* processes pay just as little regard to *reality*. They are subject to the pleasure principle; their fate depends only on how strong they are and on whether they fulfill the demands of the pleasure-unpleasure regulation" (SE, 14:187, italic JdM). The problem with this, however, is that Freud, in his interpretation of the unconscious drives, maintains the instrumentalist *reality principle* as a last, indisputable criterion. According to this reality principle, immediate satisfaction must give way to labor because this makes satisfaction safe as a future good (SE, 12:223–24): in this sense, given that the tension created by the musical piece is only resolved in the final synthesis, the sonata form, too, is under the domination of this principle.

However, Freud shares Schopenhauer's and Nietzsche's criticism of the modern philosophy of consciousness, such as it is expressed, for example, in the works of Descartes and Kant, when he maintained that *"the ego is not the master in its own house"* (SE, 17:143). In Freud's vision unconscious desires, which are not so much destroyed as placed in safety by the reality principle, are master. On the other hand, every psychoanalytic endeavour is directed at strengthening the conscious subject: "Where id was, there ego shall be. It is a work of culture—not unlike the draining of the Zuider Zee" (SE, 22:80). For this reason, the compulsion to repetition, which leads to the undermining of the conscious subject, cannot be understood by Freud in any other terms than those of regression and illness.[13] The experience of repetitive music remains at best only an apparent experience, or, as Lyotard expresses it, a *musica ficta* (Lyotard, 1980, 118).

A similar tendency is apparent with Adorno, who was strongly influenced by Freud. Although, as we saw in section 2.5, Adorno radically criticizes modern, instrumental subjectivity; for him the subject also remains the model wherefrom aesthetic experience is analyzed and assessed. Although he is exceptionally pessimistic concerning the present possibilities for the development of an autonomous subjectivity, the now-impossible autonomous subject remains Adorno's ultimate criterion of a dialectical critique that thereby necessarily obtains a negative character. For him, music, as we remarked in the previous chapter, can no longer signify any form of happiness in contemporary society as a whole. At best, as in the case of Schönberg's music, it embodies the saddening knowledge of nonidentity. Hereby it becomes—once again employing Lyotard's terminology—a *musica fingens*.

Adorno's sharp critique of the false appearance of jazz, expressed in psychoanalytical terminology, is easily applied to repetitive music. What he opposes in jazz is "the constant repetition of the simplest things" (Adorno, 1982, 80) that results in "the immobility of an always-identical spatial movement instead of a temporal movement" (Adorno, 1982, 82). This implies that a mythical repetition takes the place of a real development: Adorno's critique is especially directed at the pseudo-character of the liberating effect that is ascribed to the improvisation. In reality, in the case of jazz the subject is sacrificed to the collective (Adorno, 1982, 96). The same accusation is sometimes directed toward repetitive music. Here, too, the practitioner is absorbed in a musical process that has a strong collective character. Adorno describes the pseudosatisfaction achieved by jazz as a symptom of perversion, as an impotent and therefore anxious subjectivity. The *Tiger Rag,* he commented, "simultaneously expresses the grumbling roar of the tiger and the fear of being eaten or castrated by it" (Adorno, 1982, 106–7). Jazz, which, according to Adorno, is primarily popular among the young who have not completely subordinated themselves to the reality principle, is a compromise between aesthetic sublimation and social adaptation: "In this way, jazz is a false dissolution of art: instead of utopia being realized, it disappears from sight" (Adorno, 1955, 159, 161).

In his critique of jazz, Adorno allies himself to Nietzsche's critique of the decadent character of the "powerless yearning" (*ohnmächtig sehnsüchtiger*) heroes of Wagner's operas (Adorno, 1982, 107). If we extend this Nietzschean critique of jazz to repetitive music, then we could conceive of it as an expression of decadence, that is, of a life-denying culture.[14] In this case repetitive music would be nothing other than a "remedy for a handicapped reality" (WDB, 3:833), an opiate that, like Wagner's operas and 'hot jazz,' liberates us from the disciplining labor of the Will.

Although there are good arguments for this interpretation of repetitive music as a symptom of decadence, the question remains as to whether or not the experience of repetition is hereby exhaustively understood.[15] The specified interpretation is completely contained by the perspective of the reality principle. The question is whether or not it would be possible to understand the repetitive experience *from within* the pleasure principle, thus from unconscious desires. From among the members of the Frankfurt School, Marcuse, in *Eros and Civilization* (1955), has attempted to "pervert" (and thereby to *verwinden*) Freud's theory by relativizing the contradiction between life- and death-drives: "If the instinct's basic objective is not the termination of life but of pain—the absence of tension—then paradoxically, in terms of instinct, the conflict between life and death is the more reduced, the closer life approximates the state of gratification" (Marcuse, 1970,187). According to Marcuse, this would demand an re-eroticization of man's relationship to the Other, that is, a return to the polymorphous perversity of the child. Then, just as Schiller demanded with respect to the Romantic project, the aesthetic play would take precedence over the "need to perform." Interpreted in this manner, repetitive music could be understood as a liberating experience *par excellence*.

In the eighties, Mertens (1980) and Kurzawa (1982), taking the libidinal philosophy of Deleuze and Lyotard as their starting point, have tried to come to a more positive assessment of repetitive music.[16] In this process they agree with Lyotard's criticism of Adorno: "We must leave behind us the alternative of appearance, *musica ficta*, and the alternative of knowledge acquired only with difficulty, *musica fingens*, and, in their place, propose a changeable game of tonal intensities, a work of art which parodies nothing: *musica figura*" (Lyotard, 1980, 118). According to Mertens, the concern of libidinal philosophy is no longer to see repetitive music as a representation for the representing subject, but rather as a pure presence of intensities. Quoting Deleuze's *Différence et Répétition*, Mertens maintains that "The singular intensities find themselves in a process which is always in movement and displacement, and which produces itself at every moment. These intensities have no other content than themselves: 'Each intensity wants to be itself, has itself as goal, and repeats and imitates itself'" (Mertens, 1980, 152). Mertens finds that

this self-generating aspect of libidinal intensities is preeminently characteristic of repetitive music whereby, as we remarked above, the issue
is one of processes that, after the composer has initiated them, appear to
unfold themselves:

> In musical terms this libidinal content is only really expressed in Amer-
> ican repetitive music which is characterized by *repetition* and by a
> *process* which can be directly appreciated. The process shifts attention
> from the *content* of the change to its *mobile play*. In repetitive music, the
> change itself is the content, such that one receives the suggestion of a
> completely unbounded and freely exchanging stream of energy. . . .
> The anonymity of the impersonal process in repetitive music is further
> emphasised by the repetition which is maintained for so long that it
> can no longer be intended as recognition, but rather turns against Ego-
> constancy itself. (Mertens, 1980, 155–56)

One can ask oneself if these reinterpretations of repetitive music
from within the pleasure principle can be regarded as fruitful in every
respect. Marcuse's utopian revision of Freud, developed under the influence of the radical psychoanalyst Wilhem Reich, has in any case had
to endure much criticism from his colleagues in the Frankfurt School.
Fromm, for example, accused Marcuse of reducing the individual, by
placing the pleasure principle as central, to a system of easy-to-manip-
ulate wishes and desires such as this was so cogently described by Hux-
ley in *Brave New World* (cf. Jay, 1973, 110–11). Laermans, in a sharp critique of Lyotard's, Guattari's, and Deleuze's "desirology," has pointed
out that in many ways these authors "remain prisoners in the discourse
that they actually want to undermine" (Laermans, 1982, 7). The affirmation of the "desires- and power-machines" by libidinal philosophers
is actually an affirmation of the consumer society and leads, according
to Laermans, using the words of Benjamin, straight to the "Abyss of aestheticism" (*Abgrund des Aesthetizismus*) (Laermans, 1982, 13). The call to
splinter the subject "while modern man is already for a long time no
longer an individual or personality, let alone a Subject, but rather an
amorph whole without unity," can receive little sympathy from Laermans. Mertens appears to share this critique when—reaching back to
psychoanalytic terminology—he can finally do nothing other than interpret the "state of innocence" that repetitive music engenders in the
listener as a "psychic regression" (Mertens, 1980, 156–57). Mertens' reason for reaching this judgment is that, like Laermans, he conceives of libidinal philosophy in the last analysis as a symptom of the illness of the
late-capitalist consumption society (Mertens, 1980, 158).

3.8 THE MOMENT OF THE ETERNAL RECURRENCE

Although I largely share Laerman's and Mertens' critique of libidinal philosophy, I would, in the case of repetitive music, nonetheless warn against the danger of throwing the baby—the innocence of the repetitive experience—out with the murky, libidinal bathwater. As is the case with many (post)modern phenomena, repetitive music possesses an ambivalent character that gives the lie to every attempt at one-dimensional interpretation. Although the repetition in repetitive music can be understood as a symptom of passive nihilism, of a decadent agreement with the loss of creative subjectivity, it can equally be interpreted as an experiment (which, like all experiments, is not free from a certain danger—cf. 2.7 above) that, in the light of the bankruptcy of a specific subject-centered tradition, attempts to develop new forms of aesthetic subjectivity.

I will try to clarify this point by thinking through the experience of repetition in repetitive music from the perspective of Nietzsche's doctrine of the Eternal Recurrence, something that was already announced by the *Fragment an sich*. In my discussion of Nietzsche's philosophy in chapter 1, I remarked that one of the most significant differences with Schopenhauer lay in the affirmative character of Nietzsche's thinking. In his doctrine of the Eternal Recurrence of the Same, Nietzsche, unlike Schopenhauer and Freud, thinks of repetition not from the perspective of displeasure, but rather from that of pleasure. Acceptance of the doctrine of the Eternal Recurrence implies an aesthetic imperative: to so behave that one would desire that everything be repeated countless times. After all, as Zarathustra speaks: "But all joy wants eternity,—wants deep, deep, deep eternity!" (Z, 244). In this context, repetition, in contrast to its position in Schopenhauer and Freud, is not thought of as a regressive phenomenon directed at avoiding displeasure, at the total elimination of tension, stimulation, and thereby of subjectivity as such, but rather as a progressive phenomenon in the literal sense, directed at the eternal repetition of the moment.

In his interesting analysis of Nietzsche's doctrine of the Eternal Recurrence, Visser makes this remark: "If one considers the eternal return from the perspective of displeasure, then everything becomes neutral, indifferent. If, on the contrary, one considers the eternal return from the perspective of pleasure, then nothing is neutral" (Visser, 1989, 314). As a progressive phenomenon, that is, considered from the perspective of the future, the Eternal Recurrence of the Same means that the ultimate is demanded of initiative. Viewed from this perspective, the "surrender" to the experience of repetitive music is not a life-denying flight from reality, but rather an experiment by the subject in the radical affirmation of life.

The doctrine of the Eternal Recurrence makes it possible for us to reinterpret several of the other aspects of experiencing repetitive music that I have identified. In the foregoing I remarked that repetitive music does not make a teleological, that is, a remembering and anticipating attitude possible. This, too, was a negative formulation wherein the experience of repetitive music was understood from the perspective of a teleological experience. From within the doctrine of the Eternal Recurrence of the Same, we can now positively argue that repetition opens the dimension of the *endless little moment* that Nietzsche announced as a higher reality and truth, which, according to him, flashes into existence from the eternal flood of Becoming (KSA, 9:502). Considered positively, the nonteleological experience of repetitive music means the complete affirmation of the here and now, which is freed from its crushing links with the past and the future. "The moment redeems from the fixation on the past by purging the old. But it just as much redeems from a desire that equally devalues the present, the moment: the desire for the constantly new" (Visser, 1989, 314).[17]

In the Eternal Recurrence of the Same the completeness of the endless little moment achieves a simultaneous expression. Because each moment repeats itself endlessly, it simultaneously places us in eternity (cf. 1.9).[18] Repetitive music thereby carries us into a radically other experience of time than that provided by teleological music: while teleological experience supports the view of time wherein it is understood as a sequence of now-moments, in repetitive music the passage of time is simultaneously the endless little moment. The moment of the Eternal Recurrence opens the view to both the past and the future. In the words of Zarathustra: " 'Behold this gateway, dwarf!' I went on: 'it has two aspects. Two paths come together here: no one has ever reached their ends. This long lane behind us: it goes on for an eternity. And that long lane ahead of us—that is another eternity. They are in opposition to one another, these paths; they abut on one another: and it is here at this gateway that they come together. The name of the gateway is written above it: 'Moment'" (Z, 178).[19] We are dealing here with what, following Lyotard, we could refer to as *intensive time*. Kurzawa, who applied this notion in his analysis of repetitive music, maintains: "The moment can never 'establish' or 'situate' itself. It must constantly disappear, or, something which comes to the same thing, it must constantly arrive, it must simultaneously go and come without cessation, 'be already past and yet still arriving.' The moment comes and goes, and, given that it simultaneously comes and goes with other moments, one can say that 'it returns,' never, however, in the present, but rather in a time which is simultaneously the past and the future" (Kurzawa, 1982, 11).

This other view of time has important implications for the concept of repetition. In the linear view of time, as it is expressed in teleological music, the repetition always points to an original example (e.g., Plato's empirical objects are always repetitions or copies of the unchangeable example of the Ideas; cf. 1.1 above). The inferior character that is traditionally ascribed to repetition is closely connected to the suspicion of being "merely" a copy. The doctrine of the Eternal Recurrence of the Same radically breaks through this logic of origins and, with reference to the notes of the musical piece, makes it impossible to differentiate between the original and a copy (cf. Kurzawa, 1982).[20] In repetitive music the intensity of the moment replaces the representative character of the notes in a teleological composition, which always points to an origin.

Alongside intensity, another essential aspect of experiencing repetitive music comes to the surface: when the tones of the musical work are taken out of the traditional teleological-representational context, they appear in a different form. They become, as it were, liberated from their bondage to an instrumental reason and recoup their contingency and chance, their nonbeing intended by the human subject. In the words of Zarathustra: " 'Lord Chance'—he is the world's oldest nobility, which I have given back to all things; I have released them from servitude under purpose" (Z, 186). Hereby repetitive music makes it possible to become "what we have not yet become: *good neighbours of what is closest to us*" (KSA, 8:588). Repetitive music opens another experience of reality on both sides of the instrumentalist reality principle that, in Western culture, also in music, has become dominant.[21] This other experience implies no denial of subjectivity—after all, the concern here is an experience of human subjectivity in and through a reflexive relationship between people and things—but rather a radical critique of the subjectivism that in previous centuries has decisively determined experience.

In chapter 6, by examining the theme of chance in John Cage's music, I shall try to further explicate this aesthetic subjectivism and the experience of things that it has generated, an experience that I have here merely sketched out. The perspective of the Eternal Recurrence, however, makes it clear in advance that the specified "other" experience must not be understood as a "new" experience. After all, the doctrine of the Eternal Recurrence means a break with the modernist cult of the new that is also embodied in teleological music (see also 0.2 and 0.4 and Vattimo, 1988, 164 ff.). The "other" experience, which we undergo in Cage's music, is only comprehensible as the result of a perverting *Verwindung* of the repetition in the teleological experience. One could also say that only in the deconstruction of the teleological experience is a space for the "other" experience created.[22]

Before I examine the musical experience any further I will address, in the following two chapters, the issue of whether or not, in poetry and painting, experiences can be noted similar to those that I have presented here in the context of repetitive music. In pursuit of this aim I shall spend more time on Heidegger's hermeneutics, which has been addressed in passing in previous chapters, and which, in a certain sense, can be viewed as an heir of the Romantic project, and, more especially, of Nietzsche's elaboration of it. Given that the psychoanalytic conceptual apparatus can be useful to us with respect to articulating the "other" experience of aesthetic subjectivism, psychoanalysis, too, only this time more extensively, will once again be addressed. As psychoanalysis remains partially tributary to instrumental rationality, the boundaries of its usefulness with respect to the interpretation of the aesthetic will hereby once again emerge.

4

The First and the Last Word

Every philosophy conceals another philosophy; every opinion is also a hideaway; every word is also a mask.
—Friedrich Nietzsche

This chapter wanders around some words of Gerrit Achterberg, one of the most passionate poets of twentieth-century Dutch poetry. These words enable me to speak about the poetic word in a more general sense, and about what connects and separates poetry from philosophy and science. One can only speak when one has words available, and words can only appear within a particular horizon of experience. In this chapter, this horizon is constituted by philosophical hermeneutics and psychoanalytic theory and practice; my sources are primarily the works of Heidegger, Freud, and Lacan. The aim is to clarify some of the assumptions that steered my conceptual wanderings in the previous chapters.

The reason I bring psychoanalysis and hermeneutics into a dialogue with one of Achterberg's stanzas is that interesting ideas in both psychoanalytic and hermeneutic literature are developed, inspired by the poetic word. Moreover, psychoanalysis and hermeneutics appear to share a number of fundamental assumptions. The Dutch philosopher IJsseling, in an article published in 1969, has pointed out four remarkable parallels between Lacan's psychoanalysis and Heidegger's hermeneutics. In the first place, *language* occupies a central position for both Lacan and Heidegger: "For both Heidegger and Lacan language is a structure which, on the one hand, is more original than humans and their world because both humans and their world derive their basic rules from it. . . . On the other hand, language exists and functions only within human speech" (IJsseling, 1969, 263–64). In the second place, Lacan's psychoanalysis and Heidegger's hermeneutics both have the tendency to *decenter the subject:* as IJsseling expressed it, man "when he speaks, is more the subordinate than the subject of his words" (ibid., 265). In the third place, according to IJsseling, there is an overcoming of metaphysics in both Heidegger and Lacan, something that implies "an ending and a final completion of philosophy . . . in modern science and technology" (ibid., 265). Finally, IJsseling unravels "a certain parallelism . . . between the 'un-thought' and the 'un-said' in Heidegger, which really remain un-thought and un-said, and the 'unconscious' in Lacan which is not derivable, cannot be made conscious, and is merely acknowledged" (ibid., 265).

IJsseling's interpretation has not been without influence in the Dutch-speaking world: for example, we encounter it in striking fashion in Antoine Mooij's 1975 work on Lacan: *Taal en verlangen* (*Language and Desire*).[1] In this chapter, the specified parallels form the background against which an interpretation of one of Achterberg's stanzas will take place. However, I shall argue that the convergence of psychoanalysis and hermeneutics that IJsseling sketched out ultimately ends in a fundamental divergence. The point of divergence concerns the questions as to whether the poetic word constitutes a *domain* of knowing or, in the final analysis, is merely an *object* of another sort of knowing, philosophical or scientific.

This distinction can be easily clarified by reference to Antoine Mooij's *Language and Desire*. Mooij prefaces this introduction to Lacan's psychoanalytic theory with the following stanza from Gerrit Achterberg's poem "Bread and Circuses" (*Brood en spelen*, Achterberg, 1979, 929):

> The word has the first and the last word.
> In between, an ideal shatters into slivers,
> series of generations reproduce themselves,
> the characteristics of which I had to inherit.

> 't Woord heeft het eerste en het laatste woord.
> Daartussen valt een ideaal aan scherven,
> planten zich reeksen generaties voort,
> wier eigenschappen ik moest overerven.

The question at issue is whether we should regard Achterberg's stanza as an illustration of Mooij's scientific explication of Lacan's work, or whether we should regard this entire explication as an explanation, an interpretation, of the sense or meaning that the stanza offers us.[2] It will be argued that in psychoanalysis—explicitly in Freud's work, more ambivalently in Lacan's work—the poetic word is ultimately reduced to a pure object and illustration of psychoanalytic, that is, scientific, knowing. Heidegger, in contrast, following the Romantic movement and, more especially, Nietzsche, conceives of the poetic word as a domain of truth whereby the task of the thinker is to guard in thought what has been revealed in the poetic word.

It would be easy to dismiss the specified distinction as a marginal difference compared with the real agreements between psychoanalysis and hermeneutics. However, this small difference has destructive consequences for each of the four parallels specified by IJsseling: the poetic word, which brings psychoanalysis and hermeneutics together in this text, simultaneously sows the discord that causes their irreconcilable separation.

That which follows is a *philosophical discourse* concerning poetry, psychoanalysis, and hermeneutics: I do not submit poetic evocation, but rather argumentation. However, I permit myself to be guided by the poet's word. It must be understood as an interpretation of Achterberg's words that I quoted above. It is an interpretation that gives the first and the last word to the poet and that gradually unfolds itself in the discursive space that is created by his words.

4.1 THE RHETORIC OF THE UNCONSCIOUS

The word has the first and the last word.

't Woord heeft het eerste en het laatste woord.

The first line of Achterberg's stanza embodies in a fortunate manner what psychoanalysis and hermeneutics have in common with poetry: a particular openness for the *magic of the word*. "Words," maintains Freud in his *Introductory Lectures on Psychoanalysis*, "were originally magic and to this day words have retained much of their ancient power" (SE, 15:17). The magic that is ascribed to the word is closely connected to the view that, in the final analysis, it is not the speaker who takes over the word, but rather the word that takes possession of the speaker. Language, not man, has the first and the last word. The quotation from

Freud already indicates that we are not here concerned with a *modern* conceptualization: we have already remarked in chapter 2, following Weber, that the modern period is characterized by a disenchantment (*Entzauberung*) of the world. For this reason, ascribing magical powers to the word sounds rather archaic to us and appears to emerge from an unjustified hypostatization of language. Such a view reminds us of a superseded metaphysical and religious past.[3]

Perhaps even a *pre*-metaphysical past. The commencement of the disenchantment of the word appears to go hand in hand with the commencement of Western metaphysics. Prototypical of this disenchantment is the transition from the *mythos* to the *logos* such as this was completed in Plato's work. As we already remarked in chapter 1, in a number of places Plato makes rather condescending comments about art: in the Ion it sounds more scornful than affirmative that the poet "is never able to compose until he is inspired, and is besides himself and reason is no longer in him" (Ion, 534b). With the banishment of the poet from the Republic, Plato also appears to have excluded (belief in) the magic of the word from Western metaphysics and the science that it supports (cf. 1.1 above).

Nonetheless, Freud maintains that "to the present day . . . the word has maintained much of its magical power."[4] In the space that was excluded by metaphysics, poetry has cherished the magical power of the word and enabled it to survive over the centuries. Since the Romantic period, it appears that one can even speak of a resurgence of (the belief in) the magic of the word. The poetry of Hölderlin and George, Rimbaud and Mallarmé, and, pregnantly, of Achterberg, demands the reclaiming of the cognitive space that has been taken from it by metaphysics. The poet appears to have found a worthy ally in the psychoanalyst. To use Mallarmé's expression, psychoanalysis, just like poetry, gives "the initiative to the word." This applies to both the *practice* of the therapeutic dialogue and the psychoanalytic *theory* of the unconscious.

In the therapeutic dialogue, the word has the first and the last word in the sense that "nothing takes place in psychoanalytic treatment but an interchange of words" (SE, 15:17). Just as we could refer to a poem as a *talking event*, psychoanalysis, as a much-quoted utterance of one of Freud's patients has called it, is a *talking cure*. But, in a second, more striking sense, in poetry and therapeutic practice the word has the first and the last word. The analysand commits himself to free association: without exception, he is expected to say everything that *enters his mind*.[5] Just as in the archaic view another voice is speaking through the poet, in the therapeutic dialogue another voice emerges: that of the unconscious. The "voice" of the unconscious does not speak directly to us any more than does the voice of the gods in the words of the poet or the oracle. "The unconscious is what *is missing* in the story because it cannot be told in a direct fashion. But what cannot be told in a direct fashion is indirectly available, in errors, slips of the tongue, dreams, etc." (Mooij, 1975, 105—italics JdM). While, in normal communication, errors and slips of the tongue are put to one side as irrelevant and irrational disturbances of the conversation, the orientation in therapeutic dialogue and poetic inspiration is precisely aimed at giving voice to the unconscious. For this reason, both therapy and poetry stand in a position of tension with everyday language: "The poet and the analyst . . . thus create in the context of the analytical session (or the poetic bundle) *another* language: deviant, malformed, subversive in comparison with 'normal' communication" (Mehlman, 1976, 119).

In the psychoanalytical (*meta*)*theory* of the unconscious, too, certainly in the Lacanian version, the word has the first and the last word. At the theoretical level the primacy of language repeats itself, as we remarked in terms of the therapeutic dialogue, and, also at this level, in a dual meaning. In the first place, according to Lacan, the unconscious is structured as a language: "L'inconscient, c'est le discours de l'Autre: il est structuré comme une langage" (É, 7). According to Mooij, this utterance can, among other things, be read as: "That which escapes from a particular story nonetheless remains marked by the story in which it can find no entrance. The unconscious, therefore, is not amorphous and unstructured, but rather exhibits a coherence. This coherence is different from that of the (conscious) story, but the unconscious nonetheless provides, by virtue of this coherence, a story, *un discours de l'Autre*. This story is to be interpolated in the lacunas which the conscious story provides" (Mooij, 1975, 130–31). Therefore, Lacan can also maintain that the unconscious is a chain of terms (*"une chaine signifiante"*—É, 798).

For this reason it is also possible to speak literally of a *rhetoric* of the unconscious. Lacan identifies the pattern, characteristic of the unconscious, of the condensation and shifting of the literary figures of the metaphor and the metonym (cf. Freud, SE, 4:279–309, and É, 799). This makes the psychoanalytic interpretation into a signifying art that is closely related to literary interpretation. "In this light, interpretation is the filling in and out of the empty spaces which the story shows, and of which its malformations give evidence, whereby at the same time the *sense* of these empty spaces can be given" (Mooij, 1975, 105). The meaning of the story—to use the metaphor developed in chapter 1—is not written in stone but slips with the context (just as the meaning of

Achterberg's words slip in the process of my interpretation). This implies that the interpretation of the analysand's story is not so much a *reconstruction* as a *construction* of the past. On the basis of what the story has to say to him, the analysand designs a new "look" at his past, and, at the same time, thereby understands himself in new, future possibilities. Therefore, as a construction, the psychoanalytic interpretation is above all things a *poiēsis,* a creation of imagination.

This view of interpretation breaks down the wall between fact and fiction. The relativization of this distinction can, without exaggeration, be called one of the most fundamental insights of psychoanalysis. In his *An Autobiographical Study* from 1925 Freud maintained that psychoanalysis took a determined direction when he discovered that neurotic symptoms do not so much arise from events that have really occurred, but rather from phantasies and wishful thinking (SE, 20:33–34). After he had discovered that it is impossible to distinguish between phantasies and memories, he was no longer interested in the reconstruction of events from the past through the exposure of repressed memories, but rather in investigating the phantasies of the analysand (Ellenberger, 1970, 488).[6] For this reason one could call psychoanalysis a science of fiction. However, it must not thereby be forgotten that the object of this science—if I may express it in such paradoxical terms—is formed by "real fictions." The unconscious phantasies that are at issue here are constitutive for the life story of the human individual. They make that individual what he is: a being who desires.

The primacy of language in the theory of the unconscious can be discussed in another way. The unconscious, in Lacan's view, is not only structured as a language but, at the same time, language forms "the conditions of the possibility of the unconscious" (Lacan, 1970, 8). The unconscious is not an ontogenetic or phylogenetic older layer "under" the linguistic consciousness, as Freud appears to assume in his genetic approach, but rather it is the correlation of the linguistic culture (Mooij, 1975, 132). Using a term from Heidegger, Mooij states that the conscious and the unconscious are of the same origin (*gleichursprünglich*) (Mooij, 1975, 132).

4.2   SPEAKING LANGUAGE

In Heidegger's philosophical hermeneutics, too, the first and the last word in interpretation is given to the word. The hermeneutic interpretation, just as the psychoanalytic, is open to what the text has to say to us, something that assumes that the text has its eloquence. In "Language" (1950) Heidegger gives an expression to this eloquence that appears to satisfy Achterberg's words: "Language speaks" ("Die Sprache spricht") (L, 190). This expression appears somewhat strange to us: after all, language is a human instrument; speaking is a human activity wherein man expresses his feelings, makes propositions, and communicates. For several centuries there has been widely held consensus about this fact in linguistics and philosophy. Heidegger does not deny that language "remains unmistakably bound up with human speaking" (OWL, 125), no more than the structuralist Lacan denies that the language (*langue*) can only be actualized in concrete human speech (*parole*). According to Heidegger, the consensus that exists in linguistics and philosophy, to the extent that it is directed at constructing a metalanguage, a metalinguistics, is correct (*richtig*). But what is correct does not necessarily have to be the complete or the primary truth. The usual linguistic view, according to Heidegger, misses language itself: as little attention is paid to the *working* of language in everyday language as in scientific language. The transparency of language ensures that we do not notice these effects. Just as is the case with every human tool, language appears to be self-evident. Only at the moment that language fails, when we cannot think of a word and are momentarily speechless, are we forced to consider the effects of language.

In *On the Way to Language,* Heidegger wants "to speak about speech qua speech" ("Die Sprache als die Sprache zur Sprache bringen") (OWL, 112). In this case, the concern is a purely spoken language, that is, speech that is freed of its usual instrumental function. According to Heidegger, "what is spoken purely is the poem" (L, 194).[7] One of the poems that Heidegger considers in *On the Way to Language* is Stephan George's poem "*The Word (Das Wort)*." In this poem we encounter a line that throws light on the meaning that Achterberg's words engender:

> Where word breaks off no thing may be

> Kein ding sei wo das wort gebricht

Nothing may be where the word is missing. The poet "uses" no words: the poetic word calls into existence. Accordingly, poeticizing is before everything else a *naming* (L, 198).[8] It names things, that which exists, and therefore brings them into the light. The essence of language is *Sage*. Heidegger takes the etymology of the term as a clue:[9] " 'To say,' related to the Old Norse '*saga*,' means to show: to make appear, set free, that is, to offer and extend what we call World, lighting and concealing it"

(OWL, 93). It is not that the word "is," it *gives* us a world: "We do not mean 'There is the word'—we mean 'by virtue of the gift of the word there is, the word gives' " (OWL, 88).

To actually understand Heidegger's view of language, we need to see it against the background of the question concerning Being, which always dominated his thoughts (although, as we shall shortly see, from a changing perspective). "Being" is a concept with a long history in Western metaphysics. This term was used from antiquity onward to point to what beings have in common and what makes them beings. In other words, it is an *ontological* concept (*on, ontos* is the Greek word for being).[10] Now, there is an ambiguity connected with the concept 'Being'; it can occur as both noun and verb. As noun, it indicates something that *is*, a being (entity). However, Heidegger argues that one cannot say of Being that it *is* (or one must view 'is' as being transitive; cf. ID, 62). Being is no being, but rather the occurrence of the appearance of being. It is the temporal process of the illumination of being: Being is "the presentation of what is present." In this connection, Heidegger also sometimes uses the term *Lichtung* (the lighting process, or, more literally: an open space in the woods), which initially makes it possible that something appears (emerges): "But the lighting itself is Being" ("Die Lichtung selber ist das Sein") (BW, 211).

According to Heidegger, the happening of Being, or *Lichtung*, is closely connected with language: it is in the purely spoken language that the 'being' (this term is used here not as a noun but as a verb) of Being happens and that the beings become present. The *Lichtung* of Being happens in language, something that is expressed in the formula: "the Being of language—the language of Being" (OWL, 72). The Being of language is that it makes Being: language, in other words, has *ontological implications*. In George's words: no thing may be where word breaks off. For this reason, Heidegger in the "Letter on Humanism" calls language "the house of Being" (BW, 193). The word has the first and the last word because it forms the privileged place of the happening of Being.

The poet who listens to what the word has to say to him shares in the privilege of the word and hears Being. His word brings Being into the open. Heidegger views this openness or, as he calls it, non-concealment (*aletheia*) as the truth of Being (cf. BT, sect. 44). For this reason, Heidegger, in *"The Origin of the Work of Art"* (1950) refers to poetry as "setting-into-work of truth" ("Stiftung der Wahrheit") (BW, 186). Language gives man the privilege of standing in the openness of Being. Thus, Heidegger can also maintain: " 'Being'—that is not God and not a cosmic ground. Being is farther than all beings and is yet nearer to man than every being, be it a rock, a beast, a work of art, a machine, be it and angel, or God" (BW, 210).

4.3   THE SPEECHLESS POET

We have now understood the first line of the stanza as follows: the word brings being into the light, it signifies its closeness, it indicates its presence. Nothing exists for us without the poetic word. But in the psychoanalytic dialogue, too, there is nothing beyond the "redeeming" word (cf. Lacan, 1975, 61). The word sets both the analysand and his world in the present. However, although the word has the first and the last word, Achterberg continues:

> In between, an *ideal* shatters into slivers
>
> Daartussen valt een *ideaal* aan scherven.

The stanza's second line appears to devalue the omnipotence of the word established in the first line. An ideal shatters into slivers between the first and the last word.

Against the background of Heidegger's conceptualization of Being we could interpret this ideal that shatters into slivers as the ideal of immediately re-presenting Being. The quotation that ended the previous section continues: "Being is the nearest. Yet the near remains farthest from man" (BW, 210). The word calls things into the foreground but simultaneously hides the origin: the happening of Being wherefrom beings originate. The language in which beings are disclosed is thus simultaneously a domain that conceals. Given that language is the house of Being, this concealing constitutes the essence of language. Because the word is not something that *is*, but rather something that *gives*, the poet lacks sufficient vocabulary to articulate the poetic word itself (OWL, 88). With respect to the origin, the word continually disappoints, and, for this reason, there is a certain melancholy discernible in George's words:

> So I renounced and *sadly* see:
> Where word breaks off no thing may be
>
> So lernt ich *traurig* den verzicht:
> Kein ding sei wo das wort gebricht

In his commentary, Heidegger maintains: "An 'is' arises where the word breaks up" ("Ein 'ist' ergibt sich, wo das Wort zerbricht") (OWL, 108).

In the poet's namings, the beings are brought into the light; however, what remains unspoken in these namings is the Being itself that makes a being "be." Accordingly, Heidegger states in his commentary that a being appears there where the Word shatters into slivers. " 'To break off' here means that the sounding word returns into soundlessness, back to whence it was granted" (OWL, 108). With respect to Being, the poet is speechless. Although the poet can eloquently articulate his understanding of an indisputable lack (of Being)—the capacity to do this ensures that, not in the last instance in Achterberg's work, the poetic word fascinates us!—he lacks the word necessary for naming the lack. IJsseling expresses this as follows in his doctoral thesis concerning Heidegger: "This Being is what is unsaid and unsayable. For this reason, man is never definitively finished with speaking, the last word does not exist for him" (IJsseling, 1964, 70). It is not only Being that, in the poetic word, is concealed by the appearing into the light of beings; the beings conceal each other. The ideal that shatters into slivers between the first and the last word is accordingly *also* the ideal of the word-that-says-everything, the definitive word that is simultaneously the first *and* the last word.

In psychoanalysis, too, we encounter this thematic of the unreachable ideal of complete meaning. In the psychoanalytic perspective, speaking always necessarily implies a certain *frustration* (É 252). Mooij, summarizing the thematic, puts it as follows: "The story is a *presentation*, that is, a contemporaneous making present of man and world. In the story, both the story-teller and his world are specified as present: something is told about something or someone. Naming, however, is: not naming: through explication, something else is left in the shadows. Something or someone is (in terms of certain aspects) unveiled, but, at the same time, concealed (in terms of other aspects). The story is an unveiling and a concealing simultaneously" (Mooij, 1975, 92–93). Achterberg's words evoke that which disappears from between the words, that which remains unconscious:

> The Word has the first and the last word.
> *In between,* an ideal shatters into slivers . . .

> 't Woord heeft het eerste en het laatste woord.
> *Daartussen* valt een ideaal aan scherven . . .

The empty spaces (pauses of meaning) *between* the words, as we can interpret Achterberg's words, dispossesses us of the illusion of "a full speech" (*une parole pleine*).

More fundamentally, with the acknowledgment of the impossibility of full speech, the ideal of the "omnipotent" speaking subject shatters simultaneously into slivers. If the word has the first and the last word, then the speaking subject cannot be, as a long tradition maintains, the origin or center of speech. Freud articulated this pictorially with the formula "*the ego is not the master in its own house*" (SE, 17:143; cf. 3.7 above). In the light of Heidegger's terminology, we can read this as follows: the I is no longer master in the house of his language because this linguistic house is ultimately not *his* house, but rather the house of *Being*.

The imagery that Achterberg maintains in the second line, throws a closer light on the identity of the ideal that shatters into slivers. It is not exclusively, not even in the first instance, a word: after all, it shatters into slivers *between* the words. That which does not belong to the domain of language is often indicated as *image*. Moreover, the issue here is that of an extremely fragile image, as fragile as our reflection in water. This reflecting surface does not *shatter into slivers* due to unbridled violence, but rather due to a simple whispering of the word. However, despite this fragility, the image is extremely tempting, as Narcissus experienced when staring at his own reflection. Lacan, who in his work thematicized the decentering of the subject in a far more emphatic manner than Freud did, therefore used, perhaps not coincidentally, the imagery of the mirror when he spoke about the forming of the subject's identity.[11]

Just as is the case with his structuralist colleague Piaget, for Lacan the subject is not something that is given in advance, but rather something that comes into being (cf. 2.1 above). The mirror stage (*stade du miroir*) plays a crucial role in this coming into being. For the infant (between the sixth and the thirtieth month), the mirror-image provides the first complete image of itself. According to Lacan, this image has priority over the other images that the infant has of itself and that show the child as a crumbled body (*un corps morcelé*). Identifying itself with the mirror-image provides the basis of the infant's identity: "The jubilant assumption of its mirror-image by the tiny human infant which, in its *infans*-stadium is a being which is still completely trapped in motor impotence and dependence upon nurturers, is something which will consequently, in an exemplary situation, appear to show us the symbolic matrix wherein the I (*je*) is poured in a primordial form before it becomes objectivized in the dialectic of identification with the Other and before language has provided it with its function as subject" (É, 94). The primordial 'I' that comes into being in this manner, and that is identified with what Freud called the ideal ego, is called the *imaginary* by Lacan. It is a product of an imaginary identification because the child postulates itself as equal to something that it is not: the image in the mirror. It is thus a false image and a misunderstanding (*méconnaissance*). Nonetheless, this misunderstanding forms the conditions of possibility for the forming of the subject. Without this first, imaginary identification, later forms of identification would be impossible, while, simultaneously, this imaginary identification condemns the individual to an alienating destiny: "The most important point is that this form, even before its social determination, situates the instantiation of the *Ego* (*moi*) in a line of fiction which can never be completely recuperated by any individual—or, rather, which will only asymptotically facilitate his becoming a subject . . . " (É, 94).

The alienating becoming-a-subject takes on its definitive form once language enters the order. The linguistic order, comprising the totality of differentiated signifiers, provides the child with a name. This name makes possible a symbolic identification that replaces the imaginary identification. In the transition from the imaginary order of the image to the symbolic order of language, the sharing (*fente*) between the infant and his mirror-image is definitively established (*re-fente*). "The subject is not something which exists, but rather the coming into existence because the (future) subject intrudes himself into language and permits himself to be marked by it. The subject does not create language, but rather language creates the subject" (Mooij, 1975, 128). "The subject is no origin or center, but rather his position is eccentric with respect to the symbolic order, which constitutes the center. Herein is contained the injury towards the narcissism of a particular self-explanation by man" (ibid., 147).[12] With the entrance into language the imaginary ideal ego (*Ideal-Ich*) that the subject has constructed from himself is completely shattered. In its place comes the symbolically marked identity that is paid for with the loss of immediacy. This loss creates the fundamental lack that forms the basis of the desire that is characteristic of human existence. The ultimate acquisition of an own identity marked by language thus brings with it a fundamental yearning for the Other that is as unsatisfiable as it is unquenchable (ibid., 126).[13]

By emphasizing the eccentric character of human subjectivity and the unquenchability of human desire, Lacan, in his own way, associates with the Romantic tendency that is characteristic of nineteenth- and twentieth-century philosophical anthropology. In chapter 2 I remarked that Scheler and Plessner, the founders of contemporary philosophical anthropology, give a central place in their work to the eccentric character of human existence. According to them, humans, in contrast to animals, not only stand opposite to their environment, but also to themselves. Accordingly, man often experiences himself as a stranger and knows the desire "to become himself" (see Plessner, 1965, 288 ff.). For this reason, people strive for a completion of themselves.

In Heidegger's thinking, too, especially at the time of *Being and Time*, this transcending of the self plays an important role. He maintains that the human There-being (*Dasein*) should be understood as *projection (Entwurf)*, a task that is always yet to be realized (BT, 185). Only when human *Dasein* authentically places itself in relation to its temporariness (something that is constantly thwarted by its tendency to inauthentical engagement with the beings present in the world) can it realize itself as projection. Just as Nietzsche before him, Heidegger specifies the authentic manner of being-ahead-of-oneself-in-the-present with the term "Moment" (*Augenblick*) (BT, 387; cf. 3.8 above). Lacan, too, underlines man's "temporary" character: according to him, this temporary character is associated with the entrance into the symbolic order and the associated surrender of the Oedipal desire to immediately coincide with (the desire of) the mother. Mooij comments: "Because, in the surrender (*Versagung*) of the immediate presence a promise is simultaneously specified with the prohibition: one day, when you're bigger. In this way, the future is opened up, and, subsequently (*nachträglich*), what has happened can be seen as the past and the now as the present. In place of the *'nunc stans'* of the immediate presence, the ecstasies of time are established" (Mooij, 1975, 143–44).

That which distinguishes Lacan's view of man from the philosophers named above is his radical emphasis on the unquenchable character of desire and the insubstantial character of the subject of this desire.[14] Lacan considers human existence as really being a frustration and the desire for unity as being in the strict sense imaginary and thus unfulfillable.[15] The acknowledgment of the eccentric character of man means an injury for whoever ascribes an absolute autonomy to the subject. This injury raises the question of the origins of the human subject's phantasies of omnipotence.

4.4 HEIDEGGER'S GENEALOGY OF THE SUBJECT

> The word has the first and the last word.
> In between, an ideal shatters *into slivers*

> 't Woord heeft het eerste en het laatste woord.
> Daartussen valt een ideaal *aan scherven*

The interpretation until now shows us that the autonomy of the speaking subject is a false ideal, an idol, an image that shatters into slivers between the first and the last word. Nonetheless, this false ideal has a long history. Between the first and the last word

> series of generations reproduce themselves . . .

> planten zich reeksen generaties voort . . .

In "The Age of the World View" Heidegger presents a penetrating genealogy of subjectivism.[16] The concept 'subject' has more than one meaning: depending upon the context, it means a part of a judgment distinguished from the predicate, a grammatical subject of a sentence, or, more generally, an "I" that stands in contrast to an object or an external world. According to Heidegger, the concept of the 'subject' has such a wealth of meaning because it is a reflection of its etymological history in Western metaphysics. The concept is derived from the Latin *subjectum*, which is actually a translation of the Greek *hypokeimenon*. In "The Age of the World View" Heidegger elaborates upon the shifting meaning that the concept has undergone. For the Greeks, *hypokeimenon* (literally, "that which is underneath") referred to what "is merely available to us and which as such simultaneously constitutes the basis for its durable characteristics and its variable circumstances" (HW, 106–7). According to Heidegger, the *hypokeimenon* formed a "self-sufficient, unshakeable basis of truth in the sense of certainty" for the Greeks (HW, 107). As such, the *hypokeimenon* means the base that underlies every knowledge. In the Platonic and Aristotelian metaphysical tradition, this *hypokeimenon* was more specifically defined as "idea" (Idea) or *"ousia"* (substance). Initially, *hypokeimenon* thus had no specific relationship with man or the "I." According to Heidegger, the term *hypokeimenon* (*subjectum*) has maintained this nonanthropocentric meaning in the metaphysical tradition until modern philosophy.

It was Descartes who originated a radical shifting in the meaning of the term by conceiving of the *subjectum* as a *human* subject. What is interesting with this development is that the connotations attached to the older meaning have not disappeared, but rather have been absorbed in the new meaning. Descartes, just as the metaphysical tradition before him did with respect to the nonanthropocentric *subjectum*, conceived of the human subject as the basis of truth. In addition, however, the subject received from Descartes the significance of being the *indisputable certainty* of this truth. This receives expression in the famous Cartesian formula, *ego cogito (ergo) sum*. For Descartes this means that at the same time as man thinks (and for Descartes this is in the first place: presenting or re-presenting something), he is himself also constantly and indisputably present. "The *subjectum*, the basic certainty, is the at all times guaranteed simultaneously represented being of the representing subject together with the represented human or non-human being, that is, the objective" (HW, 109).[17] It is hereby made clear that, for Descartes, an object is at all times necessarily in contrast to the human subject: for him, the object exists merely as a being represented for a human subject. For Descartes, the basic certainty is thus not, as is the case in the entire metaphysical tradition before him, formed by something outside of the individual (be that the Idea, substance, or God), but rather by the indubitably always representable and represented *me cogitare = me esse.*[18]

In this manner, the genealogy of the concept 'subject' throws a first light on the way that the "human subject" was surrounded with phantasies of omnipotence, namely, by an expropriation of what originally constituted its basis.

4.5   UNVEILING AND CONCEALING BEING

> In between, an ideal shatters into slivers,
> series of generations reproduce themselves,
> the characteristics of which I had to inherit.
>
> Daartussen valt een ideaal aan scherven,
> planten zich reeksen generaties voort,
> wier eigenschappen ik moest overerven.

The history of the concept 'subject' may be considered exemplary for the entire history of Western metaphysics. According to Heidegger, this history is actually characterized by what he refers to as a fundamental *forgottenness-of-Being (Seinsvergessenheit)* or, in his later work, *abandonment-of-Being (Seinsverlassenheit).* That which is forgotten in forgottenness-of-Being is the ontological distinction (*Differenz*) between Being and beings (ID, 46–47). In the metaphysical tradition, the question concerning Being is misunderstood as a question relating to beings, and, more especially, concerning the highest being that functions as foundation for all other beings. Because, in Western metaphysics, the distinction between the theological question concerning the highest being and the ontological question relating to the Being of beings is not made, Heidegger chose to designate this tradition as an ontotheology (ID, 31 ff.). The forgottenness-of-Being is not a coincidental characteristic of metaphysics. On the contrary, it constitutes the conditions of its possibility: Being thereby remains *unthought*. It is this forgottenness-of-Being that the "I" in Achterberg's stanza had to inherit.

However, on the basis of what I have already said concerning the human subject's status of subordination to language and Being, it would not be correct to dismiss forgottenness-of-Being as a failure of this human subject. According to Heidegger, this abandonment-of-Being happens to man as a destiny of Being (*Geschick des Seins*) (BW, 210). The forgottenness-of-Being comes from the nature of Being's own happening. As was remarked above (4.3), the happening of Being is a process that is simultaneously one of unveiling and concealing: Being, conceived as the occurrence that unveils beings, itself remains concealed in this unveiling. In other words, Being is characterized by both positivity and negativity. Nothing is without Being, but considered from within the perspective of beings, this Being is nothing rather than a something.

Expressed in a nonanthropocentric terminology, the happening of Being can be designated an "auto-transmission" of Being. However, as the history of the *subjectum* makes clear, this transmission is not singular: there are many different destinies (*Ge-schick-te*) of Being. Together, they form the history (*Geschichte*) of Being. Given that understanding constitutes an essential part of Being, Being-as-history can also be understood as the history of the thinking of Being. In the thoughts concerning Being, an original truth (non-concealment) of Being emerges into the lighting process; at the same time, Being is necessarily concealed in its happening. Reasoning from within the human subject's phantasies of omnipotence, one could view this inherent negativity of this happening-of-Being as a deficiency (*Mangel*). However, thinking from within Being, Heidegger speaks of its restrained wealth. Restrained, because this wealth of Being first unfolds itself in the history of Being's self-explanation. For this reason, Achterberg's words can also be read in a more positive manner:

> The Word has the first and the last word.
> In between, an ideal shatters *into* slivers

> 't Woord heeft het eerste en het laatste woord.
> Daartussen valt een ideaal *aan* scherven,

an ideal, namely, that first twinkles in the glittering of language's slivers.

However, according to Heidegger, the relationship between negativity and positivity is not always equal. In his analyses of the history of
metaphysics—his analysis of the *subjectum* makes a good example—he
shows how the specified negativity, the forgottenness-of-Being, has increasingly come to dominate thinking. According to him, this can be
seen from the history of the concept 'truth' in Western thought. With respect to the truth of Being, Heidegger understands the meaning
accorded to Being in the different periods of the thinking of Being. He
maintains that the pre-Socratics understood the truth to be the non-
concealment (*aletheia*) of Being. The concept of nature (*physis*) among the
pre-Socratics was employed by Heidegger as an example of this view
(cf. Heraclitus' famous comment concerning nature that is accustomed
to hide itself; Heraclitus, in Kirk and Raven, 1987, 193).

The most important transformation of the concept of truth, mark-
ing the birth of metaphysics, took place in Plato's Theory of Ideas. It is
perhaps true that the Platonic Idea, like the interpretations of the truth
of Being after Plato, maintains the old connotation of non-concealment.
Plato viewed the Idea in the first instance as the light in which beings
participate and which first makes them beings (we find this particularly
lucidly expressed in the myth of the Cave in *The Republic* VII.514a–521c).
But, on the other hand, Plato considered Being as constituting something that can be *beheld* (at least by the philosopher). It is conceived as
something that *is*, as being. Given that Plato's attention was primarily
directed at the highest being (the Idea of the Good), ontotheology actually commences with Platonism. The truth is now viewed as *correspondence* between thinking and Ideas.

The history of the concept of truth reaches a new phase in
Descartes' subjectivism. The indisputable *cogito* of the human subject ensures that the truth can no longer only be viewed as correspondence, but
that it must be simultaneously seen as providing the foundation of the
certainty of this correspondence (cf. 4.4). According to Heidegger, in the
"Copernican" turning toward the transcendental subject in Kant's transcendental philosophy, this anthropocentric subjectivism was further
radicalized, reaching its pinnacle in Hegel's philosophy.[19] For Hegel, Being and the Absolute Spirit are ultimately identical with human consciousness. According to Heidegger we are at this point the furthest removed from ontological difference. However, the completion of
metaphysics is actually achieved in Nietzsche's thinking. During the
1930s Heidegger dedicated a series of lectures to Nietzsche's thinking
(see N 1 and 2). In the nihilistic announcement of the death of God

(viewed as the highest being, which provides the foundation of all beings), Nietzsche, according to Heidegger, radically affirms the end of metaphysics. However, as the completion of metaphysics, Heidegger considered Nietzsche's thinking as still completely belonging to metaphysics. According to Heidegger, Nietzsche's substantial critique of Plato leads to an *inverted* Platonism (N 2:22, see 1.9). He finds that Nietzsche remains ensnared in the subject-object polarity that is characteristic of modern metaphysics. Nietzsche's doctrine of the Will to Power is even susceptible of being viewed as the most extreme expression of Cartesian subjectivism because Nietzsche gives the *Übermensch* the task of subordinating no less than the totality of reality to his Will.[20]

According to Heidegger, modern science and technology, too, in contrast to their positivistic self-conception, are not opposed to the metaphysics of the subject, but rather are their ultimate expression: "In the planetary imperialism of technologically organized humanity, human subjectivity reaches it peak, from where it will descend to the level of organized uniformity in order to establish itself at that point. This uniformity, after all, is the most certain instrument of the complete, that is, technical, domination of the earth. The modern liberty of subjectivity disappears completely in the objectivity associated with it" (HW, 111).

Modern technology, just as the old *technē*, remains a method of unveiling, but in contrast to the old technique wherein nature (*physis*) was *assisted* to unveil itself, modern technology consists of challenging nature to appear (QT, 296). In calculating thinking, beings are exclusively considered from the perspective of their utility and availability: not only the certainty of the knowledge concerning the objects with which the subject surrounds himself, but, above everything, their *controllability*, too, is central in modern science and technology.[21]

Heidegger adopts an especially critical standpoint with respect to this history of increasing forgetfulness-of-Being: in 1929, with the publication of *Being and Time*, his aim was already a destruction (*Destruktion*) of metaphysics. However, this destruction should not be viewed as exclusively destructive, driven by an "imaginary" illusion to return to *pre*-metaphysical thinking or a *pre*-metaphysical method of production. What it *does* involve is an undermining of the empty representations of metaphysics in order to recuperate metaphysics's original experiences of Being. The issue is one of reflecting on the essence of the various phases of metaphysics, including, therefore, the essence of modern technology. Given that every metaphysics is an ontology, Heidegger, in *Being and Time*, views this task as a *fundamental ontology* (BT, 34). In the retrospective introduction to "What is Metaphysics?" a text that had been written in 1930, Heidegger elucidated this fundamental ontology by referring to the image provided by Descartes wherein philosophy is represented as a tree wherefrom metaphysics forms the roots. Fundamental ontology is not so much directed at these roots as at the *ground* wherein they are rooted: Being. Therefore, fundamental ontology necessarily goes *beyond* metaphysics because it is directed at what metaphysics makes possible.

After the famous reversal (*Kehre*) in his thinking, which occurred in the 1930s and 1940s under the influence of Nietzsche's radical thinking, Heidegger no longer spoke about his work in terms of a fundamental ontology. The dimension of the happening of Being, which is central in his writings following his about-turn, forms an abyssal (*abgründige*) dimension that precedes every (ontological) establishment and that, as such, does not permit or require any establishing provision of evidence (WG, 174, 308). The term "fundamental ontology," according to the later Heidegger, was still too heavily influenced by subjectivist metaphysics. In *Being and Time* it was postulated that humans constitute the exclusive point of access to Being because they are the only beings that pose questions concerning Being (BT, 25). Only man experiences the miracle of miracles: that being *is* (GA, 7:307). The individual receives this privileged position from the early Heidegger not only because (ontically considered) he *is*, but, moreover, because his existence is based upon a certain (not necessarily explicated) ontological understanding of this Being. Man, moreover, possesses the capacity to understand the Being of the other beings in a manner that is just as original as his understanding of his own existence (BT, 33).

After the reversal, and especially in the reflections about language that were brought into the discussion earlier, Heidegger considers man *from within Being* (cf. note 12, above).[22] The question is then rather how Being and its truth present themselves to human beings: the issue is one of thinking of Being (*Denken des Seins*). Heidegger no longer views this thinking as thought that provides a foundation for metaphysics, but rather as thought beyond metaphysics. In contrast to the imperialist thinking of modern metaphysics, it is thinking that presents itself as being open for the experience of Being. According to Heidegger in his "Letter on Humanism," Being's thinking demands a certain "release." We could say that "thinking of Being" expresses both subjective and objective genitive (BW, 194). This terminology, however, is actually insufficient because it is rooted in the subject-object dichotomy of metaphysical thinking. Heidegger's reflection concerns a Between (*Zwischen*) that on a primeval level makes possible the meeting of object and subject.

Despite important shifts in Heidegger's philosophical development, the reversal in Heidegger's thinking should not be viewed as a
radical departure: in the later writings dealing with thoughts concerning Being, man also occupies an important place. Understanding, as
was already remarked above, belongs to Being. For the later Heidegger,
man who understands Being still remains *Da-sein*, that is, the "There"
of "Being" (VS, 108). The individual is suitable for thinking about Being, thanks to the purely spoken man stands in "the truth of Being" (BW,
216). It is perhaps true that the word has the first and the last word, but
without man there would be no speech and thus also no possible lighting of Being. Man, as Heidegger varies the relationship with the authentically nameless, is hereby, however, not the master but rather "the
shepherd of Being" (BW, 221).

Moreover, the reversal does not mean a real departure for Heidegger because it concerns a reversal in thinking of Being itself: "The reversal is in play within the matter itself" (P, xviii). It is a step back
(*Schritt zurück*), a recalling of Being (an *andenkendes Denken*), an atten-
tive listening to what in the said—the metaphysical pronouncements—
has, in the past, remained unsaid. Being's thinking is therefore an historical thinking, a kind of recollection (*Gedächtnis*). Hereby, Heidegger
reaches back to the Greek myth of Mnemosyne, the daughter of Heaven
and Earth and mother of the Muses, including that of history: Clio.

Recalling the history of Being is for Heidegger a counterweight
against the forgottenness-of-Being that authoritatively determines
Western metaphysics. It is an interrogation of what must always necessarily remain unthought in thinking: the difference between Being and
beings. The historical character of thinking is something that Heidegger shares with Hegel. The Heideggerian "overcoming" of metaphysics, however, differs in essence from the Hegelian *Aufhebung* of
traditional metaphysics in absolute knowledge. Recalling Being, because of the simultaneously unveiling and concealing character of Being, continuously remains a thinking that leaves something fundamentally unthought. For this reason, Heidegger speaks (at least in several
places in his work) not of an "overcoming" (*Überwindung*) of metaphysics, but rather of a *Verwindung* (cf. for example, ID, 25). The concern here is a recalling of the hidden traces that Being has left behind in
the history of metaphysics, especially what has remained unthought.[23]
The emphasis that Heidegger hereby makes with respect to the inexhaustible wealth of Being once again unveils his spiritual alliance with
the Romantic project.[24]

4.6 THE ETERNAL LACK

Psychoanalysis, just as much as the Heideggerian hermeneutics, is characterized by a radical *historicity*, although while Heidegger concerned himself with the collective history of thinking, psychoanalysis made the individual biography central. However, in this respect, too, the attention is directed to a diagnostic history of the either systematically forgotten or repressed past. This diagnostic history, like the Heideggerian *Gedächtnis*, has as its objective an openness toward the repressed artefacts of the past and, thereby, reestablishing a simultaneous openness toward the future.

In psychoanalysis, too, especially in its Lacanian variant, one can recognize a fundamental *unthought*. This unthought is part of the constitution of the subject: entrance into the symbolic order of language is necessarily combined with the genesis of the unconscious. To employ a term originally used by Heidegger in another context, both this linguistic entrance and the unconscious are of the same origin (*gleichursprünglich*) (Mooij, 1975, 132). Lacan linked this splitting of the subject with Freud's obscure but nonetheless primary thesis of primal repression (cf., for example, É, 816; cf. note 15, chapter 1). According to Lacan this primal repression should not so much be viewed as an actual event that once upon a time, in some mythical past, occurred, but rather as the condition of the possibility of both consciousness and unconscious. In Moyaert's words: "It is the *Urverdrängung* which installs the radical and unremovable barrier between preconsciousness (the subject of knowing) and the unconscious (the domain of truth, which is actually the domain of an absence)" (Moyaert, 1983, 190). Viewed from the metatheoretical perspective, the psychoanalytic dialogue can never have full speech (*parole plein*) in mind but rather only the acknowledgment of the fundamental unknowableness of the unconscious.

Supporters of psychoanalysis have not been hesitant in emphasizing that this discipline should be understood as an overcoming of a dominant tendency in Western metaphysics. Psychoanalysis is especially venomous with respect to the philosophy of consciousness, as practiced by Descartes and Husserl, for example: "The central position of language is a spear-point which psychoanalysis aims at every philosophy which seeks its starting-point in consciousness. Consciousness no longer has the privileged place accorded to it by a particular philosophical tradition. It is more important, however, that the misunderstandings which are inherent to this tradition can be recognized: I am not as I think I am, and: I am not the same one who thinks that he is as the one who is" (Mooij, 1975, 205). In psychoanalytic metatheory, too, just as in Heidegger's later hermeneutics, a place is made for a negativity, a fundamental lack of meaning, which can never be terminated, but rather can at the most only be acknowledged.

4.7   THE POET ON THE COUCH

The Word has the first and the last word.
In between, an ideal shatters into slivers,
series of generations reproduce themselves,
the characteristics of which I had to inherit.

't Woord heeft het eerste en het laatste woord.
Daartussen valt een ideaal aan scherven,
planten zich reeksen generaties voort,
wier eigenschappen ik moest overerven.

The preceding reading of this stanza from Achterberg in the light of hermeneutics and psychoanalysis has shown a number of remarkable parallels between these traditions of thought. The granting of the primacy of language, the decentering of the speaking subject, the claim to have superseded traditional metaphysics, and the acknowledgment of the fundamental unthought, makes it tempting to propose with IJsseling that "Lacan's psychoanalysis and Heidegger's thought ultimately have just about the same in mind" (IJsseling, 1969, 284). The insignificant (but therefore, philosophically speaking, no less fatal) words "just about" in this sentence, however, make us suspect that we are not faced with complete identity in this case. What is it that remains unsaid in this argument?

In my opinion, this unsaid something is closely connected with what has constantly accompanied the preceding explication of hermeneutics and psychoanalysis: the poetic utterance of the word. Is it not this poetic dimension that falls away in the words 'just about'? The tiny difference covered here by the words 'just about' appears on closer inspection to undermine the totality of IJsseling's argument of parallelism. As was posited in the introduction, the point of divergence (*Differenz*) concerns the question as to whether the poetic word, in the "final" analysis, is conceived as a *domain* of knowing or as an *object* of another sort of knowing. Both Freud and Heidegger have commented upon this issue in a number of places.

Freud, in items scattered in his *oeuvre*, often concerned himself with literature. The first publication completely devoted to an aesthetic issue appeared in 1907 with the title *Delusions and dreams in Jensen's "Gradiva."* Jung had drawn Freud's attention to the novella *Gravida*, written by the Danish author Wilhelm Jensen, because a number of remarkable dreams appeared in the work (cf. Jones, 1955, 2:382). Seven years before this Freud had published *The Interpretation of Dreams*, a work that he always considered as his most important contribution to psychoanalysis. In Freud's famous expression, the dream is the royal road (*via regina*) to knowledge of the unconscious (SE, 5:609).

What is noteworthy about Freud's 1907 analysis is that for the first time in a publication he analyzed dreams "that have never been dreams at all—dreams created by imaginative writers and ascribed to invented characters in the course of a story" (SE, 9:7). He made a number of explicit comments concerning the question of the "truth of art" in his introductory remarks: he complained that "science and the majority of educated people" did not believe in the theory, developed in *The Interpretation of Dreams*, that dreams possess meanings that can be explicated. The only exceptions, he continued, are writers and poets: "But creative writers are valuable allies and their evidence is to be prized highly, for they are apt to know a whole host of things between heaven and earth of which our philosophy has not yet let us dream. In their knowledge of mind they are far in advance of us everyday people, for they draw upon sources which we have not yet opened up for science" (SE, 9:8). The literary person is here conceived by Freud as a colleague of the scientist: both elucidate meaning concerning the motives and the desires of the individual. If we consider psychoanalysis to be the science of fiction, then literature becomes *science fiction* and Jensen, author of *Gravida*, becomes the Jules Verne of the human sciences (cf. Mehlman, 1976, 121).

While, in the introduction to his analysis of *Gravida*, Freud states the opinion that literary works of art are a domain of knowing, in the conclusion he maintains that they can also be nothing more than the *object* of psychological knowing. After subjecting the dreams and the history of the protagonist's illness to a discerning analysis, an analysis that, as is so often the case with Freud, reads like a detective novel, he poses, at the end of his argument, the question as to whether or not the insight that enables the author to present his "phantasy" in such a manner that we can analyze it as a real history of illness can actually be called knowledge in any real sense. Freud answers himself in the negative. Although both psychoanalysis and literature delve into the same sources, their methods are in contradiction with one another:

> Our [i.e., the psychoanalytic—JdM] procedure consists in the conscious observation of abnormal mental processes in other people so as to be able to elicit and announce their laws. The author no doubt proceeds differently. He directs his attention to the unconscious in his own mind, he listens to its possible developments and lends them artistic expression instead of suppressing them by conscious criticism. Thus he experiences from himself what he learns from others—the laws which the activities of this unconscious must obey. But he need not state these laws, nor even be clearly aware of them, as a result of the tolerance of his intelligence, they are incorporated within his creations. (SE, 9:92).

In this quotation Freud appears once again to accept the old Platonic aversion to the poet by pejoratively labeling the author as nothing other than a mouthpiece for *another* voice. The author may well speak the truth, but he does not know what he is talking about. This results in Freud finally condemning Jensen's *Gravida* to an illustrative existence: the work of art as illustration of the truth of psychoanalysis. In the form of a well-chosen quotation at the beginning of a study, for example.

The pejorative tone that already comes through in Freud's analysis of *Gravida* becomes dominant in the article "Creative Writers and Daydreaming," which was published one year later in 1908. In this article, he compares poetic imagination with the day-dreams and phantasies of children's games. He appears to reach back to a strict *distinction* between fact and fiction in this article, and conceives of poetic imagination as a phenomenon of regression, a return to the imaginary world of children's play. In this vision, the phantasizing person, poet or daydreamer, turns away from the reality that does not satisfy him: "We lay it down that a happy person never phantasies, only an unsatisfied one. The motive forces of phantasies are unsatisfied wishes, and every single fantasy is the fulfillment of a wish, a correction of unsatisfying reality" (SE, 9:146). Further in his article, Freud remarked that what a phantasy and a dream have in common is that the desire that underpins them is repressed, therefore unconscious, and that they can only be expressed in a mutilated form. The meaning of the phantasy, literary phantasies included, can only be unveiled in psychoanalytic interpretation. In this article, Freud gives only the first word to the poet, emphatically reserving the *last* word for the scientist.

The poetic word as domain and as object of knowing: we meet both views in Freud's work. This ambivalence with respect to art and

artist appears on closer inspection to be a symptom of a more fundamental ambivalence that permeates Freud's complete *oeuvre*. On the one
hand, as is clear in the foregoing, psychoanalysis is a form of hermeneutics: an interpretation of language that is open to articulation in the voice
of the Other. Alongside this, we regularly find a causal-deterministic approach in his work. Mooij, too, underlines this in a later study: "The
hermeneutic approach is equally filled out by Freud with an approach
wherein terms such as 'power,' 'energy,' and 'psychic apparatus' function. . . . The energetic approach does not direct itself at the consistency of sentences . . . but attempts to explain changes in these by
correlating them with energetic changes or alterations within a presumed psychic apparatus. This approach . . . can therefore also be called
causal-deterministic" (Mooij, 1982, 85).

The is not the place to examine the origins of this causal-
deterministic component of psychoanalysis, but it should be emphasized that it cannot be dismissed as an early and moreover temporary
influence upon Freud's thinking. In *Beyond the Pleasure Principle*, an important metapsychological study dating from 1920, Freud still articulated the opinion that psychoanalysis would be tremendously benefited
if it could completely express its clinical findings in the terminology of
chemistry (SE, 18:60). Equally, this influence cannot be dismissed as a
regrettable metapsychological addition to an otherwise independent
and valuable therapeutic practice. On the contrary: it may be postulated
that the causal-deterministic approach, an explanatory method that,
like all positivism, is directed at control, ultimately permeates the
"essence" of the entire therapeutic conceptualization. Earlier, I quoted
Freud's opinion that the ego is not master in its own house (SE, 22:80).
However, as we also have noticed, against this he placed the following
therapeutic imperative: "Where id was, there ego shall be" (SE, 22:80; cf.
3.7). Even the most ingenious Lacanian interpretation cannot displace
the commonsense meaning of these words: psychoanalytical therapy is
directed at strengthening the ego at the expense of the unconscious.
Therapeutic surrender to free association is ultimately only a method of
achieving the *self-determination* of the subject. It is, to use an adage from
ego psychology, regression in the service of the ego.

On the basis of this "will to master," the therapy is necessarily
more than merely an acknowledgment of the fundamental unknow-
ability of the unconscious. This is something that IJsseling, and in his
wake also Mooij and Moyaert, occasionally appears to disavow. These
various factors make it clear that Freud (with Nietzsche and Heidegger
we could say: at the crucial moments of difference) can characterize the

poetic surrender to the word as nothing other than an *impotence*. The artist is "once more in rudiments an introvert, not far removed from neurosis. He is oppressed by excessively powerful instinctual needs. He desires to win honour, power, wealth, fame and the love of women; but *he lacks the means for achieving these satisfactions*" (SE, 16:376—italic, JdM). It is sometimes with an undertone of sorrow that Freud corrects the artist, perhaps because this correction sometimes touches the master stylist that Freud himself is (in the same way that Plato's condemnation of the artist also touched his own unique artistic style). It speaks volumes in this respect that Freud discouraged the poet Rilke from undergoing an analysis in order that his poetic gifts should not be damaged. However, none of this makes his rejection of art less distressing.

In a subtle manner, Lacan, in his *retour à Freud*, has also returned to the above-mentioned ambivalence. Of course, Lacan, in his emphasis of the primacy of the symbolic order, strongly resists Freud's biological interpretations, and, more strongly than Freud, he places the emphasis on the decentering of the subject that flows from the symbolic order. And in a number of other places in his work Lacan appears no longer to view free association as a method, but rather to conceive of it as an almost surrealist goal in itself, and also to conceive of the symptom as a poetic object. But even with Lacan the control-strategy plays a substantial role. This does not only appear, in stylistic terms, from Lacan's sometimes ludicrous attempts at formalization: the control-strategy finds expression with Lacan, in contradiction to his affirmation of the primacy of the symbolic order and the decentering of the subject, in the fact that with respect to therapy he, too, is ultimately directed at "the arrival of the redeeming word." The analytic conversation is directed at a complete reintegration of the (unconscious) past (Lacan, 1975, 18–20). Despite all emphasis on alienation, the psychoanalytic conversation presumes the possibility of a full speech (*parole plein*). That Lacan hereby notes that this complete speaking, in the current alienating culture, is *exclusively* possible in the therapeutic conversation, does not in any way detract from this point (Lacan, 1975, 269).

If we emphasize this aspect of psychoanalysis, then it becomes clear that psychoanalysis is ultimately strongly indebted to the metaphysical tradition. And it is precisely the rejection of art that, in the "final" analysis, brings psychoanalysis into the long chain of metaphysics. This is especially clear where psychoanalysis makes the complete speaking of the subject its categoric imperative. What is involved is bringing, through the medium of "the last word," the unthought under the dominion of the subject. In this connection, it is noteworthy that Lacan, in contradistinction to his use of Heideggerian terms, rests far more on a Hegelian conceptual scheme (as it was mediated in France by Kojève). In this perspective, psychoanalysis is not an overcoming of metaphysics and, in a strict sense, not even a resolute *Verwindung*, but rather, as part of modern science and technology, an aspect of its completion.[25] Mooij, in the last part of *Language and Desire*, does appear to acknowledge this: "Reflection on Lacan's foundation concepts opens one's eyes to the fact that he, too, is bound to the tradition against which he apparently sets himself" (Mooij, 1975, 216).

4.8 POETICIZING AND THINKING

Is it the indebtedness of psychoanalysis to the metaphysical tradition that ensures that, despite the noted agreements between hermeneutics and psychoanalysis, the few words that Heidegger affords to the latter are completely negative? In Heidegger's perspective, psychoanalysis occurs at the level of beings. It is perhaps true that psychoanalysis criticizes a particular metaphysical school, namely that of the philosophy of consciousness, but it does not bring into question metaphysics (and the forgetfulness of Being) as such. Against this, Heidegger has an attitude toward the poetic word that is fundamentally different from the mainstream of metaphysical tradition, including the psychoanalytic. Other than in this tradition, poeticizing and thinking are for Heidegger closely related (EM, 131 ff.): both of them belong to the *Sage*, the articulation of language. Coming from the "same origin," they both unveil the truth of Being (GA, 7:311–12).

This does not mean that poeticizing and thinking are the same for Heidegger: "One can only speak of identity through difference. Poeticizing and thinking appear most purely identical in their care for the word, but, at the same time, these activities are actually completely separated from each other." The thinker and the poet "live next to each on deeply separated mountains" (GA, 7:312). How should we understand the distinction between thinking and poeticizing? The text of *What Is Metaphysics?* contains only this brief and rather puzzling clue: "The thinker speaks Being. The poet names the Divine" (GA, 7:312). In his later writings, Heidegger continuously drew attention to the relationship between poeticizing and thinking.

In one of the articles that Heidegger dedicated to Hölderlin, he was more precise about how the poetic word works: "The poet names the gods and names all things in what they are" (HEP, 304).[26] The poetic word creates a house for the gods (see De Mul, 1996a). This refers to the poet's profound solidarity with the occurrence of Being: the appearance of Being occurs preeminently during the hearing of the poetic word. The manner whereby Being achieves articulation in the poetic word is, as I remarked in section 4.2, above, a naming. The theme of the fundamental unthought makes it clear why this is so: "The experience of Being at the edge of its unspeakability permits only a naming, it does not tolerate explication (*Erörterung*)" (Aler, 1970a, 151). In pure, that is, authentic speaking, the mystery of Being is *evoked*. If we can present the working of the poetic word as the opening up of the mystery of Being, then it is the task of the thinker to guard this experience of Being. In the thinker's recalling, attention is paid to what is unveiled in the poetic word. The poet's naming announces destiny (*Geschick*); the poet makes it public as the appearance of Being (Aler, 1970a, 151). It is, following Achterberg, the task of the thinker to inherit the revelation of the poetic word.

With Heidegger—and in this respect he follows Schelling's Romantic conception of the relationship of poetry and philosophy— poeticizing and thinking are not located in a subordinate relation; the poet and the thinker are committed to each other in the same dialogue. In this dialogue, between the first and the last word, the restrained wealth of Being unfolds itself. The interpretation of Achterberg's words in this chapter can in the same way be understood as my attempt as a philosopher to enter into a dialogue with the poet. Between Achterberg's first and last word the discursive intermediate space opens that makes it possible for us to recall the brilliance of his words.

4.9   FROM METAPHYSICS TO METAPHORICS: THE PYRRHIC VICTORY OF POSTMODERN PHILOSOPHY?

In the preceding sections it has become clear that Heidegger once again ascribes to poetry the truth-constructing competence that was denied it by the philosophical tradition and, ultimately, also by psychoanalysis (cf. 1.1). This places him in the Romantic tradition and, more especially, in spite of his critique of the putative metaphysical character of Nietzsche's philosophy, in Nietzsche's footsteps.

However, in contrast to Nietzsche, with Heidegger there is no question of a rehabilitation of the metaphor. In fact, with Heidegger the metaphor is remarkably absent, not only in his interpretation of poeticizing but also in his interpretation of thinking. This cannot be considered as totally unexpected. Given that he maintains the opinion that the metaphorical can only be present in the metaphysical (PR, 48; cf. 1.1), and, in his work after the reversal, is directed at a nonmetaphysical thinking, he is more or less forced to exclude the metaphorical from this thinking. His attempt to think about metaphysical and metaphorical speech *before* their differentiation can for this reason be understood by him as nothing other than an *authentic* articulation of Being. According to Heidegger, nonmetaphysical thinking makes no use of images or other representations of Being, but rather is directed at an 'immediate' "insight in that, which is" (*Einblick in das, was ist*). Therefore he also does not call the *Lichtung* an image of Being, but rather emphatically proposes: "But the lighting itself is Being" (*Die Lichtung selber ist das Sein*) (BW, 211; cf. EM, 11). Also, when Heidegger in "The Thing" specifies the appearance of Being in expressive terms as the fourfold (*Das Geviert*) of earth and sky, divinities and mortals, then, according to him, this should be understood as nonmetaphorical (PLT, 165–86). According to Duintjer, his style therefore appears to be "cerebral, heavy, and abstractly imageless," which Duintjer associates with Heidegger's "constant fixation on 'das Denkerische'" (Duintjer, 1988, 111).[27] This makes understanding and following Heidegger's attempts at nonrepresentational thinking inconceivably difficult, too.

On the basis of what was said in chapter 1 concerning the inherently metaphorical character of language, it is, however, doubtful whether (following) such an imageless thinking is possible at all.[28] With Nietzsche, and in his footsteps, Derrida, we can pose the question as to whether or not every speaking and writing is inextricably entangled with a particular metaphoric so that there can be absolutely no question of an "authentic" speaking on either side of the metaphoric (cf. note 9, chapter 1). From the preceding explication of Heidegger's thinking it can at least be remarked that he, too, did not escape from the metaphorical. The ocular character of a number of the metaphors that Heidegger used, especially those that are expressed in the light-metaphoric of the *Lichtung*, even places him emphatically—although in a completely idiosyncratic manner—in the metaphysical tradition that has been built upon Plato.

With Heidegger there appears to be a question of a "forgottenness" of the metaphorical character of the terms wherein he deals with Being. The result of such a forgottenness (or should we here speak of a suppression?) of the metaphorical aspect of language is something I interpreted in chapter 1 as a *fossilization*. In my opinion, such a fossilization is the basis of the substantiation of the happening of Being that is characteristic for the ontotheological tradition (cf. 4.5). Heidegger's suppression of the metaphoric in favor of the authentic articulation of Being appears to me to run a similar danger. Just as the preceding metaphysical tradition, Heidegger demonstrates the tendency to proffer particular metaphors (those of the *Lichtung* or the *physis*) as authentic and thereby to reserve them for Being. It should be self-evident that I do not hereby seek to argue that Heidegger's thinking should simply be added to the metaphysical tradition. His *Verwindung* of the metaphysical tradition has opened paths to another, nonmetaphysical thinking that gives much food for thought. What I do wish to say is that, by virtue of his suppression of the metaphorical character of thinking, he threatens to become entangled in a "metaphorics" that demonstrates a repetition of the metaphysical process of fossilization.

It appears to me that an indication for this is to be found in the massive, occasionally even totalitarian character of Heidegger's thought to which various critics have referred (cf. Welsch, 1987, 207–13; De Mul, 2000). The totality of contemporary culture, according to Heidegger, is characterized by a *complete* and *uniform* dominance by technology, something that he refers to as *the* completion of *the* metaphysics (HW, 111; see 4.5). In my opinion, with this massive line of thought Heidegger remains fundamentally indebted to the totalizing tradition against which he has set himself (cf. 0.6 and 2.7). The pluralism that is characteristic of contemporary, postmodern culture seems completely unknown to him. The totalitarian character of his writings gives his repeated call to arrive at another form of thinking an impotent, perhaps even fatalistic character. Put bluntly, the only thing left for Heidegger is a 'released' waiting without expectation (G, 42), or, at most, the lament that only a God can now save us.[29]

In chapter 1 I argued that the metaphor, as it appears in Nietzsche's work, forms the expression of an *ontic differentiation* of a reality that is constantly transforming itself. In his writing Nietzsche attempted to avoid the danger of fossilization by a strategic use of the metaphor (cf. 1.10). With Nietzsche, expressive language is constantly of a particularly ironic sort: it opens tempting panoramas and, simultaneously, it disturbs—partially through the multiplicity of images that pour out upon the reader—in a self-critical manner, the philosophical illusion of unity that it engenders (cf. also what has been said in 0.3 above, concerning Romantic irony). Against this, in Heidegger's "cerebral, heavy, and imageless-abstract" thinking, every irony is unknown. A fruitful further elaboration of Heidegger's version of the postmodern *Verwindung* of metaphysics demands an ironic reading of his ponderous metaphorics in order that it does not result in a pyrrhic victory.

The surrealist painter René Magritte could be a useful guide for us in this respect. In his paintings, inspired by Heidegger, he has constantly attempted, time after time and in a highly pregnant manner, to address the miracle of miracles: the mystery that Being *is*. However, the ironic style that he thereby maintains makes one think more of Nietzsche's 'gay science' than Heidegger's leaden seriousness. When, in what follows, I once again refer to psychoanalysis, then, remaining loyal to Magritte's deconstructivist humor, this will not occur without the necessary irony. Did Nietzsche have a premonition of Magritte's "surrealistic hermeneutics" when, in *The Gay Science,* he stated the expectation that perhaps even laughter may yet have a future (GS, 74)?

5

Disavowal and Representation

The work of the Belgian surrealist René Magritte takes us to the boundaries of the aesthetic domain. It forces the observer to abandon his attitude of passive viewing and invites him to reflect upon those questions that, precisely because of their everydayness and banality, generally escape our observation. Among such questions is that of visual representation and the relationship between the visual signifier (*signifiant*) and the signified (*signifié*). This epistemological connotation of Magritte's work has not escaped philosophical interest. Most especially, the painting *La trahison des images* from 1929 (figure 14) has elicited a large number of commentaries, of which Foucault's *This Is Not a Pipe* (Foucault, 1983) is perhaps the most well known.

What strikes the reader in the various interpretations is that the title of *La trahison des images* rarely enters into the discussion. This is remarkable because the titles of Magritte's works deliver a valuable contribution to the question at issue and for precisely this reason they

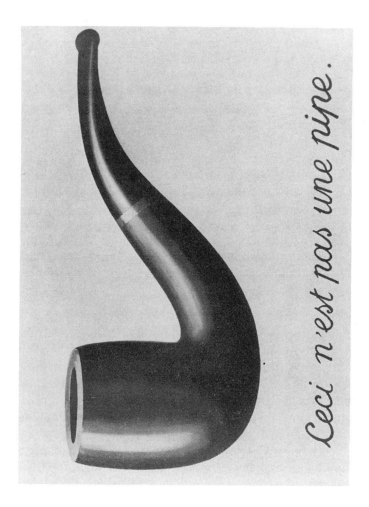

Ceci n'est pas une pipe.

FIGURE 14

La trahison des images, René Magritte, 1928–29, oil on canvas, 59 × 80 cm. Collection of W. N. Copley, New York.

demand their share in the interpretation. However, because of their puzzling character the titles conjure up considerable resistance against their inclusion in the philosophical discussion. Magritte, commenting about this, said: "The titles of the paintings are not explanations and the paintings themselves are not mere illustrations of the titles. The relationship is poetic, that is, it merely illuminates a number of the characteristics of the objects involved, characteristics which are generally ignored by consciousness" (Magritte, 1979, 259). For an analysis that is directed at the reception accorded to Magritte's work, the titles offer a tempting starting point precisely because they unveil something about what remains unconscious in perception. This is especially relevant for *La trahison des images* because the title points to a problem that appears to be closely connected to that of representation. The title of the painting of a pipe that appears not to be a pipe brings us onto the terrain of disavowal: it points at a disavowal of the image.[1]

The close connection between representation and disavowal, and the fact that these activities extend themselves to the boundaries of our thinking, makes them exceptionally difficult to "master." We exist in the fortunate circumstances, however, of being able to make an appeal to psychoanalytic theory, in which the entanglement of disavowal and representation have a privileged position, for our studies of the relationship. The texts in which Freud, and in his footsteps the French psychoanalyst Mannoni, dealt with disavowal (*Verleugnung*) in the context of fetishism especially deserve our attention.[2] These texts will function as a guiding thread in the following study of the expressive commentary that *La trahison des images* provides of the relationship between disavowal and representation in the experience of mimetic fine arts.[3] Further, an inverse movement will be initiated from the beginning of my argument by my use of Magritte's commentary to interrogate the psychoanalytic conception of this relationship from within. My interpretation of *La trahison des images* also bears traces of texts by Derrida, Barthes, and Irigaray concerning the question of representation. And, just as *La trahison des images* has unavoidably inserted itself into the ordering of language, these traces have carved themselves into the working history of the painting, the never-drying veneer of the aesthetic image that the painting embodies.[4]

5.1 MAGRITTE'S PIPE: YES, I KNOW, BUT STILL . . .

In their texts both Freud and Mannoni stand still for a moment when considering the remarkable feelings they experienced when, for the first time, they were confronted in their psychoanalytic practice with the phenomenon of disavowal. Freud begins one of the articles he wrote about this phenomenon with the words: "I find myself for a moment in the interesting position of not knowing whether what I have to say should be regarded as something long familiar and obvious or as something entirely new and puzzling" (SE, 23:275). Mannoni expresses the same sentiment when, in *"Yes I know, but still . . . ,"* he maintains that, confronted with the phenomenon of disavowal, one "feels oneself catapulted between a feeling of banality and a feeling of extreme surprise" (Mannoni, 1969, 11). It is precisely this feeling we experience when we are confronted with *La trahison des images* for the first time. The naive style shows us an unmistakable representation of a pipe, with a text underneath it reading "This is not a pipe." The shock occasioned when we perceive this similarly carries us into the remarkable borders of extreme banality and alienation.[5] The shock, namely, resides not only in the first banal amazement concerning the apparent contradiction (that is, that a painted pipe is actually not a pipe), but it also concerns the fact that we were amazed, that, despite our knowledge of the fact that a painted pipe is not actually a pipe, we were nonetheless shocked at the moment that the painting made us aware of this knowledge.[6] Without the annotation, we realize in surprise, we would believe that what we observe really *is* a pipe.

The experience of *La trahison des images* makes us conscious of a characteristic that we must assume is inherent to every aesthetic observation of a mimetic work of art, namely, the simultaneous existence of two mutually exclusive mental attitudes. In the aesthetic observation of these objects we know that what we are seeing is unreal, that it is a fiction: simultaneously, we deny this knowledge and abandon ourselves to the reality of what we are observing. This disavowal of the images (in favor of the real object they signify) brings us to the *sine qua non* of the mimetic experience. Without the mechanism of the simultaneous existence of a quantum of knowledge and a belief that is irreconcilable with that knowledge (that is a particular form of not-knowing), the mimetic experience appears to be impossible. If the knowledge component is lacking, then we find ourselves in the legendary situation of the observers of the first film performance in Paris' *Grand Café* who ran in panic from the approaching train that they saw on the screen. The knowledge component appears in this instance to have been completely absorbed in the affective component. If the affective component is lacking, then equally we cannot speak of an aesthetic experience. In Mannoni's words: "Anyone who, unprepared, attends a Chinese performance runs the risk of seeing the play as it is and the actors as they are. Viewed objectively, it is certainly theatre, but it is without the theatrical effect" (Mannoni, 1969, 161).

An important part of twentieth-century fine arts, especially that part such as abstract art that rejects the mimetic, appears to unconsciously remove itself from the boundaries of the hybrid relationship of believing and knowing (cf. 2.3). The strength of *La trahison des images* resides in the fact that it makes us conscious of this simultaneous existence of the knowledge and faith components, and, what is perhaps an even more important effect, it saturates us with the complete not-self-evidentness of this relationship. After all, we are confronted with the question as to how it is possible that two mutually exclusive attitudes can be simultaneously present in our minds.

La trahison des images does not provide an answer to this question. The pleasure that the painting affords us cannot really be described as anything other than an especially perverse and subversive pleasure. It is a shocking pleasure that does not intend to please and to explain, but rather to disturb (a pleasure that may be called characteristic for the entire tradition of the no-longer-fine arts). Magritte's painting is directed at a *Verwindung* of the mimetic tradition (cf. note 18 of the Introduction and 3.8). It is a deconstructivist practice that, in a shocking manner, makes us conscious of what must remain partially unconscious in the mimetic experience: the very process of representation. The unreflected continuity of presenting the presence of an absent object by means of a sign forms the condition of the possibility for every mimetic experience. The subversive character of Magritte's deconstructivist labor lies in becoming conscious of this disavowal of representation that is so necessary for the mimetic experience. In this becoming conscious, wherein the two mutually exclusive attitudes are brought together in one movement of thought, the representative appearance of the mimetic experience is withdrawn.[7] The mimetic experience becomes—and this differentiates Magritte's work from abstract art wherein the mimesis was "simply" abandoned—invalidated from within.[8]

The fact that *La trahison des images* provides the observer with a certain desire, despite this *Verwindung* of mimetic experience, constitutes its perverse character. This pleasure forms an indication of the existence of another aesthetic "space" beyond traditional representation. It is this space, opened up by desire, that intrigues me.

5.2   SEXUAL AND AESTHETIC DISAVOWAL

Is it pure coincidence that Freud, when speaking about perversion, also bumps up against the entanglement of disavowal and representation? He worked out several aspects of this relationship more closely in his analysis of fetishism. Fetishism, in Freud's view, is based upon the fact that the analysand, almost always male, "does not acknowledge that a woman does not have a penis, something which, as proof of the possibility of being himself castrated, is most unwelcome" (SE, 23:203). The analysand, for this reason, denies his sensory perception that the female does not possess a phallus and maintains a firm grip on the contrary conviction. According to Freud, however, the denied perception continues to be influential and, for this reason, the fetishist attributes the role of the phallus to something else, another bodily part or an article of clothing. We could express it as follows: the fetish presents the phallus as being present. In this connection, Freud speaks about the formation of a compromise between two contradictory attitudes that is related to dream-work. The fetish forms a compromise between the sensory perception that establishes the female's absence of a phallus and the wish to preserve this phallus for perception. The fetish makes it possible that the belief in the presence of a female phallus is "maintained, but also given up" (SE, 21:154).

Octave Mannoni offered the assumption that this fetishization of the absent female (mother) phallus stands "for all forms of belief which, despite falsification by reality, remain intact" (Mannoni, 1969, 12). The structural agreement between sexual and aesthetic disavowal is indeed remarkable. After all, in aesthetic perception, one of the forms of belief to which Mannoni refers, an object is by a sign equally posited as present on the grounds of its absence. A painted object (for example the pipe in *La trahison des images*) forms an aesthetic "fetish," a compromise form between knowledge of an object's absence and the disavowal of this knowledge, and thereby makes it possible to preserve the absent object for perception. In the case of both sexual and aesthetic disavowal we travel—the term 'fetish' does not appear to have been arbitrarily chosen—in the terrain of the magical (or, more rigorously, that of the "magic of belief" that precedes the "belief in magic"—Mannoni, 1969, 29). What is remarkable is that in both instances disavowal, despite its irrational character, plays itself out "in full daylight" (ibid., 30). Neither the sexual fetish nor the painted object possess anything mysterious; at the same time, they are able to carry us into a magical experience.

In the foregoing comments I remarked, and this appears to call a halt to the specified analogy between sexual and aesthetic disavowal, that, in aesthetic perception and simultaneously with the experience of disavowal (the magical compromise between knowing and wishing), we have access to knowledge of the object's absence. In the case of *La trahison des images* this is the absence of the real pipe. This knowledge, as I also remarked, does not in any way effect aesthetic disavowal. This appears to distinguish aesthetic disavowal from sexual disavowal wherein this knowledge-component is absent. In "An Outline of Psychoanalysis," however, Freud points to a simultaneous existence of disavowal and knowledge in sexual fetishism:

> The creation of the fetish emerged from the intention to destroy the evidence of possible castration so that one could avoid the fear of castration. When the woman, just as other living beings, possesses a penis, then one does not have to fear the further possession of one's own penis. Now, we encounter fetishists who have developed the same fear of castration as non-fetishists and who thus react in the same manner. In their behaviour they thus express two mutually exclusive attitudes: on the one hand they deny the reality of their perception of no penis being present with female genitals, and, on the other hand, they acknowledge a woman's lack of a penis and draw the correct conclusion from this acknowledgement. Both attitudes exist side-by-side for an entire life without their influencing each other. (SE, 23:203)

The phenomenon of the mutual existence of two mutually exclusive attitudes is presented by Freud with the term 'splitting of the Ego' (*Ich-spaltung*). The emergence of this splitting shows that the disavowal of perception by the fetishist is not complete; the acknowledgment is, after all, present in consciousness. In this case, the fetish(ism) is only partially developed: "It does not control the object-choice with exclusion of everything else, but rather leaves room for a more or less normal behaviour and sometimes even reduces itself to a modest role or a simple announcement of its presence. The distinction between the Ego and reality is, accordingly, never completely successful for the fetishist" (SE, 23:203). Aesthetic perception is capable of a similar description. The observer of *La trahison des images* surrenders to the imaginary presence of the object but, simultaneously, he realizes this surrender and precisely thereby elevates the experience to an aesthetic one. Just as, according to Freud, sexual fetishism mostly reduces itself to a modest role or simple announcement of itself (and the sexual goal of genital reproduction is preserved), so does the observer who is captured by the aesthetic experience leave open a path for a complete reproduction of knowledge. In this manner, both forms of fetishism remain under the domination of instrumental representation, which is in the service of the reality principle (see SE, 12:213–26 cf. 3.7 and 4.7). The shock that *La trahison des images* engenders is only temporary the trusted frameworks of perception quickly recover. Awakened from his aesthetic "dream" the hand faultlessly goes to the ashtray and the observer smokes his pipe with satisfaction.

When fetishism becomes acute, sexual activity removes itself from reproduction. The fetishist pulls himself free from the dominance of the sexual goal. In analogous fashion, the aesthetic observer, when he finds himself in the same situation of acute fetishism, retreats into his "disinterested pleasure" and thereby escapes from the domination of instrumental representation. In both cases, *fore-pleasure* overmasters *end-pleasure* and the perception becomes *perverse* (for the italicized terms, see Freud, SE, 7:209 ff.; in relation to the aesthetic *Jokes and Their Relation to the Unconscious*, SE, 8). In both cases we can therefore speak of an acute *aestheticism*. That is, the pleasure of looking becomes a goal in itself, cut off from the everyday practice of looking, which is guided by the demands of sexual reproduction and utilitarian representation.

A description of these forms of fetishism that, as in the case of Freud, finds its ultimate criterion in the demands of the reality principle, cannot veil its pejorative tone. However, the pleasure that the fetishist experiences in the sexual and aesthetic game can equally not be hidden. But it is a pleasure that cannot be represented in an order wherein sexual reproduction and utilitarian representation are the central terms. It is, in the different meanings of the word, a nonrepresentative pleasure. A theoretical approach—assuming, as Nietzsche has argued, that it always finds its origin in the 'factories of use' (KSA, 1:299)—can situate this pleasure at best in an atopos. The theory is here made into a detour, perverted by its object it can only evoke the pleasure at the moment that it stumbles and sets its understanding teeth into its own tail. Is it only irony that *La trahison des images* hereby shows theory its tail?

5.3   THE PERVERSION OF AESTHETICISM

The subversive character of *La trahison des images* is formed by the fact that the painting breaks through mimetic pleasure. Starting from the order of representation, it is shown that that order is empty. By no longer permitting word and image to support each other, the naive-realistic conceptualization of the representation is raped from within and "in broad daylight." The signifiers (the image of the pipe, the painted text) only point in a negative manner to each other, and, thereby, they become, as it were, meaningless. The painted sentence not only makes us realize that the image of the pipe is not really a pipe, but, at the same time, it makes us realize that the sentence refers to itself: the painted sentence, too, is not a real pipe. The signified (the "real" pipe) disappears completely from the field of view. Foucault, in his essay concerning Magritte, formulates this as follows: "Magritte allows the old space of representation to rule, but only at the surface, no more than a polished stone, bearing words and shapes: beneath, nothing" (Foucault, 1983, 41).

La trahison des images shows us a remarkable characteristic of the sign, about which, in structuralist semiology after De Saussure, too, there has been substantial speculation. The language-sign was conceived by De Saussure as a relation between sound (the signifier) and concept (the signified): the meaning-content of a sound is determined by the relation that it maintains with the other sounds that belong to the same system. The definition that De Saussure gives can be called differential because he conceives of the sign as an internal and external difference: internally, the sign is determined by the difference between the signifier (*signifiant*) and the signified (*signifié*); externally, it is determined by the difference between the signifiers and the signifieds themselves. Radicalizing this differential language-definition from De Saussure, poststructuralists such as Derrida, Lacan, and Barthes postulate that the signifier and the signified do not form a fundamental unity of sign, but rather that the signified emerged from the articulation (that is, combination and substitution) of the signifiers. A signified, it is maintained, always points to other elements and thereby also always finds itself in the position of signifier. A consequence of this point is that the signified always postpones itself: every signified is part of a referential game that never comes to rest. In contrast to what the traditional "metaphysics of the sign" argues, the signifier, according to poststructuralists, does not represent a signified that already contains meaning within itself, but rather it is a derived phenomenon, an effect of the systemic play of signifiers.[9]

In *La trahison des images* one could express this by saying that this referential game becomes frantic, as it were. In the negative reference the referential function of the representation, which, following De Saussure, is placed in parentheses by the poststructuralists, is completely removed.[10] The referential game becomes an endless repetition without origin, a simulacrum. The observer is involved in a domain from which it is impossible to escape. On a psychic level, this is expressed in the simultaneous experience of the attitudes, necessarily separated for the aesthetic experience, of knowing and believing. The observer becomes conscious of the splitting of his Ego. Nonetheless, and this is precisely what is remarkable about the experience, this becoming conscious is not, as one would expect, combined with pain or fear. The "threat of castration" that, in this instance, concerns the object of our experience (the "real" pipe), is, after all, acute in the experience of the short circuit of the signifiers in *La trahison des images*. In contrast to this, the deconstruction delivers a certain desire, a form of desire with which perhaps only perversion can provide us.

Derrida maintains: "Perversity consists precisely in sacralizing the representerer or the signifier" (Derrida, 1976, 296). When the signifiers no longer represent the signified, but rather only and purely signify each other (that is, are prisoners in a pure intertextuality), then they become self-lovers, a fetish. Magritte, in *La trahison des images*, completes the transition from a partial fetishism of the aesthetic experience to a total fetishism of aestheticism. The belief-component is eliminated in favor of an especial desire for knowledge of "the sliding (*glissement*) of the signifier over the signified" (É, 502). The dominance of the signified, which is intrinsic to naive realism, is here foresaken in favor of a desire for the dominance of the signifiers. Speaking in the context of literary texts about the pleasure (the sexual *jouissance*) of a game wherein the ultimate meaning continuously retreats, Barthes in *De l'œuvre au texte* says: "The Text, on the contrary, practices the infinite deferment of the signified, is delatory; its field is that of the signifier and the signifier must not be conceived of as 'the first stage of meaning,' its material vestibule, but, in complete opposition to this, as its *deferred action*. Similarly, the *infinity* of the signifiers refers not to some idea of the ineffable (the unnameable signified) but to that of a *playing*" (Barthes, 1984a, 158).

On the terrain of visual signifiers, *La trahison des images* refers to the extreme limits of this game, this *jouissance*: the imaginary turning point wherein the process of signification (*signifiance*) becomes submerged in showing the senselessness of the representation. The mimetic-aesthetic experience, which necessarily involves a belief-component, is here abandoned in order that the path be made free for an aestheticistic knowledge that concerns itself entirely with signifiers. Not only are the signifiers that are traditionally presented as imaginary or artistic dragged into this aestheticism: the pipe in the ashtray, too, is made into an element of a referential game without any basis.

5.4 THE PHALLUS AS TRANSCENDENTAL SIGNIFIER

In the foregoing I have been guided by the analogy Mannoni noted between sexual and aesthetic disavowal. Through this reasoning, I came upon the trail of a mysterious relationship between sexual and epistemological representation. This relationship, which continues to emerge in unexpected places in modern philosophy,[11] is also argued by Lacan, with a reference to the poststructuralist reading of Freud, on more theoretical grounds. We should briefly follow this detour because it makes it possible to approach *La trahison des images* from a somewhat different angle, in the hope that a combination of perspectives will provide more "depth" to the image with which we are concerned.

Lacan's return to Freud is strongly influenced by De Saussure's structuralist linguistics. This led Lacan to interpret the problematics of castration as a complex that marks the entrance of the individual into the symbolic order. In Lacan's view, the individual, who initially exists in an imaginary order of immediate experience, only receives the status of subject when he enters into the symbolic order (cf. 4.3). In this chain of terms, the individual and the objects of his experience are represented, proposed as present in their absence. The narcissistic identification with the mirror-image (which ensures that in an imaginary manner one continues to coincide with the Other) is thereby relieved by the acknowledgment of the other-ness of the (symbolically articulated) Other. The reality (*réalité*) of the subject is thus already a symbolically marked reality. From this, the poststructuralist character of Lacan's position is apparent: the meaning of an experience is not given in advance, but rather it is an effect of the chain of signifiers. The meaning slides, as we have already seen, into the *jeu de signifiants*, the infinite play of the signifiers.

Just like Freud, Lacan, too, puts a strong emphasis on the role that the phallus plays in the transition from the imaginary to the symbolic stage. However, he thereby firmly resists a possibly naturalistic interpretation of the castration complex. For Lacan, the phallus is "not a phantasy . . . equally not an object . . . and even less the organ which it symbolizes" (É, 690). For him, the phallus is actually the signifier that preeminently marks the transition from the imaginary to the symbolic stage. According to him, this is also the reason that Freud chose a term for this signifier that points to the simulacrum that, in Antiquity, was the phallus: "After all, it is the signifier, to the extent that it constitutes the conditions of their possibility, which is destined to indicate the effects of the signified in their totality" (É, 690).

The phallus forms the third term that transforms the dual relationship of the mirror-stage, which is characteristic of the imaginary order, into the triangular relationship, which is characteristic of the symbolic order. It is "the tiniest difference" that indicates "what the child is
not, what the mother does not have and the father (presumably) does
have" (Mooij, 1975, 142). In Mooij's words, a double distancing emerges:
"In the first place, there arises a separation from the initial two-in-one
whereby a chasm (*une béance*) appears between what are now two relations, two terms, and whereby a void (*un vide*) emerges in the place
where originally the two-in-one existed (*une place vide*). Hereby, the lack
(*le manque*) emerges which is introduced by the insatiability of desire. In
the second place, a separation emerges between what is now a relationship between two terms and what names this relationship. The third
term therefore creates a double distinction, internally between the two
relations, and externally between the relation and its symbolic representation. We can summarize this function as: differentiating representation" (Mooij, 1975, 142).

Thus, with Lacan, the phallus functions as a transcendental signifier, that is, as the condition of the possibility of every production of
meaning. It is the signifier that opens up the entrance to the (symbolic)
order of representation and thereby introduces a desire that cannot be
satisfied. But, simultaneously, for Lacan the phallus also remains the
specific symbolic signifier that indicates the penis (cf. Weber, 1978). This
explains why Freud—and Lacan with him—gives a privileged role to
the castration complex in relation to entering into the symbolic order.
Moreover, it explains why, in psychoanalytic theory, the representation
of both sexes and the representation of meaning in general cannot be
separated from one another.

5.5   POSTMODERN SCHIZOPHRENIA

Now we return to the pleasure of fetishizing the signifiers. This has become clear: it is a paradoxical pleasure. The insight that the signifiers
only cherish themselves, that every access to the signified is cut off
("castrated"), really makes us suspect the opposite: a cutting pain. To
place this pleasure we should first actually—a new detour—more
closely delineate the distinction between aesthetic belief and aesthetic
knowledge.

Here, too, it is Mannoni who suggests the direction we should
take. He maintains, associating himself with Lacanian topology, that be-

lief continuously assumes "the support of the Other" (Mannoni, 1969, 33). In "The Comic Illusion or the Theatre Seen from the Perspective of the Imaginary," he explicates this through an analysis of the 'primitive' belief in masks and theatrical illusion. In the theater, he argues, everything is done to maintain the theatrical illusion while everyone knows that it is an illusion. Here, the issue is thus one of "classic" aesthetic disavowal: an "imaginary credulous one" is always present.

Concerning this point, Mannoni remarks:

> Even though we are not ourselves the victim of a theatrical illusion or of the illusion of masks, it nonetheless appears that we gladly see someone who believes in such illusion. Everything appears to be done to produce this illusion, but it must be by someone else. As if we should conspire with the actors. Here, we see who the "you" was in "you could say" whereby the playful illusion is expressed. After all: formerly, "one believed in the masks." . . . "Formerly" means, as we could suspect, "as a child." An explanation, perhaps rather simplistic but not therefore completely inaccurate, now imposes itself as it were. Something, something from that child that we once were, still lives on in us, somewhere hidden within the Ego, perhaps in that place which Freud, following Fechner, correctly calls the theatre of the dream (and why precisely this metaphor?). This hidden part of our Self could thus be the place of the illusion, that which we actually do not yet really know what it is. (Mannoni, 1969, 164)

Although Mannoni here explicitly speaks of the theater, his description can, without too many problems, be applied to the illusion that appears in the perception of mimetic fine arts. Belief in representation, that is, in the possibility to immediately perceive reality itself through the transparent window of the painting, rests equally upon the credulity of an Other. Of course, we know that a painting constitutes an imaginary representation of reality, but we conspire with the painter, as it were, to lead this Other up the garden path, or better: to lead him behind the window. Once again, an irrational process that occurs in broad daylight.

If this explanation is correct, then it offers us the opportunity to more closely present the transition from the hybrid coincidence of belief and knowledge in aesthetic perception to the "absolute" knowledge of aestheticism. This transition would occur at the moment that the observer himself takes the place of the Other. Mannoni describes this transition by reference to a passage from Casanova's biography. It is the story of a person who believes in his own fabrications, someone who no longer possesses the phallus by magic but rather by deception.

According to Mannoni it is precisely here that the transition to complete fetishism occurs and knowledge is completely abandoned:

> We can actually see that the place of the Other is now occupied by the fetish. If this is missing it creates unrest, as occurred with Casanova, when credulity goes by default. But Casanova imagines that he knows who believes and who does not believe. Even if he actually makes a mistake, the problem can still be posed in terms of belief. After the fetish has been established, belief disappears. We then no longer know how the question sounds and we could say that it is precisely the goal of the fetishist to escape from every question. While everyone enters the terrain of belief with the *Verleugnung*, it is precisely this terrain which those who become fetishists, at least insofar as it involves their fetish, leave. (Mannoni, 1969, 32)

We may assume that the perverse power now rests upon the fact that the painting brings the observer into the position wherein he realizes that he is himself credulous. He coincides in an imaginary manner, as it were, with the Other to whom he originally ascribed belief and thereby causes the implementation of the fetishism of the signifiers. The signifiers cease to mean the Other. If we remain within Freudian terminology then we cannot fail to conclude that psychosis is hereby quite close. We surrender ourselves to an unverifiable and uncontrollable process of meaning that must lack an ultimate signified (*signifié transcendental*). We are confronted with what Moyaert presented as a schizophrenic discourse:

> The schizophrenic discourse cruelly teaches us that our discourse does not derive its support or its meaning from the presence of a final signified or an ideal semantic form which can unite all discourse. In a confrontation with schizophrenia our discourse, too, is in its turn pulled along with and written into a game of signifiers without any ultimate basis or sense. In this manner, each of his discourses loses every foundation or point of reference. In my discourse knowing collides with a radical not-knowing which ridicules my certainties: the schizophrenic "futilizes" my knowledge to a play of signifiers. (Moyaert, 1982, 151)

In an analogous manner, Magritte's *La trahison des images* could be called a schizophrenic metaphor. In the circular play of the signifiers (the words and the image), every access to the Other of the signifiers (the signified, the "real" pipe) is cut off. To use another of Moyaert's terms, a *demetaphoricization* occurs (Moyaert, 1982, 142). The circular play of the signifiers, the purely negative reference to the words and the image, creates a vacuum where previously belief pointed the Other to "his" place. Where first a metaphorical leap to the other side of the signifiers stood, there now only exists the endless metonymy of signifiers. In other words, *La trahison des images* surprises us with the realization that the painting (and mimetic art in general) is not a window through which we can gaze at the Other, but, rather, a glass stained by signifiers that betrays nothing except its one-dimensional surface.

With the help of what we have learned so far, let us approach more closely the pleasure of complete fetishism, the aestheticism wherein the observer of *La trahison des images* finds himself. The aestheticism, which permits us once again to coincide with the imaginary Other, removes the fear of castration because thereby the signified disappears completely from view and thereby can no longer be experienced as a loss. In this context, with respect to the analogous position wherein schizophrenia finds itself, Moyaert remarks:

> Every possible vulnerability occasioned by the indestructible presence of the Other (or the other) disappears given that his discourse is just as much a code of the message as a message of the code; and this has as consequence the fact that the subject of the psychosis himself takes the place of the Other and thus himself becomes the Other. The schizophrenic can peacefully maintain himself in a world of signifiers which, in his narcissistically inflated omnipotence, he can manipulate freely and without any risk. (Moyaert, 1982, 151)[12]

Complete fetishism appears in this manner to be characterized by a double pleasure. In the first place, fetishism is released from the metaphorical leap in the dark: it remains on the surface, escaping from the fear of the loss, the Lack (*le manque*). Here, pleasure is essentially negative, based upon the absence of fear. But, at the same time, there is the other pleasure of manipulation. It coincides with the Other, dominates the game from within because the fetishist has himself become part of it. Expressed in a classic Freudian image: he experiences an oceanic relation with the Other. A return to "the paradise of pure immediacy" takes place.

The observer of *La trahison des images* finds himself equally, even if only temporarily, in this circular play of the signifiers. He becomes, as it were, absorbed into the surface of the canvass. His belief in the signified makes way for an absorption in the process of meaning (*signifiance*). The knowledge-component takes the place of believing, but it is a knowledge of a special sort wherein the negation (the not-knowing of belief) is eliminated. This lack of the negation constitutes the radical otherness of the pleasure that is opened up by *La trahison des images*. In Barthes' words, it is "a pleasure without separation" (Barthes, 1984a, 164). However, in terms of psychoanalysis, it is also therefore continuously an *imaginary* pleasure. For the same reason, it is a pleasure that can never be adequately contained within the schemas of representation, just as ultimately the pleasure of sexual fetishism can never be adequately understood from within the schemata of sexual reproduction. Although postmodern experience is a parasite upon modern experience, it unlocks a pleasure that is never completely understandable from within the perspective of the reality principle (cf. 3.7 and 3.8).

5.6   SUPERFICIALITY FROM DEPTH

With this last remark we have returned to a place where the detours had already brought me, something that makes clear the circular character of these paths. We have to confirm that, in our attempts to bring it under the dominance of our theoretical "instinct to master" (*Bemachtigungstrieb*), we have constantly and repetitively pushed the pleasure from the other—postulated—aesthetic order out in front of us. Examining it from the order of the representation, that which falls outside is literally nonrepresentative.[13] The image that *La trahison des images* presents to us appears at this point to converge with the imaginary constructs of the poststructuralists who have crossed our paths. After all, the poststructuralists postulate that an immediate experience—and must it not be admitted that this experience is the imaginary travel-goal of my wanderings?—is impossible within the symbolic order. Hereby, in the last analysis, the fetishistic pleasure is only comprehensible as a regression to an imaginary past. Lacan does speak, it is true, about a third order, that of the real (*le réel*), but it is conceived by him as the impossible: it is impossible to reach or take on and is ultimately inaccessible. Does not Magritte appear to say the same when he magically removes the "real pipe" right in front of our eyes?

Nonetheless, this "psychoanalytic" interpretation does not appear to agree with the light-footed pleasure that *La trahison des images* awakens in me. Does not the pipe appear predominantly to succumb under the weight of these sombre theories concerning "the Lack"? Without doubt it is a charged interpretation. For this reason it is tempting, having arrived at this point, to continue the reverse movement—with Magritte toward psychoanalysis—to ensconce ourselves in the experience that *La trahison des images* offers us, and from this position to question the theory. In the foregoing I called *La trahison des images* the embodiment of the limit of the game of signifiers. This limit forms the boundary between the three-dimensional space of the *signifiance* (which is constantly characterized by the metaphorical leap toward 'the other' of the signifiers) and the flat surface of the circular (metonymical) dominance of the signifiers. Magritte shows us, where poststructuralism criticizes the dominance of the transcendental signified, that the "chain of signifiers" is the rattling herald of a new dominance: that of the transcendental signifier and the Eternal Lack. The legitimate question that *La trahison des images* presents to us is whether making the signifier absolute is not a new prison, a new columbarium built with the rubble of the old dungeon?[14]

The paths of the different poststructuralists (whom I have previously too simplistically summarized under one heading) appear here to separate. If Magritte here stands opposite Lacan, then Derrida and Barthes find themselves on his side. Samuel Weber, in his commentary concerning the meaning of the phallus in Lacan's work, points, following Derrida, to the danger of making the signifier absolute: "Making the signifier absolute . . . removes at the same time, however, its specific and determining difference, and thereby makes it a signified" (Weber, 1978, 124). The phallus, the Eternal Lack, moreover emerges as a signified to which every signifier ultimately refers. One way of putting this is to say that at this point Lacan's sexual metaphor fossilizes and access to every space outside the phallic representation is made theoretically impossible. Put another way: when the phallus disappears as a specific signifier because it is made absolute, then the other of the phallus also disappears: desire. And it is precisely this desire around which the circular movement of Magritte's *La trahison des images* "revolves."

But how should this desire be evoked? In any case, Magritte does not have the destruction of representation as his goal. In *La trahison des images* it remains demonstratively present—after all, does the naive-realistically presented pipe not always remain a pipe? It appears that Magritte here tries to support Derrida's comment that "we can pronounce not a single destructive proposition which has not already had to slip in the form, the logic, and the implicit postulations of precisely what it seeks to contest" (Derrida, 1981, 280–81). Magritte's strategy is not destructive. However, he lets the instrumentalist representation stumble momentarily in favor of the acute shock that momentarily isolates the image from the differentiating chain of signifiers.[15] At those moments the thing, as Kaulingfreks expresses it in his study of Magritte, is "undifferentiatedly present, without determination. It just is there, and hereby, as it were, it is no longer a thing. In its conveyed isolation, in the presence, it emerges as a mystery" (Kaulingfreks, 1984, 111). Shocked by the negative references of image and caption in *La trahison des images* (cf. note 5, above), we learn during a moment the mystery of "the experiential ground of pure presence" of the pipe (Kaulingfreks, 1984, 45). This mystery forms, to use Heidegger's notions, the "miracle of miracles: that Being exists" (GA, 9: 307).[16] Magritte himself commented about this mystery: "The mystery is not *one* of the possibilities of reality. The mystery is what is absolutely necessary if reality is to exist" (quoted by Kaulingfreks, 1984, 46).

Hereby, if I may permit myself such an expression, representation momentarily "gets wasted." Or, as one can express it in French, *"la représentation casse sa pipe."* Although it is preeminently art that provides us with this mysterious experience, it is not restricted to art: "the thought whereof a pipe and the caption 'this is not a pipe' are the terms . . . [s]uch thoughts evoke 'de jure' the mystery, while 'de facto' the mystery is evoked by a pipe in an ash-tray" (Magritte, 1979, 530). The pipe is at that moment Lacan's *object petit a,* the first lost partial-object, the—according to Lacan—"forbidden" last link in the chain of desire. Against this, in the experience of the mystery there is no question of a lack, but rather of an abundance (*a plus-de-jouir*). The desire is not primarily the result of an unremovable lack, but rather the transcendent openness or disclosedness (*Erschlossenheit*) wherein the world, the Being of being, appears to us. This desire constitutes the conditions of the possibility of the neighborliness of things of which Nietzsche speaks (KSA, 8:588; cf. 3.8). Breton, at least with respect to this point, was correct: Magritte gives *lessons in things.*

All of this appears remarkably superficial and banal. But it is perhaps for precisely this reason that it escapes from "depth psychology." The remarks concerning banality and alienation by Freud and Mannoni are an indication of this point. Magritte explicates far more explicitly his view that psychoanalysis is not able to explain the mystery:

> Art, to the extent that I understand it, removes itself from psychoanalysis: it evokes that mystery without which the world would not be able to exist, that is, the mystery which one must not confuse with every problem, no matter how difficult. No sane person believes that psychoanalysis can explain the mystery of the world. The nature of the mystery destroys curiosity. Psychoanalysis has just as little to say about works of art which evoke the mystery of the world. (Magritte, 1979, 558; cf. 2.4)

If this analysis remains on the surface, then this is because things show themselves precisely at this point. Perhaps we should also interpret the title of the painting from this thought. That which Magritte makes an issue of in *La trahison des images* is the disavowal of immediate experience, the disavowal of appearance as luster, as the tempting appearance of Being. But, and this too makes the painting clear: afterwards, when theory dominates this experience, the experience is denied and understood as a regression, as a return to an imaginary past. A similar wilful "superficial" reading of *La trahison des images* reminds us of Nietzsche's hymn to the Greeks: "O, the Greeks! They knew how to live. What is required for that is to stop courageously at the surface, the fold, the skin, to adore appearance, to believe in forms, tones, words, in the whole Olympus of appearance. Those Greeks were superficial—*out of profundity*. And is not this precisely what we are again back to, we daredevils of the spirit who have climbed the highest and most dangerous peaks of present thought and looked around from up there—we who have looked *down* from there? Are we not, precisely in this respect, Greeks? Adorers of forms, of tones, of words? And therefore—*artists?*" (GS, 38). Perhaps the greatest achievement of *La trahison des images* resides in its boundless superficiality—out of profundity.

6

The Oldest Nobility
in the World

Once man needed a God, now he is delighted by a
world-disorder without God, a world of chance, horror,
ambiguity and seduction.

—Friedrich Nietzsche

The *Fragment an sich*, composed by Nietzsche in 1871, is a fascinating
composition for a number of reasons. Not only does the repetition-
notation without an end-signal point forward to the dominant role that
the "Eternal Recurrence of the Same" will play in both his later philosophy and twentieth-century repetitive music, as was explicated in chapter 3, but also the extremely fragmentary character of the composition
anticipates in a number of ways the future of Western culture.[1] This
applies in the first instance to Nietzsche's own later writings. While an
important part of nineteenth-century philosophy is characterized by
a strong compulsion, Nietzsche confronts us, most especially in the
middle period of his development, with an extremely fragmentary collection of aphorisms. In the foregoing (see 0.1 and 1.8) we have already
remarked that, according to Nietzsche, the fragmentary is characteristic
for the Romantic and that, despite his expressed preference for the
("healthy") classical style, he thereby betrays his Romantic attitude.
That this is not a purely stylistic affair is demonstrated by the aphorism
wherein Nietzsche calls the compulsion to systemize a lack of honesty
(TI, 470). The fragmentary character of his work, like his radical

metaphoric, is connected with the contents of his philosophy. The fragmentary style forms the expression of the insight that, with the death of God, the world has lost its coherence and unity.

That which brings the semiologist Roland Barthes and the composer John Cage together in this chapter is their Nietzschean predilection for the fragment. Barthes' texts, too, possess a remarkably fragmentary character and, just as with Nietzsche, this cannot be explained as a purely stylistic preference. Barthes consciously chose the fragmentary manner of writing to prevent his texts from achieving a closed character or being traced back to a last, enduring meaning. In *A Lover's Discourse. Fragments* he motivated the choice to construct his book as a series of alphabetically ordered fragments as follows: "It is the very principle of this discourse (and of the text which represents it), that its figures cannot be *classified*: organized, hierarchized, arranged with a view to an end (a settlement): there are no first figures, no last figures. To let it be understood that there was no question here of a love story (or of the history of a love), to discourage the temptation of meaning, it was necessary to choose an *absolute insignificant* order" (Barthes, 1979, 8). The fragmentary manner of writing, just as Romantic irony, is directed at preventing a "fossilization of language."

The beloved fragment does not permit itself to be inserted into the columbarium of concepts. It is a puzzle that creates the persistent but misleading suggestion that it is part of a coherent whole. In *Roland Barthes by Roland Barthes* Barthes remarks about the fragment that: "Every piece is a unity in itself and yet it is nonetheless each time nothing more than an intermediary space between the pieces around it: the work is only made of pieces which fall outside" (Barthes, 1975, 98).

With Barthes, just as with Nietzsche, considerations of content and style are difficult to separate. Writing fragmentarily makes it possible to achieve the proper "tone": "The fragment," remarks Barthes, "is a condensing not of thoughts or wisdom, or of truth (as in the maxim), but of music: the 'tone' comes to replace the argument" (Barthes, 1975, 98). With respect to the fragmentary character of his work, he points to a close relationship with Romantic music: "That person who has best understood and implemented the aesthetic of the fragment (before Webern) is perhaps Schumann: he called the fragment 'intermezzo,' in his work he composed more and more 'intermezzi': everything which he made was finally 'inserted,' but between what and what? What will that say, a series of only interruptions?" (Barthes, 1975, 98).

That which Barthes here writes about Schumann's work is, in my opinion, even more applicable to Cage's work. While by Schumann the fragments are still combined by the tonal system, with Cage the fragmentation touches the smallest distinctive unit of the music: the tones. Many of Cage's "compositions" appear to be completely beyond musical coding: each tone comes to stand on its own. The internal relationship of the musical and the discursive fragment explicated by Barthes is expressed by Cage in the texts that he wrote, wherein he often used the same method of fragmentation as in his compositions. Cage himself commented about his writing style: "I hope to let words exist, just as I have attempted to let sounds exist" (Cage, 1968, 151).

In this chapter, I will confront the works of Cage and Barthes with each other from the perspective of the fragmentary. Hereby, it will not only become clear what it is that binds them to each other, but also what separates them: their evaluation of *chance*. Cage uses chance to achieve a fragmentation. Flipping coins during composition to determine the following note, switching on arbitrary radio stations during the performance, leaving aside the contribution from the performers so that the coincidental sounds inside and outside the concert hall emerge into the foreground—these are merely a few examples of the appeal that Cage makes to chance so that the fragment can appear as a fragment. In his texts, Barthes only comments in passing about chance, preferably in unremarkable subordinate clauses, in parentheses or quotation marks, but the tone in these instances is without exception negative or at least suspicious. In his early work, he defined the structuralist activity as a "battle against chance" (Barthes, 1977, 217), in connection with Eisenstein's films he called chance crude, "a signifier on the cheap" (Barthes, 1984a, 69), and in his introduction in the narratology he even called it a myth and declared that art does not know any noise (Barthes, 1984a, respectively 80 and 89). For this reason, even a text such as *A Lover's Discourse. Fragments* wherein the fragmentation is at its greatest is nonetheless deliberately organized alphabetically. He chooses deliberately for a *moderate* arbitrariness: "Hence we have avoided the wiles of pure chance" and frustated "the power of chance to engender monsters" (Barthes, 1979, 8).

In the elaboration of this "smallest difference" between Cage and Barthes we must, of course, not lose sight of nuance. Cage, too, knows of moderate arbitrariness, for example, when he explains his predilection for mushrooms by the fact that they come just before "music" in the dictionary. However, in Cage's work, this moderate arbitrariness is just as much overshadowed by the affirmation of the radical arbitrariness of chance.

When clarifying Cage's radical affirmation of chance I shall not only refer to Barthes' (post)structuralist semiology, but also to Foucault, whose archaeology provides a framework in which Barthes' semiology can be historically situated, and to the works of Nietzsche and Heidegger. Against the background of the interpretation of Nietzsche's and Heidegger's works in previous chapters, I shall, in the last sections of this chapter, briefly examine a number of remarks that these philosophers have made concerning chance.

6.1 BARTHES' BATTLE AGAINST CHANCE

The origin of Barthes' battle against chance must be sought in the so-called first semiology ("science of signs") that he developed in the 1960s. This semiology was strongly influenced by structuralism, most especially by De Saussure's structuralist linguistics. For Barthes, structuralism does not so much represent a school or movement as an activity, "the controlled succession of a certain number of mental operations" (Barthes, 1977, 214).[2] This activity is not confined to the reflexive use of language, but rather is inherent in every production of meaning (*signification*). Structuralist theory is directed at such a reconstruction of (natural or cultural) objects that the structuring rules that determine their functioning are made apparent. This structure of functional relationships is not pregiven, but rather is the result of a theoretical construction; it concerns an imitation without original, a *simulacrum* (Barthes, 1977, 214). As Barthes expresses it, in the structuring activity intelligence is added to the first object. The goal of the structuring activity is therefore not a copy but the making intelligible of the first object. A simulacrum is a *composition*, a controlled manifestation of functions, a homologous object. This is no less applicable to the intellectual composition of reality as found in science, adds Barthes, than to literary, representational, and musical composition (Barthes, 1977, 215).[3]

Barthes distinguishes two basis-operations with respect to the structuring activity: dissection (*découpage*) and articulation (*agencement*). The object is dissected into its smallest elements, elements that, in themselves, do not have any meaning but whereby the substitution by another element introduces a change in the meaning of the whole. The phonemes in verbal language here constitute a clear example: in themselves, the letters k and t have no meaning, but the substitution of the k for a t in the word 'book' completely changes the meaning of the word. The operation of dissecting into distinctive elements produces a first, diffused condition of the simulacrum. Here, we are equally not concerned with an anarchy of elements: every element, together with every other element, forms a paradigm, "an intelligent organism."

Articulation, the second typical operation in the structuring activity, consists of formulating rules that regulate the combination of elements and the association of those combinations. In other words, in this step the rules of syntax are established, the rules that, through their constant operation, make it appear to us that an object is constructed and therefore meaningful. At this point we stumble into the origin of Barthes' suspicion regarding chance. He calls articulation a battle against chance because every element of an object constructed by man answers to a code (Barthes, 1977, 217). The rules of association—in this connection Barthes also employs the traditional term 'form'—ensures that the object in question cannot be viewed as a pure effect of chance, but rather appears as a meaningful whole. In structuralist activity man constitutes meaning. From Barthes' analysis, man appears as a *homo significans* (Barthes, 1977, 218).

De Saussure was the first to methodically apply this structuring activity to a science, linguistics. This successful application of the structuralist method imposed a strongly linguistic brand upon the first semiology. "However great the diversity, the irregularily, the disparity even of current research in semiotics," explains Julia Kristeva, "it is possible to speak of a specifically semiotic *discovery*. What semiologists discovered in studying 'ideologies' (myths, rites, moral codes, art, etc.) as sign-systems, is that the *law* is governing. Or, if one prefers, the *major constraint* affecting any social practice lies in the fact that it signifies; i.e., that it is articulated *like* a language" (Kristeva, 1975, 47). This tempts Barthes into inverting De Saussure's view of the relationship of semiology and linguistics. In the *Elements of Semiology* we read: "linguistics is not a part of the general science of signs, not even a privileged part, it is semiology which is part of linguistics: to be precise, it is that part covering *great signifying unities* of discourse" (Barthes, 1984b, 79). The linguistic centrism that is derived from this position is characteristic for French philosophy after phenomenology and existentialism. Lévi Strauss, Lacan, Althusser, Barthes, and Metz, to name just a few, have applied the linguistic method to a number of nonlinguistic domains of reality such as (respectively) relations of kinship, the unconscious, the economy, fashion, photography, and films.[4]

6.2 THE SEMIOLOGY OF MUSIC AND THE BOUNDARIES OF VERBAL LANGUAGE

If we wish to construct a conversation between Barthes and Cage, then it would appear that an appropriate manner would be an application of

Barthes' semiology to music. However, various problems hereby arise. Not only do we not find any encouragement in Barthes' work for a semiology of music (even though he regularly speaks of music), but, in contrast to other branches of semiology, the semiology of music has not to date really emerged. Given that there appears to be much to say for a semiology of music, this appears, at first sight, to be a remarkable fact. After all, music, just like language, appears remarkably easy to dissect into the smallest distinctive elements—the tones, that is, sounds determined by a constant frequency. In addition, it is also the case that here, too, the substitution of a particular note in a composition by another note results in a change in the total musical sound and sequence. However, although interesting semiotic analyses have been carried out with respect to musical syntax, the semiology of music appears, in contrast with a number of other branches of semiology, to face insurmountable problems with respect to the question of semantics.

In order to elaborate upon these problems I should examine in more depth several of the conceptual differentiations that are characteristic of Barthes' first semiology. At the foundation of semiology one finds De Saussure's differential definition of signs. As was explicated in the preceding chapter, De Saussure defined the sign as a unity of signifier (*signifiant*) and signified (*signifié*): an acoustic image and a concept. In the linguistic sign *tree*, the acoustic image 'tree' and the concept "tree" are united with each other. The relationship between signifier and signified is completely arbitrary in natural languages: the acoustic image 'tree' is neither more nor less able to express the concept "tree" than 'arbre' (French), 'Baum' (German), or 'boom' (Dutch). The sign is based upon a convention. De Saussure's definition of signs can be called differential for two reasons. Not only is there the just referred to *internal* difference between signifier and signified, but, moreover, there is an *external* difference: signifiers and signifieds never exist alone, but rather they derive their existence from their difference from other signifiers and signifieds.[5] De Saussure has expressed this double difference with rather pretty imagery: a sign is comparable to a form cut out of paper. The upper and lower part of the cut-out form can be compared with the signifier and the signified in the sign: they literally constitute the two sides (the internal difference) of the same coin. The place that the cut-out form occupies with respect to the rest of the paper (which, like a puzzle, is once again divided into separate forms) forms the external difference and constitutes the value that the sign possesses in the total system.[6]

In the first semiology interest is primarily directed at the 'vertical' relationship between signifier and signified. For this reason, the issue of *denotation* and *connotation* is central in the first semiology.[7] Each system of attributing meaning (*signification*) contains a relation between signifier and signified (stated by Barthes to be respectively the levels of expression and content—cf. Barthes, 1984b, 149 ff.). The signifier denotes the signified: the acoustic sound 'tree' denotes the mental representation "tree." The sign as a whole, however, again functions as a signifier or signified at a higher level of attributing meaning. The sign tree can be used in its totality, for example in an allegory, as a *signifier* that denotes the signified 'life.' In this case, the sign of the first is hollowed out, as it were, and (largely) filled with the signified of the second order.[8] According to Barthes, with respect to the signified we enter in that case into the terrain of myth and ideology, and with respect to the signifiers the terrain of rhetoric. But the sign tree can also function as *signified* in an attribution of meaning of the second order. When the semiologist speaks about this sign in the framework of his theories, for example. In that case we enter the territory of the metalanguage.

If we compare the musical sign with the linguistic sign, then a number of important differences become immediately apparent. Thus, for example, musical "language," unlike verbal language, is not only, and not even primarily, linear-discursive, but rather is based on simultaneous sounds, on harmony. However, the most important difference between musical and verbal language is undoubtedly to be found in the area of the *denotative* and *referential* function of language. If we wish to speak about music in terms of meaning, then we should realize that this meaning is of a fundamentally different order from the meaning of language. If the musical signifier, the sound, already denotes something, then, unlike the case in verbal language, it is not a concept that is being signified. If we wish to bring musical signifiers into a connection with the content of thoughts, then the issue, to quote Nietzsche's paradoxical definition of music (from Wagner), is one of "a system of thought without the abstract form of thought" (KSA, 1:485). As we have already remarked in chapter 1, Nietzsche presents such a system of thought as *mythical.* What is characteristic of the myth is precisely the lack of the type of articulation that is characteristic of the *logos* of verbal language (cf. Langer, 1976, 204 ff.).

No less problematic is the referential function of musical language. If, with music, we can already speak of a reference to a nonmusical reality, then this occurs in an essentially different manner than in the case of the linguistic signifier. In the literature of the semiotics of music the referential function of musical "language" is investigated at various levels of meaning by respectively interpreting it as index, symptom, signal, and arbitrary sign (cf. note 6, chapter 2).

Nattiez, who with *Foundations of a Semiology of Music* (1975) produced one of the most impressive attempts to provide the foundations of a semiotics of music, tried to place its referential function in safety by conceiving of it as a system that elicits emotional content via *indexical* paths. Now, indices, just like symptoms, are by definition nonintentional signs. For this reason, according to De Meyer, indices and symptoms cannot be considered as belonging to music to the extent that we view it as the intentional production of sounds (De Meyer, 1982). The most that one could do is view bad playing or singing as an index or symptom of a badly tuned instrument or the performer's lack of expertise. Self-evidently this does not remove the fact that intentional signs, too, can elicit indexical reactions such as, for example, the traditional cheerfulness elicited by the major scale or sadness by the minor scale.[9] However, whoever attempts to conceive of music entirely in terms of indexical signs surrenders to a rather problematic musical "behaviorism" (cf. Ruwet, 1972) that not only too easily ignores the temporally and culturally bound character of the indexical reactions—for example, that which is viewed as dissonant is dependent upon historical developments and differs between cultures—but, at the same time, it narrows the meaning of music in an unjustifiable manner.[10]

According to De Meyer, although auditory *signals* (the sound of the doorbell, for example), in contrast to indices, do possess an intentional character, they equally do not form a sufficient condition to be able to speak of music given that music always assumes a certain code (even it is self-evidently so that coded sounds can appear as signals—in the case where someone hearing the national anthem being played views this as a signal to stand up, for example).

The most fruitful semantic approach is perhaps to view music as a *symbol*. In this instance, the assumption is that an analogy exists between the musical sign and the nonmusical (psychic or physical) reality. In the simplest case, such an iconic function can appear as musical *onomatopoeia* (for example, as imitation of gurgling mountain brooks, bad weather and storm, the beating of a heart, etc.). However, with Schopenhauer we can doubt whether or not we have actually obtained a grip on the essence of music with such a "painting music" (*malende Musik*) (Schopenhauer, 1977, 2, sect. 219; cf. my comment concerning Beethoven's Sixth Symphony in note 3, chapter 3). We could also, however, view the analogy metaphorically. The theme of knocking in Beethoven's Fifth Symphony can then be understood, for example, as the "knocking of destiny at the door" or—as Nietzsche does—the "endless melody" of Wagner's operas as a symbol of the infinity of Becoming. By Adorno, too, as was earlier remarked, there appears to be a similar sort of symbolic view of music when he attributes a (conventionally determined) homology with social reality to the musical form (see 2.5).

However, the question remains whether we are justified to speak of semantic content in these cases. After all, it is impossible to understand music as a system of arbitrary signs in the sense of verbal language, that is, as a system of signs based upon convention that concretely refer to the reality outside of that system. The untranslatability of the musical "language" is undoubtedly connected with this (Langer, 1976, 234). We could maintain, with Rilke, that instrumental music is the language wherein all languages fall silent. This insight leads to doubt concerning Barthes' starting point that verbal language constitutes the foundation of *all* possible systems of signs.[11] In *Semiotics of Music*, which appeared in 1980, Schneider devastatingly concludes: "Semiotics is certainly a science—but not a science of music" (Schneider, 1980, 241).

The view that music as a whole cannot be conceived in terms of the example of verbal language, something that is at the basis of Schneider's critique, is shared by many contemporary musical theorists. Langer, quoted earlier, is also of the opinion that musical symbolization is not reducible to the discursive symbolization of verbal language (Langer, 1976, 204 ff.). This view, incidentally, is not new; it is rooted in Romantic aesthetics. In preceding chapters we have already remarked that Schopenhauer and Nietzsche strongly emphasized the distinguished character of music in relation to language. Music, maintains Nietzsche in *The Birth of Tragedy out of the Spirit of Music*, in its complete unboundedness does not need the image and understanding, but rather merely *tolerates* their presence alongside it. Nietzsche, incidentally, does not stand alone with this view. For many Romantics, music forms the preeminent paradigm for all the arts, including literature and poetry (see Neubauer, 1986, 10).

We could naturally ask ourselves if Schopenhauer's and Nietzsche's inclination to elevate expressive music above language does not constitute a Romantic (over)reaction to the foregoing aesthetics of music. In the eighteenth century, just as in the recent semiology of music, musicology and the aesthetics of music were conceptualized from within language. Thus, for example, Johann Nicolaus Forgel remarked in his three-part *Musikalisch-kritische Bibliothek* (1778 and 1779), that "musical pieces of a particular length share with language the rules of order and the organization of ideas" (quoted in Neubauer, 1986, 22). Perhaps Schneider has this eighteenth-century tradition in mind when he maintains: "The traditional historical musical science offers accentuations and concepts which the questions raised—and partially rejected—by semiotics more relevantly pose and answer" (Schneider, 1980, 241). At the end of the book quoted earlier Nattiez, too, expresses the anxious suspicion that he achieved nothing other than "having re-formulated the great truths of classical musicology in a new terminology" (Nattiez, 1975, 400).

6.3   THE ARCHAEOLOGY OF THE EIGHTEENTH-CENTURY SEMIOLOGY OF MUSIC

The idea that twentieth-century structuralism, which includes Barthes' semiology, reached back past nineteenth-century subject-centered philosophy to eighteenth-century mimetic models was also presented by Foucault in *The Order of Things* (1966). This "archaeology of the human sciences"—as the subtitle reads—offers an interesting framework for examining the apparently discontinuous development of ideas about music. In his archaeology Foucault analyzed the successive epistemes—which he presented as Kantian historical *a priori's*—that have determined Western thinking since the Renaissance.[12] In his discussion of structuralism, Foucault points out that this approach reaches back to the emphasis on the linguistic system that is characteristic of the classical episteme. Foucault even speaks of a return of language: "At this point, where the question of language arises again which such heavy over-determination, and where it seems to lay siege on every side of the figure of man (that figure which had once taken the place of Classical Discourse), contemporary culture is struggling to create an important part of its present, and perhaps of its future" (Foucault, 1974, 382–83).[13]

If we accept Foucault's periodicization then the eighteenth-century aesthetics of music belongs to the classical episteme. Foucault also presented this classical episteme as the episteme of representation (*representation*). Foucault does not consider representation as an activity carried out by the subject. According to him, in the classical episteme representation is viewed as an immediate expression of things. The representations were not understood as the product of a knowing subject, but rather as an order that was given by God simultaneously and in full congruence with the order of things. In the words of Leibniz, these two orders exist in a *harmonia praestabilita*.

This epistemic organization has important implications for knowledge in the classical episteme: it is viewed as a correct ordering of linguistic signs (*mathesis*). In this ordering, which can be situated in a tableau, the order of things immediately becomes clear (cf. the passage concerning the *mathesis universalis* in 0.5 above). In principle, the universal order of things is completely given with the universal ordering of language. When Foucault provocatively maintained that man did not yet exist in the classical episteme, this means that there was not yet a place arranged for man as a representing subject *outside* the tableau. However, the activity of representation can be represented just as little *within* the tableau. Man emerges in the tableau as just one being among the many that make up *the great chain of Being*.[14]

Foucault expressively explicated this by reference to a famous painting by Velasquez. According to him, the representation presented in the foregoing sentence forms the authentic theme of *Las Meninas*. The painting shows us the painter Velasquez pausing in front of a canvas that he is painting. Neither the picture on the canvass nor what is being painted is visible to us. The subject of the painting is in the place from where we are viewing *Las Meninas*. Moreover, this is also the place where Velasquez stood when he painted *Las Meninas*. Because of the presence of a mirror on the back wall we are nonetheless permitted a glance at the represented subject: vaguely but unmistakably it shows us the royal couple. Foucault argued that Velasquez's painting shows the impossibility of the classical episteme to represent the activity of representation itself. This activity is now divided into three functions that are representable: the production of the representation (the painter), the represented object (the royal couple), and the perception of the representation (the observer who looks on from the doorway). "But there, in the midst of this dispersion which it is simultaneously grouping together and spreading out before us, indicated compellingly from every side, is an essential void: the necessary disappearance of what is its foundation—of the person it resembles and the person in whose eyes it is only a resemblance. This very subject—which is the same—has been elided. And representation, freed finally from the relation that was impeding it, can offer itself as representation in its pure form" (Foucault, 1974, 16).

Gerard Broers, in an interesting philosophical study of the music of Wagner, Schönberg, and Cage has attempted to interpret the tonal system, as it originated at the beginning of the eighteenth century, from within Foucault's view of the classical episteme. The tonal system, which had occupied a dominant position in musical production from about 1750 until late into the nineteenth century, was first formulated by Rameau in his *Traité de l'harmonie* (1722) (cf. 3.3). It is a remarkably ambivalent work. On the one hand, Rameau conceives of music as a phenomenon based upon natural laws, while on the other hand he presages later structuralism with the view, in tension with the first conceptualization, that music forms an order that is based upon arbitrarily chosen generative principles (cf. Neubauer, 1986, 83).[15] Broers interprets the tonal system in terms of Foucault's concept of the classical episteme:

> Music, too, does not escape its own episteme which, in the case of Baroque music, is the episteme of representation. The music is representation of feelings. In the music, the emotions, the affections, become clearly recognizable and are separated from each other in sound. Roughly in the same way as nature in the tableaux of Linnaeus are restlessly absorbed in the representations, the composer exerts himself in order that the melodic, rhythmical, and harmonic conventions be so dextrously possible employed so that a good representation of the effect is achieved. He was *not* concerned with giving stature to his own subjectivity, measuring himself, as it were, against the musical parameters which go beyond him as would occur in the nineteenth century. (Broers, 1982, 31–32)

Analogous with Velasquez's painting, we could add, the representation (of feelings) is central to the tonal system, but the system simultaneously excludes the representation of the activity from the representation.

Against the background of Broers' interpretation we can understand why Leibniz defined music as "an expression of the universal harmony which God brought into the world" (cf. Haase, 1963, 25). Just as the ordering of language in the classical episteme immediately represented the order of things, the musical *mathesis* relates itself to the world. If we listen to music, maintains Leibniz, then we enjoy an harmonious, mathematical ordering that we can nonetheless not completely comprehend: "Musica est exercitium arithmeticae occultum nescientis se numerare animi" (Leibniz, 1934, 241). It is important to hereby underline that there is here no question of a naive mimetic theory. Music does not constitute an imitation of objects from the world by a representing subject, but rather expresses the universal laws that are the foundations of total reality by purely musical means.[16] Hawkins, in his *A General History of the Science and Practice of Music* (1776), expressed this "formalism," which is intrinsic to classical episteme and which assumes that all musical proportions are based upon harmonious relationships in the universe—a view that dates back to Pythagoras—as follows: "In short, there are only a few things in nature which music is capable of imitating, and those are of a kind so uninteresting, that we may venture to pronounce that as its principles are founded in geometrical truth and seem to result from some general and universal law of nature, so its excellence is intrinsic, absolute, and inherent, and, in short, resolvable only to be attributed to His Will who has ordered everything in numbers, weight, and measure" (quoted in Neubauer, 1986, 172).

Broers substantiates his Foucaultian interpretation of the tonal system by an interpretation of the clavier as a musical tableau:

> The musical material itself is also completely charted, classified in a tableau on which from now on all available tones are given: the keys of the clavier. Not that the clavier was new, but rather the manner in which from now on it is tuned, and since when it (mostly) remains tuned, namely, the octave divided into 12 equal semitones. This well-tempered tuning system makes it possible that each of the 12 tones can be the basis of a musical piece, and that all of those pieces can be in tune that is, with an imprecision similarly divided across the entire octave, performed on that instrument. In such a piece all chords have a *function* (centrifugal or centripetal) with respect to the tonic or with respect to the tonic chord, because this music is largely harmony. (Broers, 1982, 32)

J. S. Bach's *Wohltemperierte Klavier*, written in the same year as Rameau's *Traité de l'harmonie*, shows the possibilities of the tonal system: it consists of preludes and fugues in every key from the chromatic octave in major and minor.

Broers' interpretation of the tonal system appears at first sight to be in contradiction to my earlier interpretation. After all, in section 3.3, I indicated that the sonata form, comparable with the central perspective, is a form wherein reality in its entirety appears to the listening *subject*. This is only an apparent contradiction, however. The tonal system such as Broers interprets it forms a system of conditions on the basis of which the articulated expression by a subject first becomes possible. With the help of De Saussure's distinction we could propose that logically the tonal system (the musical *langue*) precedes the possibility of concrete, subjective musical representation (the musical *parole*). Just as in the example of painting the order of the (perspectivist) representation formed the conditions of possibility for the appearance of the representing subject, so the tonal system forms the conditions of possibility of subjective musical expression. Paradoxically enough, the expression in both cases means a breakthrough in the timeless purity of the system. The creation of Romantic, expressive music by the individual creative genius presumes the (structural) representation of the classical episteme and simultaneously means a radical undermining of this system of representation.[17]

6.4 THE SONATA FORM AND THE EPISTEME OF MAN

According to Foucault, Kant's philosophy marks the entrance of modern episteme. In his archaeological analysis of modern episteme, which reminds us of Heidegger's genealogy of the subject (cf. 4.4), Foucault argues that Kant's transcendental philosophy destroys the classical episteme, and that the human subject becomes the foundation of everything that is, and that the entire world becomes the representation of this human subject.[18]

This is clarified in an exemplary manner by the development of the sonata form, which is characteristic of the tonal system. During the nineteenth century the sonata form came under enormous pressure, the development increased in scope and radicality, and thereby also the harmonic vagueness. The changed function of the development is expressed in different ways: the number of modulations increased, as well as the distance between the keys, and the duration wherein the transitions were made became shorter and shorter. The development, the most "subjective" part of the composition, took on a more important place, something which also had an influence on other parts of the sonata form. The number of themes in the exposition increased and the distinction between exposition and development became vaguer. Beethoven, especially in his later string quartets, transformed the tonal system in an incomparable manner to a brilliant expressive medium of subjective feelings. This makes Beethoven, as Barthes remarked, the first composer with a development.

In further developments, the "objective" codes of the totality come under increasing pressure. After 1850 we can therefore also speak of drifting tonality. Wagner played an important role in this development. He decoded the total system right up to its most extreme boundaries and, with respect to the musical composition, could only "hold it together" by virtue of the nonmusical concept of the *Gesamtkunstwerk*. According to Nietzsche the decadence of Wagner's music primarily resides in this point:

> The commencement with Wagner is hallucination: not from sounds, but from gestures. Hereby he first seeks the semiotics of sound. If you want to admire him, then you should see how he hereby goes to work: how he separates, how he creates tiny units, how he inspires them, drives them out, makes them visible. But then his competence is exhausted: of the rest, nothing is suitable. How paltry, how uncertain, how amateuristic is his manner of "developing," his struggle to at least mix together that which has not separated. (KSA, 6:27–28)

It was Schönberg who completed the decoding of tonality in his free atonal period. In the atonal music all twelve tones of the octave receive "identical rights" for the subject that expresses itself. It appears that here the emancipation of the Romantic subject finds its completion. In the free atonal work there is no longer an internal teleology that regulates the progress of material development from within; subjective expression receives total dominance in favor of the unity of the work. Perhaps Nietzsche's criticism of Wagner is even more applicable to Schönberg's early work:

> The totality is no longer a totality. But that applies to every decadent style: time and again the anarchy of the atoms, degradation of the Will, "freedom of the individual," in moral terms—extended to a political theory: "*identical* rights for everybody." Life, *identical* inspiration, the vibration and exuberance of life, compressed to the smallest elements, what remains *poor* in living. Everywhere paralysis, difficulty, rigidification *or* enmity and chaos: and both become increasingly clear as the organizational form becomes higher. The totality no longer lives: it is adjusted, worked out, artificial, an artistic product. (KSA, 6:27)

6.5 THE MUSICAL DOMINION OF THE SUBJECT

Once again we encounter here the ambivalent character of the Romantic project. The emancipation of the Romantic subject, the announcement of radical freedom leads to a situation wherein, by virtue of a lack of rules and laws, freedom turns against itself. Subjective freedom becomes subjective arbitrariness: because every tone is of equal value a total lack of value and disintegration of the musical material is threatening.

Looking at the recent history of music it becomes possible to distinguish two answers to this threatening musical nihilism, with the seed of both found in Nietzsche's work. In the first place there is the possibility to restrain the subjective arbitrariness by a renewed objective organization. The goal here, following Nietzsche, is to create a music in the Great Style: "To become master of the Chaos which man is; to suppress his Chaos, to become form: logically simple, unambiguous, mathematical, to become law, that is the great ambition here" (KSA, 13:246; cf. Section 1.8 above). This path leads to the serial music of the later Schönberg and the radical total serialism of Stockhausen and Boulez.

In Schönberg's serial music (also referred to as twelve-tone music or dodecaphony) the game of the musical signifiers is determined in advance by a choice for a particular sequence of the twelve tones such that every tone of the equally tempered scale only emerges once.

During composition all twelve tones should be used before any single tone may be repeated. The chosen trope can be subjected to all sorts of treatments, such as transposition, reflection, and inversion, but it remains determinant for the entire composition. However, there is a fundamental difference here with the determination of the tonal system. While in that case one can speak of an immanent teleology that arises from the nature of the octave itself and that ensures that the music plays itself, as it were, in the "freischwebende Mathematik" (Adorno, 1984, 116) of the twelve-tone music, the determination is completely external. It is imposed on the material from outside by the composer and often inaudible for the audience. In his *Philosophy of New Music* Adorno expressed this as follows: "Music is the result of a process which determines the material and which does not permit itself to be seen" (quoted in Mertens, 1980, 120).

This makes it an urgent question as to whether or not the Great Style that Nietzsche desired is realized in this music. Here, there is actually no longer a question of a reconciliation of the parts and the whole, the general and the exceptional. The Belgian composer and musicologist Wim Mertens, in his illuminating analysis of twelve-tone music, remarked about this:

> The unity of part and whole is realized in the dodecaphony at the expense of an isolation of the parts: after all, the whole no longer grows organically out of the parts, but rather it is imposed from outside so that the parts are separated and the whole crumbles. The principle of the total differentiation of material ceases to exist: the ubiquity of the variation ensures that nothing really changes. . . . Schönberg's work is described as dissonant. On the one hand the dissonant stands for the total emancipation of the Romantic subject, but, on the other hand, it denies this subject by virtue of the determining, externally imposed dodecaphonic system of composition. The absolute dynamic of subjective pathos thus comes to be equal to its objective leveling out. The subject determines the music according to a rational system but becomes itself the object of the system. The equalization of all twelve tones in the series makes each expression virtually impossible and must necessarily lead to subjective indifference. (Mertens, 1980, 121)

The emancipation of the Romantic subject thus leads to the objective sound material being made absolute, and, simultaneously to an atomizing of the separate sounds. These elements thus liberate themselves from the structure that is imposed upon them. However, the idea of "work" is hereby saved. The composing subject no longer perhaps functions as the expressive content of the musical sign, but it does still do so as musical form. In this sense the subject, just as it arose in Romantic music, maintains its dominance. Broers remarked in this context that:

> Western culture as the exploitative and systematic organization of nature achieves its audible counterpart in music, where a process of musical domination now takes possession of nature. An old dream: it appears that the complete organization of music will be realized. . . . No longer hindered by classic convention, music becomes . . . controllable by the composer in all its facets. Schönberg, by performing this program, has brought the hidden tendency of Western artistic music onto the surface: he is the *Aufklärer* of music. (Broers, 1982, 36–37)[19]

Boulez's and Stockhausen's total serialism means a further radicalization of the path begun by Schönberg. In 1951 they respectively produced *Structures*, a work for two pianos, and *Kreuzspiel*, a composition for oboe, bass clarinet, piano, and percussion. Both works were composed following strict serial principles. Not only the pitch, as with Schönberg and Webern, but also the duration of the tone, its strength and timbre are predetermined in detail by the entire composition. Just as the painter Stella in his strict formalist period, Boulez and Stockhausen no longer see themselves as creative artists, but rather as engineers (cf. 2.3). The sound material is subjected to *scientific* research and the composer, as if he were Leibniz's God, makes exuberant use of arithmetical and mathematical series.

The early work of John Cage connects quite closely to this serial tradition in twentieth-century music. Cage, born in 1912 in Los Angeles, studied piano and composition with Henry Cowell, who, as composer, publisher, and propagandist, played an exceptionally important role in the development of a specifically American musical tradition. As a composer, Cowell experimented with, among other things, the direct plucking, stroking, and hitting of piano strings, techniques that Cage would later follow in his compositions for *prepared piano*. In the 1930s, however, he was still strongly influenced by Schönberg, who had fled from Nazi-Germany and established himself in Los Angeles. From 1935 to 1937 Cage studied with Schönberg. However, Schönberg was rather ambivalent with respect to Cage, accusing him of a total lack of feeling for harmony and considering him more of an inventor than a composer (see S, 261).

Early compositions, such as *Sonata for solo clarinet* (1933), can be listened to as miniature essays in twelve-tone serialism (cf. Griffith, 1981,

3). The "lack" of feeling for harmony encouraged Cage to an exploration of rhythmic structures. The *Quartet* and *Trio*, originating in 1935 and 1936, presage the repetitive music of composers such as Reich. In this connection, important works are the *Constructions in Metal I, II and III*, which were composed between 1939 and 1942. The compositions for percussion and piano converge in works for prepared piano (1943–48). These compositions are remarkable because they are not organized from within a particular harmonic system; sound and silence are structured as temporal intervals. Cage called this idea, which he saw preeminently embodied in the music of Satie and Webern, "the only new idea in music since Beethoven" (in Griffith, 1981, 11). The harmonic vagueness was underlined, under the influence of Cowell's techniques of composition and Duchamp's *Ready Mades*, by the preparation of the piano by fixing pieces of wood, paper, rubber, and metal between the strings. It is characteristic of Cage that he did not extend these experiments to an *oeuvre*, but left them as fragments and began to explore new paths.

In the manifesto *The Future of Music: Credo* (1937), wherein Cage pleaded for a radical exploration of sound, he wrote:

> I believe that the use of noise to make music will continue and increase until we reach a music produced through the aid of electrical instruments which will make available for musical purposes any and all sounds that can be heard. Photo-electric, film, and mechanical mediums for the production of music will be explored. Whereas, in the past, the point of disagreement has been between dissonant and consonant, it will be in the immediate future, between noise and so-called musical sounds. The present methods of writing music, principally those which employ harmony and its reference to particular steps in the field of sound, will be inadequate for the composer, who will be faced with the entire field of sounds. New methods will be discovered, bearing a definite relation to Schönberg's twelve-tone system and present methods of writing percussion music and any other methods which are free from the concept of a fundamental tone. (S, 3–5)

With this call to the exploration of all sounds, Cage appears to set himself in the tradition of the increasing control of nature. The reference to Schönberg would appear to confirm this. For Cage, the issue is one of *organizing* sound (S, 6). In his manifesto, he explicitly connects music to social development. In agreement with Adorno's theory of musical reflection, he understands the development of new methods in combination with social development: "Schönberg's method is analogous to a society in which the emphasis is on the group and the integration of the individual in the group" (S, 5).

However, the development of "methods which are free from the concept of a fundamental tone"—a call Cage soon will rise to, leads to a fundamental break with this striving for organization and control. In the manifesto, this is already expressed in the appreciation for improvisation in jazz (S, 5).[20] In compositions for *prepared piano*, this fundamental alteration is introduced by the abandonment of traditional musical notation. Musical notation is no longer an exact symbolic representation of sound, but rather forms a set of indications for the performer, who enjoys great freedom in the performance of these indicators. Before attempting to explicate Cage's break with the preceding musical tradition, I want to pause momentarily by the further development of the presently unwilling tools of semiotics that I have chosen to use.

6.6 BARTHES' SECOND SEMIOLOGY AND THE DEATH OF THE COMPOSER

In the foregoing I interpreted musical development from the Romantic period as an example of the ideas of domination that are characteristic of the modern "episteme of man." At the same time I indicated that, according to Foucault, structuralism, to which Barthes' first semiotics also belongs, constitutes a break with this modern episteme. According to Foucault, the structuralist sciences disrupt the subject centrism of this episteme by focusing on the structural level, which is condition of the possibility of the subject's consciousness and experiences. Language is no longer conceived as a medium in which to express *a priori* meanings in the subject, but rather is attributed to the material conditions of possibility of meaning as such.[21] This does, indeed, imply an important break with tradition.

Nonetheless, on the grounds of Barthes' definition of structuralist activity, we could ask ourselves if structuralism really has managed to liberate itself in all respects from the modern episteme. Frank has convincingly argued that structuralism in any case remains in the tradition of the modernist will to control. After all, the structuralist analysis is directed at discovering the rules according to which phenomena appear and that make it possible to control these phenomena (Frank, 1984, 36).[22] According to Frank, poststructuralist theories that have been elaborated since the 1960s by French philosophers such as Derrida and Kristeva, can be viewed as attempts to free structuralism from these ideas of control by emphasising the uncontrollability of the system (Frank, 1984, 37).

Barthes' second, later semiology should be understood in this context. He puts the development of his second semiology in relation with what he refers to as the "great affair of modern science": the disintegration of the linguistic sign (cf. 5.3). It is primarily the writings of Lacan, Derrida, and Kristeva that make Barthes aware of the remarkable inconsistencies in semiology's concept of the sign. If the sign is differential, that is, if it is determined by a difference, then can we still speak of the unity of the sign? Are not the signifier and the signified constituted on the basis of a trace that they contain of all other elements in the system? A signifier or a signified only has value in relation to what it itself is not. At the level of the signifier, this is not such a problem because most of the sign systems are built up from a finite number of signifiers (thus, verbal languages only have a limited number of different phonemes). However, the number of signifieds is in principle infinitely great. For this reason, the value of a signified remains in essence undetermined. The signified constantly points to other signifieds and thus, as it were, becomes itself a signifier. An indicatory game thus unfolds that never comes to rest. An infinite web appears that Derrida refers to as *text*. Such a text has no ultimate transcendental signified (*signifié transcendental*). This disintegration of the linguistic sign has radical consequences for the first semiology. A semiological analysis can no longer be a vertical analysis that leads from signifier to signified, but rather becomes a never-ending horizontal analysis of the sliding of the signifiers (Lacan, É, 502; cf. 4.1 and 5.3 above). The primacy shifts from the denotation to the connotation. In order to show this difference in "meaning," Barthes, in his later writings, no longer speaks of "*signification*" but of "*signifiance*."

An important consequence of the second semiology is the much-discussed "death of the Author." "The 'author'," maintains Barthes in *The Death of the Author* (1968), "is a modern figure, a product of our society insofar as, emerging from the Middle Ages with English empiricism, French rationalism and the personal faith of the Reformation, it discovered the prestige of the individual, of, as it is more nobly put, the 'human person'" (Barthes, 1984a, 142–43). Within the modern episteme the author functions as a transcendental signified: "To give a text an author is to impose a limit on that text, to furnish it with a final signified, to close the writing. . . . [w]hen the Author has been found, the text is 'explained'—victory to the critic" (Barthes, 1984a, 147). Hereby, Barthes points to an important counter-movement: "In France, Mallarmé was doubtless the first to see and to foresee in its full extent the necessity to substitute language itself for the person who until then had been supposed to be its owner" (Barthes, 1984a, 143).[23] Over against the literature of the Author, Barthes places multiple authorship of the text. Along with the Author, traditional literary criticism is brought into the balance: "In the multiplicity of writing, everything is to be *disentangled*, nothing *deciphered*; but rather the structure can be followed, 'run' (like the thread of a stocking), at every point and at every level, but there is nothing beneath; the space of writing is to be ranged over, not peirced; writing ceaselessly to evaporate it, carrying out a systematic exemption of meaning" (Barthes, 1984a, 147).[24] Barthes' comments concerning multiple writings possess a strong Nietzschean undercurrent. The quotation continues: "Imprecisely this way literature (it would be better from now on to say *writing*)—by refusing to assign a 'secret,' an ultimate meaning, to the text (and to the world as text)—liberates what may be called an anti-theological activity, an activity that is really revolutionary since to refuse to fix meaning is, in the end, to refuse God and his hypostases—reason, science, law" (Barthes, 1984a, 147).

In the article *"De l'oeuvre au texte"* (1971), written several years later and wherein Barthes' love for the fragment receives expression, the shift from the first to the second semiology was more closely explicated. Contrary to the old theory of literature that is based upon the literary work, a finalized whole that finds its ultimate meaning in the author, the text is only perceivable as a work in progress. "The text," maintains Barthes, in the spirit of Romantic irony (cf. 0.3 above),

> practices the infinite deferment of the signified, is dilatory; its field is that of the signifier and the signifier must not be conceived of as the "first stage of meaning," its material vestibule, but, in complete opposition to this, as its *deferred action*. Similarly, the *infinity* of the signifier refers not to some idea of the ineffable (the unnameable signified) but to that of a *playing*; the generation of the perpetual signifier (after the fashion of a perpetual calender) in the field of the text (better, of which the text is the field), is realized not according to an organic process of maturation or a hermeneutic course of deepening investigation, but rather according to a serial movement of disconnections, overlappings, variations. (Barthes, 1984a, 158)

Expressed in the terminology of the first semiology we could postulate that the text is overcome by a constant connotation that repeatedly subordinates to a *Verwindung* every threatened "fossilization" of meaning into a denotation, or, alternatively, "deconstructs" it from within.

The reading of the text is fundamentally unique and simultaneously permeated with quotations, references, echoes, in brief, various forms of linguistic use. Every text can only be conceived as an intertext of other texts. It is not a nonlinguistic context (the biography of the author, the sociocultural reality) that is determinate, but the relations that the text maintains with other texts. Every text is in fact a fragment of an endlessly sliding text. Barthes speaks about this pleasure in a terminology that is derived from Freud and Lacan, but he constantly perverts it in a manner comparable to the manner in which Magritte perverts psychoanalytic ideas (cf. the preceding chapter). For Barthes, text and desire are not contradictory, they merge into one another. Desire is not, as with Lacan, the result of a lack (or even a Metaphysical Lack), but a productive desire, understood in Nietzschean terms, that creates from immeasurable abundance (cf. 1.5–6).[25] The issue is not one of passive consumption of the text, but rather an active playing along with it. In this playing along, musical connotations can be noted: " 'Playing' must be understood here in all its polysemy: the text itself *plays* (like a door, like a machine with 'play') and the reader plays twice over, playing the Text as one plays a game, looking for a practice which re-produces it, but, in order that that practice not be reduced to a passive, inner *mimesis* (the Text is precisely that which resists such a reduction), also playing the Text in the musical sense of the term" (Barthes, 1984a, 162).

The second semiology not only makes it possible to look at classical literature from a completely different perspective (Barthes' reading of Balzac's novella *Sarrasine* in *S/Z* offers an excellent example of this), but, in addition, it opens the ears for "another" experience of tonal music. This music, too, is understood no longer as an expression of a subject—we could speak here, metaphorically, of the "death" of the Composer—but as a musical intertext that appears to autonomously perform itself. For Barthes, the musical text in the second semiology even achieves a paradigmatic meaning. Musical text has the advantage over literary text because the denotation can only reside with difficulty in the musical structure. After all, the process of connotation, characteristic of the (inter)text, which ultimately excludes every denotation, appears in its most radical form in music (cf. note 2, chapter 2). It is not without irony that the musical characteristic that frustrated the development of a semiology of music that is oriented to linguistics has now made music the shining example of literature. The Romantic "revenge" of music against verbal language appears to be hereby repeated.

The connotative sliding is preeminently applicable to the classical musical "text" such as the sonata form where every signifier constantly points to the other notes within the text. The emancipation of music from language that, as we noted above, entered into nineteenth-century aesthetics, appears to repeat itself in the second semiology. Just as in the Romantic era, music becomes a model for literature. An important plus for this model is that the musical signifier does not play its game at the expense of its physical reality. In contrast to the apparently transparent linguistic sign, the musical signifier is not primarily transcendent but immanent. We could call the musical "text" a *pure* connotative system, a pure "*signifiance.*" In section 6.2, I remarked that Nietzsche presented music, in comparison with language, as a mythical system of thought, and that Barthes maintains that the myth is characterized by connotation. If we short-circuit these ideas then we could claim that the purely connotative character of music constitutes it mythical character (cf. Lévi-Strauss, 1975, 14 ff.). Instrumental music can be viewed as a system of pure connotation, that is, a system in which every potential denotation is immediately completely connoted and the denotation is infinitely postponed.[26] In this case, the musical meaning resides completely in the internal organization of the musical signifiers and, therefore, music becomes pure form.

Barthes notes parallels between the development of literary and musical texts.

> The history of music (as a practice, not as an "art") does indeed parallel that of the Text fairly closely: there was a period when practicing amateurs were numerous (at least within the confines of a particular class), and "playing" and "listening" formed a scarcely differentiated activity;[27] then two roles appeared in succession, first that of the performer, the interpreter to whom the bourgeois public (though still itself able to play a little—the whole history of the piano) delegated its playing, then that of the (passive) amateur, who listens to music without being able to play (the gramophone record takes the place of the piano). We know that today postserial music has radically altered the role of the "interpreter," who is called on to be in some sort the co-author of the score, completing it rather than giving it "expression." The Text is very much a score of this new kind: its asks from the reader a practical collaboration. Which is an important change, for who executes the work? (Barthes, 1984a, 162–63)

Barthes gives the following answer to this question: "there is one place where this multiplicity [of the reading—JdM] is focused and that place is the reader, not, as was hitherto said, the author. The reader is the space on which all quotations that make up a writing are inscribed without any of them being lost: a text's unity lies not in its origin but in its destination" (Barthes, 1984a, 148). Analogously, we could argue that the complexity of the music finds its destination in the listener.

A question that Barthes' second semiology raises is whether or not he remains confined in the metaphysics of unity and the subject, although here *another* subject is pushed forward. The creative activity of the Romantic genius is transferred by Barthes to the performer and the listener whereby these figures are ascribed all of the characteristics that the genius of an Author first possessed.[28] I shall attempt to clarify this by confronting Barthes' second semiology with Cage's later aleatory compositions.

6.7 CAGE'S TOTAL ALEATORIC

The year 1951 is exceptionally important in recent musical history. Not only did Boulez's *Structures* and Stockhausen's *Kreuzspiel* mark two high points in the development of total serialism, but, in addition, it was the year that Cage broke radically with serialism's ideas of control in his compositions *Music of Changes* and *Imaginary Landscape nr. 4*. Compared with total serialism, these works of Cage may be considered as a possible explication of the second Nietzschean answer to the threatened musical nihilism that consists of a radical affirmation of chance. If we compare the manner of composition that Cage adopted in these works with those of Boulez and Stockhausen, then no greater contrast appears to be possible. While, as we remarked above, in the serial compositions of Boulez and Stockhausen every aspect of the composition is fixed in advance, Cage, in his compositions, significantly turns away from predetermined determinations and gives the preference to chance.[29] In *Music of Changes*, a composition for piano, Cage uses the centuries-old oracle of the *I Ching*, the Chinese Book of Changes. By repeatedly throwing tree coins in the air, the composition was almost totally determined by chance. The operations of chance, namely, determine the ordering of the sixty-four cards upon which the elements of the composition (pitch, duration, consonance, dynamic, etc.) are written.[30]

Music of Changes is a piece that we could already refer to as an aleatory composition. But, although the composition was determined to an important degree by chance, the performer is still expected in the traditional manner to follow the completely written score. In *Imaginary Landscape nr. 4*, also written in 1951, Cage radicalizes the role of chance in the performance by letting the performer, too, apply coincidental operations. Thus, in the performance of *Imaginary Landscape nr. 4*, the fourteen radios that are set by the performer to arbitrary stations determine to an important degree the ultimate "soundscape." The performance of this composition becomes just as much a surprise to the composer as to the performers and the audience. This postserial music of Cage's appears to satisfy the demand of the performer's co-authorship that Barthes formulated in *From Work to Text*.

However, Cage goes a step further. In his most radical aleatory composition, *4'33"*, written for solo piano (but in fact able to be performed with every possible instrument) and first performed in 1952 in Woodstock, there is absolutely no noted sound at all. Thus, maintains Cage, it is a piece which consists of three parts in none of which sound is produced in an intentional manner. The only concrete indication consists of the opening of the keyboard's cover and then, four minutes and thirty-three seconds later, closing it again. The performance consists of all the sounds emanating from the performer, the audience, and the external world during this period.

Despite the radically contrary technique of composition, there is a remarkable agreement between the total serial work of Boulez and Stockhausen and Cage's aleatory compositions.[31] In total serialism, too, despite the total domination of the composer, the end-result practically appears not be perceived in advance (although, theoretically, it is predictable). By cutting out the internal teleology the soundscape is made independent (Mertens, 1980, 129). Boulez had already acknowledged this in 1952 when he defined serialism and aleatoric as *parallel inverts*. In his study of serialism, Sabbe, the Belgian musicologist, remarked about this: "Cage cultivates discontinuity and the subsequent indetermination by under-determination, the serialists do it by over-determination: one by anticipating little, the other by anticipating so much that everything can happen at any moment" (quoted in Mertens, 1980, 131). However, despite this agreement in indetermination of the sound material, there are fundamental differences with respect to the intentions of both parties.[32] Where, in serialism, indetermination appears in opposition to the attempt to make the subjective work-concept safe (that which only works because the composing subject subordinates himself to the autonomy of the composed work), Cage's aleatoric is precisely aimed at undermining that work-concept. Even more radically than Barthes, Cage moves in his aleatory experiments "from work to autonomous (musical) text."

6.8   NIETZSCHE, HEIDEGGER, AND THE WORLD OF CHANCE

When Gerard Broers, in his already cited study concerning Wagner, Schönberg, and Cage, from a Nietzschean perspective concludes that Cage's music is preferable to Schönberg's impressive *oeuvre*, he hastened to add that Cage's work "occasionally cannot be enjoyed unless one has a good book at hand" (Broers, 1982, 34). This comment is not incomprehensible within the experiential horizon that is formed by the tonal tradition and the passive aesthetic pleasure that it answers. The question, however, is whether or not we are being fair to Cage's "work." The aesthetic pleasure that this work elicits is of an essentially different nature than traditional aesthetic pleasure. Just as the music of those repetitive composers discussed in chapter 3, Cage's music demands an essentially other, nonteleological listening attitude. However, the provision of listening pleasure is perhaps not the most important aim of Cage's music: this type of music, even more than repetitive music, encourages reflection. We are dealing here with a type of music that gives food for thought.

Cage himself has regularly attempted to articulate this reflective aspect of his music in readings and articles.[33] He formulates his program as follows: "To liberate sound from psychic intentions. Sound is sound, man is man. Let sound be itself rather than a vehicle for human theories and emotions" (quoted in Mertens, 1980, 132; cf. S, 71). The issue is one of liberating sound from the domination of the human subject. The fragmentation of isolated elements forms a first step for this, something that the aleatoric still shares with serial music. However, where serial music still holds in this respect to an external organization via the composer, at this point the affirmation of chance in Cage's aleatory music implies a radical break with teleology and subjective representation. In answer to the question as to what he is attempting to achieve with writing music, Cage says: "a purposeful purposelessness or a purposeless play" (S, 12). This description makes one think of Derrida's description of deconstruction as a *stratégie sans fin*, a strategy without end/aim.[34] We see here an inversion of the Kantian idea that in art the issue is a "purposiveness without a purpose" (*Zweckmässigkeit ohne Zweck*) (CJ, 65/KU, B31). While, according to Kant, a hidden efficiency of nature appears in the free play of the imagination, Cage's aleatory music evokes precisely the purposelessness of the world. Viewed from a teleological perspective, the result is a destruction of meaning and symbolization, in brief: nonsense. We are concerned here not only with a radical aesthetics of music, but, at the same time, with a no less radical ontology (Griffith, 1981, 38 ff.).

Just as Schopenhauer before him and Reich after him (cf. 3.5), Cage appeals to Eastern ideas in his attempts to explicate this ontology. The lessons of his Zen master, Dr. Suzuki, play an especially important role in his writings and readings. In this context, he also used the philosophy of the Book of Changes, the *I Ching*.[35] Cage also regularly reaches back to Western mystics such as Meister Eckhart in order to clarify his worldview (cf. Griffith, 1981, 21). At the moment, I do not

wish to examine in more depth Cage's self-expressed sources of inspiration, but I will attempt to explicate the philosophy embodied in his music with the help of some comments concerning chance of Nietzsche and Heidegger.

In chapter 1, I remarked that Nietzsche placed the "Innocence of Becoming" in contrast to the rigid columbarium of theoretical knowledge. His thinking was primarily directed at breaking out of the "fossilization" in order that this innocence of Becoming, which had been affected by the metaphysical tradition, might be experienced. According to Nietzsche, it is important in this respect to surpass the goal-rational thinking that is characteristic of modern times (KSA, 10:245). It is in this context that he speaks of chance. In *Thus Spoke Zarathustra* we read: " 'Lord Chance'—he is the world's oldest nobility, which I have given back to all things; I have released them from the servitude under purpose" (Z, 186). While the metaphysical tradition and Christianity hope to discover a purposeful process in the chaotic chance of the world, Nietzsche pleads for an affirmation of chance. Against those who believe in the simultaneous existence of a world of goals and a world of chance, Nietzsche postulates in *Daybreak* that all goals are imaginary: "so there is only one realm, that of chance accidents and stupidity" (D, 81).[36] "A little wisdom is no doubt possible; but I have found this happy certainty in all things: that they prefer—to *dance*" (Z, 186). Affirming the world of Becoming means acknowledging that the world is a dance-floor of divine chance: "O sky above me, you pure, lofty sky! This is now your purity to me, that there is no eternal reason-spider and spider's web in you—that you are to me a dance floor for divine chances, that you are to me a god's table for divine dice and dicers!" (Z, 186).[37]

According to Nietzsche the complete instrumentalist culture can be viewed as a "battle against chance" that is directed at taming and damming chance: "The total history of nature demonstrates a decline of the *fear of chance, of uncertainty, of the unexpected*. Culture, that means learning *to calculate*, learning to think in causal terms, learning to foresee, learning to believe in necessity. . . . Today, man goes to war against this 'evil'—he even abolishes it" (WDB, 3:626). Barthes' structuralist battle against chance appears to me to be a good example of the struggle about which Nietzsche speaks here. The battle against chance has not been without success: "Where everything is made a goal, that is where chance makes way as if it becomes afraid" (WDB, 3:1106). But, in a certain sense, this success is only apparent: the contingency of our existence is not really controllable. Moreover, fending off chance implies the loss of our creativity. Only the one who opens himself to what occurs by chance is able to authentically create.

In the era of calculation, however, man increasingly cuts himself off from chance: "*Men of chance.*—The essential part of every invention is the work of chance, but most men never encounter this chance" (D, 167). Nonetheless, according to Nietzsche, there is a boundary to the calculation of life: "Yes, there is a measure of the feeling of certainty, the possibility of a belief in law and calculation, where it enters consciousness as disgust—where the *passion for chance,* for *uncertainty,* and for the *unexpected* suddenly appears as desirable" (WDB, 3:626).

It is the realization of the contingency of our existence that primarily echoes in the foregoing quotations concerning chance. Nietzsche acknowledges that existence as it is could have been different, and, for this reason, that it is only a possible existence (cf. Vuyk, 1990, 163). Though we sometimes think as calculating people, we never completely control our own existence: it often occurs by chance, as a gift or destiny—and it is characteristic of the ambivalence of our existence that it is not infrequently simultaneously gift *and* destiny. The issue for Nietzsche at this point is that, despite the contingency of our existence, we must accept responsibility for it.

In the early Heidegger we encounter a number of comments concerning chance that betray a relationship with Nietzsche. In *Being and Time* it is made clear that what we ordinarily refer to as chance can only coincide with the openness (*Erschlossenheit*) of There-being. The openness to chance (*Zufall*) brings There-being into the facticity of its existence (BT, 346). Just as Nietzsche, Heidegger relates the openness for chance with a manner of existence that is permeated by a deep realization of the contingency of our existence. To exist means to be thrown into an existence that we have not chosen for ourselves (BT, 174). Like Nietzsche, Heidegger at this point calls for the acceptance of this existence as one's own existence despite the fact that one is not oneself its foundation. Only by 'authentically' existing in this manner can one open oneself to new possibilities, that is, to exist as *project* and thereby become what one is (BT, 185; cf. 4.3). Only in this case do we have a future in an authentic sense (cf. note 17, chapter 3). "Apparently poorer but nonetheless richer in coincidence" (G, 61) applies to those who acknowledge the contingency of existence. The Being of beings can only appear in openness toward what coincidentally occurs.

With the later Heidegger, in contrast to Nietzsche, the acknowledgment of contingency appears to become a certain passivity or even fatalism (cf. 4.9). In his lectures of 1929–30 Heidegger already maintains that the Being of beings can only *occur* to us if we are able to wait resignedly (*Gelassen*) (GM, 510).[38] Heidegger's monolithic critique of mod-

ern technology's *Will to Will,* which is, according to him, the inevitable and most extreme form of Nietzsche's *Will to Power* wherein the subjectivism of the metaphysical tradition finds its completion (N, 1:37–46), only permits as alternative the attitude of *not-willing,* a waiting without any form of expectation (G, 42). From a Nietzschean perspective, one could ask oneself if he does not thereby enter a path that leads inevitably to one or another form of passive nihilism. Even disregarding this, the question is whether or not radical resignation is a possibility for human beings, given that they, as Nietzsche expresses it, would rather have *nothingness* than *not* to Will (GM, 299; cf. note 25, Introduction).

But is there an alternative here? Is there a 'willing' conceivable that does justice to the chance of existence (cf. Vuyk, 1990, 130)? Nietzsche's *Verwindung* of the metaphysical opposition of fatalism and chance could help us find a way. In section 1.9, with reference to Kundera's reflections on Nietzsche's Eternal Recurrence of the Same, I remarked that this doctrine can be understood as an expression of the preparedness to bear the highest possible responsibility, even for what occurs as destiny. In Nietzsche's view an *amor fati* is needed if we are to be able to bear the contingency of our existence. This "passion for destiny" must not be understood as a vulgar fatalism. Accepting the contingency of existence causes fatalism to invert itself and opens a space for creativity and freedom. By not living along the edges of the contingency of our existence, but rather by accepting it, it becomes possible to give form to what happens to us. The *amor fati* leads to a *Verwindung* of the metaphysical contradiction between necessity and chance: "The most extreme fatalism is nonetheless identical with *chance* and that which creates" (KSA, 11:292; cf. Fink, 1960, 89, and note 36, above).

Against the background of this *Verwindung,* it becomes clear that we do not, as Heidegger does, necessarily have to interpret Nietzsche's theory of the Will to Power as the consequence of the modern inclination toward transcendental subjectivity. From the *amor fati* idea we could also present the Will as the expression of the preparedness to accept for ourselves the contingency of existence. In his study concerning the *Homo Volens,* from which I already have quoted several times, Vuyk has interpreted Nietzsche's conception of the Will in the following manner:

> The issue may never be one of removing the essential chance of the powers which direct existence. People are just not able to attribute necessity to these powers. However, what we can do is acknowledge their existence—something which presupposes both sensitive experience and rational investigation—and in that respect to take a position. A position which neither activates nor curbs these powers, but which

does indicate our relationship to them. In the total power-field, we can affirm some and ignore others. In this manner, we give form to the relationships between our Selves and the power-field which motivates us so that these relationships attribute an identity to the Self. This process of *becoming conscious* of what occurs in and around us, and of selection from the totality by means of *affirmation* and *negation*—I would like to propose that, from now on, we refer to this as 'willing'. (Vuyk, 1990, 179)

On the grounds of this interpretation we should not necessarily view the *Great Style* as the expression of the Will to subjugation of everything desired by the human subject—in such a case, total serialism would be the preeminent candidate for the qualification *Great Style*—but rather as the giving form to "the relationships between our Selves and the power-field which motivates us" from the insight into the chance or contingency of our existence. In this case, the predicate Great Style is more accurately applicable to Cage's aleatory experiments than to the works of the total serialists (cf. Broers, 1982, 57).

The experience of Being's coincidentality—which had already led the Greeks to pose the question as to why there was something rather than nothing—is an ambivalent experience: it divides us "between surprise about the beauty of the world and amazement about its diabolical nature" (Oudemans, 1980, 259). In the *aesthetic* experience of chance this surprise and amazement appear to associate in a conflicting harmony (cf. 0.3 above). Such an experience, as it is evoked by Cage's music, for example, could be called sublime because, in Kant's paradoxical formulation, it provides us with a 'negative pleasure' in the chaotic and purposeless character of the world. (CJ, 98 ff./KU B76 ff.; cf. 0.3 above). In the first of his *Duineser Elegien* Rilke (1975, 2–3) formulated this experience as follows:

> For Beauty is nothing but
> the beginning of awesomeness which we can barely endure
> we marvel at it so because it calmly disdains
> to destroy us

> Denn das Schöne is nichts
> als des Schrecklichen Anfang, den wir noch grade ertragen,
> und wir bewundern es so, weil es gelassen verschmäht,
> uns zu zerstören.

The "elevated" character of the sublime work of art resides in the fact that it temporarily reconciles us with the tragic irony of destiny (cf. 1.6).

Where we usually live along the tragedy of our existence because the re-alization of its tragic dimension paralyzes our behavior, the sublime work of art enables us to momentarily stand eye to eye with the insub-stantial nature of our existence without tumbling into lethargy. These sublime experiences are rare, but, just as every momentary experience, they cast their light far beyond themselves.

It appears to me that something that is characteristic of these 'ele-vated' experiences is that they enable us to go beyond ourselves in the direction of the Other. Just as in the moment of love and the altruistic deed, in the sublime aesthetic experience our relation with things, ani-mals, and people is freed from the crushing bonds of purposefulness that they inevitably possess in everyday experience. In the sublime ex-perience, the Other appears to us in its Being-Other (cf. N, 1:107–14). In the foregoing we saw that, in his music, Cage attempts to permit the sound to be itself rather than making it a vehicle of human theory and feeling (cf. S, 71). This formulation of Cage reminds us of the manner in which Heidegger defines the phenomenological attitude in *Being and Time*: "to let that which shows itself be seen from itself in the very way in which it shows itself from itself" (BT, 58). We could interpret both Cage's aleatory music and the later Heidegger's reflection on Being as a radicalization of this phenomenological attitude (cf. Aler, 1970a, 128).[39] Just as is the case with Heidegger's later philosophy, Cage's mu-sic reflects the nonintentionality of the subject whereby the "intention-ality" of Being is enabled to appear (cf. IJsseling, 1964, 39; Griffith, 1981, 31). Here there is no longer any question of a representation of beings, but rather of a pure "coming-to-presence of the Presence." Expressed in Barthes' semiological terminology, we here reach the "zero-grade" of music, the uncoded presence of sounds.[40]

This dimension of the Being of beings cannot be understood as ob-jective reality. Considered from the perspective of objectiveness, Being is a Nothing (cf. 4.5). "Nothingness, as the negative of Being, is the ulti-mate opposite of pure negativity. Nothingness is never nothing and equally it is not something in the sense of an object; it is Being itself, to the truth of which man is exposed when he has overcome himself as subject, that is, when he no longer presents beings as objects" (ZW, 112–3). The Being of the sounds that Cage wants to allow to appear in 'his' compositions (actually we should speak here of "compositions of the world") also really has the character of Nothingness rather than an objective something. Cage announces this dimension with the concept of *silence* (in this regard it is noteworthy that he gave the title *Silence* to one of his collections of essays and readings). Nonetheless, this silence should not, as is the case with Eco, be viewed as the most extreme form of modernist destruction of the past (cf. note 37, chapter 2). What Cage calls silence constitutes the totality of sounds that are not intended by the human subject. Sound is that which "happens *to be* in the environment," maintains Cage, "and it is only called silence because it does not form part of a musical intention" (quoted in Kostelanetz, 1971, 146). What we call "chance" in Cage's music is what escapes the tendency to control and which follows like a shadow the musical practice that is characterized by control.[41]

6.9   THE AEOLIAN HARP

Cage's (implicit) aesthetics has been disputed from various positions and with various degrees of severity. A fellow composer such as Boulez, agreeing with Schönberg's judgment regarding the talents of his student Cage, with respect to composing, chose the *ad hominem* argument and maintained that Cage's "orientally coloured aesthetic" only serves to disguise the fundamental weakness of his composition technique. Boulez, as we mentioned in note 32, above, is prepared to permit chance a role but he is "fundamentally opposed to the dismissal of the composer when he [i.e., Cage—JdM] introduces operations of chance which have every possibility of being uninteresting, which destroy every notion of vocabulary" (Boulez, 1975, 111). With Adorno, this critique achieves a metaphysical charge; he accuses Cage of resignation with respect to contingency; Cage removes the aesthetic subject from the organization of contingency (Adorno, 1979, 329). In the continuation of his earlier quoted critique of the Romantic and dadaist glorification of nature, Adorno accuses Cage of breathing new life into the dangerous myth of a reconciliating nature to which critical subjectivism and historical development is sacrificed (cf. 2.5). Thereby, Cage could open the way to an inhuman musical practice and even, perhaps, an inhuman society. Boulez even goes so far as to suggest that Cage's music frees the way for, and that the music itself is ripe for, a fascist society (see Broers, 1982, 57).

Apart from Cage, Nietzsche, Heidegger, and Barthes have also been accused of announcing an inhumane or even antihumane ideology. In the case of Barthes, his declaration of the Author's death has been a particular bone of contention. In this case, the reproach is certainly not correct. Because Barthes replaces the ideology of the Author with the ideology of the Reader he remains within the domain of a theoretical humanism. He could, not without reason, present himself as the true humanist:

> it is derisory to condemn the new writing in the name of a humanism hypocritically turned champion of the reader's rights. Classical criticism has never paid any attention to the reader; for it, the writer is the only person in literature. We are now beginning to let ourselves be fooled no longer by the arrogant antiphrastical recriminations of good society in favour of the very thing it sets aside, ignores, smothers, or destroys; we know that to give writing its future, it is necessary to overthrow the myth; the birth of the reader must be at the cost of the death of the Author. (Barthes, 1984a, 148)

As became clear in the foregoing, the critique of subject-centrism in Nietzsche, Heidegger, and Cage is more radical than in Barthes. Cage acknowledges this in no uncertain terms: "The *Music of Changes* is more inhuman than human" (S, 36). However, the question remains as to whether this music can also be referred to as *anti*-human. The answer is self-evidently dependent upon what one understands by the term *humanism*. If one thereby means the modern metaphysics of the subject, wherein the totality of reality is reduced to pure objectivity, then it is indeed possible to speak of an antihumanism with respect to Nietzsche, Heidegger, and Cage. However, if we understand the determination of the *being* (*Wesen*) of man under the term *humanism*, then we could equally justifiably refer to it as a humanism "in the extreme sense" (*im äussersten Sinn*) (BW, 222). Given that Ex-istence (*Ek-sistenz*) toward Being is characteristic for the essence of man, this is not, according to Heidegger, exclusively determined from man himself (cf. BPh, 51). Against the traditional definition of man it could be argued that it is precisely the *humanitas* that it fails to accord sufficient value to (BW, 210). Does the dignity of man not reside precisely in the transcendental openness with respect to the Being of beings? Because of the subject-centric connotations of the term *humanism*, it would perhaps be preferable here to speak of a metahumanism, a humanism that points beyond itself to a more all-embracing dimension wherein man is taken up—as a link in the *great chain of Being* (cf. Cousineau, 1972, 51).

It is clear that for Nietzsche, Heidegger, and Cage the issue is not so much one of giving up the notion of subjectivity, but rather, in Heidegger's words, of a new definition of the *Konstellation von Sein und Mensch* (ID, 21). The critique of subjectivism that is found in Nietzsche's doctrine of the Eternal Recurrence of the Same, in Heidegger's thinking of Being, and in Cage's aleatory music should not be understood as a goal in itself, but rather as a deconstruction that makes space available wherein we can experiment with new forms of subjectivity.[42] Such experiments are not without risk. But, once more agreeing with Van Tongeren's argument, our situation is inevitably "critical": life *is* experimentation. Definitive answers are not available to us: "The determination of the essence of man never can be an answer, but is in essence a question" (*Die Bestimmung des Wesen des Menschen ist nie Antwort, sondern wesentlich Frage*) (EM, 107). Whoever misunderstands the risk or does not engage in the experiment alienates himself from his own project (Van Tongeren, 1984, 361; cf. 2.7 above).

Whether such experiments with subjectivity make us susceptible to a fascist society, as Boulez suggests with respect to Cage's aleatory music, is something that I seriously doubt. The fragmentary, ambiguous, deconstructive, and ironic character of Nietzsche's and Cage's work cannot in any way be combined with a totalitarian worldview or politics (cf. Deleuze, 1983, 31). Moreover, they are in no way concerned with a representation of this or that political idea; they present, in a fundamental manner, the issue of a "politics of representation" that forms the basis of modern (whether or not totalitarian) politics (cf. Wallis, 1984, xvi). If one wishes to impose a political label per se on their activities, then it is possible that the term 'anarchism' would come closest to their position. In any event, Cage, in his writings, quite regularly quotes Thoreau's comment that "that government which does not govern, is the best".[43] As I pointed out in section 4.9, I have my own objections with respect to the totalitarian tendency in Heidegger's thinking. However, Heidegger's persistent emphasis on the *questioning* character of philosophy is difficult to reconcile with the totalitarian inclination to definitive answers.

I also cannot unquestioningly agree with Adorno's accusation that Cage and company sacrifice historical development to the myth of a reconciliating nature. When the constant search for the new is understood as historical development, then Cage, Heidegger, and Nietzsche, not without reason, place question marks by this notion, and their work, just as that of Derrida who is allied to them, can be presented as a "strategy of delay" (IJsseling, 1990; cf. 0.5). And, although they certainly do reach back to the Romantic hope for a reconciliation with and through nature, such a reaching back may not be understood as a flight to tradition. "The flight to tradition, a mixture of humility and pretension," maintains Heidegger, "is, when done for itself, not able to achieve anything except the closing of one's eyes and a blinding with respect to the historic *moment*" (ZW, 96). For Cage, Heidegger, and Nietzsche the issue is one of a *Wiederholung* of the Romantic inheritance in the light of man's contemporary situation (cf. note 21, Introduction).

When, in this context, Cage, Nietzsche, and Heidegger reach back to the Romantic concept of nature, then this should not be understood as an 'agrarian reaction' or as a nostalgic desire for the period before modern technology. The issue is one of reflecting upon the meaning of Romantic desire for a reconciliation with nature in the light of modern technology. Cage's experiments with electronic music—his *Imaginary Landscape nr. 1* marks the commencement of this genre—are an indication that a *Wiederholung* of the Romantic question concerning the relation of man and nature (*physis*) does not have to mean a flight into the past, but rather that it has a future. In Cage's "ecological" aesthetics the "photographic negative" (Heidegger) is made audible: an ensemble of man *and* nature.

We find this other dimension of the relationship between nature and technology expressed in the image of the Aeolian harp. The Aeolian harp, which enjoyed tremendous interest in the Romantic period, is an instrument that consists of an open frame over which a number (five to twelve) of catgut strings of various thickness are stretched. The wind is directed through a number of screens so that it plays the strings. The Aeolian harp constitutes the symbol of the desire for a harmony of man and nature. It is an instrument made by man but made to sound by *physis*. It forms an expression of the pantheistic desire that is unique to the Romantic (cf. 0.2 above). In his poem "The Aeolian Harp" Coleridge expressed this questioningly as follows:

> And what if all of animated nature
> Be but organic harps diversely framed,
> That tremble into thought, as o'er them sweeps
> Plastic and vast, one intellectual breeze,
> At once the Soul of each, and God of all?

This image recalls Heraclitus' image of the lyre as the tension-filled unit of opposites (Heraclitus, in Kirk and Raven, 1980, 195 ff.). Whoever hears the disgruntled noises that *animate nature* produces today will have difficulty suppressing his doubts concerning this *one* "intellectual breeze" that directs everything. But, as we have seen, doubt concerning the reality of this unity also belongs, in an even more pronounced manner since Nietzsche's announcement of the "Death of God," to the essence of Romantic desire.

But the unachievable character of the ideal of a tension filled unity does not render impotent its capacity to elevate us beyond ourselves.

Even if this Romantic desire does not change our finite world, in the moment of the desire that world does appear essentially different to us. It remains the same and at the same time becomes completely different. Does not the living paradox of Romantic desire reside in this? In one of his many anecdotes concerning his Zen master, Dr. Suzuki, Cage expresses this as follows: "Before studying Zen, men are men and mountains are mountains. While studying Zen, things become confused. After studying Zen, men are men and mountains are mountains. After telling this, Dr. Suzuki was asked, 'What is the difference between before and after?' He said: "No difference, only the feet are a little bit off the ground' " (S, 88). Nietzsche, too, in my opinion, expresses this in his poem "World Wisdom" (Welt-Klugheit) (GS, 43):

Do not stay in the field!	Bleib nicht auf ebnem Feld!
Nor climb out of sight.	Steig nicht zu hoch hinaus!
The best view of the world	Am schönsten sieht die Welt
Is from a medium height.	Von halber Höhe aus.

To lift us a little bit off the ground in order that we experience the beauty of the world—does not the wonder of Romantic desire reside in this?

Afterword:
Virtual Romantics

Perhaps one of the most paradoxical insights of philosophical hermeneutics is that a distance in time should not be regarded as an obstacle for a fruitful understanding of a text (or a painting, a piece of music, or any other cultural artefact), but quite the contrary as the very condition of its possibility. According to philosophical hermeneutics, understanding cannot and should not aim at an objective reconstruction of the meaning of the interpreted text. Objective interpretation is impossible, because understanding is a dialogical process that is characterized by a fusion of the different horizons of the interpreted text and the interpreter (cf. Gadamer, 1986, 305 ff.). In this dialogical process of understanding new meanings arise that exceed the horizons of both the interpreter and the interpreted text. The greater the distance between these horizons, the more original these meanings may be. This is not the only reason that the impossibility of objective understanding should not distress us. After all, our dialogue with the past is generally not motivated by a sheer antiquarian desire for knowledge, but by a practical interest in finding answers to topical questions. We interpret texts from the past in order to transcend our own finite horizon of understanding and to enhance our orientation in the present world. Obviously, this does not imply a plea for the very opposite of objective understanding: sheer *subjective* arbitrariness, which merely multiplies the prejudices of our horizon of understanding. In order to prevent this, it is important that we always try to remain open to what texts and other cultural artifacts from the past have to say to us. In other words, fruitful interpretations require sensitivity for the otherness and the unfamiliarity of that which is interpreted.

I FROM ROMANTIC TO DIGITAL DESIRE

Fortunately, being sensitive to unfamilarity is not always a difficult task. As I experienced while preparing the English edition of this book, even when an author looks back at his own texts written in a not so distant past, an experience of unfamiliarity may easily occur. My present horizon of experience is not exactly the same as the one I had at the moment of writing these texts. As a result, rereading them revealed new meanings that I did not intend when I wrote the book.

The lectures and articles that constituted the raw material of this book were written between 1983 and 1990. The first Dutch edition of the book appeared in 1990, followed by a second edition in 1991 and a third, revised edition in 1995. If I had to rewrite it completely today, I surely would fit the pieces of the jigsaw puzzle together in different ways and, moreover, I would leave aside some of them and add others. Since the publication of the first edition other subjects have attracted my attention and thinking and writing about them has had implications for my view on Romantic desire.

The research immediately following the writing of *Romantic Desire* was still narrowly connected with the contents of this book. Some of the articles I published consisted of elaborations of themes discussed in *Romantic Desire* (cf. De Mul, 1993a and 1996a). However, the main project in these years consisted of a comprehensive reconstruction of Wilhelm Dilthey's unfinished *Critique of Historical Reason* and an analysis of its effective history in twentieth-century philosophy, especially in the work of Heidegger, Gadamer, and Derrida.[1] The reconstruction—and, inevitably, reinterpretation—of Dilthey's analysis of the 'tragedy of finitude' enabled me to further elucidate the Romantic image of divided man and culture that inspired my wanderings through (post)modern culture in *Romantic Desire*. The study of Dilthey's *Critique of Historical Reason* also helped me to clarify the nature of the development of our horizon of understanding (cf. De Mul 1997d), and it underpinned my conviction that philosophical interpretation of classical texts should ultimately contribute to an *ontology of the present*. As man and world are not stable entities, but characterized by an eternal flux—Dilthey's hermeneutic ontology resembles Nietzsche's "metaphorical ontology" quite closely in this respect—the interpretation of the present is the never-ending task of philosophy.[2] This is especially the case in (post)modern culture, which is characterized by an increasingly quickening change. For that reason it was not that surprising that the study of Dilthey's work lead me to a study of the probably most important event of our time: the *information revolution*.

That information and communication technology (ICT) already is rapidly changing our world and that we are as yet only confronted with the beginning of this revolution is generally recognized by now (De

Mul, 1998). Certainly, not everyone will agree with Alvin Toffler (1980), who regards the information revolution as as fundamental as the Agricultural Revolution in the Neolithic Era and the Industrial Revolution in the nineteenth century, but it is clear that it is not easy to overestimate the far-reaching implications of this revolution. Since the development in 1946 of the ENIAC, the first electronic computer, the computer has started to colonize and transform our society, our culture, and even our bodies and minds. Especially in the last fifteen years, with the massive distribution of the personal computer and the rampant growth of worldwide computer networks more and more aspects of our lives are affected by information technology.

In my philosophical work since 1993 my main concern has been the analysis and interpretation of the conceptual and ontological implications of ICT. Digital technologies not only bring about new social and cultural practices, but they also have fundamental implications concerning our conceptualization of the world and ourselves. ICT, like previous forms of mastering nature, serves to fashion not only objects outside ourselves but human subjects as well (cf. Barglow, 1994, 2).

Rereading *Romantic Desire* from the perspective of the information revolution—a perspective virtually absent in the book—not only threw new light on the contents of this book, but on ICT as well. Of course, this afterword is not the right place to discuss the complex relationship between (post)modernism and ICT at length.[3] Here I will restrict myself to one specific reading of information technology as an embodiment of Romantic desire. In the following sections I will to argue that the Romantic oscillation between enthusiasm and irony, which profoundly characterizes (post)modern culture, also marks the reflections on digital technology, and, moreover, that (the design of) digital technology *itself* is marked by it.

2   (POST)MODERN ROMANTICS

In order to develop my thesis, I first have to return briefly to Schlegel's idea that inspired me in the foregoing explorations in (post)modern culture, and elaborate it on two aspects that remained underdeveloped but that are crucial for a "Romantic interpretation" of ICT: finiteness and ambiguity.

In the introduction of this book, I took Schlegel's definition of Romantic art as an eternal oscillation between enthusiasm and irony as a clue for my interpretation of the Romantic movement as a whole. I have argued that in Romantic art and philosophy enthusiasm for experiencing infinity is accompanied by the consciousness that this is an unachievable ambition. This leads to Romantic irony, which self-critically disturbs the illusion of an actual realization of the desired state of beatitude.

A central motive in this Romantic strategy is the consciousness of the *finiteness* of human experience and human life. Obviously this consciousness did not begin with Romanticism. The idea that we, as human individuals, only occupy a very small part of the world space and the realization that our lives take place between a definite beginning and ending is perhaps as old as humanity itself. After all, it is the price Homo sapiens pays for being reflexive. This consciousness is very difficult to bear. Being finite not only means that we have to face our mortality, but also that there is always a spatial and temporal distance between us and our world, our fellow men and even ourselves (cf. the remarks on human eccentricity in 4.3).

Human culture has always had as one of its main aims the overcoming of human finiteness. For many centuries religion has been a successful strategy. In Western culture Christianity for many centuries offered the comfort that our finiteness is only temporal, and will be overcome completely in an eternal afterlife. However, since the beginning of modern culture, for many people this strategy has lost its credibility. The development of the scientific worldview and the growth of the historical consciousness, together with the secularization of society and the disenchantment of the world, inevitably has lead to the "death of God" (cf. 1.7). This process resulted in a radicalization of the consciousness of finiteness.

The alternative that has been developed in modern culture has been the overcoming of our finiteness in space and time with the help of science and technology. This strategy was not completely new. From the dawn of human culture, technology, no less than religion, aimed to bridge temporal and spatial distances. An alpha-technology such as writing, for example, is not only a means of communication with our contemporaries, but also a technology that helps us to bridge the distance in time that exists between us on the one hand and our ancestors and descendants on the other. Likewise, beta-technologies like the telescope and the car can be conceived of as attempts to bridge spatial distance. As Peter Weibel, reflecting on the psychological impact of modern media, remarks: "Technology helps to fill, to bridge, to overcome the insufficiency emerging from absence. Every form of technology is teletechnology and serves to overcome spatial and temporal distance. However, this victory over distance and time is only a phenomenological aspect of the (tele)media. The real effect of the media lies in over-coming the mental disturbances (fears, control mechanisms, castration complexes, etc.), caused by distance and time, by all forms of absence, leave, separation, disappearance, interruption, withdrawal or loss" (Weibel, 1992, 73–74).

The achievements of the scientific and technological revolution have been very impressive. However, from the very beginning there have been doubts about this modern strategy to overcome our finite-ness. Not only did the disadvantages of technological rationality soon come to the fore, which emphasized the limits of human control over na-ture, but also the final beatitude promised by science and technology of-ten happen to be projected into an ever-receding future (cf. 0.6 and 2.5). In this sense, as already Nietzsche sharply has argued, the modern strat-egy turned out to be a secularized version of Christian teleology.

In the case of the Romanticists the clear consciousness of human finiteness did prevent them from falling into a naive belief in the possi-bility of realizing final beatitude. As I have argued, Romantic irony em-bodies a fundamental openness toward infinity and it does not so much destroy the desire for eternity and an enthusiasm for beatitude, as keep it alive and thus prevent us from falling into despair.

In the foregoing chapters I have tried to show that Schlegel's def-inition of Romantic art as an eternal oscillation between enthusiasm and irony offers us an elucidating view on the fundamental *ambiguity* of (post)modern culture. However, this does not imply a simple equa-tion of modernism and enthusiasm on the one hand, and postmod-ernism and irony on the other. The relationship between the two turned out to be more complex. In the first place we noticed that mod-ernism, although driven by enthusiasm, is itself characterized by a process of differentiation that functions as a source for postmodern doubt concerning modernistic pretensions to totality and unity. Sec-ondly, postmodern irony—like Romantic irony—presupposes mod-ernistic enthusiasm not only as its counterpoint, but also as its starting point of inspiration. This is so even when, as in the case of deconstruc-tivism, the real—perhaps for human beings too real—possibility of in-comprehension is emphasized. After all, deconstructive interpreta-tions, as we find them in the work of Derrida, still aim at an openness to the otherness of what is suppressed in the metaphysical striving for all-embracing truth.

For this reason I have preferred in the book to use the term *(post)modern* instead of speaking of modern and postmodern culture as different and separated entities. And it was also for the same reason that—using a phrase of Heidegger—I described postmodern criticism of modernism as a *Verwindung* of modernism, a radicalization of the inherent disintegrating tendencies of modern metaphysics, a contortion that, although it occurs in modern thinking is nonetheless aimed at recovering from modern thinking's limitations (cf. 0.6). A similar idea lies behind Lyotard's conception of postmodernism as a therapeutic rewriting of modernism, in which concealed possibilities of this tradition come to the fore (Lyotard, 1991). Lyotard compares such a rewriting with the way a psychoanalyst listens to the story of the analysand (cf. 4.1). Also in this case, an openness to what is suppressed is aimed at.

This being said, it is clear that, living in a (post)modern culture, we are not facing a simple choice between a modern and a postmodern point of view. Our task is rather to find ways to cope with the ambiguity that characterizes almost every single aspect of our (post)modern culture and life. In the introduction I quoted Eco, who remarks that with the modern, anyone who does not understand the game can only reject it, but with the postmodern, it is possible not to understand the game and yet take it seriously (see 0.8). Because of the fundamental ambiguity of (post)modern culture we might add that in our present culture it is possible that we *do* understand the game and take it seriously nevertheless![4] Being ambiguous, it can be playfully and seriously at the same time. Which is—we might vary Eco's words—the very quality (the risk) of ambiguity.

But it is not only our (post)modern culture that is ambiguous. Like beauty, ambiguity is in the eye of the beholder. (Post)modern human beings themselves are characterized by a fundamental ambiguity in their understanding of the world and themselves. What distinguishes human life in (post)modern culture from modern and premodern life is that we have become conscious of the eternal contradiction between human finitude and the desire for eternity, which for many centuries has been concealed by a metaphysical hope that this desire actually can be satisfied. It is a consciousness that is extremely difficult to bear. Ambiguity can be conceived of as the (post)modern cultural answer to this "unhappy consciousness." Ambiguous cultural and technological artefacts function as a fetish as described by Freud (cf. 5.2). They enable the mutual existence of two mutually exclusive attitudes ('splitting of the Ego') so that, as a consequence, the desire for eternity is "maintained, but also given up" (SE, 21:154).

This fundamental ambiguity of (post)modern culture and technology can be found in a very intensified form in the domain of information technology.

3 THE (POST)MODERN COMPUTER

When we study the cultural reflections on ICT, two ambiguities soon come to light. In the first place we notice two mutually exclusive types of interpretations of the nature of the computer. In the first, ICT is regarded as a part of, even as the completion of, the process of modernity, whereas in the second, ICT is interpreted as the embodiment of post-modernity. According to Sherry Turkle these different conceptions of ICT were brought about by the remarkable changes the computer itself has gone through in the past decades (Turkle, 1995, 29–49). On its introduction in the forties, the computer seemed the perfect embodiment of the modern worldview. The computer was seen as a transparent technology that enables us to reduce complex phenomena to a conveniently arranged and controllable whole of mathematical algorithms. In this sense it is clearly the outcome of the modernist dream of a *mathesis universalis* (cf. 0.5). The digital code of the computer realizes Leibniz' intention to create a universal language that is able to absorb every significant statement or piece of reasoning in a logical calculus (cf. Heim, 1993, 37). Moreover, the digital code reduces words, images, and music to a universal series of ones and zeros (cf. Lanham, 1993). This "informatization of the worldview" can be conceived of as a transformation of the mechanization of the world picture, which reached its peak in modernity (cf. Dijksterhuis, 1964; De Mul, 1999).

This modernist conception of the computer can still be found in the MS-DOS operating system that dominated the first generation of personal computers in the eighties. It enables the skilled user to master the computer at an elementary level down to the last detail. The relationship of the user with his computer is abstract here, formal and monological. The user instructs his computer by keying in commands that are characterized by a strict syntax and a wealth of exact parameters. The Macintosh computer by Apple, which was introduced in 1984, radically abandoned the modernist aesthetics of the MS-DOS computer. With the Macintosh, the user is separated from the operating system by a graphic interface. He is forced to take things "at interface value" (Turkle, 1995, 23). By using his mouse, the user double-clicks on icons in order to activate facilities. Here, the contact is concrete, concerning content and dialogue-like. The user simply deletes a file by 'dragging' it to an illustration of a wastepaper basket and enters into a dialogue with the computer by selecting the possibilities relevant to the context, which the computer shows him. The MS-DOS computer permits to use only one application at a time, but the Macintosh user can 'zap' to and

fro between the different windows that all give access to a specific application. In this respect the Macintosh resembles the pluralism of postmodern society and transforms his user to a *Homo zappens*. Many of the
more or less elitist postmodern theories and practices concerning the
decentering of subject and text, the deconstruction of linearity and
the dissemination and multiplication of meaning, seem to find their
massive realization in the digital domain.

Turkle interprets the transition from the modern to the postmodern approach of the computer as that from *calculation* to *simulation*. In
her view, there is much more at stake here than the development of a
new kind of *interface:* the change is symptomatic of a broad cultural
change happening at the moment. Though I agree with Turkle's char-
acterization of the two different approaches, I do not think that what we
are facing is a simple transition. In the postmodern computer, behind
the postmodern screen we have to take at interface value that there is
still the modernist calculation going on. The different approaches to ICT
are anchored in the ambiguous (post)modern nature of the computer itself. Already in the famous Turing Test—a game in which a person has
to find out with the help of a series of questions whether the answers
given to these questions are formulated by another human or by a
computer—the idea of the computer expressed a fascinating amalgam
of *calculation* and *simulation*.

The hybrid operating system of Microsoft, MS-Windows, perfectly
embodies this ambiguous nature of the computer. On the surface it is a
(more or less aggressive) imitation of the graphic interface of Macintosh,
with the distinction that it still gives access to the underlying MS-DOS
operating system. In fact, Microsoft Windows is a perfect metaphor for
our present (post)modern culture as a whole, which shows the same
ambiguous mixture of modern and postmodern layers. Already the
windows metaphor itself is hybrid. On the one hand it reminds us of the
modern metaphor of knowledge as a transparent window, suppressing
the sensual nature of every medium of knowledge, language included
(cf. Jay, 1994, 503). On the other hand, because of its scaling powers the
graphical interface directs our attention toward the very materiality of
the sign and in doing so deconstructs the very transparency of the computer window. As Richard Lanham has argued, this ambiguity leads to
a constant oscillation of looking *through* and looking *at* on the computer
screen (Lanham 1993, 42–44).

The second ambiguity we are confronted with in the literature on
ICT concerns the evaluation of the merits of the computer. On the one
hand there is a tendency, rooted in the Enlightenment's belief in
progress, to welcome the computer as a "healing magician" that will re-

alize our wildest dreams and desires (cf. Moravec, 1988; Kelly, 1994; Paul and Cox, 1996). On the other hand, demonic experiences with modern technologies have lead to the conception of the computer as the ultimate embodiment of all those forces that are undermining Western culture (cf. 2.5). Though no one denies that multimedia information technologies offer immediate access to a flood of images, texts, and sounds, critics observe that this does not lead to an increase of involvement, but rather to apathy and indifference. According to some of these critics, ICT not only is an assault on human identity and community, because it transforms our world in one huge electronic panopticon, but it will ultimately lead to the replacement of man by computers and might even result in his extinction (cf. Slouka, 1995).

In this (post)modern "dialectic of digital Enlightenment" (cf. 2.5) the two ambiguities mentioned do not necessarily overlap each other exactly. The predominantly positive evaluations of ICT by the representitives of the "Californian ideology" that fill cybermagazines like *Wired* not only show a strange mix of hippie ideals of the sixties and hard-core capitalism (cf. Barbrook and Cameron, 1995), but it is a strange mix of modernist and postmodernist ideas and motives as well. We find modernist beliefs in human autonomy and control almost seamlessly joined with the postmodern insight that digital worlds inevitably run "out of control" (Kelly, 1994). On the other side of the spectrum we find negative evaluations of the postmodern "aesthetics of simulation" consisting of the same strange mix of modernist and postmodernist ideas. This confirms the ambiguous status of ICT. Both interpretations have their own value. In (post)modern culture the computer is the main medium in which we project our ontotheological dreams for infinity (cf. 4.5), and at the same time it embodies our ironical doubts about these utopian dreams.

4   DIGITAL DREAMS

I will try to elucidate my romantic interpretation of the ambiguity of information technology by focusing on the way it expresses itself in three prominent digital technologies: hypertext, virtual reality, and artifical intelligence.

Seen from a sheer technical point of view *hypertext* is nothing more than a database of texts (and in the case of hypermedia also of images and sounds), that enable a nonsequential reading and writing. An early example of this technology is Ted Nelson's Xanadu, which, in conceptual form, was already introduced in the early sixties.[5] Xanadu as envisioned by Nelson not only consists of a worldwide database of information comprising video, music, and voice as well as texts, it also comprised a royalty payment system and an organization along the lines of the franchising network of McDonalds. Nelson's hypertextual dream clearly reflects the modern desire for total accessibility: "At your screen of tommorow you will have access to all the world's published work: all the books, all the magazines, all the photographs, the recordings, the movies" (Nelson, 1993, preface). Hypertext, as Michael Heim comments on Nelson's prophesy, emulates a divine access to things. It promises to provide the human subject with an *omniscience* that once was attributed to God.

However, the fact that the name of Nelson's project was inspired by a poem of the Romantic poet Coleridge has been an omen. Time and again Nelson promised that Xanadu was about to be completed, but the project is still underway. As Benjamin Woolley remarked, "Like a preacher impatiently awaiting the arrival of Judgment Day, he was still predicting that Xanadu, or at least the software needed to build it, was just six months away in 1990. Six months after he said it (I was there; I heard him), it still was not, but by that time most who had heard about it hardly cared: it was the concept that mattered, not its realization" (Woolley, 1992, 158).

By now Nelson's Xanadu seems to be fully outclassed by the World Wide Web, which embodies much of Nelson's dream. The question remains whether hypertext really fulfills the almost religious dream of omniscience. One cannot deny that the amount of information available on the web already is overwhelming. But for finite beings as we are the result is rather information overload than omniscience. Because of the hypertextual structure of the information, we sense a totality and a closure that always remains outside our reach. In this sense the pathological connotation of the term *hyper* in hypertext is not without reason. " 'The hypertext reader,' Terence Harpold remarks, "*reads the text as would an obsessional, insofar as he believes in the link,* in its promise of a relation between lexias, and, ultimately, in the closure, saturation or saturability that founds the link as a navigational tool" (Harpold, 1994, 209). Instead of fulfilling the desire for closure, hypertext turns out to be a never ending detour.

Here we notice a remarkable convergence between hypertext and deconstructivistic notions of intertextuality.[6] Hypertext turns out to be a materialization of Barthes notion of the text:

> The text practices the infinite deferment of the signified, is dilatory; its field is that of the signifier and the signifier must not be conceived of as the "first stage of meaning," its material vestibule, but, in complete

> opposition to this, as its *deferred action*. Similarly, the *infinity* of the sig-
> nifier refers not to some idea of the ineffable (the unnameable signi-
> fied) but to that of a *playing;* the generation of the perpetual signifier
> (after the fashion of a perpetual calender) in the field of the text (bet-
> ter, of which the text is the field), is realized not according to an organic
> process of maturation or a hermeneutic course of deepening investi-
> gation, but rather according to a serial movement of disconnections,
> overlappings, variations. (Barthes, 1984a, 158)

In this sense hypertext is the very opposite of a divine access to things.
It consists of an "anti-theological activity, an activity that is really revolutionary since to refuse to fix meaning is, in the end, to refuse God
and his hypostases—reason, science, law" (Barthes, 1984a, 147; cf. 6.6
above). Whereas in the case of Barthes intertextuality is revolutionary
in the sense that it opposes the dominion of the classical, linear, and teleological text and its claim to a final, all-embracing meaning, under the
absolute rule of hypertext the deferment of meaning would result in a
restless indifference.

Similar ambiguities we find in the related techniques of *telepresence* and *virtual reality*. Here again we encounter the (post)modern ambiguity of information technology. On the one hand, virtual reality is the
outcome of the realist tradition of pictorial representation that started
with the central perspective in the Renaissance (Penny, 1994; cf. 2.2). The
invention of photography in the nineteenth century added photoreal-
ism to the representation, and film motion. Virtual reality in turn adds
navigation, immersion, and interaction to the cinematic representation.
On the other hand, in virtual reality the postmodern simulation
reaches—for the time being—its peak as well. With Baudrillard we
could argue that virtual reality is no longer a mode of representation,
but rather a form of disappearance of reality (cf. note 19, Introduction).
However, as the oxymoron "virtual reality" already suggests, within the
ambiguous realm of this technology the metaphysical opposition between reality and illusion loses much of its traditional meaning (see 3.8
above; cf. De Mul, 1997a). If virtual reality is "an event or entity that is
real in effect but not in fact" (Heim, 1993, 109) the question arises to
what extent "factual reality" still can be distinguished from "effective
reality." At least the very notion of reality should be reconsidered.

Another ambiguity in telepresence and virtual reality brings us
back to the theme of finiteness. These technologies are perfect examples
of the human desire to overcome spatial and temporal finiteness, as well
of the unachievability of this desire. With the help of a datahelmet and
datagloves the user can be virtually present at another place on earth (or

outer space) or in a fully computer-generated cyberworld, for example in a virtual (re)construction of the past.[7] In the first case the user is represented by a telerobot, equipped with artificial senses and limbs, that enable him not only to immerse himself in the distant environment, but also to navigate through it and interact with it. In the second case the immersion, navigation, and interaction take place in a computer-generated world. Apart from the practical uses of these technologies—imagine a fireman rescuing victims in a burning house with the help of a telerobot, or a surgeon practicing a difficult operation on a simulated patient—they are expressions as well of the human desire to obtain two other divine qualities as well: *omnipresence* and *omnipotence.*

But also in this case the ontotheological desire cannot be realized through the medium. Although the virtual world we design seems to realize our dream of omnipotence, we start to realize that because of the complexity of the digital domain (which causes unintended interferences of programs), the impact of chance (e.g., spontaneous mutations of programs, due to errors in copying files) and deliberate opposition of other users (the rapidly growing field of cybercrimes), this domain finally turns out to be as uncontrollable as our ordinary world. Moreover, though the telepresent subject in principle might travel virtually to all thinkable places in the universe in an instant, this still is far removed from omnipresence.

Cybereuphoria has an answer to this objection as well. We can find it in the domains of *artificial intelligence* and *robotics* and it is called: downloading the human mind into the computer. Along this line Hans Moravec develops some amazing ideas about the overcoming of human finiteness in his fascinating book *Mind Children: The Future of Robot and Human Intelligence.*

He imagines a robot brain surgeon equipped with billions of microscopic small electric and chemical sensors and a supercomputer. This machine proceeds as follows. After opening the brain case the robot starts scanning the first few millimeters of brain surface and with the help of high-resolution magnetic resonance measurements it builds a three-dimensional chemical map, while arrays of magnetic and electric antennas collect signals that are rapidly unraveled to reveal, moment to moment, the pulses flashing among the neurons. Next, the computer makes a simulation of this portion of the brain and tests its accuracy by comparing the signals in the simulation with the original ones. Because the patient is conscious, in a "test drive" the simulation is connected to the actual brain and is fine-tuned. When the simulation has reached a state of sufficient perfection, the simulation is established permanently and the cells in the superfluous tissue are excised.

Layer after layer the brain is simulated, then excavated. Eventually your skull is empty, and the surgeon's hand rests deep in your brainstem. Though you have not lost consciousness, or even your train of thought, your mind has been removed from the brain and transferred to the machine. In a final, disorienting step the surgeon lifts out his hand. Your suddenly abandoned body goes into spasms and dies. For a moment you experience only quiet and dark. Then, once again, you can open your eyes. Your perspective has shifted. The computer simulation has been disconnected from the cable leading to the surgeon's hand and reconnected to a shiny new body of the style, color and material of your choice. Your metamorphosis is complete. (Moravec, 1988, 110)

In Moravec's view with the help of this technique our desire for eternity will be a big step nearer to its realization. Not only will we become immortal—we can make backups of our mind and transfer them to a new cyborg body as soon the old one is worn out or damaged, but we will also be able to merge our brains with other ones or make more copies of ourselves (the digital version of the splitting of the Ego). Omniscience and omnipresence seem to come within the reach of finite man. But the decisive step yet has to come. In a world populated by artificial intelligences that zip about, a human mind would lumber about in a massively inappropriate body simulation. "We might then be tempted to replace some of our innermost mental processes with more cyberspace-appropriate programs purchased from the AIs, and so, bit by bit, transform ourselves into something much like them. Ultimately our thinking procedures could be totally liberated from any traces of our original body, indeed of any body. But the bodiless mind that results, wonderful though it may be in its clarity of thought and breath of understanding, could in no sense be considered any longer human" (Moravec, 1992). This is not yet the endpoint of Moravec's vision. He expects that not only will human minds merge, but those of other species as well. In this way our future will be able to benefit from and build on what the earth's biosphere has learned through its multibillion-year history: "Our speculations ends in a supercivilization, the synthesis of all solar-system life, constantly improving and extending itself, spreading outward from the sun, converting nonlife in mind. Just possibly there are other such bubbles expanding from elsewhere. What happens if we meet one? This process, possibly occurring now elsewhere, might convert the entire universe into an extended thinking entity, a prelude to even greater things" (Moravec, 1988,116).

Here I will not discuss the question whether Moravec's ideas about the downloading of minds are practicable or will (for the greater part) remain science *fiction* (see for an overview of the philosophical and scientific arguments pro and con, Paul and Cox, 1996, 172–92). Nor will I discuss the moral merits of Moravec's book.[8] In the context of my discussion of the Romantic dimension of the digital revolution, I just want to point to the peculiar oscillation between enthusiasm and irony in Moravec's project.

In the foregoing chapters we have noticed that the ideal of "overcoming man" plays a persistent role in the Romantic tradition. However, even in Nietzsche's radical prophesy of the *Übermensch* the "overcoming" aims at another type of *man* and not so much at his extinction. Similarly, in the postmodern prophesy of the "death of man" (cf. Foucault, 1974) this death does not concern man as a species, but a specific metaphysical conception of man.[9] Moravec's vision can be conceived of as a fundamental radicalization of the Romantic prophesy insofar he predicts a real end of the life of the species Homo sapiens. It radicalizes Nietzsche's idea that man only is a rope, stretched between ape and *Übermensch*. In Moravec's vision this *Übermensch* will be build not out of carbon, but out of silicon instead.

Though at first sight it might seem that Moravec's prophesy overcomes the Romantic oscillation between enthusiasm and irony in favor of the former, it finally confirms the fundamental unachievability of the human desire for eternity. After all, the "overcoming" of man as envisioned by Moravec would—ironically—result in the total dissolution of the *subject* of desire. This should not surprise, as finite man is characterized by an "eternal lack" (cf. 4.6). We cannot abolish this lack without abolishing men themselves.

Obviously, the result of such an extinction could be new subjects of desire, having new objects of desire as well. Perhaps they will desire to be finite, as once the gods of the Olympus did when they observed man. Simulating the past history of finite man (and all the possibilities that have not been realized) the infinite cyberbeing might come to the insight that the "eternal lack" of this peculiar species, and the very finiteness and fragility of its beatitude, in the end has been its greatest blessing.

Virtually speaking, of course.

Notes

INTRODUCTION

1. Perhaps the argument presented in this book could be better expressed in a hypertext form (see Kolb, 1994). However, most chapters were published earlier as separate readings or articles in a traditional, linear form: see the Acknowledgments. The texts of these prior publications have been reworked and, in most cases, drastically altered. Should the reader choose an idiosyncratic trajectory to follow in this present text, he can orient himself by referring to the various interconnected references in the different chapters.

2. The term *aesthetics* was introduced around the middle of the eighteenth century by Alexander Baumgarten in his two-volume (1750 and 1758) publication *Ästhetica*. The term, for Baumgarten, referred to both the science of sensory knowledge, in accordance with the etymology of the Greek concept *aisthēsis,* and the science of fine art. Although Baumgarten, whose philosophy of art was completely dependent upon the antique tradition, contributed little to the development of modern aesthetics, subsequent to his publications, as we shall see further in this current volume, the connection between art and sensory knowledge became something of a constant. In the *Critique of Pure Reason* (1781) Kant's use of the term *aesthetics* still has the sense of (transcendental) research into the contribution of sensibility toward scientific knowledge. At the time of his first critique, Kant still considered a study of (aesthetic) taste based upon *a priori* grounds to be impossible. Only in 1787, in a letter to his publisher, did Kant make reference to a third *a priori* principle, i.e., the feeling of pleasure and displeasure, alongside the capacity for knowledge and will (see Kulenkampff, 1974, 113). Kant elaborated, in the *Critique of Judgment* (1790), the transcendental analysis of this third *a priori* in the form of an analysis of the aesthetic judgment of taste. It can be stated without exaggeration that this transcendental analysis marks the commencement of modern aesthetics.

3. The fact that Kant, in his *Logic* (A25) and in a letter to Carl Friedrich Stäudlin, his publisher, remarked that the third question has a central place in *Religion within the Borders of Pure Reason* appears to contradict what has just been asserted. However, he wandered two different pathways in answering the third question. In the text concerning religion, answering the question concerning a possible reconciliation between nature and freedom, he made a traditionally Christian appeal to an almighty being (*allvermögendes Wesen*) that had established "an ultimate goal for all things" (*Endzweck aller Dinge*) (*Religion*, BA vii).

We could call the other answer to the third question, as it is formulated in the *Critique of Judgment*—whereby art is accorded the capacity to effect the reconciliation between nature and freedom—the secular or anthropocentric answer, and this is more in agreement with the Copernican switch to human subjectivity that is developed in Kant's transcendental philosophy.

4. Besides the *aesthetic* revolt against the primacy of theoretical reason—which is central to this book—in post-Kantian philosophy there is also a broad resistance to the primacy of theoretical reason on the basis of a *practical* (i.e., moral-political) conception of philosophy. In the nineteenth century, this resistance took a characteristic form in the work of Fichte and Marx, while in the twentieth century the works of the American pragmatists, the early Heidegger, the later Wittgenstein, Gadamer, Habermas, and Rorty are examples of a similar practical philosophy (cf. Bernstein, 1983). This tradition reaches back to, among others, Aristotles' defense of practical philosophy against Plato. Much post-Kantian philosophical discussions and polemics appears to be a consequence of the fact that primacy was accorded to different experiential domains. Depending upon whether theoretical, practical, or aesthetic reason is postulated as the basic model of experience, essentially different *worldviews* can be distinguished (Dilthey, 1914–1996, vol. 8; cf. De Mul, 2000).

5. Although the following characteristics are derived from the writings of German representatives of the Romantic movement, which flowered in England, France, and Germany in the period 1790 to 1850, my concern here is not so much with a description of a particular historical period, but rather with the stipulation of a specific worldview that is not restricted to the Romantic but that, as I will subsequently argue in this current work, is, in certain ways, *still* constitutive for our present experience.

6. With respect to Kant one can also speak at a theoretical level of a bankruptcy of moral-political reasoning: "The so-called 'formalism' [of the Kantian ethic—JdM] is an expression of the impotence of moral reason. And moral reason is impotent because it considers the concept of a goal without controlling the resources necessary to realize it and, in a decisive manner, even abandons the problem of such realization" (Marquard, 1962, 365–66). According to Marquard, the Kantian switch to aesthetics should primarily be understood as a reaction to this impotence of moral reason (*ibid.*, 367). For this reason, the project toward an aestheticization of the worldview is, from its inception, connected to the realization of a cultural crisis. In sect. 0.3 of this Introduction I shall more closely examine this fundamental characteristic of the Romantic project.

7. In this connection, Schelling's philosophy of nature has been of decisive importance for the Romantic movement (Knittermeyer, 1929, 101). Spinoza's pantheistically interpreted concept of nature, too, has made its mark on the concept of nature found among the Romantics. This concept forms a clear schism between the otherwise closely connected German Romantic and Idealist movements. In contrast to Schelling, Hegel, and more especially Fichte, spoke out forcibly against the sanctification of nature.

8. In the *Allgemeine Übersicht der neuesten Philosophischen Literatur* (1797; a revisited version was published in 1809 under the title *Abhandlungen zur Erläuterung des Idealismus der Wissenschaftslehre*), Schelling had already expressed

this insight, postulating that spirit is only spirit "if it *makes itself an object*, that is, if it becomes *finite*. Therefore, it cannot be infinite without becoming finite, nor can it (for itself) become finite without being infinite. It is therefore neither the one nor the other alone, neither finite nor infinite, but rather within it is the original *union of the infinite and the finite*" (W, 1:367).

9. The desire for the absolute is expressed in the Romantic tendency to abolish the boundaries between art, religion, and philosophy (see Novalis, 1989), and, in addition, to make the boundaries permeable between the different genres within art. Schelling expresses the expectation that "philosophy, in the same manner as, in the youth of science, it was born and nurtured from within poetry, just as all other sciences which eventually freed themselves from it, will return with all the other streams, after its completion, to the general sea of poetry from whence it sprang" (W, 3:629). Because Schelling understands that such a transformation of philosophy and science into poetry is not immediately realizable, he maintains that an intermediate form is necessary. Accordingly, he finds that, just as, in the pre-Socratic experience, philosophy and poetry were one and the same mythology, the future transition of philosophy into poetry will take the form of a new mythology that will not be the work of one singular poet, but, rather, of a whole generation of poets (W, 3:629). In chapter 1 we will see that Nietzsche similarly speaks of the necessity of a new mythology.

10. Furst understands traditional irony, in the first place as the so-called Socratic irony, which, at least according to its place in the Platonic dialogues, is borne by the belief in the possibility of perceiving absolute truths. Socrates, presenting himself, in an ironic manner, as a fool, shows the ignorance of his conversational partners. For him, irony is primarily a didactic *method* that leads those partners to the truth. For the Romantic, irony is much more than a method: "In short, far from *using* irony, as the traditional ironist does, the romantic ironist *is* ironic. His irony is the instrument for registering the obdurate paradoxicality of a universe in eternal flux" (Furst, 1984, 229).

11. While it is true that Schelling, following Winckelmann, postulates that the expression of the work of art is one of "nobel simplicity and silent greatness," he immediately adds that this also applies "where the greatest tension and grief or joy is expressed" (W, 3:620). It is probable that no single Romantic artist has more effectively succeeded in representing this contradictory harmony of the beautiful and the sublime than the painter Casper David Friedrich.

12. In the *Critique of Pure Reason* Kant had already pointed out that transcendental imagination "is a blind but indispensable function of the soul, without which we should have no knowledge whatever, but of which we are scarcely ever conscious" (CR, 112/KrV, A78). Kant posited this transcendental imagination as the original root of sensibility and understanding (CR, 61, 92/KrV, A15, A50). His reflections concerning the imaginative power of the artistic genius in the *Critique of Judgment* appear to be a result of this notion of transcendental imaginative power. In connection with the fundamental place of transcendental imagination and its relation to artistic imagination in Kant's work, see Heidegger, KM, especially 130–63, and Mörchen's dissertation, under Heidegger's supervision entitled *Die Einbildungskraft bei Kant* (Mörchen, 1928).

13. In "The Meaning of the Theory of the Unconscious for a Theory of the No-Longer-Fine Arts" Marquard has attempted to interpret these no-longer-fine arts on the basis of Hegel's thesis of the "death of art" (Marquard, 1968). According to Marquard, this thesis does not mean that art, after, according to its own highest determination, being relegated to the past, will cease to exist, but rather that, because of the modern world's characteristic disintegration (*Entzweiung*) of subject and object (which is expressed in the internalization of religion and the demythologizing of the external world) it can no longer be the expression of their identity. However, according to Marquard, this does mean that art also finds new possibilities: art becomes no-longer-fine art and, then, ultimately, no-longer-artistic art. This latter finds its expression in the increasing reflexivity of the modern arts. In the conceptual arts of the 1960s and '70s, for example, it appears that this *sensual* aspect of art has completely disappeared. The positive evaluation that Marquard attaches to the *ironic* character of art after the death of art is difficult to reconcile with the spirit of Hegel's aesthetics. Hegel, after all, emphatically resisted the ironic character of (Romantic) art: "But if irony is the keynote of representation, then the most un-artistic principle is maintained as the true principle of the work of art. For there are partially coarse, partially contentless, and partially styleless persons introduced because the substantial appears to be puny in them, and, finally, the already mentioned passion and unresolved tension of spirit are also involved. Such creations cannot awaken any authentic interest" (Ä,1:104).

14. Pannwitz uses the concept in his book *The Crisis of European Culture* as a synonym for Nietzsche's concept of the *Übermensch*. Nietzsche, who is considered by many to be the "grandfather" of postmodernism, really appears hereby to have stood by the cradle of this concept (cf. Welsch, 1987, 12–13). De Onis, most probably independently of Pannwitz, introduced the concept in his book *Antologia de la Poesia Espanola e Hispanoamericana (1882–1932)* (De Onis, 1934, xviii). For De Onis this concept refers to the transition phase from early modernism to what he refers to as *ultra-modernism* in Spanish poetry. For the further development of the concept, see also Köhler, 1977. For Toynbee, the concept *postmodern* appears, in his monumental *A Study of History*, as referring to the period after 1875, wherein politics in terms of national states gives way to global interaction (Toynbee, 1947, 39).

15. This "neuzeitliche" modernism must be distinguished from the modernism in the visual arts that first appeared at the end of the nineteenth century and was primarily expressed in the large number of *-isms*—such as impressionism, cubism, futurism, and expressionism—in modern art. Later in the introduction I will also argue that these two forms of modernism share a certain kinship. In chapter 2 artistic moderns are more closely dealt with.

16. According to Heidegger the term *modern worldview* is, in fact, a pleonasm because the world first became a view in modernism: "There was no medieval worldview which became a modern worldview, but rather the fact that the world *became a view* is a distinguishing characteristic of Modern Time" (ZW, 90; cf. 4.4). In "The Digitalisation of the Worldview" I have analyzed this

characteristic phenomenon of modernism in terms of the paradigmatic example of photography (see De Mul, 1997a).

17. This also applies to Habermas' contemporary modernism. It is perhaps true that the intersubjective tack brought to fruition in Habermas' philosophy meets a number of important objections directed against *traditional* subjectivism, but, nonetheless, it ultimately remains a form of subjectivism that contains the pretension of providing a foundation.

18. In German, *Verwinden* means equally *to recover from*, as with illness, and *to fold/crush together* or *to contort*. In connection with the *Verwindung der Metaphysik*, Heidegger writes: "In the leap-off, the leap does not shove the leaping-off realm away from itself, rather in leaping the leap becomes a recollective appropriation of the *Geschick* [common fortune] of being" (PR, 94). The issue concerns a contortion that, although it occurs in modern thinking, is nonetheless aimed at recovering from modern thinking's limitations. We meet a similar *Verwindung* in Magritte's paintings, which, although they are based on the conventions of representation, simultaneously undermine these representations from within (see 5.1). In order to prevent the loss of the double connotation of the concept of *Verwindung*, I chose to leave it untranslated in the following pages. See 1.9, 3.8, and 4.6.

19. This aspect is probably most pregnantly underlined by Baudrillard. In an interview concerning the development of the mass media he summarized it as follows: "The last phase, and this is what most interests me, is the phase wherein one can no longer speak of reproduction—after all, reproduction still contains a message—but rather of a phase wherein every reference to reality disappears. In such a case, the media is no longer a method of reproducing reality but becomes *a form of disappearance* of reality" (Lutz, 1983/84).

20. For this reason, the postmodern positive reevaluation of the past is not, in my opinion, in tension with the thesis—which is also frequently connected with postmodernism—of the end of history. When the past is conceived of as a grab bag from which, according to desire, one may pick, or even *must* pick because otherwise the silence falls, then one parts from the modernist metanarratives wherein it is assumed that particular ends (the absolute, emancipation, reintegration) can be realized (cf. 6.9).

21. When I speak of the topicality of the Romantic project, it must not be understood as a nostalgic appeal to return to the nineteenth-century Romantic worldview. I am concerned with what Heidegger presented as a "coming back understandingly to one's ownmost 'been' " (BT, 373), that is, an interpretative retrieval (*Wiederholung*) of the Romantic past from the position of our contemporary (post)modern experiential horizon. The Romantic past is not conceived, therefore, as a pure past (*Vergangenheit*), that is, as something that was but is no longer (BT, 444), but rather as something that continues in our present experience. By interpreting the Romantic past from the position of our contemporary experiential horizon, I hope to increase understanding of our current experiences (see 3.8). One could, following Gadamer, compare such "a fusion of horizons" with the fusion of different metals, whereby the new metal possesses

characteristics that the separate metals did not possess (Gadamer 1986, 305 ff.). In contrast to what Gadamer is occasionally, under the influence of Hegel, tempted to do (see Gadamer, 1975, 272; 1986, 419), I do not believe that this process of interpretation leads to an increasingly more encompassing conceptualization. Our radical finiteness ensures that it is inevitable that much remains unthought. See 4.5 and De Mul, 1991 and 2000.

22. In chapter 5, with a discussion of Freud's theory of the splitting of the Ego (*Ich-Spaltung*), I shall more extensively address the question as to how it is possible that two mutually exclusive starting points can appear in a single experience.

23. As Vuyk, in an interesting essay concerning the aestheticization of the worldview, correctly remarks, this (by the Romantics cultivated) interest for the aesthetic is not otherwise restricted to the postmodern: "Most of the great philosophers of the 20th century have made aesthetic subjects a theme in their thinking: Heidegger, Sartre, Adorno, Marcuse, Gadamer, Foucault, Derrida—to mention only a few. Today, it has become almost a criterion of greatness in a thinker that he (or she) has addressed the terrain of aesthetic appreciation" (Vuyk, 1988, 174).

24. As we shall see in chapter 4, this shifting is clearly seen in the development of Heidegger's thought. Where he still cherished the pretension, in the period of *Being and Time,* to provide a foundation, through a *fundamental ontology,* for all the characteristic phenomena of the human existence (*Dasein*), such as science and art, his later work increasingly took on the form of a *dialogue* with art.

25. "Although Heidegger surmised something of human discord, amongst other reasons because he did not assume that humanity finds itself in a process of progress from finiteness to infinity, we are still of the opinion that he did not comprehend the core of the issue because he conceived the discord of reality and unreality as a given in relation to which man can practice his strength" (Oudemans, 1980, 245; see, in connection with this "released strength," 6.8).

26. In several places Oudemans does appear to acknowledge this longing—where, for example, he states that Gadamer correctly points out that hope is a human manner of experience sui generis that cannot be judged exclusively according to an objectivizing sense of reality. In this connection, he even states that "although it is certain that what will happen to us will destroy our hope, we nonetheless continue to hope for the good life, and that is obvious, because it is literally true that without hope, we cannot live" (Oudemans, 1980, 257). In contrast to Oudemans, I do not wish to put the emphasis on the (self-evidently foredoomed to failure) total realization of hope in the future, but rather on the fact that hope *offers* us a future (see, in this connection, the distinction made between "being oriented toward the future" and "having a future" that is made in 3.8).

I   FROZEN METAPHORS

1. For this reason, Kant, in the *Critique of Pure Reason,* applies the term *transcendental* to all knowledge not so much occupied with the objects-in-itself, as

with our cognition of these objects, to the extent that this mode of cognition is possible *a priori* (CR, 59/KrV, A12). The characteristically modern philosophical shift to transcendental subjectivism, which was, in important respects, already prepared in the (otherwise mundane) philosophy of Descartes, will, in chapter 4, be more extensively examined in the context of Heidegger's analysis of the concept of *subjectivity*.

2. Thus, for Kant, space and time are not objective qualities of objects, but rather *a priori* forms of human reason. Seen from a transcendental perspective, therefore, they are subjective. However, given that beings can only appear to the human subject as phenomena in space and time, these forms possess empirical reality (cf. CR, 72/KrV, A28).

3. *"The Man Who Came from the Cold,"* originally written in Dutch, had not been previously published. At the end of the 1970s, Delpeut published poetry in, among others, Dutch periodicals such as the *Revisor* (vol. 5 [1978], nos. 1 and 5; vol. 6 [1979], no. 1) and *Tirade* (vol. 23 [1979], nos. 245/249). The English translation of the poem has been authorized by the poet.

4. That this tradition should not be considered as monolithic is apparent, for example, in the fact that, in the Middle Ages, rhetoric, as part of the trivium, still belonged to the process of intellectual formation. In the Renaissance, rhetoric even experienced a considerable flowering. However, with Descartes' commencement of modern philosophy rhetoric became increasingly discredited.

5. In the following chapter I shall deal more thoroughly with the background of this characteristic phenomenon of modern, autonomous art.

6. In his annotations in the *Critical Edition* (*Kritische Studienausgabe*) of Nietzsche's works, Giorgio Colli points to the fact that, in many cases, the posthumously available fragments are much less metaphoric than the works published during Nietzsche's life. This indicates that the metaphor has primarily a strategic goal in Nietzsche's published works (cf. KSA, 13:651 ff.).

7. This Romantic theory concerning the metaphorical origin of language had already been expressed in 1772 by Herder in his publication, *On the Origin of Language.*

8. Because the metaphorical illusion precedes every word, it can be postulated: "It is not correct that we can lie because we speak, but rather we can speak and think because we lie" (Noerr, 1985, 170).

9. The dependence of metaphysics upon metaphors has been more recently argued by Derrida. In *White Mythology: Metaphor in the Text of Philosophy,* originally published in 1971, Derrida argued that metaphysics, in its attempt to ban metaphoricism and to realize an 'authentic' speech, continues to pay tribute to at least one metaphorical track that, within metaphysics, must always remain unconsidered (Derrida, 1982a, 219). Unlike what Nietzsche appears to do in the early works that were just discussed, Derrida does not defend a one-sided reduction of the concept in relation to the metaphor or of metaphysics in relation to rhetoric. He conceives of their relation to each other as a mutual embrace that makes it impossible for one of the two opposites to achieve a definitive primacy. The *Verwindung* of the opposition between appearance and truth, which Nietzsche realizes in his later works (and which comes into the discussion in

section 9 of this chapter), brings his views of the relation between metaphor and metaphysics closer to the standpoint adopted by Derrida.

10. Admiration for Heraclitus is a constantly recurring theme in Nietzsche's work. In *Philosophy in the Era of the Greeks* he had already made his admiration clear for "this lightning flash from Efese": "Heraclitus called more loudly than Anaximander that: 'I see nothing other than words. Do not let yourselves be fooled! It lies in your brief gaze, not in the essence of things, if you think that you see certainty in the sea of becoming and decaying. You maintain the names of things as if they are durable, unchangeable: but even the stream in which you step for the second time is not the same as with the first occasion'" (KSA, 1:822–83). In *Ecce Homo,* written shortly before his collapse, Nietzsche maintained that, close to Heraclitus, he feels "warmer and more well than anywhere else." The doctrine of the Eternal Recurrence of the Same, which, as we shall later see, he regarded as the most exalted formulation of Becoming, "could possibly already have been taught by Heraclitus" (EH, 81, 99).

11. I derive this term from Visser (1989, 209). In this connection, Visser quotes a crucial fragment from 1881 which, although written eight years later than "Über Wahrheit und Lüge im aussermoralischen Sinn," closely relates to the implicit ontology of this essay: "we are not subtle enough to perceive the probably *absolute stream of occurring:* the *enduring* exists only thanks to our gross organs, which summarize and originate a plan that, *precisely,* in this fashion, does not exist. The tree is in each moment something *new,* we affirm the *form* because we are not able to perceive the subtlety of an absolute movement" (KSA, 9:554).

12. On the basis of the foregoing it appears to me that Heidegger's thesis—which will shortly enter this discussion—that Nietzsche's doctrine of the *Wille zur Macht* is the completion of transcendental subjectivism (see 4.5) is, to say the least, one-sided because it takes insufficient account of the break with subjectivism that Nietzsche's philosophy established. It is perhaps true that Nietzsche occasionally appears unable to withstand the temptation to substantiate the Will to Power in apodictic terms, thereby making it the authentic *subjectum* ("This world is the Will to Power and nothing beyond this!"—KSA, 11:611), but in other places, where he refers to the Will to power as an interpretation, a human metaphor (BGE, 52–53), he appears to be truer to the "abysmal" (KSA, 5:346) dimension of becoming. In addition, in section 9 of this chapter I shall argue that the doctrine of the Will to Power, which is central to Heidegger's interpretation of Nietzsche, actually plays a subordinate role in comparison to the Doctrine of Eternal Recurrence given that, according to Nietzsche, the affirmation of Becoming finds its purest expression in this latter doctrine.

13. In the Nietzsche literature a number of different work and developmental periods are distinguished. In the most common, which we come across in Nietzsche's work itself, three periods are noted (see Pütz, 1975, 23–24). At the beginning of *Thus Spoke Zarathustra,* Nietzsche states: "I name you three metamorphoses of the spirit: how the spirit shall become a camel, and the camel a lion, and the lion at last a child" (Z, 54). The camel symbolizes the first period

wherein Nietzsche is still weighed down by Schopenhauer's metaphysics and Wagner's music. In the second, "positivistic" period, symbolized by the lion, commencing with *Human, All Too Human* (1876) and continuing to *The Gay Science* (1882), Nietzsche reveals himself to be a radical sceptic who, philosophizing 'with the hammer,' liberates himself from the burden of the metaphysical tradition but is not thereby able to operate creatively. The essay form of the earlier works gives way to a strongly aphoristic style. In the third period, commencing with *Thus Spoke Zarathustra,* the aesthetic ontology and the affirmation of art are once more taken up, but they are now liberated from the metaphysical heritage and nourished by a "higher naivety": "The child is innocence and forgetfulness, a new beginning, a sport, a self-propelling wheel, a first motion, a sacred Yes" (Z, 55). The metaphorical character of Nietzsche's work reaches an "equally poetic as thoughtful" (Heidegger) pinnacle in *Thus Spoke Zarathustra.* In the later works, the essay form returns in some writings. In the *Nachlass* from the 1880s there are a number of designs for a systematic magnum opus (in connection with which, among others, the title *Will to Power* appears). Ultimately, Nietzsche abandoned this plan for a systematization of his philosophy (see, e.g., KSA, 12:8). In my opinion, the reason for this abandonment must be sought in the fact that Nietzsche appreciated that the metaphorical character of reality would not permit itself to be fixed in a system without harming this, its most essential, characteristic.

14. In a supplement—published in 1844—to his magnum opus *The World as Will and Representation,* Schopenhauer expressed this insight into the fundamental futility of existence in a magisterial way:

> In endless space countless luminous spheres, round each of which some dozen smaller illuminated ones revolve, hot at the core the infinity of space there are innumerable light-giving spheres, round each of which about a dozen smaller spheres revolve, hot at the core and covered over with a hard cold crust; on this crust a moldy film has produced living and knowing beings: this is empirical truth, the real, the world. Yet for a being who thinks, it is a precarious position to stand on one of those numberless spheres freely floating in boundless space, without knowing whence or whither, and to be only one of innumerable similar beings that throng, press, and toil, restlessly and rapidly arising and passing away in beginningless and endless time. Here there is nothing permanent but matter alone, and the recurrence of the same varied organic forms by means of certain ways and channels that inevitably exist as they do. (Schopenhauer, 1966, 3)

Nietzsche begins his essay *"Über Wahrheit und Lüge im aussermoralischen Sinne"* with a paraphrase of this text, and continues: "In this way could someone have imaginatively constructed a fable and yet failed to have illustrated it sufficiently, how pitiful, shadowy and fleeting, how aimless and arbitrary human intellect appears within nature; there have been ages when it was not present; when it is no longer present, there will be nothing which has occurred" (KSA, 1:875).

15. Above everything that belongs to what must be forgotten is the Dionysian nature of man: the instincts. In his analysis, in *The Genealogy of Morals*, of this process of actively forgetting the instincts, Nietzsche gives an interesting explanation for the origin of unconscious desires. As a consequence of the repression of instinctual urges, "they had to depend on new, covert satisfactions. All instincts that are not allowed free play turn inward. This is what I call man's interiorization; it alone provides the soil for growth of what is later called man's *soul*" (GM, 217). Eric Blondel, in a splendid study concerning Nietzsche's use of the metaphor, remarks that this view of active forgetfulness and the origin of the unconscious shows a strong agreement with Freud's concept of repression and his explanation for the unconscious by virtue of a primal repression (Blondel, 1977, 153; cf. Freud, SE, 12:66 ff.). Blondel also points to the fact that the primal repression, in both Nietzsche and Freud, possesses a strong metaphorical character: for both of them, the issue is one of metaphorical transfer (in Freud's terminology: a *Verdichtung*) wherein the distinction between consciousness and the unconscious is constructed. Lacan's interpretation of unconscious repression as a metaphorical process pregnantly underlines the relationship of Nietzsche's and Freud's views of the concept of repression (Lacan, É, 493–528; see also, in this connection, 4.1 and 4.6).

16. Blondel notes here, too, a remarkable agreement between Nietzsche and Freud. The plastic, metaphorical power about which Nietzsche speaks corresponds, according to Blondel, with the plasticity of the libido, that is, the capacity of the libido to transform both the object and the means of satisfaction (Blondel, 1977, 172). In this respect, Nietzsche offers a preview of Freud's sublimation theory. See 0.3 and 4.7.

17. See 0.2 for Schiller's use of the term *naive*. There is, however, an important difference between Schiller's and Nietzsche's use of the term: where, for Schiller, that which is naive is an expression of the original harmonious unity with nature, Nietzsche views the "naive" Homeric culture as a world of appearances that had as their purpose the goal of masking the terrors of existence.

18. In his study of the orgiastic cult of Dionysius, which originated in Thrace, whereby, in a religious-sexual ecstasy live sacrificial animals were torn limb from limb before being eaten, Schröeder argues that circa 1000 B.C., at the time of the Dorian migration, the cult began its triumphal passage through Greece but met resistance from the dominant Apollonian culture. This conflict led to a certain amount of assimilation of Dionysius in the Olympian religion, whereby, the cult of Dionysius gradually lost its more barbaric characteristics. After the temporary balance between Dionysius and Apollo in the tragedies, Dionysius was transformed into "the delicate wine-god, the playful youth with luxuriant locks and dark, violet-colored eyes, the youngster with a soft, almost feminine beauty, of fine, thoughtful appearance, the Dionysius such as Couperus [a Dutch, early-twentieth-century author of romantic, and sometimes decadent novels—JdM] drew him in his profoundly poetic work" (Schröeder, 1919, 23–24).

19. For Nietzsche, other than for the Platonic tradition, art is, for this reason, no mimesis, imitation of nature, but rather its metaphysical supplement (B, 113–14).

20. In *The Birth* Nietzsche makes a terminological distinction, which is not found in the cited preparatory study, between the truth of science and the tragic wisdom that is characteristic of pre-Socratic (and his own) philosophy (B, 88). This tragic wisdom is not the tempting illusion of scientific truth that entered the world with Socrates, but rather a comprehension of eternal suffering as the basis of everything that is.

21. In this manner, tragic irony is completely transformed by Socrates into a purely didactic stylistic method in the service of reaching philosophical Truth. Cf. what was remarked in 0.3 concerning the contradiction between Socratic and Romantic irony.

22. In *The Birth* Nietzsche had already commented: "The tremendous courage and wisdom of *Kant* and *Schopenhauer* carried off the most difficult victory: victory over the optimism that lurked within the essence of logic, which in turn forms the basis of our culture" (B, 87).

23. In a posthumously available fragment Nietzsche defines this phenomenon as follows: "What does nihilism mean?—*That the highest values lose their value*. There is no goal. There is no answer to the 'why' " (W, 3:557). Nietzsche specifies this nihilism as *passive* nihilism, distinct from the *active* that, as we shall shortly see, he personally propagated.

24. The first version of *The Birth*, which consists of roughly the first fifteen sections of the published book (and which, with the title *Socrates and the Greek Tragedy*, is present in KSA, 1:601–40), restricts itself to an interpretation of Greek tragedy's development. The second part of the book, wherein Nietzsche speaks about the rebirth of tragedy in Wagner's music, forms a report concerning his conversations with Cosima and Richard Wagner about the first part, whereby contents were related to the actual state of affairs in culture. A number of themes in this second part, for example the exaltation concerning German culture, appear to be strongly Wagnerian, and, after Nietzsche's break with Wagner, formed, together with the latter's music, the target of his critique of modern culture.

25. As Nietzsche, in his later work, begins more and more to identify with the Dionysian, his biography and his teachings become more and more entangled with each other. The last letters Nietzsche sent to Cosima Wagner at the beginning of January 1889, signed with the name Dionysius, mark his definitive entrance into the Dionysian realm of insanity.

26. In *The Genealogy of Morals* Nietzsche remarked that Schopenhauer understood Kant's conceptualization of the unselfishness of aesthetic experience in a most un-Kantian manner because "he too responded to beauty from an interested motive, even out of the strongest, most personal interest, that of the tortured man seeking release from his torment" (GM, 240).

27. In the *Aesthetics*, Hegel maintained that "for us, art, according to its highest determination, is something from the past" (Ä, 1:22). "Art invites us to a reflective consideration, not with the goal that we once again bring it to the foreground, but rather so that we may, scientifically, understand what it is" (*ibid.*, cf. De Mul, 1993a). This view of the death of art cannot be grasped

separately from Hegel's rejection of the image in favor of the concept, an argument to which I referred in section 1.1 of this chapter.

28. In "Über Wahrheit und Lüge," too, Nietzsche maintained the distinction between the real nature of things and the appearance of metaphysical knowledge that we possess of those things. In *The Birth* he speaks, in so many words, of a world "behind phenomena" (B, 80). In *Thus Spoke Zarathustra* he appears to have this aspect of his earlier philosophy in mind when he writes: "Once Zarathustra too casted his deluded fancy beyond mankind, like all afterworldsmen. Then the world seemed to me the work of a suffering and tormented God. Then the world seemed to me the dream and fiction of a God; coloured vapour before the eyes of a discontented God" (Z, 58).

29. Given that the "herausdrehung des Platonismus" consists not so much in postulating a new truth alongside of—or in place of—that provided by metaphysics as the evocation of another experiential domain via a deconstructive "dissolution" of a number of fundamental metaphysical opposites, I consider, following Vattimo, this Heideggerian term *Verwindung* applicable to Nietzsche's thought (Vattimo, 1988, 168; cf. what was said concerning the term *Verwindung* in note 18, Introduction).

30. Nietzsche emphatically places himself in opposition here to the positivism that presumes facts that have an existence independent of the interpretative process: "Contrary to the positivism which stands still by the phenomena—'there are only facts,' I say: no, facts do not exist. Only interpretations. We can not specify *Factum* 'as such': perhaps it is also nonsense to want to do so. 'That's all subjective,' he says, but that is already explanation, there is nothing given for the 'subject' but only *imputed, placed behind.*—Finally, is it still necessary to place the interpreter behind the interpretation? That is already invention, hypothesis. To the extent that the word knowledge indeed has any sense, the world is thus knowable, but it continuously permits other significations, it has no simple meaning behind it but knows only countless meanings, 'perspectives' " that the world can never completely exhaust (KSA, 12:315). "Facts" are the result of the fossilization of the metaphorical interpretation: "The name, fame, meaning, the externality and the usual measure of a thing—from its origin mostly a deviation and arbitrariness, the things hang as a mantle and the essence, even the skin, feels completely strange—is, by the belief and growth thereof from generation to generation, gradually attached to the thing, as it were, grown together with it and become its substance: the appearance from the first beginning almost always becomes its essence and it works in that fashion. . . . It is enough to create new names, value-judgments, and probabilities in order that, eventually, new 'things' be created" (GS, 121–22). Nietzsche's genealogy is directed at exposing the origin, the process of becoming of these "things" in order that the self-evident nature might be undermined.

31. In my opinion, Fink is correct when he maintains that this doctrine comprises Nietzsche's most fundamental thought (Fink, 1960, 83). There are a number of reasons as to why this thought has not always had the attention it deserves in the reception accorded to Nietzsche's work. In the first place, this "highest formula of affirmation that can possibly be attained" (EH, 99) occupies

only a modest place in his published work. "Concerning the Übermensch, Zarathustra speaks to *everyone*, concerning the death of God, to only *a few*, and concerning the Eternal Recurrence of the Same only to himself," writes Fink, who conceives of the intimate character of the doctrine as evidence for its fundamental importance in Nietzsche's later thinking. In the second place, the doctrine of the Eternal Reccurrence has been placed in the background by a number of philosophers, Jaspers, for example, because it is considered to be contradictory. Although, from the standpoint of metaphysics, there may well be something to say for this criticism, it misses precisely what makes Nietzsche's thinking so interesting: his attempt to develop a nonmetaphysical reflection. In the third place, National-Socialist interpreters such as Bäumler have reduced the doctrine, for political purposes, in favor of the conception of the Will to Power. Although Heidegger justifiably pointed out that a meaningful interpretation of Nietzsche's philosophy must also do justice to the doctrine of the Eternal Reccurrence (he criticizes Jaspers and Bäumler because they failed to do this—cf. N, 1:21 ff.), even he ultimately understands the doctrine primarily in terms of the Will to Power.

32. In this second case it is of less significance whether the doctrine is "true" or not (a question, incidentally, that cannot be answered outside of metaphysics), than what its effect is: "Is it *true*, or, more to the point: does one believe that it is true—then *everything* changes and turns around, and *all* previously applicable values become devalued" (letter to Overbeck, 1884, quoted in Visser, 1989, 277).

2   THE PATH OF AUTONOMY

1. Habermas interprets the origins of modern aesthetics in Kant's work: "In the initial phase of this process, there emerged the cognitive structures of a new domain, one quite distinct from the complex of science and knowledge and that of morality. And the task of clarifying these structures subsequently fell to philosophical aesthetics" (Habermas, 1996, 47; cf. 0.1 above).

2. In the other forms of art, a similar process of emancipation in the direction of autonomy and purity of aesthetic methods has occurred. Music found itself in a relatively favorable starting position because it is hardly mimetic in character. In the seventeenth and eighteenth centuries there were a variety of attempts, however, to understand music in terms of a mimetic aesthetics (cf. 6.3). In the Wagnerian *Gesamtkunstwerk*, too, music is made subordinate to the totality. Nonetheless, in Eduard Hanslick's *Vom Musikalisch-Schönen* (1854), a formalist conception of music was already defended, a defense wherein music was conceptualized as a system of sounds that stands completely apart from the encircling world. Literature's specific medium has hindered its leaving behind *mimesis* and *expressiveness*. According to Clive Bell, one of the leading formalist aestheticians at the beginning of this century, literature can for this reason never become a pure art-form. Only in marginal phenomena such as Kurt Schwitters's dadaist poetry and the concrete poetry of the 1960s was the mimetic function of

language breached. However, in the latter case typography was often accredited with a mimetic function. Apart from this, the modernist conception of the literary work as an autonomous totality, as it is defended in the *New Criticism*, for example, connects closely with the developments in pictorial art and music.

3. The choice for Piaget and Stella was not an arbitrary one. In his theory of rationalization, Habermas allies himself quite closely with Piaget and his student Kohlberg. Cf. Habermas, 1983; Habermas 1984, 1:67 ff., 72, 140; and Habermas, 1987, 9, 30, 140. Stella's work until 1970 belongs to the most puritan expression of modern, autonomous art.

4. The Kantian starting point that knowledge of reality is never a passive reflection of reality, but rather that it always presupposes one or another construction, is something that Piaget shares with Nietzsche. However, while for Nietzsche, as we have seen in chapter 1, this led to the view that all knowledge is interpretation, Piaget attempts to maintain the notion of objective knowledge.

5. Piaget also refers to this stage as the egocentric, but this term is rather misleading because, strictly speaking, there is at this stage no question of an ego distinct from the surrounding world.

6. With the help of De Saussure's terminology, Piaget distinguishes between various semiotic functions: (1) *indices*, that is, signs whereby the signifier (*signifiant*) is connected through a causal relation with the signified (*signifié*) (for example, the smoke that signifies the fire); (2) *symbols*, whereby signifier and signified are separated from each other but where the latter stands in a particular analogy to the former (in a child's game, for example, a white stone can stand for white bread); and (3), *signs* in a more restricted sense whereby signifier and signified are also separated from each other, but, in this case, whereby their relation is conventional and accordingly arbitrary (thus, the word 'tree' signifies the object 'tree' not by virtue of an analogy but because of convention). According to Piaget, indices already play an important role in the first weeks following birth but the other two semiotic functions only become apparent from approximately the second year of life on (Piaget, 1983, 115). De Saussure's semiology will be more extensively dealt with in chapter 5 and 6, in which (post)structuralism will be discussed.

7. This aspect reminds us of the anthropological theories of Scheler and Plessner. In Plessner's terminology animals organize their actions from a center and, in this sense, they stand against the world. According to him, people distinguish themselves from animals because they can not only distance themselves from the external world but also from this center of experience. Plessner speaks, in this context, of *eccentric positionality* (Plessner, 1965, 288 ff.). Piaget also refers to this characteristic distancing with the concept of *decentering*. In this case, Scheler speaks of the human *Weltoffenheit* (Scheler, 1988, 38). That the human eccentric position is closely connected with man's linguistic character is something that will become clearer during the discussion of Heidegger's and Lacan's ideas in chapter 4.

8. According to Weber this process of social rationalization is characterized by *structural differentiation, formalization* and *universalization* of the separate structures, and an increasingly efficient theoretical and practical *control* of reality.

9. For this reason it is not surprising that in formalist art criticism only completely abstract works, wherein every trace of mimesis and expression have been eliminated, are understood to be *pure* paintings (cf. Bell, 1914 and Fry, 1920). However, the first generation of abstract artists often maintained more or less mystical mimetic theories. Abstract art was viewed by artists such as Kandinsky and Mondrian as a 'portrayal' of spiritual reality (cf. Kandinsky, 1959; also see Stolniz, 1960, chapter 10). A good overview of this aspect of modern abstract art is offered by the catalogue of the exhibition *The Spiritual in Art. Abstract Paintings 1890–1985*, which was held in the Municipal Museum, The Hague, in 1987 (Weisberger, 1986). Contemporary abstract artists such as Frank Stella, however, emphatically reject mystic theories of portrayal à la Kandinsky (see the following section).

10. This discussion raises echoes of the *Querelle des anciens et des modernes* which took place at the end of the eighteenth century. In contrast to "les anciens," who considered classical art as an unachievable ideal, the modernists argued that progress in art was most certainly possible. However, in most cases this claim had relevance exclusively to *technical* developments in painting. Many modernists even acknowledged that progress in technique could go hand in hand with the loss of aesthetic values.

11. Gablik's model also appears to be supported by the developmental model, from Michael Parsons, of the development of the individual's aesthetic reception. In his model, which was inspired by Piaget and Kohlberg, Parsons distinguishes five stages in aesthetic development that can be respectively be referred to as associative, mimetic, expressive, formalist, and interpretive. Parson's theory appears to be an affirmation of the homology in individual and historical development postulated by Piaget (see Parsons, 1987; cf. De Mul, 1988, 1997b).

12. Stella's pathos of purity finds a nice expression in an anecdote about a man who most definitely did not love modern art, and most especially did not love abstract expressionism. The man said to him that it would already be an achievement if the painters succeeded in setting paint to the canvass in a manner such as it was in the [paint-]tubes. "And that," continues Stella laconically, "is what I've attempted since then to do. I try to keep the color identical to how it is in the tube" (quoted in Gachnang, 1989, 212).

13. Cf. William Rubin's essay in the catalogue of this exhibition (Rubin, 1970).

14. The modernist perspective, as it is represented by Gablik, has been present in a dominant manner in the last decade of art historical literature. Following the remarkable return to figuration in postmodern painting, the interest of art historians in the long-marginalized realistic tendencies in twentieth-century art has once again grown.

15. In his diary, Tristan Tzara provides a good record of these "happenings" *avant la lettre:* "1916 July 14. For the first time anywhere. Waag Hall. 1st Dada night (Music, dances, theories, manifestos, poems, paintings, costumes, masks). In the presence of a compact crowd Tzara demonstrates, we demand the right to piss in different colors, Huelsenbeck demonstrates, Ball

demonstrates, Arp *Erklärung* [Statement], Janco *meine Bilder* [my pictures], Heusser *eigene Kompositionen* [original compositions], the dogs bay and the dissection of Panama on the piano and dock—shouted poem—shouting and fighting in the hall, first row approves second row declares itself incompetent to judge the rest shout who is the strongest. . . . Boxing resumed: Cubist dance, costumes by Janco, each man his own drum on his head, noise, Negro music/trabatgea bonoooooooooo ooooooo/ 5 literary experiments: Tzara in tails stands before the curtain . . . and explains the new aesthetics: gymnastic poem, concert of vowels, bruitist poem, static poem chemical arrangement of ideas, 'Biriboom, biriboom . . . vowal poem, a a ò, i e o, a i i." (quoted in Ades, 1974, 14). An interesting overview of dadaism, by one of those involved with the movement, is provided by Richter, 1964.

16. In 1918, Picabia joined the dadaists in Zurich, after a period in New York, where, together with Marcel Duchamp, he was a member of the group of avant-gardists surrounding the photographer Alfred Stieglitz. A year later, together with Tristan Tzara, he played an important role in the founding of the Dada Movement in Paris.

17. Sigmund Freud, too, in his still remarkably topical study *Civilisation and Its Discontents* (1930), argued that the increasing rationalization of man in no way eliminates the darker side of human character. One can rather speak of a repression that, according to him, necessarily leads to outbursts that become more serious as that repression increases.

18. Lemaire, in his earlier quoted work concerning landscape paintings, came to a similar conclusion: "In this way, the appearance of the landscape in the West between 1400 and 1550 is simultaneously an expression of the subordination of the world-space to the Will of a calculating and all-seeing man and a sign of a certain estrangement between man and his environment, of a loss of intimacy and self-evident belonging between man and his landscape" (Lemaire, 1970, 25).

19. This formulation betrays a certain influence of Freud's psychoanalysis on the philosophy of surrealism (cf. Spector, 1974, 146 ff.). Breton and his friends did indeed exhibit considerable interest in Freud's psychoanalytic theories. Not only did the surrealists find in psychoanalysis a confirmation of their thoughts concerning the liberating force of love, humor, and art, but painters such as Dali, Masson, and Magritte also made enthusiastic use of Freudian symbols. In addition, a number of personal contacts between surrealists and psychoanalysts such as Lacan occurred. Nonetheless, there are also fundamental differences between the worldviews of surrealism and psychoanalysis. The most significant difference is undoubtedly the fact that while psychoanalysis as therapy is ultimately directed at curbing unconscious urges and bringing them under the guidance of rational consciousness (I shall explicate on this point in 4.7), the surrealist strove for the liberation of the unconscious from the dominance of rationality. From the beginning, the dadaists had a much more skeptical attitude toward psychoanalysis. Tzara, for example, wrote in his 1918 Manifesto: "Psychoanalysis is a dangerous illness, it pacifies the tendency of the individual to resist reality and systematizes the bour-

geoisie" (Tzara, 1986, 174). The surrealist Magritte also always maintained a critical reserve with respect to psychoanalysis for the same reason (cf. the epigraph at the beginning of Chapter 5).

20. This pronouncement from Breton's *The Political Position of Surrealism* points up the relationship that surrealists felt for both Marxism and communism. Many surrealists, Breton among them, became members of the Communist Party. However, it soon became clear that there were irreconcilable differences between the various worldviews. Other than the communists, who acknowledged the primacy of a social revolution, the surrealists strove for a total change of mentality. The surrealists also rejected the communists' bourgeois aesthetic conceptualizations that had led, in the countries where the "proletariat" had established a dictatorship, to a reactionary social-realism. On the other side, the communists distrusted the "idealism" and "elitism" of the surrealists (cf. Alquié, 1969, 56 ff.). Because the differences between the communist and the surrealist worldviews ultimately proved larger than the agreements, the cooperation between communists and surrealists was primarily a series of arguments and scandals (cf. Nadeau, 1964).

21. Max Ernst especially, in his *frottages,* which came about by rubbing with chalk or pencil over a piece of paper that had been laid over a rough surface, experimented with chance operations (cf. Rubin, 1986, 82). In chapter 6, on the basis of the work of John Cage, I shall examine this characteristic phenomenon of avant-garde art more extensively.

22. The philosophy of surrealism, which I present here merely in a number of catchwords, was not systematically developed by the surrealists themselves. This was not only because such a systematicization can not be reconciled with the surrealist rejection of rational ordering, but, more especially, because in the movement *pratiquer la poésie* was always paramount. Using the philosophy of Plato, Descartes, and Hegel as his primary referential context, Alquié (1969) offers an interesting reconstruction of the philosophy of surrealism.

23. In addition to the works of the specified philosophers, I make grateful use, in this section, of Jay's *The Dialectical Imagination* (Jay, 1973), which provides a lucid overview of the work of the Frankfurt School's first generation of theorists, and also of the articles that Jay (1985) and Keulartz (1986) wrote about Habermas' theory of aesthetics and its relationship to Adorno's and Benjamin's theories.

24. Concerning the *striving* for control, according to Adorno and Horkheimer, there is, however, a clear continuity between the mythical and the rational view of the world: "The myths, as the tragedians came upon them, are already characterized by the discipline and power that Bacon celebrated as the 'right mark' (Adorno and Horkheimer, 1973, 8). Seen from this perspective, the tendency to control is not, for Adorno and Horkheimer, a specifically modern characteristic, but rather a striving inherent to human nature that reminds us of Nietzsche's doctrine of the Will to Power.

25. On this point, despite substantial differences with respect to numerous other points, there is an striking parallel between the *Dialectic of Enlightment* and

the views of Heidegger and Foucault. Heidegger, in his analysis of technology in "The Overcoming of Metaphysics," has pointed out that, in modern times, man has become the ultimate raw material of 'calculating thinking' (VA, 1:84; cf. also 4.6). Foucault has made clear in his genealogies of punishment and sexuality how the human body, in modern time, has become the object of techniques of discipline (Foucault 1977 and 1984). In the *Dialectic of Enlightment*, Adorno and Horkheimer have expressed their admiration for the radical manner in which De Sade in his perverse novels and Nietzsche in his teachings of the Will to Power exposed the real nature of modern culture:

> Not to have glossed over or suppressed but to have trumpeted far and wide the impossibility of deriving from reason any fundamental argument against murder fired the hatred which the progressives (and they precisely) still direct against Sade and Nietzsche.[. . .] Inasmuch as the merciless doctrines proclaim the identity of domination and reason, they are more merciful than those of the moralistic lackeys of the bourgeoisie. 'Where do your greatest dangers lie?' was the question Nietzsche once posed himself, and answered thus: 'In compassion.' With his denial he redeemed the unshakable confidence in man that is constantly betrayed by every form of assurance that seeks only to console. (Horkheimer and Adorno, 1973, 118–19).

26. This "thingification" affects language, too, which becomes a unidimensional instrument of control in place of a dialogue in the true sense of the word. Adorno and Horkheimer already see forerunners of this decline in Homer's *Odyssey* wherein Odysseus escapes from Cyclops by naming himself "No-body." It is true that Odysseus defeated Cyclops, but only at the price of self-denial and a fundamental mutilation of language (Adorno and Horkheimer, 1973, 69).

27. With this statement of Stendhal, Adorno, together with Nietzsche (cf. 1.8), turns against Kant's view that aesthetic enjoyment constitutes a *disinterested* pleasure. It is precisely as a promise of future happiness that art is of such great importance. In this sense, Adorno, too, associates himself with the Romantic project, although in his case the ironic component, the insight into the unachievability of its aims, appears to completely eclipse the hope. Given also that this view of irony pre-dominates in postmodernism (cf. 0.2), it is not surprising that Adorno's theory of aesthetics is currently in great vogue among postmodernist thinkers.

28. It is remarkable that, despite his rejection of the vulgar-Marxist reduction of a work of art to an ideological *content* reflecting class interests and his emphasis on the autonomy of art, Adorno here maintains a *formal* mimesis-function for art. In note 9 we saw that a number of "formalist" artists also maintain this theory of mimesis.

29. "By affirmative culture is meant that culture of the bourgeois epoch which led in the course of its own development to the segregation from civilization of the mental and spiritual as an independent realm of value that is also considered superior to civilization. Its decisive characteristic is the assertion of

a universally obligatory, eternally better and more valuable world that must be unconditionally affirmed: a world essentially different from the factual world of the daily struggle for existence, yet realizable by every individual for himself 'from within,' without any transformation of the state of fact. It is only in this culture that cultural activities and objects gain that value which evaluates them above the everyday sphere. Their reception becomes an act of celebration and exaltation" (Marcuse, 1968, 95).

30. In 6.5, in association with an analysis of the work of Schönberg's American "student," John Cage, I shall provide a more extensive explication of Schönberg's twelve-tone technique.

31. According to Adorno avant-garde art underwent the same fate. Regardless of the extent to which it resisted autonomous art, it was not long before it, too, found its way into the museum and thereby became neutralized.

32. Using Heidegger's conceptualization of poetic language, which, with respect to its purpose, is closely allied to Benjamin's theory of language, I will expand upon this theme in chapter 4.

33. In surrealism Magritte, especially, has employed the stylistic medium of the shock in his work. I will expand on this point in chapter 5.

34. Here I can not go into more detail concerning Benjamin's analysis of the philosophical and cultural implications of the reproducibility of photography and film. For a more detailed discussion of these implications in relation to digital imaging, see De Mul, 1997a.

35. Honesty compels that it be mentioned here that Habermas himself emphatically postulated in his speech that the prospects for realizing his alternative are not favorable. However, he appears to attribute this rather to the pre-, anti- and postmodern tendencies in contemporary Western culture, which are antagonistic to modernism, than to specific characteristics of modern rationalization itself (cf. Habermas, 1996, 53 ff.).

36. As was the case with the first retrospective in 1970, the catalogue contained an informative text by Rubin (see Rubin, 1987).

37. We encounter a similar line of thought with Eco. After he drew attention, in the quotation given above, to the modernist destruction of the past, he commented about modern avant-garde: "The avant-garde destroys, defaces the past: *Les Demoiselles d'Avignon* is a typical avant-garde act. Then the avant-garde goes further, destroys the figure, cancels it, arrives at the abstract, the informal, the white canvas, the slashed canvas, the charred canvas. In architecture and the visual arts, it will be the curtain wall, the building as stele, pure parallelepiped, minimal art; in literature, the destruction of the flow of discourse, the Burroughs-like collage, silence, the white page; in music, the passage from atonality to noise to absolute silence (in this sense, the early Cage is modern)" (Eco, 1983, 66–67). However, in chapter 6 I shall argue that Cage's composition 4'33" (which consists of four minutes and thirty-three seconds of silence) can with equal justification be interpreted as the expression of a postmodern experience.

38. In this connection, Stella also speaks of a blending of materialism and immaterialism: "The roots of 1960s abstraction, so thoroughly grounded in the

abstraction of the North, in the encouraging antimaterialism of Mondrian, Kandinsky, and Malevich, must be reinforced with energy drawn from the realism of the South—the thorough, stubborn materialism of Cézanne, Monet, and Picasso" (quoted in Beeren, 1988, 2).

39. Martis writes of the *"avant-garde"* in this respect, but, as the subsequent text of the quotation makes clear, he uses the term as a synonym for "modernism."

40. Andy Warhol's pop art is in my opinion an excellent example of this point. Although he made use of numerous avant-garde techniques such as (photo)montage and thereby brought life into his work, he did not bother to criticize the consumer society that he portrayed. The existing society is for him nothing more than a possible object of aesthetic repetition. It is perhaps true that an aestheticization of everyday reality was thereby achieved (for example by elevating cans of Campbell's Tomato Soup to an aesthetic object), but in such a case it appears primarily to be what Adorno and Habermas specified as a "false dissolution" of art that merely confirms the consumer society in its existence. This critique does not remove the aesthetic qualities of Warhol's work, which are undoubtedly closely connected to the Apollonian qualities of the consumer society's aesthetics.

3   THE ART OF FORGETTING

1. This expression appears to be a variant of Leibniz's remark "Music is unconscious exercise in mathematics such that the spirit does not know that it counts" (*Musica est exercitium arithmeticae occultum nescientis se numerare animi*) (*Epistolae* 241). Cf. 6.3.

2. Even Nietzsche, who tried with "the greatest exertion of the mind, to overcome metaphysics," speaks of the "human, all-too-human" necessity to return to metaphysics after such a victory. "*Then*, however, he needs to take a *retrograde* step: he has to grasp the historical jusitfication that resides in such ideas, likewise the psychological, he has to recognize that they have been most responsible for the advancement of mankind and that without such a retrograde step he will deprive himself of the best that mankind has hitherto produced.— In regard to philosophical metaphysics, I see more and more who are making for the negative goal (that all positive metaphysics is an error), but still few who are taking a few steps back; for one may well want to look out over the topmost rung of the ladder, but one ought not to want to stand on it" (HH, 23; cf. my remarks in 1.10, with reference to Wittgenstein's imagery of the ladder). Such a work of art could only be produced by the *Übermensch*, while for us, as "Ultimate Men," metaphysics, just as much as art, is a necessary supplement so that we can live with our finitude.

3. Perhaps Schopenhauer had Beethoven's 1808 Sixth Symphony (the Pastoral) in mind when he offered his critique of this "painting music." The Pastoral consists of four movements that have the titles: *Erwachen heiterer Gefühle bei der Ankunft auf dem Lande, Szene am Bach, Lustiges Zusammensein der*

Landleute, Gewitter, Sturm, and *Hirtengesang. Frohe, dankbahre Gefühle nach dem Sturm.* As a sort of apology for these mimetic titles, Beethoven added to the score the motto "More expression than painting" (*Mehr Ausdruck als Malerey*). (Höweler, 1975, 91).

4. One would perhaps expect to note an admiration for Beethoven in Schopenhauer's work, a composer who, in the words of the musicologist Solomon, more than any other "placed the tragic in the centre of his heroic style" and who "made death, destruction, fear, and aggression components of musical form." Perhaps his critique of "painting music" prevented Schopenhauer from appreciating Beethoven's work (Baum, 1984, cf. note 3, above).

5. In the following exposition I present the complex development of the tonal tradition in a somewhat simplified manner. In 6.3, I shall return to this exposition and provide some additional comments with rather more nuance.

6. This theme also plays an important role in the dadaist "aesthetics of spontaneity" that was discussed in the previous chapter. Tzara even defined Dada as an "abolition of memory" (Tzara, 1986, 178).

7. Similar effects appear in the visual arts, for example in the so-called op art (optical art). In the work of artists such as Bridget Riley, visual effects such as vibrations or wave-effects are achieved by a refined grouping of lines, squares, ellipses, spheres, etc., and by systematically perpetrated changes of form. In both repetitive music and op art a state of awareness is created wherein particular visual or auditory motives quite clearly come to the surface although, in objective terms, they occupy a relatively unimportant place in the composition.

8. That this similarity is not coincidental is proven by the conceptual history of the term *unconscious,* which, via the philosophy of Nietzsche and Eduard van Hartmann's *Philosophy of the Unconscious* (1869), refers back to Idealist philosophy, something to which Schopenhauer's philosophy of the Will also belongs (see Marquard, 1969; cf. what was noted in 0.3 concerning the relation between Freud and Schelling).

9. In *The Unconscious* (1915) Freud explains this further as follows: "The processes of the system *Ucs,* are *timeless;* i.e. they are not ordered temporally, are not altered by the passage of time; they have no reference to time at all. Reference to time is bound up, once again, with the work of the system *Cs.*" (SE, 14:187).

10. Cf. Piaget's opinion, discussed in the previous chapter, concerning the adualism of early youth. According to the genetic approach in psychoanalysis, unconsciousness is a "remnant" of the earlier experience of reality. In the next chapter, incidentally, we shall see that in lacanian psychoanalysis a nongenetic approach to the unconscious is developed.

11. It is not improbable that Freud was influenced by Nietzsche when he developed the line of thought that I shall elaborate below. As a right-minded citizen of Vienna at the time of the fin-de-siècle Freud was familiar with Nietzsche's work and, according to various comments in his own work, he felt a close affinity to the philosopher (cf. among other SE, 14:15–16, and SE, 20:60). Cf. note 9, above.

12. In chapter 5 I will more closely address the issue of the inability of psychoanalysis to present this 'perversion' in anything other than a negative fashion, conceived as it is as a disavowal of reality. At the same time I shall examine more closely the difference between aesthetics and aestheticism that I maintain here.

13. Given that, in the context of therapy, Freud ascribes a healing effect to repetition, one can equally speak of a certain ambivalence in Freud's approach to it. In the therapeutic dialogue the traumatic experience that is the foundation of the neurosis is repeated at the verbal level, whereby it becomes an object of the instinct to master (*Bemächtigungstrieb*) of the conscious subject (cf. Kurzawa, 1982, 11).

14. With respect to its contents, Philip Glass's opera *Akhnaten* could be called a good example of this point. The opera deals with the decline of the Egyptian Pharaoh Achnaton (1372–54 B.C.) who broke with the existing polytheistic religion in favor of the Sun God, Aton. This engendered much resistance, not least because Achnaton neglected the worldly politics of the Egyptian empire in his religious struggle. In the final scene from the opera we see the spirits of the "powerless yearning" of Achnaton and his family, wandering through the ruins of the city that he had built for Aton before joining themselves to his father's burial procession. Compare the remark concerning the relationship between decadence and Plato's "Egypticism" in 1.7. However, the foregoing criticism does not in any way detract from the fact that Achnaton's *Hymn to the Aten* constitutes one of the most beautiful arias that twentieth-century opera has produced.

15. One can of course address a similar question to Adorno's extremely rigid interpretation of jazz. I restrict myself here to repetitive music.

16. Laermans has pointed out that, despite the fact that it originated in an essentially different philosophical context, the libidinal philosophy of Deleuze and Lyotard demonstrates a remarkable agreement with Marcuse's Freudo-Marxism (Laermans, 1982, 8, 13).

17. This appears to contradict the earlier comment about the progressive, future-oriented character of the affirmation of the Eternal Recurrence. However, it is necessary to consider in this context that, in the affirmation of the doctrine of the Eternal Recurrence, the issue is not so much being oriented toward the new, but rather the wish that the *now* should be endlessly repeated. Visser, who also speaks of this putative contradiction, made a distinction in this context between *being purely oriented toward the future* and *having [a] future* (Visser, 1989, 315).

18. This theme already plays an important role in Nietzsche's 1874 work "On the Uses and Disadvantages of History for Life" (cf. 1.6). In this work Nietzsche provides a sharp critique of the historic consciousness that was characteristic of the nineteenth century, aiming at both the Hegelian and the historicist variants. Further, Nietzsche defended in the work the proposition that "there is a degree of sleeplessness, of rumination, of historical sense, which is harmful and ultimately fatal to the living thing, whether this living thing be a

man or a people or a culture" (H, 62). Nietzsche elaborates this proposition in a critical analysis of the three forms of writing history which, according to him, emerge from the historical understanding: the *monumental* (whereby the past is used as a template for future behavior), the *antiquarian* (wherein the past is employed as a justification for the present), and the *critical* (wherein events are evaluated by critically reviewing their antecedents). Although each of these forms of historical understanding possesses some utility for life, an overabundance of historical understanding leads to deceptive analogies and to the mummification or even destruction of life. In that case, only an *un-* or *supra-*historical attitude can provide salvation: "He who cannot sink down on the threshold of the moment and forget all the past, who cannot stand balanced like a goddess of victory without growing dizzy and afraid, will never know what happiness is—worse, he will never do anything to make others happy" (H, 62). The suprahistorical individual is the individual "who sees no salvation in the process and for whom, rather, the world is complete and reaches its finality at each and every moment" (H, 66).

19. Visser remarks that the implicit view of time that emerges from Nietzsche's imagery of past and future, standing together under the gateway of the moment, colliding with each other, shows a similarity with the view of time that Heidegger tried to explicate in *Being and Time*. In this context, Visser also points to Heidegger's book about Nietzsche wherein the experience of the moment is interpreted in terms of the 'analytics of There-being" (*Daseinanalytik*) from *Being and Time* (Visser, 1989, 307; cf. N, I). It can be added that in *Being and Time*, where the notion of the moment plays an important role, Heidegger had already explicitly related himself to Nietzsche in order to explicate his own views of time and historicity. In this connection, however, Heidegger did not point to the experience of the moment in *Thus Spoke Zarathustra* but to "The Uses and Disadvantages of History for Life." According to Heidegger, the reason why history can be useful or disadvantageous for 'life' resides in the temporariness (*Zeitlichkeit*) and historicity of the human way of Being: There-being (*Dasein*). Heidegger argues that the three forms of writing history that Nietzsche distinguishes answer the three ecstasies of the temporariness (and thereby historicity) of There-being. There-being possesses a future existence through the determined disclosure of already chosen possibilities. Next, There-being is open to the "monumental" possibilities of existence. In the repetitive expropriation of thrown possibilities the possibility is simultaneously present for the "antiquarian" maintenance of "dagewesen Existenz." In the unity of future and past, the present (*Gegenwart*) is also disclosed. However, this "making present" (*gegenwärtigen*) simultaneously implies a making nonpresent (*entgegenwärtigung*) of the inauthentic present of the fallen-ness of Being. In this sense, the monumental-antiquarian writing of history, in its authentic form, is necessarily a critique of the present. Heidegger's conclusion is: "Authentic historicality is the foundation for the possibility of uniting these three ways of history" (BT, 449).

20. In the case of the digital sampling of sounds and images, a dominant technique in today's popular culture, we see a similar disappearance of the

distinction between original and copy (cf. Mitchell, 1994; De Mul, 1997a). This characteristic seems to be one of the main constituents of the aesthetics and metaphysics of postmodern culture.

21. Philosophical reflection can engender the same experience. In the conceptual "deconstruction" of the logic of origins another space is opened, as it were, for another experience of things. Or, as Nietzsche expressed it in *Daybreak:* *"The more insight we possess into the origin the less significant does the origin appear; while what is nearest to us,* what is around us and in us, gradually begins to display colours and beauties and enigmas and riches of significance of which earlier mankind had not an inkling" (D, 31).

22. Cf. what has already been remarked concerning the *Verwindung* in 0.6 and 1.9.

4   THE FIRST AND THE LAST WORD

1. For explicit references to IJsseling see Mooij, 1975, 93, 128, 230, 239, and 261. References to Heidegger are to be found, among other places, on pages 39, 101, 132, and 211.

2. In his preface to *The Genealogy of Morals,* Nietzsche referred to part three of the book as an explanation of a single sentence in his (poetic) work *Thus Spoke Zarathustra* (GM, 157).

3. Achterberg's stanza has an indisputably strong religious-Christian connotation. It points to the first stanza of Hymn 1 in Jan Wit's Dutch translation (Wit, 1973, 1). Translated in English:

God has the first word.
In the beginning
He permitted the light to win,
He still continues to speak.

God has the first word.
Before we entered the world,
He already called us by our names,
His calling is still heard.

God has the last word.
What He said in antiquity,
shall be heard at the end of time
everywhere in His Kingdom.

God stands at the beginning
and will come at the ending.
His word is in its Being
the origin, the goal, and the meaning.

God heeft het eerste woord.
Hij heeft in den beginne
het licht doen overwinnen,
Hij spreekt nog altijd voort.

God heeft het eerste woord.
Voor wij ter wereld kwamen,
riep Hij ons reeds bij name,
zijn roep wordt nog steeds gehoord.

God heeft het laatste woord.
Wat hij van oudsher zeide,
wordt aan het eind der tijden
in heel zijn rijk gehoord.

God staat aan het begin
en Hij komt aan het einde.
Zijn woord is van het zijnde
oorsprong en doel en zin.

The biography of Achterberg also makes it clear that religious experience is a significant motive in his poetry. Although my concern here is with a intertextual interpretation rather than an reading of the stanza from within Achterberg's biography, this chapter suggests that it also possesses a particular magical-religious dimension when viewed from the first mentioned perspective.

4. This raises the question whether a secularized view of language is ever able to completely leave this magical-religious inheritance behind it. In *Twilight of the Idols* Nietzsche expresses the expectation that we will not be able to lose God as long as we believe in grammar (TI, 483).

5. This is undoubtedly an important point of connection with the surrealist *écriture automatique*. Cf. what I remarked in 2.4, concerning the relation between surrealism and psychoanalysis. It is not improbable that surrealist literature had some influence on Lacan's views of language. In any event, he maintained close relations with a number of Parisian surrealists.

6. In a 1984 study that caused a furor, Masson argued that, with this development, Freud capitulated to the Victorian indignation consequent to his earlier view that emotional disturbances always emerged from *really* experienced sexual violence. Even if this criticism is justified (recent research into the frequency of incest appears to confirm Freud's earlier views), then quite clearly the significance of Freud's thesis that unconscious phantasies play an important role in our life experience is in no way removed. The most that one can argue in this case is that Freud incorrectly specified *all* memories in terms of unconscious phantasies. In connection with Masson's critique, see note 19, chapter 2, where the critique of the dadaist Tzara, that psychoanalysis soothes the human tendency to resist reality to sleep and thereby systematizes the bourgeoisie, is quoted.

7. On the basis of this definition, incidentally, not all poetry is poetic. The opposite of the poem, that is, the purely spoken, is not moreover formed by prose: prose *can be* just as poetic as poetry. In even more general terms, Heidegger maintains in *The Origin of the Work of Art* that "the essence of art is poetry" (*Dichtung*) (BW, 186).

8. With this emphasis on the evocative character of the word, Heidegger's view of language shows a certain relation with Benjamin's mimetic view of language (cf. 2.5).

9. Heidegger often uses the etymology of a word to orient himself with an interpretation. Although he does not maintain etymology as an argument in the strict sense, it does form a reference in his vision for unraveling a particular syntactical structure or coherence.

10. Although Heidegger, for reasons that will be discussed below, no longer used the concept 'ontology' at the time he wrote "*Language*" (1950), it is useful to me at this point in my attempt to clarify Heidegger's position.

11. The distinction that Lacan makes between the imaginary and the symbolic order combines with that made between image and word: "The imaginary order is connected with the image, the symbolic order with the word" (Mooij, 1975, 71).

12. The later Heidegger terminologically expresses the eccentric position of the individual when he replaces the concept *Existenz* from *Being and Time* with the term *Ek-sistenz*, which refers to the protrusion of the individual toward the light of Being (BW, 213).

13. The fundamental desire to be identical with the Other is persistently present in Achterberg's poetry. It sounds almost imploring (Achterberg, 1979, 126):

Yet, nonetheless, the word must exist which coincides with you.	En nochtans moet het woord bestaan dat met u samenvalt.

The tragic appreciation that the fulfilment of this desire would mean the abandonment of one's own symbolically marked identity, and for this reason that it is a fundamentally unfulfillable desire, resonates equally in Achterberg's poetry (Achterberg, 1979, resp. 409, 150):

I can meet only words, never again you.	Ik kan alleen woorden ontmoeten, u niet meer.
That I am able to find a last name for the beloved so that I can blind the universe before I become nameless myself.	Dat ik bij machte ben te vinden een laatste naam voor de beminde, om dit heelal mee te verblinden voordat ik zelve naamloos word.
It is my only shortcoming.	Het is mijn enige tekort.

Heidegger specifies the transcendental orientatedness of There-being toward Being—he defines Being as "the transcendens pure and simple" (*das transcendens schlechthin*) (BT, 62), or, in Lacanian terms: the desire (toward the Other) as such—with the same term as Achterberg when he speaks of the necessity of learning "to exist in the nameless" (BW, 199).

14. This applies in any case to Lacan's (meta)theoretical position. Hereafter we shall see that the Lacanian practice must proceed from the possibility of a "redeeming word" because without this possibility therapy would lose its meaning.

15. The unfulfillable character of desire is for Lacan closely connected with the metonymic character that he ascribes to it: it consists of a constant *shifting* of the object of desire. In agreement with Nietzsche I wish to stress the metaphorical dimension of desire. Desire creates future possibilities and thereby makes possible the transcending of intraworldly being (cf. 1.5 and 6.8).

16. Heidegger uses the concept 'genealogy' in *Being and Time* in order to present an ontological analysis of the different possible modes of Being (BT, 31). In this connection, see also Nietzsche's application of the concept, discussed in note 30, chapter 1.

17. Kant, who shares Descartes starting point in this respect, expresses this subjectivism in the conceptualization of transcendental apperception, the "I

think," which, according to him, necessarily accompanies all of our representations (cf. CR, 153/KrV, B131 ff.).

18. In the previous two chapters we have seen how this turning toward subjectivity was achieved in the development of the central perspective and the tonal system. In this respect, also cf. my analysis of photography in De Mul, 1997a.

19. For this reason, Mooij correctly points out that, in the case of Kant, the adjective "Copernican" is somewhat misleading because Copernicus rejected the geo-and anthropocentrism of the Ptolemic worldview while Kant made human subjectivity the foundation of all philosophy (Mooij, 1975, 207). The ultimate question that absorbs transcendental philosophy is, after all, "What is Man?" (*Logic*, A25; cf. 0.2 above).

20. Although Heidegger is still very enthusiastic about Nietzsche in his 1936/1937 Nietzsche lectures (as we saw in sect. 1.9, in these lectures he even speaks of Nietzsche's twist out of Platonism (*Herausdrehung des Platonismus*)), his tone becomes increasingly critical in the following lectures. His primary accusation is that Nietzsche, with the doctrine of the Will to Power, remains locked in ontological nondifferentiation. It is perhaps true that Nietzsche appreciated the inexhaustibility of beings (something that, in agreement with Visser, I described in chapter 1 with the term 'ontic differentiation'), but, according to Heidegger, he did not continue through to the hidden depths of Being itself (cf. Visser, 1989, 209, 211). This ensures that Nietzsche, most especially in the doctrine of the Will to Power, ultimately remains completely indebted to the metaphysical tradition. I have already argued in chapter 1 that Heidegger's critique does not appear to me to be completely legitimate: he gives too great an emphasis to the doctrine of the Will to Power and also interprets the doctrine of the Eternal Recurrence, wherein Nietzsche most convincingly manifests himself on the boundaries of metaphysical thinking, completely in terms of Power (cf. notes 14 and 37, chapter 1). Perhaps Heidegger is correct when he maintains that Nietzsche, *within* the perspective of the doctrine of the Will to Power, shows a strongly anthropocentric tendency to consider art, just like Plato, in terms of *human production*, but I am of the opinion that Nietzsche's struggle—set out in chapter 1—to free things from subordination to the human goal and to bring humans into neighborliness with things reveals a nonmetaphysical line of thought that is closely related to Heidegger's view that humanity should be the shepherd of the Being of beings (BW, 210). In chapter 6 I shall examine this relatedness of theirs in more depth. A possible answer to the above-mentioned accusation of a lack of "depth" is Nietzsche's hymn to "superficiality from depth," which will emerge in section 6.6. In section 4.9, from the perspective of Nietzsche's metaphorical philosophy, I shall make a number of critical marginal notes concerning Heidegger's thinking.

21. "All of nature," according to Kant, "is actually nothing other than the connection of phenomena according to rules" (*Logic*, A1). The totality of nature is thereby predestined to manipulable objectivity (whereby, at the philosophical level, the contemporary ecological crisis is actually prepared in advance). Heidegger regularly associates himself in his work with the concept of nature held by the Romantics, a concept that, according to him, is not oppressed by this

subjectivization. In this Romantic concept of nature, the concern is the nature that "webt und strebt," which surprises us and holds us captive as landscape (BT, 94, 100). According to Heidegger, this Romantic concept of nature is concerned with nature in an authentic sense (WG, 155). In his later philosophy, Heidegger, specifying the term with Heraclitus' word *physis*, appears more and more to identify Being with this nature in its original sense. Already in the *Introduction to Metaphysics*, published in 1935, he wrote: "Die Physis ist das Sein selbst" (EM, 1).

22. We may view the *Kehre* as a radicalization of Heidegger's phenomenological starting point to address the thing itself—and, for Heidegger, this is preeminently Being itself (cf. BT, 58; and P, xvi; in connection with this theme, see 6.8 below, and De Mul, 1997d).

23. In *Kant and the Problem of Metaphysics*, published in 1929, Heidegger already speaks of a *Wiederholung* wherein the text that is to be interpreted is not simply repeated but "revealed in its original, long-hidden possibilities" (KM, 195). After the *Kehre* the notion of *Wiederholung* remains important although it loses the connotation of a *foundation* in an original ground that it still had in *Kant and the Problem of Metaphysics* (cf. what has already been remarked concerning the term *Verwindung* in 3.8, 2.9, and 0.6; also see Vattimo, 1988, 172 ff.).

24. Cf. Schelling's view, discussed in 0.1 above, concerning the inexhaustibility which is characteristic of interpretations of a work of art.

25. Among the French structuralists, Foucault appears on this point more closely related to Heidegger. Although, in *The Order of Things* (1966), Foucault considers psychoanalysis, because of its emphasis on the autonomy of language, as a contra-science that introduces the postmodern episteme (Foucault, 1974, 373 ff.), in his later genealogical writings he increasingly conceives of it as a therapeutic "technique" in the service of the "disciplining" of the modern subject (cf. Foucault, 1977 and 1984).

26. On this basis one could argue that the religious dimension in Achterberg's work does not necessarily have to be specified by reference to his biography, but rather flows from a particular 'magical' view on poetic language. Or, as Achterberg expressed it in the first stanza of the poem *Code* (Achterberg, 1979, 604):

The life-force which thee once possessed	De levenskracht die gij eenmaal bezat
is now divided amongst the abc	verdeelt zich nu over het abc.
I constitute key-words with it	Ik combineer er sleutelwoorden mee
and open the most difficult lock to	en open naar uw dood het zware slot.
thy death.	
It is, in the verse, the configuration: God,	Het is, in 't vers, de figuratie: God,
found in the letters g, o, d,	te vinden in de letters g, o, d,
in this sequence, but not by definition,	in deze volgorde, maar niet per se,
other configurations can also do this.	ook andere formaties kunnen dat.

27. An exception should perhaps be made for *Contributions to Philosophy (About Event)* written in the 1930s but only published in 1989. The 'Sils Maria

style' of this book betrays the influence of Nietzsche, whose work he had intensively studied in that period.

28. According to his summons to people to learn "to exist in the nameless" (BW, 199), Heidegger is aware of the precarious character of his struggle. He permits himself to be tempted into making the comment that *authentic* speech is actually located in remaining silent. Cf. what we remarked in section 4.3 of this chapter regarding the speechlessness of the poet in regard to Being.

29. Cf. the notorious *Spiegel* interview published after Heidegger's death (in Neske and Kettering, 1988).

5 DISAVOWAL AND REPRESENTATION

1. *La trahison des images* is also referred to by Magritte as *L'usage de la parole.*

2. Those texts of Freud to which I refer here are "Fetishism" (SE, 21:147–57), "An Outline of Psychoanalysis" (SE, 23:139–207), and "Splitting of the Ego in the Process of Defense" (SE, 23:271–78). Those works of Mannoni that are especially important are "Yes I know, but still . . . " and "The Comic Illusion or the Theatre Seen from the Perspective of the Imaginary," both published in Mannoni, 1969.

3. The word 'mimetic' is taken here in its broadest meaning as the representation of material and immaterial things. In this sense, a part of abstract art (Mondrian and Kandinsky, for example) also exhibits a mimetic character to the extent that it refers to some kind of reality outside the painted surface.

4. The interpretation nonetheless remains incomplete and imperfect. Imperfect because the context from within which the interpretation occurs constantly remains in movement (cf. 1.1), incomplete because aesthetic ideas that are representations of the power of imagination give much food for thought without being able to be fully expressed and capable of providing insights by our concepts (Kant, KU, 193; cf. section 0.7).

5. The term 'shock' might appear too emotionally laden in relation to the observation of a painting. However, I use it with the special meaning with which Kaulingfreks accredited it in his book about Magritte: "That which is unexpected about the shock is its quality as a Trojan Horse within the fortress of intellect. The intellect becomes unsettled but recovers and adjusts itself to the disturbance. Thereby, it forgets that the violence of the shift and the events, from their existing character, are gradually and repeatedly set into an hierarchy. . . . However, the shock as a means of consciousness requires the intellect in order that it remains both unknown and new. It is only shocking in relation to a situation wherein it does not fit, and can only be shocking if there is a rational hierarchy" (Kaulingfreks, 1984, 133–34).

6. Cf. the following comment from Magritte: "It isn't about amazing someone, but rather about the fact, for example, that one is amazed by one's amazement" (Magritte, 1979, 435).

7. Here, the word 'representative' is conceived in a double meaning: not only is the mechanism of visual representation deconstructed from within, but, in addition, it thereby simultaneously loses its exemplary character within the

aesthetic domain. Concerning the relationship of these different connotations of the term 'representation', see Derrida, 1982b.

8. The subversive character of this assault on representation is even more shocking because in *La trahison des images* "commonsense is raped in broad daylight" (Thrall-Soby, 1965, 15). Magritte's preference carrying out his subversive activities in "broad daylight" distinguishes him from the French surrealists, who demonstrated a preference for the night and the occult. In this connection it speaks volumes that Magritte gave the title *Le surrealisme en plein soleil* to the manifestos he published in 1946. Cf. how this imagery of light and darkness also appears in Mannoni when he speaks of denial.

9. See for a critical evaluation of this poststructuralist credo: J. de Mul, 2000, chapter 8.

10. Because structuralist linguistics directs itself at the linguistic system (*langue*) and abstracts from concrete speech (*parole*), De Saussure can, on methodological grounds, leave the referential function of language out of consideration. Among the poststructuralists, the referential function of language as such appears sometimes to be called into question. This is combined with the ambiguity of the term *signifié:* on the one hand, this term refers to a (mental) concept; on the other hand, it can also refer to the signified object to which the sign as a totality (sound + concept) refers.

11. In the first place I am thinking here of the in every way bizarre *Gender and Character* by Otto Weininger (1980; first published in 1903). But with Nietzsche, too, sexual metaphors play a constant role (cf., for example, BGE, 31, 11; and the occasionally dizzying commentary that Derrida [1978] wrote on this work). Derrida, incidentally, points to the fact that in Heidegger's painstaking interpretation of Nietzsche's "Wie die Wahre Welt endlich zur Fabel wurde" the passages dealing with the feminine character of the Christian metaphysics belong to the few to which he does not address himself. In his Nietzschean-inspired deconstruction of Heidegger's *Verwindung*, Derrida makes this unconsidered metaphor one of his entry points (cf. 4.9).

12. One could refer to this schizophrenic discourse as the postmodern variant of passive nihilism. In my opinion, it is preeminently expressed in the writings of Baudrillard (cf. 0.3). At a theoretical level *irony* receives here the complete dominance over what, in this context, I would like to call "the *enthusiasm* of the signified." The American psychiatrist-philosopher Louis Sass has made an interesting attempt to show schizophrenia, from within Heidegger's *Being and Time*, as a radicalized "theoretical" assessment of Being whereby everything (including persons) can be conceived as merely manipulable, immediately available objects. One way of summarizing Sass's argument is to say that the schizophrenic suffers from an extremely deficient mode of understanding Being. Baudrillard's thesis of the obscene transparency of objects appears to me to be an affirmation of that which is criticized by Heidegger: the technical challenging of nature (QT, 296; cf. 4.9).

13. This is what Friedrich Schlegel presents as a "cyclical progression." We return to the place from whence we came, but we now see this place from an ironic distance.

14. Cf. 1.4 and 1.7. Owens, in an article concerning the relation between feminism and postmodernism, comes to the same conclusion when he maintains that: "postmodernists instead expose the tyranny of the *signifier*, the violence of its law" (Owens, 1983, 59). Given the phallocentric character of Lacan's theory, it is not surprising that this critique is primarily expressed by feminist theorists.

15. There is a remarkable parallel here with the tactics that a feminist such as Irigaray uses against Lacan phallocentricism. She, too, in Derrida's line, maintains that every critique absorbs the postulates of what is criticized: "If it was only her intention to inverse the order of things—if, indeed, that were possible—then ultimately history would arrive at the same point: phallocentricism. Neither her gender, nor her imaginary desires, nor her language would therein (re-)find her place" (Irigaray, 1977, 32). A similar tactic would result in "a new dungeon, a new monastery which she would build for herself." The alternative is to sabotage the phallic order from within, comparable with the manner whereby Magritte permits the order of representation to stumble.

16. The connection that, following Kaulingfreks, I make here between Magritte's view of the mystery and Heidegger's hermeneutic is also discernible in Magritte's texts. Kaulingfreks points to the fact that Magritte knew Heidegger's work and corresponded with Heidegger experts such as De Waelhens (Kaulingfreks, 1984, 47, note 26).

6   THE OLDEST NOBILITY IN THE WORLD

1. Levano interprets *Das Fragment an sich* as a humorous answer to the remark, made by his friend and fellow student Erwin Rohde, that all his compositions fragment into many pieces (Levano, 1986, 125).

2. This use of language reminds one of Piaget's structuralism, which was dealt with in chapter 2. In "The Photographic Message" (1961), Barthes explicitly appealed to Piaget when he maintained that there is "no perception without immediate categorization" (Barthes, 1984a, 48).

3. In this respect Barthes points to the structuring character of the surrealistic *écriture*, which forms perhaps "the first experience of structural literature"(Barthes, 1977, 214; concerning the surrealist collage/montage, see 2. 4–5 above).

4. Cf. section 4.1, wherein Lacan's thesis that the unconscious is structured as a language was discussed in some detail.

5. Cf. the remark in the preceding section concerning the changing of meaning by the substitution of one letter in a word. The difference in meaning of the words 'book' and 'boot' rests upon the (external) difference between the signifiers k and t.

6. Notice that De Saussure does not include the referential aspect of language, i.e., the reference to a nonlingual reality, in his definition of signs (cf. note 10, chapter 5). This arises from his methodological attempt to exclude

everything which is nonlingual from linguistics. Because my interest is not primarily linguistic, I shall examine this referential aspect in what follows.

7. For a more extensive explication of the processes of denotation and connotation, see the analysis of Barthes' writings on photography in De Mul, 1997a.

8. According to Barthes, at least at the time of his first semiology, the denotation never completely gets absorbed in the connotation, given that in such an instance there could be no question of an utterance.

9. A similar indexical view of music appears to have been at the foundation of Schopenhauer's and Nietzsche's (early) musical aesthetics (cf. 1.5 and 3.2 above). They not only conceive of music as an expression of the (transsubjective) World Will, but, in addition, they also, in comparison with other artistic forms of representation, put the emphasis on the immediacy of musical language. This immediacy is characteristic of the indexical sign. The index stands in an uncoded causal relation with its referent. In *La chambre claire* Barthes also explained the urgent working of photography by the fact that here, too, we are confronted with an indexical sign (see De Mul, 1997a). The difference between photography and music could lie in the fact that photography causally borders material phenomena while music borders the immaterial. However, for Schopenhauer and Nietzsche, given that they simultaneously attribute a symbolic function to music, it is not considered as a purely indexical sign (cf. Nietzsche, KSA, 1: 571).

10. Langer correctly points to the fact that music is not a direct form of self-expression, but rather a re-presentation of emotions. A particular piece of music that represents sadness does not necessarily elicit sadness in us (in such a case we are more like to speak of a "false sentimentality"), but rather it articulates that feeling by musical means (Langer, 1976, 222).

11. Incidentally, not all structuralists share this view of Barthes. In his introduction to *The Raw and the Cooked* Lévi-Strauss maintains that verbal language and music are sign-systems that are radically contrary to each other, that do not permit themselves to be translated into each other (Lévi-Strauss, 1975, 27). While, in a number of studies, he examined the myth from a linguistic perspective, in *The Raw and the Cooked* he analyzes it from the perspective of the musical system of signs.

12. Foucault distinguishes four epistemes: the Renaissance (1400–1600), the classical episteme (ca. 1600–1800), the modern episteme of man (ca. 1800–1950), and a postmodern episteme (not, incidentally, presented by him under this title) of which he considered structuralist thought to form a first expression.

13. To the extent that Foucault's archaeology is related to structuralism, one could argue that, in this sense, he is more a premodern than an anti- or postmodernist thinker. In any event, he distinguishes himself from other (post)structuralist thinkers by clinging to the classical representational model of the sign in his archaeology (cf. Frank, 1984, 159 ff.)

14. For this reason, according to Foucault, we must not let ourselves be misled by the apparent place that man occupies in rationalism and humanism: "Renaissance" 'humanism' and Classical 'rationalism' were indeed able to allot

human beings a privileged position in the order of the world, but they were not able to conceive of man" (Foucault, 1974, 318).

15. According to Lévi-Strauss, these two perspectives are not necessarily mutually exclusive. He finds that we can support the conventionalism of structuralism without abandoning the idea that each of the different arbitrary systems of signs is based upon particular physical and physiological characteristics (Lévi-Strauss, 1975, 21).

16. In twentieth-century structuralism this notion is further developed by Lévi-Strauss, who speaks of a universal structure that finds expression in a variety of cultural phenomena such as relations of consanguinity, linguistic systems, economic systems, and myths.

17. At the philosophical level this transition from the classical to the modern episteme can be easily read from Kant's aesthetics of music. On the one hand, with his view of "free beauty" (whereby an object is judged purely on the basis of its form, without thereby using concepts), Kant associates himself with the formalism of the classical aesthetics of music, although, because of his Copernican turn, the harmony experienced in form no longer concerns the cosmos, but rather the *human* ability to know (cf. CJ, 75, 198–99/KU, B48, B212). On the other hand, however, he maintains that music is insufficiently able to express aesthetic ideas. As an art form that merely elicits emotions, Kant, in his classification of art forms, situates it in the lowest place (see Neubauer, 182 ff.).

18. Cf. Heidegger's analysis of the subjectum in *"The Age of the World View,"* which was examined in 4.4 above. An important difference is that Heidegger considered Descartes as the founder of the modern worldview while Foucault sets the beginning of modern episteme with Kant. In Foucault's view, Descartes is a typical representative of the classical episteme that preceded the modern version.

19. These various points appear to be supportive for the thesis that Nietzsche's concept of the Great Style is a part of the process of subjectivation that is characteristic of Western metaphysics (cf. note 12, chapter 1, and note 20, chapter 4).

20. In section 3.7, we saw that Adorno condemned jazz because it would only mean a pseudoliberation from the servitude of the subject that is characteristic of modern society.

21. We encountered, in a paradigmatic manner, both characteristics of this structuralist approach—the emphasis on language and the decentering of the subject—in chapter 4 when we examined Lacan's theory, wherein it is maintained that the symbolic order precedes the human subject, which is first constituted by the insertion of the future subject in the symbolic order of language.

22. Foucault himself, in his archaeological period, also appears not to have succeeded in completely freeing himself from the modern episteme. This is primarily apparent from his Kantian conceptual framework (cf. Foucault, 1974, 340 ff.). For Foucault, in his analysis of the episteme, the issue is one of exposing the conditions of possibility, whereby the competence is ascribed to the archaeologist of gaining insight into unthought epistemic structures. In this sense it can be said that archaeology is characterized by at least two of the "doublures" that

Foucault attributes to the modern episteme: the transcendental-empirical and that of the cogito and the unthought (cf. Dreyfuss and Rabinow, 1983, 92–93).

23. In this regard, Barthes attributes an important role to surrealism, too, although his judgment of this movement has a critical undercurrent: "Surrealism, though unable to accord language a supreme place (language being system and the aim of the movement being, romantically, a direct subversion of codes—itself moreover illusory: a code cannot be destroyed, only 'played off'), contributes to the desacralization of the image of the Author by ceaselessly recommending the abrupt disappointment of expectations of meaning (the famous surrealistic 'jolt'), by entrusting the hand with the task of writing as quickly as possible what the head itself is unaware of (automatic writing), accepting the principle and the experience of several people writing together" (Barthes, 1984a, 144; cf. 2.4 and 1.1).

24. Ulmer maintains that, under the influence of this development in literature, a similar development in art criticism has developed. *Postcriticism* breaks with the "realistic criticism" which, assuming a model of correspondence with reality, aims at reproducing the literary work in a critical manner (Ulmer, 1983, 86). Postcriticism, which originates by applying artistic procedures to an existing text, produces new writings that are not essentially differentiable from the literary texts. Barthes refers to these simulacra as *anamorphoses* of the object of interpretation.

25. A parallel development occurs with Foucault when, in his genealogical period and under the influence of Nietzsche, he underlines the productivity of power and thereby gives special attention to the lust that is connected with the exercise of power.

26. Apart from functioning mythically, incidentally, this connotative system, in the case of musical quotations or parodies of style, can also function metalinguistically (cf. De Meyer, 1982, 10). In many postmodern compositions this metalinguistic function even eclipses the mythical. The result is equally comparable: in this case, too, the denotation is constantly postponed.

27. Here, moreover, we must take into account that the tonal music about which we speak was primarily a *musica practica*. In this respect, Barthes comments: "The music which one plays arises from an activity which is only fractionally auditory, and, in addition, it is manual (and therefore, in particular sense, more sensual), it is the music which you and I play, alone or with friends, with no other audience than the participants (that is, that the risk of the theater, of the struggle with hysteria, is avoided); a muscular music whereby the share of hearing is only one of ratification, as if the body hears and not 'the soul'; a music which is not played by the heart, sitting in front of the piano or standing behind the music stand, the body controls, directs, and coordinates, it must transcribe what it reads, makes the sound and the meaning, the body which registers and is not merely the translator or pure receiver" (Barthes, 1977, 149).

28. In his texts on photography Barthes at crucial points maintains the subject-object model that is characteristic of modern metaphysics. Because, on the other hand, he rejects the underlying assumptions of this metaphysics, his

last text ends in the tragic conclusion that what he has constantly attempted to achieve was actually "an *impossible* science" (see De Mul, 1997a).

29. The composer's interest in chance, incidentally, is not new. In the eighteenth century there were already experiments with chance carried out (see Griffith, 1980, 157). This appears to indicate that Cage finds himself here in a particular tradition. However, Cage's intention is completely different than that of the eighteenth-century composers. Where these eighteenth-century composers, already playing at dice, affirmed the dominance of the dominant episteme (represented in music by the tonal system), Cage, with his aleatory "compositions," as we shall shortly see, is ultimately aiming at a radical *undermining* of the musical episteme of the modern period: that of the composing subject (regardless as to whether he is conceived as composer or—as in the case of Barthes' second semiology—as listener).

30. Traditionally, the consultation of the *I Ching* leads to the formation of a particular pattern of the sixty-four possible basis-hexagrams which are then interpreted as advice for correct behavior. The dissection of reality into sixty-four basal elements and the articulation of the combinations by the oracle makes one think of the structuralist activity such as it was defined by Barthes above (cf. 6.1). The most important difference is that in the case of the *I Ching* the articulation of the combinations is ascribed to chance rather than the human subject. Cf. also Cage's description of his applications of the *I Ching* during the composition of the *Music of Changes* (S, 57 ff.).

31. A didactic problem that is linked to this poing is that in the performance of aleatory work the aleatory effects are often not audible. They are only observed if we know about the application of operations of chance. One of the strategies followed by aleatory composers to make the listener aware of these consists of carrying out more than one performance of a work during the same concert. However, the recording of the performance leads to a fixed product. Occasionally, one attempts to prevent this by giving the instruction to alter *at random* the volume, the balance, and the tone-control during the playback. To prevent the specified fixation the repetitive composers whom I discussed in an earlier chapter choose precisely for a method that is so patterned that "false perceptions," the so-called resulting patterns, are the inevitable consequence (cf. 3.5).

32. This also applies to the later works of Boulez and Stockhausen, such as Boulez's *Third Piano Sonate* (1957) and Stockhausen's *Klavierstück XI*, wherein operations of chance are applied (cf. Griffith, 1980, 157, and Mertens, 1980, 128). With Boulez and Stockhausen, given that serial composition no longer possessed a dynamic because of the abandonment of the internal teleology, chance was used as a dynamic principle. In other words, chance is here in the service of work's external organization.

33. It is interesting that here, too, Cage has often used aleatory techniques to deconstruct his discursive arguments, something that has not infrequently provided an extremely fragmentary result. He has also used these techniques to "treat" literary works such as Joyce's *Finnegan's Wake*. He appears in this fashion to realize the postcritique for which Ulmer argues (cf. note 24, above).

34. "This means that de-construction is a never-ending task without a goal (telos). The 'goal' or teleology itself is subsumed under de-construction" (IJsseling, 1968, 127). The dissection of the ambiguous French word 'fin' (end, goal) provides this double meaning.

35. In his preface to the German translation of the *I Ching* Jung remarked that Chinese philosophy—in contrast to the Western, physical scientific approach that is primarily directed at regularity—places the emphasis on chance: "The moment which momentarily is being observed is, according to the old Chinese standpoint, more of a coincidental constellation than a sharply delimited result of a casually linked chain of events. Interest appears to be directed at the configuration which is formed at the moment of observing the coincidental events and not at the hypothetical origins which apparently explain their conjunction"(Jung, n.d., xviii). "We must admit," maintains Jung, "that there is something to say for the enormous significance of chance. An incalculable amount of human energy is directed at combating and restricting the disadvantage of the danger which chance represents. But theoretical approaches concerning cause and effect frequently appear pale and musty in comparison with the practical result of chance" (Jung, n.d., xvii).

36. In a strict sense it is for this reason senseless to speak of chance, given that this word only has meaning in relation to its opposite: purposes. "Once you know that there are no purposes, you also know that there is no accident (*Zufall*); for it is only beside a world of purposes that the word 'accident' has meaning" (GS, 168). Where Nietzsche—and, after him, Heidegger—uses the concept of chance it undergoes in other words a *Verwindung:* it points in this case to the 'contingent necessity' of the world.

37. The image of the spider's web connects with the earlier quoted passage from *Daybreak*. After Nietzsche has spoken about our fear of the powerful world of the cosmic stupidity of chance, he postulates that despite the "anxiety-inducing poetry" of this neighborliness we would not want to miss it because "for these monsters often arrive when our life, involved as it is in the spider's web of purposes, has become too tedious or too filled with anxiety, and provide us with a sublime diversion by for once *breaking* the web—not that these irrational creatures would do so intentionally! Or even notice they had done so! But their coarse bony hands tear through our net as if it were air"(D, 80).

38. At the time of his activist, National-Socialist engagement, incidentally, we encounter a strongly contradictory evaluation of chance. In the *Rektoratsrede* (1933), Heidegger refers to the following quotation from Von Clausewitz: "I speak out against the frivolous hope in salvation through the hand of chance" (R, 18).

39. Because the issue of Being in *Being and Time* was still primarily approached from the analytic of There-being (*Dasein*), Being was then not considered as yet being sufficiently able to "show itself from itself" (BT, 58). It is characteristic for the approach in *Being and Time*, for example, that the concealed quality of Being is still completely understood in terms of the forgottenness-of-being of There-being's collapse into the beings of internality (cf. BT, 219 ff). In contrast to this, in the writings after the *Kehre* the concealed quality was local-

ized in "die Sache selbst" and understood as a *self*-concealing of Being. Thus, there is no longer an issue of forgottenness-of-being, but rather of an abandonment of Being. To consider this, a radicalization is demanded of the intentionality of Being which is already assumed in *Being and Time* (cf. IJsseling, 1964, 39). Being is then no longer understood as a dimension that is available to There-being when it chooses, but rather as a happening that, in a certain sense, has man at its disposal.

40. By virtue of the undermining of the subjective intentionality of Cage's aleatory compositions, the indexical determination of music, the value of which was called into question in section 6.2 because of the nonintentional character of the index, gains in significance. Cf. note 9, above.

41. We could utilize the following quotation from Heidegger to refer to total serialism's efforts to control the total sound-picture, something that, as we remarked in the foregoing, nonetheless resulted in an unpredictable sound-result: "However, as soon as the gigantic of planning, calculating, organization, and certainty transforms from the quantative into its own quality, then the gigantic and what apparently always and everywhere must be accounted to the calculating must, precisely for this reason, become the incalculable. This remains the invisible shadow which is everywhere cast over all things if man becomes the subjectum and the world becomes an image" (ZW, 95; cf. 4.4).

42. In this sense, Foucault is an heir of Nietzsche and Heidegger: "Maybe the target nowadays is not to discover what we are, but to refuse what we are. We have to imagine and to build up what we could be to get rid of this kind of political "double bind," which is simultaneous individualization and totalization of modern power structures. The conclusion would be that the political, ethical, social, philosophical [we could add: aesthetic—JdM] problem of our day is not to try to liberate the individual from the state, and from the state's institutions, but to liberate us both from the state and from the type of individualization which is linked to the state. We have to promote new forms of subjectivity by the refusal of this kind of individuality which has been imposed upon us for several centuries (Foucault, 1982, 216).

43. Cage's reaction to Glenn Branca's repetitive music, which caused an enormous uproar during the New Music America Festival in Chicago (1982), is typical of his aversion to the totalitarian. It wasn't so much the ear-blasting volume of this *Wagner Punk,* of which even die-hards from the heavy metal scene would be jealous, which disturbed Cage, as the complete ecstatic surrender of the musicians. In an interview with Mertens he commented about this:

> Yesterday evening I could not in any manner enjoy the Branca-piece. Not because it was so loud—in that respect I can bear rather a lot—but rather because in my opinion it had exceptionally negative political implications. I wouldn't want to live in such a society, a society where one asks other people to do things together in such an intensive manner. It was in no sense an enjoyable experience. Now that I think about it, I'm a bit more open towards it. Not that I would want to embrace it, but I also wouldn't want to prohibit it. . . . Branca is an example of a

person who completely determines what others should do. . . . Not a shepherd watching over his flock, but a leader who demands that everyone agrees with him. No question of any sort of freedom. The only soft, fresh wind occurred when the technique failed—the amplifier exploded. That was the only moment when the music was freed from Branca's intention. (in De Meyer, 1982, 26–7)

AFTERWORD

1. The resulting book was published in Dutch in 1993. An English translation will appear under the title *The Tragedy of Finitude: Dilthey's Hermeneutics of Life* in the Yale Studies in Hermeneutics series (De Mul 2000). See also De Mul 1991 and 1996b.

2. According to Foucault, this preoccupation with the present is a typical modern phenomenon. In his view Kant's pamphlet "What Is Enlightenment?" is one of the first examples of this ontology of the present (Foucault, 1984b).

3. Some interesting interpretations of this relationship can be found in Ulmer (1991), Landow (1992), Woolley (1992), Heim (1993), Mitchell (1994), Turkle (1995), and Poster (1995). See also De Mul (2000, 1997a, and 1997e).

4. It is against this background that we should understand the ethical dimension in (especially the later) writings of postmodern philosophers such as Derrida and Lyotard. Their postmodern playfulness does not prevent them from taking the moral implications of their plays very seriously.

5. A still earlier conception of hypertext can be found in Vannevar Bush's 1945 article "As We May Think." However, his memex machine still was based on the mechanical manipulation of microfilms instead of computer technology.

6. Cf. George Landow's *Hypertext: The Convergence of Contemporary Critical Theory and Technology*: "When designers of computer software examine the pages of *Glas* or *Of Grammatology*, they encounter a digitalized, hypertextual Derrida; and when literary theorists examine *Literary Machines*, they encounter a deconstructionist or poststructuralist Nelson. These shocks of recognition can occur because over the past several decades literary theory and computer hypertext, apparently unconnected areas of inquiry, have increasingly converged" (Landow, 1992, 2; cf. Poster, 1995).

7. A nice example is Virtual Reality Lascaux, a simulation of the famous prehistoric cave in France, developed by the Center for the Electronic Reconstruction of Historical and Archeological Sites and presented at the Biennale of Seoul in 1995. This virtual reality system not only enables the user to wander through an exact copy of the original cave, but he also can click on the prehistoric paintings and tools in order to learn more about them and there is even the possibility of a confrontation with a simulated caveman. VR-systems like these realize the old dream of traveling through time, though in a different way than many science fiction novelists imagined. After all, in VR we do not really return to the past, but we are immersed in a (re)construction of it that remains—like the historical novel—a fusion of past and present horizons.

8. Perhaps it is an exaggeration to call it, as Roger Penrose has done in his review of the book, the most dangerous book since Hitler's *Mein Kampf*, but it requires not so much imagination to think that it could result in morbid policies.

9. There is an exception. In *The Inhuman: Reflections on Time* Lyotard considers the possibility of the extinction of man in the context of the development of information technology. However, unlike Moravec, Lyotard does not understand this possibility as a challenge, but as a threat (Lyotard, 1991).

Bibliography

Achterberg, G. (1979). *Verzamelde Gedichten* [Selected Poems]. Amsterdam: Querido.

Ades, D. (1974). *Dada and Surrealism.* London: Thames and Hudson.

Adorno, Th. W. (1955). *Prismen. Kulturkritik und Gesellschaft* [Prisms: Critique of Culture and Society]. Frankfurt am Main: Suhrkamp.

———. (1958). *Philosophie der neuen Musik* [Philosophy of New Music]. Frankfurt am Main: Europäische Verlagsanstalt.

———. (1970). Ästhetische Theorie [Aesthetic Theory]. In *Gesammelte Schriften* [Collected Works], vol. 7. Frankfurt am Main: Suhrkamp.

———. (1982). Über Jazz [On Jazz]. In *Gesammelte Schriften* [Collected Works], vol. 17, 74–108. Frankfurt am Main: Suhrkamp.

———. (1984). Musikalische Schriften V [Musical Writings V]. In *Gesammelte Schriften* [Collected Works], vol. 18. Frankfurt am Main: Suhrkamp.

Aler, J. M. M. (1970a). Inleiding en commentaar [Introduction and Commentary]. In M. Heidegger, *Wat is metafysica?* [What Is Metaphysics?]. Tiel/Bussum, The Netherlands: Lannoo.

———. (1970b). Krise der Kunst—Kunst der Krise [Crisis of Art—Art of Crisis]. In *Schopenhauer-Jahrbuch:* 50–73. Frankfurt am Main: Waldemar Kramer.

Allison, D. (ed.). (1977). *The New Nietzsche: Contempory Styles of Interpretation.* New York: Dell.

Alquié, F. (1969). *The Philosophy of Surrealism.* Ann Arbor: The University of Michigan Press.

Aristotle. (1984). *The Complete Works of Aristotle.* The Revised Oxford Translation. Ed. Jonathan Barnes. Princeton: Princeton University Press.

Barbrook, R. en A. Cameron. (1995). The Californian Ideology, Http://www.wmin.ac.uk/media/HRC/ci/calif5.html.

Barglow, R. (1994). *The Crisis of the Self in the Age of Information: Computers, Dolphins and Dreams.* London/New York: Routledge.

Barthes, R. (1975). *Roland Barthes par Roland Barthes* [Roland Barthes by Roland Barthes]. Paris: Seuil.

———. (1977). *Critical Essays.* Evanston, Ill.: Northwestern University Press (Originally published as *Essais critiques,* 1964).

————. (1979). *A Lover's Discourse: Fragments*. London: Jonathan Cape (Originally published as *Fragments d'un discours amoureux*, 1977).

————. (1984a). *Image/Music/Text*, 149–54. London: Flamingo.

————. (1984b). *Writing Degree Zero & Elements of Semiology*. Suffolk, U.K.: Edmundsbury Press (Originally published as *Le degré zéro de l'écriture*, 1953, and *Élements de sémiologie*, 1964).

Baum, G. (1984). Schopenhauer und die Musik der Goethezeit [Schopenhauer and Music of the Goethe Era]. In Schirmacher, 1984: 170–74.

Beeren, W. (1988). *Frank Stella. Catalogus Stedelijk Museum no. 719* [Frank Stella: Catalogue of the Municipal Museum]. Amsterdam: Stedelijk Museum.

Behler, E. (1978). Nietzsche und die frühromantische Schule [Nietzsche and the Early Romantic Movement]. In *Nietzsche-Studien* 7: 59–96.

Behler, E. and J. Hörisch (eds.). (1987). *Die Aktualität der Frühromantik* [Actuality of Early Romanticism]. Paderborn, Germany: Ferdinand Schöningh.

Beierwaltes, W. (1982). Einleitung [Introduction]. In F. W. J. Schelling, *Texte zur Philosophie der Kunst* [Texts on Philosophy of Art], 3–49. Stuttgart: Reclam.

Bell, C. (1914). *Art*. London: Chatto & Windus.

Benjamin, W. (1973). *Der Begriff der Kunstkritik in der deutschen Romantik* (1920) [The Concept of Art Criticism in German Romanticism]. Frankfurt am Main: Suhrkamp.

————. (1974). Das Kunstwerk im Zeitalter seiner technischen Reproduzierbarkeit [The Work of Art in the Era of Its Technical Reproductibility]. In *Gesammelte Schriften* [Collected Writings], vol. 1–2, 471–508. Frankfurt am Main: Suhrkamp.

————. (1977). Der Sürrealismus. Die letzte Momentaufnahme der europäischen Intelligenz [Surrealism: Last Snapshot of European Intelligence]. In *Gesammelte Schriften* [Collected Writings], vol. 2–7, 295–310. Frankfurt am Main: Suhrkamp.

Berger, J. (1969). *The Moment of Cubism*. London: Weidenfeld and Nicolson.

Berman, R. A. (1987). Konsumgesellschaft. Das Erbe der Avantgarde und die falsche Aufhebung der ästhetischen Autonomie [Consumer Society: The Heritage of the Avant-garde and the False Overcoming of Aesthetic Autonomy]. In Bürger and Bürger, 1987, 56–71.

Bernstein, R. J. (1983). *Beyond Objectivism and Relativism: Science, Hermeneutics and Praxis*. Oxford: Basil Blackwell.

Biemel, W. (1959). *Die Bedeutung von Kants Begründung der Ästhetik für die Philosophie der Kunst* [The Meaning of Kant's Foundation of Aesthetics for Philosophy of Art]. Cologne: Kölner Universitäts-Verlag.

————. (1973). *Martin Heidegger in Selbstzeugnissen und Bilddokumenten* [Martin Heidegger in Self-Testimonies and Images]. Reinbek bei Hamburg: Rowohlt.

Black, M. (1978). Metaphor. In J. Margolis (ed.), *Philosophy Looks at the Arts: Contemporary Readings in Aesthetics*, 451–67. Philadelphia: Temple University Press.

Blondel, E. (1977). Nietzsche: Life as Metaphor. In D. B. Allison (ed.), *The New Nietzsche: Contemporary Styles of Interpretation*, 150–75. New York: Dell.

———. (1984). Nietzsches metaphorisches Denken [Nietzsche's Metaphorical Thinking]. In *Nietzsche Kontrovers* 4: 92–109.

Bönig, T. (1986). Metaphysik und Sprache beim frühen Nietzsche [Metaphysics and Language in Early Nietzsche]. In *Nietzsche Studien* 15: 72–106.

Boulez, P. (1975). *Par volonté et par hasard* [By Will and by Chance]. Paris: Éditions du Seuil.

Breton, A. (1977). *Manifestoes of Surrealism*. Ann Arbor: The University of Michigan Press.

———. (1978). *What Is Surrealism? Selected Writings*. London: Pluto Press.

Bröcker, W. (1963). *Das was kommt gesehen von Nietzsche und Hölderlin* [That Which Comes as Seen by Nietzsche and Hölderlin]. Pfullingen, Germany: Neske.

Broers, G. (1982). De Anti-Opera, of: Muziek en de grote stijl [Anti-Opera, or: Music and the Great Style]. M.A. thesis, University of Amsterdam.

Bürger, P. (1974). *Theorie der Avantgarde* [Theory of the Avant-garde]. Frankfurt am Main: Suhrkamp.

Bürger, C. and P. Bürger (eds.). (1987). *Postmoderne: Alltag, Allegorie und Avantgarde* [Postmodernity: Everyday Life, Allegory, and Avant-garde]. Frankfurt am Main: Suhrkamp.

Cage, J. (1968). *A Year from Monday*. London: Calder and Boyars.

———. (1973). *Silence: Lectures and Writings*. London: Calder and Boyars.

Carusso, P. (1974). Gespräch mit M. Foucault [Conversation with M. Foucault]. In W. Seiter (ed.), *Michel Foucault. Von der Subversion des Wissens* [Michel Foucault: On the Subversion of Knowledge], 7–31. Münich: Carl Hanser Verlag.

Coleridge, D. and S. (eds.). (1860). *The Poems of Samuel Taylor Coleridge*. Leipzig: Tauchnitz.

Colli, G., (1980). Die nachgelassenen Fragmenten von Herbst 1885 bis Herbst 1887 [Posthumous Fragments from Autumn 1885 till Autumn 1887]. In F. Nietzsche, *Kritische Studienausgabe*, vol. 13, 651–68. Berlin: Walter de Gruyter.

Cousineau, R. H. (1972). *Heidegger, Humanism and Ethics. An Introduction to the Letter on Humanism*. Leuven, Belguim: Editions Nauwelaerts.

Dahlhaus, C. (1988). *Klassische und romantische Musikästhetik* [Classic and Romantic Aesthetics of Music]. Laaber, Germany: Laaber-Verlag.

De Boer, Th. (1989). *Van Brentano tot Levinas. Studies over de fenomenologie* [From Brentano to Levinas: Studies in Phenomenology]. Meppel/ Amsterdam: Boom.

De Man, P. (1974). Nietzsche's Theory of Rhetoric. *Symposium: A Quarterly Journal in Modern Foreign Literatures*, 28:33–51.

De Meyer, G. (1982). Notities voor een communikatieve benadering van de muziek [Notes for a Communicative Approach of Music]. In

G. de Meyer (ed.), *Muziek en non-communicatie. Het geval van de minimale/repetitieve muziek* [Music and Non-Communication: The Case of Minimal/Repetitive Music]. Leuven, Belgium: Centrum voor Communicatiewetenschappen.

De Mul, J. (1985). Image without Origin: On Nietsche's Transcendental Metaphor. In P. J. McCormick (ed.), *The Reasons of Art/Art et ses raisons*, 272–84. Ottawa: University Press/Éditions de l'Université d'Ottawa.

———. (1987). Genetic Structuralism and Conceptual Relativism. In P. Weingartner and G. Schurz (eds.), *Reports on the 11th International Wittgenstein-Symposium*, 31–34. Vienna: Hölder-Pichler-Tempsky.

———. (1988). The Development of Aesthetic Judgement: Analysis of a Genetic-Structuralist Approach. *Journal of Aesthetic Education* 22.2: 55–71.

———. (1991). Dilthey's Narrative Model of Human Development: A Necessary Reconsideration of the Philosophical Hermeneutics of Heidegger and Gadamer. *Man and World*, 24: 409–26.

———. (1993a). Mark Manders in Conversation with Jos de Mul. In J. Brand, C. de Muynck, and Valerie Smith (eds.), *Sonsbeek '93*, 281–292. Gent, Belgium: Snoeck Ducaju & Zoon.

———. (1993b). Landschaft in sicht [Landscape in sight]. In F. -A. Hettig and Th. Meyers zu Slochteren (eds.), *Verwantschaften Düsseldorf/Rotterdam*, Catalogue Kunsthal Rotterdam, 12–35. Rotterdam: Rotterdamse Kunststichting.

———. (1995). Imagination without Strings: A Virtual Look in the Future of the Visual Arts. In Liubava Moreva and Igor Yevlampiev (eds.), *Paradigms of Philosophizing: Second International Conference on Philosophy and Culture*, 246–52. St. Petersburg, Russia: Eidos.

———. (1996a). Poet after the Death of God. In I. van der Cruysse and W. Shetter (eds.), *Contemporary Explorations in the Culture of the Low Countries*, vol. 9, 49–68. Lanham, Md.: University Press of America.

———. (1996b). Die Fortgang über Kant. Dilthey and the Transformation of Transcendental Philosophy. In *Dilthey-Jahrbuch für die Geisteswissenschaften*, vol. 10, 80–103.

———. (1997a). The Digitalization of the World View: The End of Photography and the Return of the Aura. In A. W. Balkema and H. Slager (eds.), *The Photographic Paradigm*, Lier en Boog: Series of Philosophy of Art and Art Theory, vol. 12, 44–56. Amsterdam/Atlanta: Rodopi.

———. (1997b). Aesthetic Development. In A. W. van Haaften, M. Korthals, and T. Wren (eds.), *Philosophy of Development: Reconstructing the Foundations of Human Development and Education*, 135–52. Dordrecht/Boston/London: Kluwer Academic Publishers.

———. (1997c). Artistic Development. In A. W. van Haaften, M. Korthals, and T. Wren (eds.), *Philosophy of Development: Reconstructing the Foundations of Human Development and Education*, 183–98. Dordrecht/Boston/London: Kluwer Academic Publishers.

———. (1997d). Structuralist and Hermeneutic Approaches to Development. In A. W. van Haaften, M. Korthals, and T. Wren (eds.), *Philosophy of Development: Reconstructing the Foundations of Human Development and Education*, 223–43. Dordrecht/Boston/London: Kluwer Academic Publishers.

———. (1997e). Networked Identities. In M. B. Roetto (ed.), *ISEA 96 Proceedings: Seventh International Symposium on Electronic Art*, 11–16. Rotterdam: ISEA96 Foundation.

———. (1999). The Informatization of the Worldview. *Information, Communication & Society* 2.1: 604–629.

———. (2000). *The Tragedy of Finitude: Dilthey's Hermeneutics of Life*. New Haven: Yale University Press (Originally published as *De tragedie van de eindigheid. Dilthey's hermeneutiek van het leven*, 1993).

De Mul, J. and M. Korthals. (1997). Postmodernism and the Reconstruction of Developmental Theory. In A. W. van Haaften, M. Korthals, and T. Wren (eds.), *Philosophy of Development: Reconstructing the Foundations of Human Development and Education*, 245–60. Dordrecht: Kluwer Academic Publishers.

De Vogel, C. (1967). *Theoria*. Assen, The Netherlands: Van Gorcum.

De Wilde, E., et al. (1982). *'60'80: Attitudes/Concepts/Images*. Amsterdam: Van Gennep.

Deleuze, G. (1983). *Nietzsche and Philosophy*. New York: Columbia University Press (Originally published as *Nietzsche et la philosophie*, 1962).

———. (1988). *Foucault*. Minneapolis: University of Minnesota Press (Originally published as *Foucault*, 1987).

———. (1994). *Difference and Repetition*. New York: Columbia University Press (Originally published as *Différence et répétition*, 1968).

Derrida, J. (1976). *Of Grammatology*. Baltimore: John Hopkins University Press (Originally published as *De la grammatologie*, 1968).

———. (1978). *Éperons. Les styles de Nietzsche*. Paris: Flammarion.

———. (1981). *Writing and Difference*. London: Routledge & Kegan Paul (Originally published as *Écriture et différence*, 1968).

———. (1982a). *Margins of Philosophy*. Chicago: University of Chicago Press (Originally published as *Marges de la philosophie*, 1972).

———. (1982b). Sending: On Representation. *Social Research* 49: 294–326.

Dijksterhuis, E. J. (1964). *The Mechanization of the World Picture*. Oxford: Clarendon Press.

Dilthey, W. (1914–1996). *Gesammelte Schriften* [Collected Writings]. Vols. 1–12: Stuttgart: B. G. Teubner and Göttingen: Vandenhoeck & Ruprecht. Vols. 13–21: Göttingen: Vandenhoeck & Ruprecht.

Dreyfuss, H. and P. Rabinow. (1983). *Michel Foucault: Beyond Structuralism and Hermeneutics*. Chicago: University of Chicago Press.

Drijkoningen, F. and J. Fontijn (eds). (1986). *Historische Avantgarde. Programmatische teksten van het Italiaans Futurisme, Dada, het Constructivisme, het*

Surrealisme en het Tsjechisch Poëtisme [Historical Avantgarde: Programmatic texts of Italian Futurism, Dada, Constructivism, Surrealism, and Czech Poetism]. Amsterdam: Huis aan de drie grachten.

Duintjer, O. D. (1988). *Rondom metafysica* [Around Metaphysics]. Meppel/Amsterdam: Boom.

Eco, U. (1983). *Postscript to The Name of the Rose*. San Diego: Harcourt Brace Jovanovich.

Ellenberger, H. F. (1970). *The Discovery of the Unconscious: The History and Evolution of Dynamic Psychiatry*. New York: Basic Books.

Féher, F. (1987). Der Pyrrhussieg der Kunst im Kampf um ihre Befreiung. Bemerkungen zum postmodernen Intermezzo [Phyrrhic Victory of Art in the Battle for Its Liberation: Notes on the Postmodern Intermezzo]. In Bürger and Bürger (eds.), *Postmoderne: Alltag, Allegorie und Avantgarde*, 13–33. Frankfurt am Main: Suhrkamp.

Fink, E. (1960). *Nietzsches Philosophie* [Nietzsche's Philosophy]. Stuttgart, Germany: Kohlhammer.

Finkielkraut, A. (1995). *The Defeat of the Mind*. New York: Columbia University Press (Originally published as *La défaite de la pensée*, 1987.

Foucault, M. (1964). La folie, l'absence de l'oeuvre [Madness, Absence of Oeuvre]. *La table ronde* 196: 11–21.

———. (1974). *The Order of Things*. London: Tavistock Publications (Originally published as *Les mots et les choses*, 1966).

———. (1977). *Discipline and Punish*. London: Allen Lane (Originally published as *Surveiller et punir*, 1975).

———. (1982). The Subject and Power. In H. L. Dreyfus and P. Rabinow (eds.), *Michel Foucault: Beyond Hermeneutics and Structuralism*, 208–16. Chicago: University of Chicago Press.

———. (1983). *This Is Not a Pipe*. Berkeley/Los Angeles: University of California Press (Originally published as *Ceci n'est pas une pipe*, 1973).

———. (1984a). *The History of Sexuality*, vol. 1. Harmondsworth, United Kingdom: Penguin (Originally published as *Histoire de la sexualité I*, 1976).

———. (1984b). "What Is Enlightenment?" In *The Foucault Reader*, ed. P. Rabinow, 32–50. New York: Pantheon Books, 1984.

Frank, M. (1980). *Das Sagbare und das Unsagbare. Studien zur neuesten französischen Hermeneutik und Texttheorie* [The Speakable and the Unspeakable: Studies on the Newest French Hermeneutics and Theory of Texts]. Frankfurt am Main: Suhrkamp.

———. (1984). *Was ist Neostrukturalismus?* [What Is Neostructuralism?]. Frankfurt am Main: Suhrkamp.

Freud, S. *The Standard Edition of the Complete Psychological Works of Sigmund Freud* (24 vols.). London: Hogarth Press and the Institute of Psychoanalysis, 1953–74.

Fry, R. (1920). *Vision and Design*. London: The Phoenix Library.

Furst, L. R. (1984). *Fictions of Romantic Irony in European Narrative, 1760–1857.* London: Macmillan.

Gablik, S. (1976). *Progress in Art.* London: Thames and Hudson.

Gachnang, J. and S. Gohr (eds.). (1989). *Bilderstreit. Widerspruch, Einheit und Fragment in der Kunst seit 1960* [The Battle of Images: Contradiction, Unity and Fragment in Art since 1960]. Cologne: DuMont.

Gadamer, H. -G. (1975). *Truth and Method.* New York: Crossroad.

———. (1986). *Wahrheit und Methode. Ergänzungen, Gesammelte Werke II.* Tübingen, Germany: J. C. B. Mohr (Paul Siebeck).

Gombrich, E. H. (1969). *Art and Illusion.* Princeton: Princeton University Press.

Goth, J. (1970). *Nietzsche und die Rhetorik* [Nietzsche and Rhetoric]. Tübingen, Germany: M. Niemeyer.

Greenberg, C. (1993). Modernist Painting. In *The Collected Essays and Criticism,* vol. 4: *Modernism with a Vengeance, 1957–1969,* 85–93. Chicago: University of Chicago Press.

Griffith, P. (1981). *Cage.* Oxford Studies of Composers, vol. 18. London/ New York: Oxford University Press.

Haase, R. (1963). *Leibniz und die Musik: Ein Beitrag zur Geschichte der harmonikalen Symbolik* [Leibniz and Music: Contribution to History of Harmonic Symbolism]. Hommerich, Germany: Eckhardt.

Habermas, J. (1973). *Legitimationsprobleme im Spätkapitalismus* [Problems of Legitimation in Late Capitalism]. Frankfurt am Main: Suhrkamp.

———. (1978). *Politik, Kunst, Religion. Essays über zeitgenössische Philosophen* [Politics, Art, Religion: Essays on Contemporary Philosophers]. Stuttgart, Germany: Philipp Reclam.

———. (1983). Rekonstruktive vs. verstehende Sozialwissenschaften [Reconstructive vs. Understanding Social Sciences]. In J. Habermas, *Moralbewußtsein und kommunikatives Handeln* [Moral Consciousness and Communicative Action]. Frankfurt am Main: Suhrkamp.

———. (1984). *Theory of Communicative Action,* vol. 1. Boston: Beacon Press (Original published as *Theorie des kommunikatives Handelns,* I, 1981).

———. (1985). *Der philosophische Diskurs der Moderne* [The Philosophical Discourse of Modernity]. Frankfurt am Main: Suhrkamp.

———. (1987). *Theory of Communicative Action,* vol. 2. Boston: Beacon Press (Originally published as *Theorie des kommunikatives Handelns,* II, 1981).

———. (1996). Modernity: An Unfinished Project. In M. Maurizio Passerin d'Entrèves and Seyla Benhabib (eds.), *Habermas and the Unfinished Project of Modernity: Critical Essays on* The Philosophical Discourse of Modernity, 38–55. Cambridge: Polity Press.

Harpold, T. (1994). "Conclusions." In George P. Landow (ed.), *Hyper/text/theory,* 189–222. Baltimore: John Hopkins University Press.

Hassan, I. (1987). *The Postmodern Turn: Essays in Postmodern Theory and Culture.* Columbus: Ohio State University Press.

Hegel, G. W. F. (1955). *Ästhetik* [Aesthetics]. Ed. by F. Bassenge. Berlin: Aufbau-Verlag.

———. (1970). *Enzyklopädie der philosophischen Wissenschaften* [Encyclopedia of Philosophical Sciences]. In *Werke* [Works] (Eds. E.Moldenhauer and K. M. Michel), vols. 8–10. Frankfurt am Main: Suhrkamp.

Heidegger, M. (1949). "Hölderlin and the Essence of Poetry." In M. Heidegger, *Existence and Being*. Chicago: Henry Regnery Company. (Originally published as "Erläuterungen zu Hölderlins Dichtung," 1944).

———. (1958). *Introduction to Metaphysics*. New Haven: Yale University Press (Originally published as *Einführung in die Metaphysik*, 1953).

———. (1960). *Essays in Metaphysics: Identity and Difference*. New York: Philosophical Library (Originally published as *Identität und Differenz*, 1957).

———. (1962). *Being and Time*. Oxford: Basil Blackwell (Originally published as *Sein und Zeit*, 1927).

———. (1962). *Kant and the Problem of Metaphysics*. Bloomington: University of Indiana Press (Originally published as *Kant und das Problem der Metaphysik*, 1929).

———. (1967). *Vorträge und Aufsätze*, 3 vols. [Lectures and Essays]. Pfullingen: Neske.

———. (1969). *The Essence of Reasons*. Evanston, Ill.: Northwestern University Press (Originally published as *Vom Wesen des Grundes*, 1929).

———. (1971). *On the Way to Language*. New York: Harper & Row (Originally published as *Unterwegs zur Sprache*, 1959).

———. (1974). Preface. In S. J. Richardson, *Heidegger: Through Phenomenology to Thought*. The Hague: Martinus Nijhoff.

———. (1975). Language. In M. Heidegger, *Poetry, Language, Thought*, 187–210. New York: Harper & Row (Originally published as "Die Sprache," 1950).

———. (1975). *Poetry, Language, Thought*. New York: Harper & Row.

———. (1976). *Wegmarken* [Road-signs]. *Gesamtausgabe*, vol. 9. Frankfurt am Main: Klostermann.

———. (1976). *Vom Wesen des Grundes* [The Essence of Reason]. In *Wegmarken*. *Gesamtausgabe*, vol. 9, 123–75. Frankfurt am Main: Klostermann.

———. (1977). *Holzwege* [Forest-roads]. *Gesamtausgabe*, vol. 5. Frankfurt am Main: Klostermann.

———. (1977). *Die Zeit des Weltbildes* [The Age of the Worldview]. In M. Heidegger, *Holzwege* [Forest-Roads], *Gesamtausgabe*, vol. 5, 75–113. Frankfurt am Main: Klostermann.

———. (1977). *Vier Seminare* [Four Seminars]. Frankfurt am Main: Klostermann.

———. (1978). What Is Metaphysics? In M. Heidegger, *Basic Writings*, 91–112. London: Routledge & Kegan Paul (Originally published as "Was ist Metaphysik?," 1930).

———. (1978). The Origin of the Work of Art. In M. Heidegger, *Basic Writings*, 143–87. London: Routledge & Kegan Paul (Originally published as "Der Ursprung des Kunstwerkes" in *Holzwege*, 1950).

———. (1978). Letter on Humanism. In M. Heidegger, *Basic Writings*, 189–242. London: Routledge & Kegan Paul (Originally published as "Brief über den 'Humanismus'," 1947).

———. (1978). *The Question Concerning Technology.* In M. Heidegger, *Basic Writings*, 283–317. London: Routledge & Kegan Paul (Originally published as "Die Technik und die Kehre," 1962).

———. (1978). Building Dwelling Thinking. In M. Heidegger, *Basic Writings*, 319–39. London: Routledge & Kegan Paul (Originally published as "Bauen Wohnen Denken," in *Vorträge und Aufsätze*, 1954).

———. (1978). What Calls for Thinking? In M. Heidegger, *Basic Writings*, 91–112. London: Routledge & Kegan Paul (Originally published as "Was heisst Denken?," 1954).

———. (1983). *Die Selbstbehauptung der deutschen Universität/das Rektorat 1933/34* [Self-Maintenance of the German University/Rectorate 1933/34]. Frankfurt am Main: Klostermann.

———. (1985). *Gelassenheit* [Release]. Pfullingen, Germany: Neske.

———. (1989). *Beiträge. Zur Philosophie* [Contributions. On Philosophy], *Gesamtausgabe*, vol. 65. Frankfurt am Main: Klostermann.

———. (1991). *The Principle of Reason.* Bloomington/Indianapolis: Indiana University Press (Originally published as *Der Satz vom Grund*, 1957).

———. (1991). *Nietzsche,* 2 vols. San Francisco: Harper San Francisco (Originally published as *Nietzsche*, 1961).

Heim, M. (1993). *The Metaphysics of Virtual Reality.* New York: Oxford University Press.

Henry, A. (1971). *Métonymie et métaphore* [Metonym and Metaphor]. Paris: Bibliothèque française et romane.

Horkheimer, M. (1988). Neue Kunst und Massenkultur [New Music and Mass Culture]. In *Gesammelte Schriften* [Collected Writings], vol. 4, 419–38. Frankfurt am Main: Fischer Taschenbuch Verlag.

Horkheimer, M. and Th. W. Adorno. (1973). *Dialectic of Enlightenment.* Norfolk: Lowe & Brydone (Originally published as *Dialektik der Aufklärung*, 1947).

Höweler, C. (1975). *Het XYZ der Muziek* [The XYZ of Music]. Bussum, The Netherlands: De Haan.

Hulten, P. (ed.). (1986). *Futurismo & Futurismi.* Milan: Bompiani.

IJsseling, S. (1964). *Heidegger. Denken en danken. Geven en zijn* [Heidegger: Thinking and Thanking, Giving and Being]. Antwerp, Belgium: De Nederlandsche Boekhandel.

———. (1969). Filosofie en psychoanalyse [Philosophy and Psychoanalysis]. *Tijdschrift voor Filosofie* 31: 261–89.

————. (1990). Jacques Derrida: een strategie van de vertraging [Jacques Derrida: A Strategy of Delay]. In Widdershoven and De Boer, 1990, 9–15.

Irigaray, L. (1985). *This Sex Which Is Not One*. Ithaca, N.Y.: Cornell University Press (Originally published as *Ce sexe qui n'en pas un*, 1977).

Jankélévitch, V. (1964). *L'ironie romantique* [Romantic Irony]. Paris: Flammerion.

Jay, M. (1973). *The Dialectical Imagination*. London: Heinemann.

————. (1985). Habermas and Modernity. In R. J. Bernstein (ed.), *Habermas and Modernity*. Cambridge: Polity Press.

————. (1994). *Downcast Eyes: The Denigration of Vision in Twentieth-Century French Thought*. Berkeley: University of California Press.

Jones, E. (1955). *Sigmund Freud: Life and Work*, 3 vols. New York: Basic Books.

Joyce, M. (1995). *Of Two Minds: Hypertext Pedagogy and Poetics*. Ann Arbor: University of Michigan Press.

Jung, C. G. n.d. Voorwoord [Preface]. In *I Tjing*, xvi–xxxiii. Deventer, The Netherlands: Ankh-Hermes.

Kandinsky, W. (1959). *Über das Geistige in der Kunst* [On the Spiritual in Art]. Bern: Benteli.

Kant, I. (1959). *Foundations of the Metaphysics of Morals* and *What Is Enlightenment?* Indianapolis: Bobbs-Merrill Educational Publishing. (Originally published as *Grundlegung zur Metaphysik der Sitten*, 1785, and *Beantwortung der Frage: Was heißt Aufklärung?"*, 1783).

————. (1968). Die Religion innerhalb der Grenzen der bloßen Vernunft [Religion within the Bounderies of Pure Reason]. In *Theorie-Werkausgabe*, vol. 8, 645–879. Frankfurt am Main: Suhrkamp.

————. (1968). *Logik* [Logic]. In *Theorie-Werkausgabe*, vol. 6, 417–582. Frankfurt am Main: Suhrkamp.

————. (1968). Zum ewigen Frieden [Toward Eternal Peace]. In *Theorie-Werkausgabe*, vol. 11, 195–251. Frankfurt am Main: Suhrkamp.

————. (1968). *Prolegomena zu einer jeden künftigen Metaphysik, die als Wissenschaft wird auftreten können* [Prolegomenon to a Coming Metaphyisics, that Could Appear as Science]. In *Theorie-Werkausgabe*, vol. 5, 113–264. Frankfurt am Main: Suhrkamp.

————. (1978). *Critique of Pure Reason*. London: Macmillan (Originally published as *Kritik der reinen Vernunft*, 1781).

————. (1987). *Critique of Judgment*. Indianapolis: Hackett (Originally published as *Kritik der Urteilskraft*, 1790).

Kaulingfreks, K. (1984). *Meneer Iedereen* [Mister Everyone]. Nijmegen, The Netherlands: SUN.

Kelly, K. (1994). *Out of Control*. Reading Mass.: Addison-Wesley.

Keulartz, J. (1986). Over kunst en cultuur in het werk van Habermas [On Art and Culture in the Work of Habermas]. In F. van Doorne and M. Korthals (eds.), *In debat met Habermas* [Debate with Habermas], 11–37. Amsterdam/ Meppel: Boom.

Kirk, G. S., and J. E. Raven. (1980). *The Presocratic Philosophers*. Cambridge: Cambridge University Press.

Kitchener, R. F. (1986). *Piaget's Theory of Knowledge: Genetic Epistemology and Scientific Reason*. New Haven/London: Yale University Press.

Knittermeyer, H. (1929). *Schelling und die romantische Schule* [Schelling and the Romantic Movement]. Munich: Reinhardt.

Koestenbaum, P. (1960). The Logic of Schopenhauer's Aesthetics. *Revue Internationale de Philosophie*, 14: 85–95.

Kofman, S. (1972). *Nietzsche et la métaphore* [Nietzsche and Metaphor]. Paris: Payot.

Köhler, M. (1977). "Postmodernismus": Ein begriffsgeschichtlicher Überblick ["Postmodernism": An Overview of the History of the Concept]. *Amerikastudien* 121: 8–18.

Kolb, D. (1994). *Socrates in the Labyrinth*. Cambridge: Eastgate Systems.

Kostelanetz, R. (1971). *John Cage*. Documentary Monographs in Modern Art. London: Allen Lane.

Kristeva, J. (1975). The System and the Speaking Subject. In Th. A. Sebeok (ed.), *The Tell-tale Sign*. Lisse, The Netherlands: Peter de Ridder Press.

Kulenkampff, J. (ed.). (1974). *Materialien zu Kants 'Kritik der Urteilskraft'* [Material on Kant's *Critique of Pure Reason*]. Frankfurt am Main: Suhrkamp.

Kundera, M. (1984). *The Unbearable Lightness of Being*. New York: Harper & Row.

Kunneman, H. (1986). *De waarheidstrechter. Een communicatietheoretisch perspectief op wetenschap en samenleving* [The Funnel of Truth: A Communication-theoretical Perspective on Science and Society]. Amsterdam/Meppel: Boom.

Kurzawa, L. (1982). Repetition und Vergessen [Repetition and Forgetting]. In M. Fahres (ed.), *Das europäischen Minimal Musik Projekt* [The European Minimal Music Project]. Utrecht, The Netherlands: European Minimal Music Project.

Lacan, J. (1966). *Écrits*. [Writings]. Paris: Éditions du Seuil.

——. (1966). Petit discours à l'O.R.T.F [Small Discours at O.R.T.F.]. *Recherches*, 3/4: 5–9.

——. (1970). Préface [Preface]. In A. Rifflet-Lemaire, *Jacques Lacan*, Brussels: Dessart.

——. (1975). *Le Séminaire I* [Seminar I]. Paris: Éditions du Seuil.

Laermans, R. (1982). Desirologie—of het mislukte afscheid [Desirology—or a Failed Farewell]. *Krisis. Tijdschrift voor Filosofie*, 9: 5–16.

Landow, G. P. (1992). *Hypertext: The Convergence of Contemporary Critical Theory and Technology*. Baltimore/London: John Hopkins University Press.

Langer, S. (1976). *Philosophy in a New Key. A Study in the Symbolism of Reason, Rite and Art*. Cambridge, Mass.: Harvard University Press.

Lanham, R. A. (1993). *The Electronic Word: Democracy, Technology, and the Arts*. Chicago and London: University of Chicago Press.

Laplanche, J. and J.-B. Pontalis. (1972). *Vokabular des Psychoanalyse* [Vocabulary of Psychoanalysis]. Frankfurt am Main: Suhrkamp.

Leibniz, G. W. (1734). *Leibnitii Epistolae ad diversos, theologici, ivridici, medici, philosophici, mathematici, historici et philologici argvmenti, e MSC. Avctoris* (cum annot. suis prim. divulgavit Christian. Kortholtus), 2 vols. Leipzig: sumtu Bern. Christoph. Breitkopfii.

Lemaire, T. (1970). *Filosofie van het landschap* [Philosophy of the Landscape]. Baarn, The Netherlands: Ambo.

Levano, Ch. (1986). Nietzsche en de muziek [Nietzsche and Music]. In G. J. Kleinrensink (ed.), *De zaak Nietzsche* [The Nietzsche Case], 112–30. Nijmegen, The Netherlands: Vriendenlust.

Levels, M. (1981). Romantische tendenzen in het werk van Sigurdur Gudmundsson en Hrein Fridfinsson [Romantic Tendencies in the Work of Sigurdur Gudmundsson and Hrein Fridfinsson]. Master's thesis. University of Amsterdam.

———. (1982). *Sigurdur Gudmundsson*. Weesp, The Netherlands. Openbaar Kunstbezit.

Lévi-Strauss, C. (1975). *The Raw and the Cooked: Introduction to a Science of Mythology.* New York: Harper & Row (Originally published as *Le cru et le cuit,* 1964).

Lutz, I. (1983/1984). Een gesprek met Jean Baudrillard [A Conversation with Jean Baudrillard]. *Skrien* 132/133 (Winter 1983/1984): 8–11.

Lyotard, J.-F. (1980). *Des dispositifs pulsionels.* Paris: Christian Bourgeois.

———. (1984). The *Postmodern Condition: A Report on Knowledge.* Manchester, U.K.: Manchester University Press (Originally published as *La condition postmoderne: Rapport sur le savoir,* 1979).

———. (1991). *The Inhuman: Reflections on Time.* Oxford: Polity Press.

Magritte, R. (1979). *Écrits complets* [Complete Writings]. Paris: Flammarion.

Mann, Th. (1977). Schopenhauer. In G. Haffmans (ed.), *Über Arthur Schopenhauer* [On Arthur Schopenhauer], 87–132. Zurich: Diogenes.

Mannoni, O. (1969). *Clefs pour l'imaginaire ou l'Autre Scène* [Keys for the Imaginary or the Other Scene]. Paris: Éditions du Seuil.

Marcuse, H. (1968). *Negations: Essays in Critical Theory.* London: Penguin.

———. (1970). *Eros and Civilisation.* Suffolk: The Chauser Press.

Marquard, O. (1962). Kant und die wende zur Ästhetik [Kant and the Turn toward Aesthetics]. *Zeitschrift für Philosophische Forschung* 16:231–43, 363–74.

———. (1968). Zur Bedeutung der Theorie des Unbewußten für eine Theorie des nicht mehr schönen Kunst [The Meaning of the Theory of the Unconscious for a Theory of the No-Longer-Fine Arts]. In H. R. Jauß (ed.), *Die nicht mehr schönen Künste. Poetik und Hermeneutik* [No-Longer-Fine Arts: Poetry and Hermeneutics], vol. 3: 375–92. Munich: Wilhelm Fink Verlag.

———. (1982). Über einige Beziehungen zwischen Ästhetik und Therapeutik in der Philisophie des neunzehnten Jahrhunderts. [On some Relations between Aesthetics and Therapeutics in the Philosophy of the Nineteenth Century]. In *Schwierigkeiten mit der Geschichtsphilosophie* [Difficulties with Philosophy of History], 83–106. Frankfurt am Main: Suhrkamp.

Martis, A. (1986). Postmodern Trans-avantgarde. In Hudson and Van Reijen (eds.), *Modernen versus postmodernen* [Modernists versus Postmodernists], 229–81. Utrecht, The Netherlands: HES Uitgevers.

Masson, J. M. (1984). *The Assault on Truth: Freud's Suppression of the Seduction Theory.* New York: Farrar, Straus and Giroux.

Matthews, G. (1972). *Plato's Epistemology.* London: Faber.

Megill, A. (1985). *Prophets of Extremity: Nietzsche, Heidegger, Foucault, Derrida.* Berkeley: University of California Press.

Mehlman, J. (1976). Zwischen Psychoanalyse und "Psychocritique" [Between Psychoanalysis and "Psychocriticism"]. In M. Curtius (ed.), *Seminar: Theorie der künstlerischen Produktivität* [Seminar: Theory of Artistic Productivity], 119–50. Frankfurt am Main: Suhrkamp.

Mertens, W. (1980). *De Amerikaanse repetitieve muziek* [American Repetitive Music]. Bierbeek, Belgium: Vergaelen.

Mitchell, William J. (1994). *The Reconfigured Eye: Visual Truth in the Post-Photographic Era.* Cambridge: MIT Press.

Mooij, A. W. M. (1975). *Taal en verlangen* [Language and Desire]. Amsterdam: Boom.

———. (1982). *Psychoanalyse en regels* [Psychoanalysis and Rules]. Amsterdam: Boom.

Moravec, H. (1988). *Mind Children: The Future of Robot and Human Intelligence.* Cambridge: Harvard University Press.

———. (1992). Pigs in Cyberspace. Http://www.vpro.nl/htbin/scan/www/vpro-digitaal/web-map/views/ hans-moravec).

Mörchen, H. (1929). Die Einbildungskraft bei Kant [Kant on Imagination]. In *Jahrbuch für Philosophie und phänomenologische Forschung*, vol. 11. Halle a.d. Saale, Germany: Max Niemeyer.

Moyaert, P. (1982). Een betekenisproductie zonder geschiedenis [Production of Meaning without History]. *Raster* 24: 135–52.

———. (1983). Taal en onbewuste. Freud en Lacan over de "Urverdrängung" [Language and Unconsciousness: Freud and Lacan on "Urverdrängung"]. *Algemeen Nederlands Tijdschrift voor Wijsbegeerte* 75: 173–91.

Musil, R. (1979). *The Man without Qualities,* vol. 1. London: Pan Books.

Nadeau, M. (1964). *Histoire du surréalisme* [History of Surrealism]. Paris: Éditions du Seuil.

Nattiez, J.-J. (1975). *Fondements d'une sémiologie de la musique* [Foundations of a Semiology of Music]. Paris: Union générale d'éditions.

Nelson, Th. H. (1992). *Literary Machines.* Sausalito, CA: Mindful Press.

Neske, G. and E. Kettering (eds.). (1988). *Antwort. Martin Heidegger im Gespräch* [Answer: Martin Heidegger Speaks]. Pfullingen, Germany: Neske.

Neubauer, J. (1986). *The Emancipation of Music from Language: Departure from Memesis in Eighteenth-Century Aesthetics.* New Haven/London: Yale University Press.

Nietzsche, F. (1920–29). *Gesammelte Werke. Musarionausgabe* [Collected Works. Musarion-edition]. Munich: Musarion.

———. (1956). The Genealogy of Morals: An Attack. In *The Birth of Tragedy and The Genealogy of Morals.* New York: Anchor Books (Originally published as *Zur Genealogie der Moral,* 1887).

———. (1969). *Thus Spoke Zarathustra: A Book for Everyone and No One.* Harmondsworth, U.K.: Penguin Books (Originally published as *Also sprach Zarathustra. Ein Buch für Alle und Keinen,* 1886).

———. (1974). *The Gay Science.* New York: Vintage Books (Originally published as *Die fröhliche Wissenschaft,* 1882–87).

———. (1976). *Twilight of the Idols or, How One Philosophizes with a Hammer.* In *The Portable Nietzsche.* New York: The Viking Press (Originally published as *Götzen-Dämmerung,* 1889).

———. (1976). *Werke in Drei Bänden.* [Works in Three Volumes]. Ed. K. Schlechta. Frankfurt: Ullstein.

———. (1980). *Sämtliche Werke. Kritische Studienausgabe* [Collected Works: Critical Edition]. Berlin: De Gruyter.

———. (1982). *Daybreak: Thoughts on the Prejudices of Morality.* Cambridge: Cambridge University Press (Originally published as *Morgenröte,* 1881).

———. (1983). The Uses and Disadvantages of History for Life. In F. Nietzsche, *Untimely Meditations.* Cambridge: Cambridge University Press.

———. (1986). *Human, All Too Human.* Cambridge: Cambridge University Press (Originally published as *Menschliches, Allzumenschliches,* 1878).

———. (1990). *Beyond Good and Evil: Prelude to a Philosophy of the Future.* Harmondsworth, U.K.: Penguin Books (Originally published as *Jenseits von Gut und Böse. Vorspiel einer Philosophie der Zukunft,* 1886).

———. (1992). *Ecco Homo: How One Becomes What One Is.* Harmondsworth, U.K.: Penguin Books (Originally published as *Ecce homo. Wie man wird, was man ist,* 1889).

———. (1993). *The Birth of Tragedy out of the Spirit of Music.* Harmondsworth, U.K.: Penguin Books (Originally published as *Die Geburt der Tragödie aus der Geiste der Musik,* 1878).

Noerr, G. S. (1985). Der Leib im Gitterwerk der Sprache [The Body in the Latticework of Language]. In P. Rippel (ed.), *De Sturz der Idole. Nietzsches Umwertung von Kultur und Subjekt* [The Twilight of the Idols: Nietzsche's Revaluation of Culture and Subject], 165–211. Tübingen: Edition Diskord im Konkursbuchverlag.

Novalis. (1922). *Die Christenheit oder Europa: ein Fragment* [Christianity or Europe] (First published around 1799). Hamburg: Bund der Buchfreunde.

Onis, F. de. (1934). *Antología de la Poesia Española e Hispanoamericana (1882–1932).* Madrid: Centro de Estudios Históricos.

Oudemans, Th. W. C. (1980). *De Verdeelde mens. Ontwerp van een filoso-fische antropologie* [Divided Man: Draft for a Philosophical Anthropology]. Amsterdam/Meppel: Boom.

Owens, G. (1983). The Discourse of the Others: Feminists and Postmodernism. In H. Foster (ed.), *The Anti-Aesthetic: Essays on Postmodern Culture.* Port Townsend, Wash.: Bay Press.

Pannwitz, R. (1917). *Der Krisis der europäischen Kultur,* 2 vols. [Crisis of European Culture]. Nuremberg: Carl.

Parsons, M. (1987). *How We Understand Art.* Cambridge: Harvard University Press.

Paul, G. S., and E. D. Cox. (1996). *Beyond Humanity: CyberEvolution and Future Minds.* Rockland, Mass.: Charles River Media.

Paz, O. (1974). *Children of the Mire: Modern Poetry from Romanticism to the Avant-Garde.* Cambridge: Harvard University Press.

Penny, S. (1994). Virtual Reality as the Completion of the Enlightment. In C. E. Loeffler and T. Anderson (eds.), *The Virtual Reality Casebook,* 199–213. New York/London: Van Nostrand Reinhold.

Peperzak, A. Th. (1981). Hybridisme [Hybridism]. *Algemeen Nederlands Tijdschrift voor Wijsbegeerte* 734: 251–67.

Piaget, J. (1972). *Insights and Illusions of Philosophy.* London: Routledge and Kegan Paul.

———. (1983). Piaget's Theory. In P. H. Mussen (ed.), *Handbook of Child Psychology,* vol. 1, *History, Theory, and Methods,* 103–29. New York: Wiley.

Plato. (1961). *The Collected Dialogues.* Ed. Edith Hamilton and Huntington Cairns. New York: Bollingen Foundation.

Plessner, H. (1965). *Die Stufen des Organischen und der Mensch* [Stages of the Organic and Man]. Berlin: De Gruyter.

Poster, M. (1995). Postmodern Virtualities. In M. Featherstone and R. Burrows (eds.), *Cyberspace, Cyberbodies, Cyberpunk: Cultures of Technological Embodiment,* 79–95. London: Sage Publications.

Praz, M. (1970). *The Romantic Agony.* Oxford: Oxford University Press.

Pütz, P. (1975). *Friedrich Nietzsche.* Stuttgart, Germany: Metzler.

Quintilianus. (1920–22). *Institutio Oratoria.* London: Heinemann.

Richards, I. (1936). *Philosophy and Rhetoric.* New York: Oxford University Press.

Richardson, S. J. (1974). *Heidegger: Through Phenomenology to Thought.* The Hague: Martinus Nijhoff.

Richter, H. (1964). *Dada. Kunst und Antikunst* [Dada: Art and Anti-Art]. Cologne: DuMont Schauberg.

Rilke, R. M. (1975). *Duinesian Elegies.* Chapel Hill: University of North Carolina Press.

Rorty, R. (1979). *Philosophy and the Mirror of Nature.* Princeton: Princeton University Press.

Rothmann, K. (1981). *Duitse Letterkunde* [German Literature]. Utrecht/Antwerp, The Netherlands/Belgium: Spectrum.

Rubin, W. (1968). *Dada, Surrealism and Their Heritage.* New York: Museum of Modern Art.

———. (1970). *Frank Stella.* New York: Museum of Modern Art.

———. (1987). *Frank Stella, 1970–1987.* New York: Museum of Modern Art.

Ruwet, N. (1972). *Langage, musique, poésie* [Language, Music, Poetry]. Paris: Éditions du Seuil.

Sanders, H. (1987). Postmoderne. Alltäglichkeit als Utopie [Postmodernity: Triviality as Utopia]. In Bürger and Bürger, 1987, 72–83.

Scheler, M. (1988). *Die Stellung des Menschen im Kosmos* [Position of Man in the Cosmos]. Bonn, Germany: Bouvier.

Schelling, F. W. J. (1907). *Werke. Sämtliche Werke* [Works: Collected Works]. Ed. K. Fr. A. Schelling. 14 vols. Stuttgart/Augsburg, Germany: Cotta.

Schiller, F. (1962). *Naive und sentimentalische Dichtung* [On Naive and Sentimental Poetry]. In *Schiller Werke. Nationalausgabe* [Schiller's Works, National Edition], vol. 20. Weimar, Germany: Hermann Böhlaus Nachfolger.

———. (1981). *Über die ästhetische Erziehung des Menschen* [On the Aesthetic Education of Man]. Stuttgart: Hanser.

Schirmacher, W. (ed.). (1984). *65. Schopenhauer Jahrbuch* [65. Schopenhauer Yearbook]. Frankfurt am Main: Waldemar Kramer.

Schlegel, F. (1882). *Seine prosaischen Jugendschriften* [His Prosaic Juvenile Writings]. Ed. J. Minor. Wien: Konegen.

———. (1975). *Kritische Ausgabe* [Critical Edition], vol. 8. Munich: Carl Hanser Verlag.

Schneider, R. (1980). *Semiotik der Musik* [Semiotics of Music]. Munich: Wilhelm Fink.

Schopenhauer, A. (1966). *The World as Will and Representation,* vol. 1. London/ Toronto: General Publishing Company (Originally published as *Die Welt als Wille und Vorstellung,* 1819).

———. (1969). *The World as Will and Representation,* vol. 2. London/Toronto: General Publishing Company (Originally published as *Die Welt als Wille und Vorstellung,* Zweiter Band, 1844).

———. (1977). *Parerga und Paralipomena.* 2 vols. In *Arthur Schopenhauer. Werke in zehn Bänden* [Arthur Schopenhauer: Works in Ten Volumes], vols. 7–10. Zurich: Diogenes.

Schröeder, J. A. (1919). *De extatische cultus van Dionysos* [The Ecstatic Cult of Dionysius]. Baarn, The Netherlands: Hollandia.

Schulz, W. (1953–1954). Über den philosophiegeschichtlichen Ort Martin Heideggers [On the Philosophic-Historical Place of Martin Heidegger]. In *Philosophische Rundschau* 1:65–93, 211–232.

Schwarz, D. (1989). Über die Möglichkeit mehrere Farbtuben [On the Posibility of Several Paint Tubes]. In Gachnang and Gohr, 1989, 209–18.

Slouka, M. (1995). *War of the Worlds: The Assault on Reality.* London: Abacus.

Solomon, M. (1977). *Beethoven.* London: Cassel & Co.

Sørensen, B. (1963). *Symbol und Symbolismus in den ästhetischen Theorien des 18. Jahrhunderts und der deutschen Romantik* [Symbol and Symbolism in the Aesthetic Theory of the Eighteenth Century and German Romanticism]. Copenhagen: Munksgaard.

Spector, J. J. (1974). *The Aesthetics of Freud: A Study in Psychoanalysis and Art.* New York: McGraw-Hill.

Stenger, N. (1991). Mind is a Leaking Rainbow. In M. Benedikt (ed.), *Cyberspace: First Steps,* 49–58. Cambridge/London: MIT Press.

Stolniz, J. (1960). *Aesthetics and Philosophy of Art Criticism.* Boston: Houghton Mifflin.

Thrall-Soby, J. (1965). *Magritte.* New York: Museum of Modern Art.

Toffler, Alvin. (1980). *The Third Wave.* New York: Morrow.

Toynbee, A. J. (1947). *A Study of History.* Abridgement of volumes 1–4 by D. C. Sommervell. Oxford: Oxford University Press.

Turkle, S. (1995). *Life on the Screen: Identity in the Age of Internet.* New York: Simon & Schuster.

Tzara, T. (1977). *Seven Dada Manifestos and Lampisteries.* London: John Calder, and New York: Riverrun Press.

Ulmer, G. L. (1983). The Object of Post-Criticism. In H. Foster (ed.), *The Anti-Aesthetic: Essays on Postmodern Culture.* Port Townsend, Wash.: Bay Press.

———. (1991). Grammatology Hypermedia. *Postmodern Culture* 1.2 (1991).

Van Haaften, A. W., M. Korthals, and T. Wren (eds.) (1997). *Philosophy of Development: Reconstructing the Foundations of Human Development and Education.* Dordrecht/Boston/London: Kluwer Academic Publishers.

Van Nierop, M. (1989). *Denken in tweespalt. Interpreteren in ambivalentie* [Thinking in Discord: Interpreting in Ambivalence]. Delft, The Netherlands: Eburon.

Van Tongeren, P. J. M. (1984). *De moraal van Nietzsches moraalkritiek* [The Moral of Nietzsche's Critique of Morality]. Nijmegen, The Netherlands: SUN.

Vattimo, G. (1985). Aesthetics and the End of Epistemology. In P. J. McCormick (ed.), *The Reason of Art/L'Art a ses raisons,* 287–94. Ottawa: University of Ottawa Press.

———. (1988). *The End of Modernity: Nihilism and Hermeneutics in Postmodern Culture.* Cambridge: Polity Press.

Visser, G. (1989). *Nietzsche en Heidegger. Een confrontatie* [Nietzsche and Heidegger: A Confrontation]. Nijmegen, The Netherlands: SUN.

Vuyk, K. (1988). De esthetisering van het wereldbeeld [Aesthetization of the Worldview]. *Revisor* 1/2: 171–83.

———. (1990). *Homo Volens. Beschouwingen over de moderne mens als willende mens naar aanleiding van Nietzsche en Heidegger* [Homo Volens: Contemplations on

Modern Man as Willing Man referring to Nietzsche and Heidegger]. Kampen, The Netherlands: Kok Agora.

Waldberg, P. (1972). *Surrealism*. London: Thames and Hudson.

Wallis, B. (ed.). (1984). *Art after Modernism: Rethinking Representation*. New York: New Museum of Contemporary Art.

Weber, S. (1978). *Rückkehr zu Freud. Lacans Ent-stellung der Psychoanalyse* [Return to Freud: Lacan's Disfigurement of Psychoanalysis]. Frankfurt am Main: Ullstein.

Weibel, P. (1992). New Space in Electronic Age. In E. Bolle (et al.), *Book for the Unstable Media*, 65–75. Den Bosch, The Netherlands: V2.

Weininger, O. (1980). *Geschlecht und Charakter* [Gender and Character]. Munich: Matthes & Seitz.

Weisberger, E. (ed.). (1986). *The Spiritual in Art: Abstract Painting 1890–1985*. New York: Abbeville Press.

Welsch, W. (1987). *Unsere postmoderne Moderne* [Our Postmodern Modernists]. Weinheim, Germany: VCH Acta Humaniora.

Whately, R. (1846). *Elements of Rhetoric*. London:

Widdershoven, G. A. M. and Th. de Boer (eds). (1990). *Hermeneutiek in discussie* [Hermeneutics Discussed]. Delft, Netherlands: Eburon.

Wit, J. (1973). God heeft het eerste en laatste woord [God Has the First and the Last Word]. In *Liedboek voor de kerken*, 1 [Songbook for Churches]. The Hague: Boekencentrum.

Wittgenstein, L. (1975). *Tractatus Logico-Philosophicus*. Frankfurt am Main: Suhrkamp.

Woolley, B. (1992). *Virtual Worlds: A Journey in Hype and Hyperreality*. London: Penguin.

Name Index

Subject Index